PREGNANT PAUSE

To my son Bill and my daughter Jill – with all my love.

Pregnant Pause
An International Legal Analysis
of Maternity Discrimination

ANNE-MARIE MOONEY COTTER
The Social Security Disability Law Firm, USA

Routledge
Taylor & Francis Group

LONDON AND NEW YORK

First published 2010 by Ashgate Publishing

2 Park Square, Milton Park, Abingdon, Oxfordshire OX14 4RN
52 Vanderbilt Avenue, New York, NY 10017

Routledge is an imprint of the Taylor & Francis Group, an informa business

First issued in paperback 2020

British Library Cataloguing in Publication Data
Cotter, Anne-Marie Mooney.
    Pregnant pause : an international legal analysis of
    maternity discrimination.
    1. Pregnant women--Employment--Law and legislation.
    2. Maternity leave--Law and legislation. 3. Sex
    discrimination in employment.
    I. Title
    344'.0144-dc22

Library of Congress Cataloging-in-Publication Data
Cotter, Anne-Marie Mooney.
    Pregnant pause : an international legal analysis of maternity discrimination / by Anne-Marie Mooney Cotter.
        p. cm.
    Includes bibliographical references and index.
    ISBN 978-0-7546-7847-2 (hardback) -- ISBN 978-0-7546-9666-7 (ebook)
    1. Discrimination in employment--Law and legislation. 2. Sex discrimination against women--Law and legislation. 3. Pregnant women--Employment--Law and legislation. I. Title.

    K1770.C684 2010
    344.01'44--dc22

                                                                    2010003968

ISBN 13: 978-0-7546-7847-2 (hbk)
ISBN 13: 978-0-367-60274-1 (pbk)

Contents

Biography

Dr. Anne-Marie Mooney Cotter, Esq. is a Montrealer, fluent in both English and French. She earned her Bachelor's degree from McGill University at age 18, her Juris Doctor law degree from one of the leading civil rights institutions, Howard University School of Law, and her Doctorate degree (Ph.D.) from Concordia University, where she specialized in Political Economy International Law, particularly on the issue of equality. Her work experience has been extensive: Chief Advisor and later Administrative Law Judge appointed by the Prime Minister to the Veterans Review and Appeals Tribunal in Canada; Supervising Attorney and later Executive Director for the Legal Services Corporation in the United States; National Director for an environmental network in Canada; Faculty for Business Law at the Law School, Law Society of Ireland; Associate at the law firm of Blake Cassels and Graydon L.L.P. with a secondment as in-house counsel with Agrium Inc. in Canada; Attorney with the Disability Law Center of Alaska; and Solo Practitioner of the Social Security Disability Law Firm. She is also a gold medallist in figure skating. Dr. Cotter is the proud mother of Bill and Jill.

Chapter 1

Introduction

> So we come here today to dramatize a shameful condition. In a sense we've come to our nation's capital to cash a check. When the architects of our republic wrote the magnificent words of the Constitution and the Declaration of Independence, they were signing a promissory note to which every (human) was to fall heir. This note was the promise that all ... would be guaranteed the unalienable rights of life, liberty, and the pursuit of happiness ... A check which has come back marked insufficient funds. We refuse to believe that there are insufficient funds in the great vaults of opportunity of this nation. And so we've come to cash this check, a check that will give us upon demand the riches of freedom and the security of justice.[1]

In our universal quest for justice in general, and appreciation for maternity issues in *Pregnant Pause*, we may learn from the immortal words of one of the greatest civil rights leaders and human rights activists Dr. Martin Luther King, Jr. This book, *Pregnant Pause*, focuses on the goal of maternity equality, and the importance of the law and legislation to combat maternity discrimination in these troubling times. The aim of this book is to better understand the issue of inequality and to improve the likelihood of achieving maternity equality in the future and ending maternity inequality. *Pregnant Pause* examines the primary role of legislation, which has an impact on the court process, as well as the primary role of the judicial system, which has an impact on the fight for maternity appreciation. This is the seventh book in a series of books on discrimination law. Other titles in the series are: *Gender Injustice*, dealing with gender discrimination; *Race Matters*, dealing with race discrimination; *This Ability*, dealing with disability discrimination; *Just A Number*, dealing with age discrimination; *Heaven Forbid*, dealing with religious discrimination; and *Ask No Questions*, dealing with sexual orientation discrimination. A similar approach and structure is used throughout the series to illustrate comparisons and contradictions in discrimination law.

Fundamental rights are rights which either are inherent in a person by natural law or are instituted in the citizen by the State. The ascending view of the natural law of divine origin over human law involves moral expectations in human beings through a social contract, which includes minimum moral rights of which one may not be deprived by government or society. The competing view is that courts operating under the Constitution can enforce only those guarantees which are expressed. Thus, legislation has an impact on the court system and on society

---

1   King Jr., Dr. Martin Luther, *March on Washington*, United States, 1963.

as a whole. Internationally and nationally, attempts have been made to improve the situation of those who are members of all minorities and outlaw maternity discrimination through acceptance and accommodation.

In looking at the relationship between *Pregnant Pause* and the law, the book deals comprehensively with the issue of maternity discrimination throughout its chapters by outlining important legislation in the area, with no particular position argued necessarily but with the intent to give the reader the knowledge to make up their own mind; also, for the most part, the countries examined were chosen because of their predominant common law background, because of their predominant use of the English language in legislation and case law, and because of their predominant role in the fight against discrimination: Chapter 1 introduces the reader to the core area of maternity discrimination; Chapters 2 and 3 cover maternity discrimination generally and pregnant pause specifically, and the United Nations, respectively; Chapters 4 and 5 examine maternity discrimination in Australia and New Zealand, and Africa and South Africa, respectively; Chapters 6 and 7 examine maternity discrimination in Canada, Mexico and the United States, and the North American situation with the North American Free Trade Agreement regarding maternity discrimination, respectively; Chapters 8 and 9 examine maternity discrimination in the United Kingdom and Ireland, and the European situation with the European Union Treaty regarding maternity discrimination, respectively; and Chapter 10 concludes this overview of maternity discrimination. If a woman chooses to step away from her career and stay home with her children, she loses out on many aspects of the labor market, including income, seniority and pension; if a woman chooses to maintain her career and place the children in daycare or with a nanny, then she, as well as her children, loses out on many aspects of motherhood, including valuable time and bonding.

The globalization process and the various economic agreements have a direct impact on people's lives as key players in the labor market today. This study seeks to comparatively analyze legislation impacting maternity discrimination in various countries internationally. It also examines the two most important trade agreements of our day, namely the North American Free Trade Agreement and the European Union Treaty, in a historical and compelling analysis of equality. Although an important trade agreement with implications for labor, the North American Free Trade Agreement has a different system from the European system in that it has no overseeing court with jurisdiction over the respective countries. Further, the provisions for non-discrimination in the labor process are contained in a separate document, the North American Agreement on Labor Cooperation. On the other hand, the European Union Treaty takes a different approach, by directly providing for non-discrimination, as well as an overseeing court, the European Court of Justice, and the treaty is made part of the domestic law of every Member State, weakening past discriminatory laws and judgments. Further, the European process actively implements equality by way of European Union legislation. North America, as the new world with its image of freedom and equality, is considered to have made great strides in civil rights. However, the American philosophy of survival of the fittest, the pursuit of materialism and the search for the fountain of youth have slowed down the process. With the advent of the European Union, the coming together of nations has had a very positive influence on the enforcement of human rights, much more so than that of North America, because of the unique European approach.

All parties must cooperate, and governments need to work with businesses, trade unions and society as a whole, so together they can create an environment where all humans can participate at all levels of political life and decision-making. Indeed, combating maternity inequality and achieving maternity equality requires a strong *Pregnant Pause* focus on maternity appreciation and equality in constitutional, legal, judicial and electoral frameworks for all humans to be actively involved at the national and international levels. According to liberal democracy, the rule of law is the foundation stone for the conduct of institutions. *Pregnant Pause* offers a defense of the notion that social reform is possible and plausible through key institutions, which include the legal system and its use of the law. For liberal democracy, the legislative system is the core for the governance of society in the way it functions toward social equality of opportunity. It is clear that if we initially reform our legislation and our laws and in the end our way of thinking, then there will be a change in the institutions of society and their functioning, which will be a major step forward in societal reform.

The law is of central importance in the debate for change from maternity inequality to maternity equality. Actionable and enforceable rights are legal norms, which represent social facts demarcating areas of action linked with universalized freedom.[2] Law is a powerful tool, which can and must be used to better society. Associated with command, duty and sanction, and emanating from a determined source, law is a rule of conduct enforced by sanctions, and administered by a determinate locus of power concentrated in a sovereign or a surrogate, the court. Therefore, the justice system and the courts play a vital role in enforcing the law. Legitimacy has subjective guarantees of internalization with the acceptance and belief in authority, and objective guarantees of enforcement with the expectation of reactions to the behavior.[3] Therefore, the law must recognize equally all members of society, in order for it to be effective. Further, in order for a law to be seen as legitimate from society's point of view and accepted by the people, in general to be followed, a process of inclusive interaction by all affected must first be realized. When creating laws, this means that input from various groups, including all humans regardless of maternity issues, is critical.

Thus, laws have two components, namely, facts, which stabilize expectations and sustain the order of freedom, and norms, which provide a claim of approval by everyone. Law makes possible highly artificial communities whose integration is based simultaneously on the threat of internal sanctions and the supposition of a rationally motivated agreement.[4] Maternity discrimination and injustice can be

---

2 Habermas, Jurgen, *Between Facts and Norms*, Massachusetts, 1998, p.xii.
3 Fried, Morton, *The Evolution of Political Society*, New York, 1967, p.23.
4 Habermas, Jurgen, *Between Facts and Norms*, Massachusetts, 1998, p.8.

undercut through the effective use of both the law and the courts. The facticity of the enforcement of law is intertwined with the legitimacy of a genesis of law that claims to be rational, because it guarantees liberty. Laws can go a long way in forbidding inequality and providing for equality; where one ends the other begins. There are two ranks of law, namely ordinary law of legislation, administration and adjudication, and higher constitutional law affecting rights and liberties, which government must respect and protect. The latter encompasses the constitutions of the various nations as interpreted by the supreme courts. Law holds its legitimacy and validity by virtue of its coercive potential, its rational claim of acceptance as right. It is procedurally constructed to claim agreement by all citizens in a discursive process purported to be open to all equally for legitimacy with a presumption of fair results. The legitimate legal order is found in its reflexive process. Therefore, we must all believe that equality is a good and necessary thing, which is essential to the very growth of society and to the ending of maternity discrimination.

Thus, conflict resolution is a process of reasoned agreement where, firstly, members assume the same meanings by the same words; secondly, members are rationally accountable for their actions; and thirdly, mutually acceptable resolutions can be reached so that supporting arguments justify the confidence in the notion that the truth in justice will not be proven false.[5] Disenchantment with the law and the legal process only serves to undermine the stabilization of communities. By legitimizing the legal process and holding up the ideals of equality in the fight against maternity discrimination, the law and the courts can bring about change.

All humans have had to fight in the formulation of laws and in the enforcement of equality in the courts. Human differences rest on economic determination and historical change. Inequality in the distribution of private property among different classes of people has been a characteristic of society. The ruling class loathes that which it is not, that which is foreign to it. The patriarchal system has freely fashioned laws and adjusted society to suit those in power, and this has traditionally been young white Anglo-Saxon Protestant men; however, women have had to juggle the roles of mother and career woman. Relationships, opportunities, attributes and preconceived notions are socially constructed and are learned through socialization processes. They are context- and time-specific but changeable, since the physical and the mental determine what is expected, allowed and valued in a given situation. In most societies, there are differences and inequalities between humans in the decision-making opportunities, assignment of responsibilities, undertaking of activities, and access to and control over resources with maternity part of the broader sociocultural context. There are important criteria for analysis, including maternity, gender, race, disability, age, religion, sexual orientation, and class, and hence all these can, alone or combined, amount to discrimination.

The concept of equality is the ignoring of difference between individuals for a particular purpose in a particular context, or the deliberate indifference to

---

5   Ibid., at p.xv.

specified differences in the acknowledgement of the existence of difference. It is important to note that assimilation is not equality. The notion of rights and of equality should be bound to the notion of justice and fairness. Legal freedom and rights must be seen as relationships not possessions, as doing, not having. While injustice involves a constraint of freedom and a violation of human dignity through a process of oppression and domination, justice involves the institutional conditions necessary for the development and exercise of individual capacities for collective communication and cooperation.[6] Discrimination is the withholding from the oppressed and subordinated what enables them to exercise private and public autonomy. The struggle must be continued to bring about psychological, sociological and institutional changes to allow all members of the human race, regardless of maternity, to feel equal and to recognize all as being so. Solidarity and cooperation are required for universal and global equality.

Though humans are mortal and civilizations come and go, from Biblical times to our days, there has been a fixed pivot for the thoughts of all generations and for humans of all continents, namely the equal dignity inherent in the human personality.[7] Even Pope John XXIII described the United Nations Declaration of Human Rights in his 1963 Encyclical *Pacem in Terris*, as 'one of the most important acts of the United Nations' and as 'a step towards the politico-judicial organization of the world community'; 'In social life, every right conferred on man by nature creates in others (individuals and collectivities) a duty, that of recognizing and respecting that right'.[8] Further, Pope John Paul II described the importance of work and of just remuneration in his 1981 Encyclical *Laborem Exercens*:

> Work bears a particular mark of ... humanity, the mark of a person operating within a community of persons .... While work, in all its many senses, is an obligation, that is to say a duty, it is also a source of rights on the part of the worker. These rights must be examined in the broad context of human rights as a whole, which are connatural with man, and many of which are proclaimed by various international organizations and increasingly guaranteed by the individual States for their citizens. Respect for this broad range of human rights constitutes the fundamental condition for peace in the modern world: peace both within individual countries and societies and in international relations .... The human rights that flow from work are part of the broader context of those fundamental rights of the person .... The key problem of social ethic ... is that of just remuneration for work done .... Hence, in every case, a just wage is the concrete means of verifying the justice of the whole socio-economic system and, in any case, of checking that it is functioning justly.[9]

---

6 Ibid., at p.419.
7 Cassin, René, *From the Ten Commandments to the Rights of Man*, France, 1969.
8 Pope John XXIII, *Pacem in Terris*, Rome, 1963.
9 Pope John Paul II, *Laborem Exercens*, Rome, 1981.

An improvement in equality of opportunity is sought for all rather than a utopian state of equality. No one should misunderstand this. Clearly, oppression exists. Rather, this book, *Pregnant Pause*, seeks to add to the list of inequalities to be considered, in this context maternity discrimination, and does not rule out other forms of injustices. Generalities are not presumed nor are they made here, for this would detract from the very purpose of this book, to bring to the forefront of discussion the reality of injustice, not to create further injustice, in the pursuit of *Pregnant Pause*.

Chapter 2
Pregnant Pause in Maternity Discrimination

Introduction

In the quest for appreciation for maternity issues in *Pregnant Pause*, this chapter will examine maternity discrimination generally, and pregnant pause specifically. All human, civil, cultural, economic, political and social rights, including the right to development, are universal, indivisible, interdependent and interrelated. Governments and others must not only refrain from violating human rights, but must work actively to promote and protect these rights. Human rights issues of discrimination continue to mar progress towards empowerment where women in particular who deal with maternity issues continue to be stereotyped and discriminated against, face systemic barriers and prejudice that prevent them from accessing the opportunities created for the achievement of equality, and continue to occupy the dual role of mother and career woman.

Maternity Discrimination Generally

The word discrimination comes from the Latin 'discriminare', which means to 'distinguish between'. Discrimination is more than distinction; it is action based on prejudice resulting in unfair treatment of people. Social theories of egalitarianism claim that social equality regardless of maternity issues should prevail. Discrimination can be defined as treatment or consideration of, or making a distinction in favor of or against, a person or thing based on the group, class, or category to which that person or thing belongs rather than on individual merit, and unfair treatment of a person or group on the basis of prejudice. Unlawful discrimination can be characterized as direct or indirect. Direct discrimination involves treating someone less favorably, because of the possession of a prohibited attribute such as maternity than they would treat someone without the prohibited attribute who was in the same circumstances. Indirect discrimination involves setting a condition or requirement that a smaller proportion of those with the prohibited attribute can comply with than those who do not have the prohibited attribute without reasonable justification.

Discrimination is to make a distinction. Commonplace forms of invidious discrimination include distinctions by maternity, gender, race, disability, age, religion, sexual orientation and class. Invidious discrimination classifies people into different groups in which group members receive distinct and typically unequal treatments and rights without rational justification. Expectations and obligations of group members are also biased by invidious discrimination. If the justification is rational, then the discrimination is not invidious. By virtue of establishing nationalism, as opposed to globalism, every government has formalized and supported discrimination. However, many governments have attempted to control discrimination through civil rights legislation, equal opportunity laws and institutionalized policies of affirmative action. Within the equal opportunities/individual merit approach can be found a spectrum of tests for discrimination. At one end of the spectrum, there is the 'equality as mere rationality', where arbitrary and unreasonable behavior is deemed discriminatory, but justifications for discrimination are accepted at face value. At the other end of the spectrum, there is the 'equality as fairness', where justifications are examined critically, the possibility of indirect discrimination is recognized, and burdens of proof may be shifted. There is a third conception of equality which goes beyond the individual merit approach but avoids the explicitly redistributive language of equality of results, the 'radical equality of opportunity', which argues for institutional and structural changes to remove the barriers to equal participation of people belonging to different groups. It involves the creation of positive duties on employers to promote equality, by reviewing employment practices and workplace organization.

Prejudice is, as the name implies, the process of pre-judging something. In general, it implies coming to a judgment on the subject before learning where the preponderance of the evidence actually lies, or formation of a judgment without direct experience. When applied to social groups, prejudice generally refers to existing biases toward the members of such groups, often based on social stereotypes, and at its most extreme, denying groups benefits and rights unjustly or, conversely, unfairly showing unwarranted favor towards others. It may be a matter of early education; those taught that certain attitudes are the correct ones may form opinions without weighing the evidence on both sides of a given question. Many prejudicial behaviors are picked up at a young age by children emulating their elders' way of thinking and speaking, with no malice intended on the child's part. Overall, prejudice has been termed an adaptive behavior by sociologists.

Affirmative action or positive discrimination is a policy or a program providing access to systems for people of a minority group, who have traditionally been discriminated against, with the aim of creating a more egalitarian society. This consists of access to education, employment, health care or social welfare. The terms affirmative action and positive discrimination originate in law, where it is common for lawyers to speak of affirmative or positive remedies that command the wrongdoer to do something. In contrast, negative remedies command the wrongdoer to not do something or to stop doing something. In employment, affirmative action may also be known as employment equity or preferential hiring. Affirmative action requires that institutions increase hiring and promotion of candidates of mandated groups. It originally began as a government remedy for past government and social injustices, and exists to change the distribution of such things as jobs, education or wealth based on certain characteristics.

Supporters of affirmative action argue that affirmative action policies counteract a systemic discrimination by providing a balancing force. A certain group may be less proportionately represented in an area, often employment or education, due, in the view of proponents, to past or ongoing discrimination against members of the group. The theory is that a simple adoption of meritocratic principles along the lines of maternity-blindness would not suffice to change the situation: regardless of overt principles, people already in positions of power are likely to hire people they know, and people from similar backgrounds; also, ostensible measures of merit might well be biased toward the same groups who were already empowered. In such a circumstance, proponents believe government action giving members of the group preferential treatment is necessary in order to achieve a proportionate distribution. A written affirmative action plan must include goals and timetables for achieving full utilization of all people, especially those from a different group, in quotas based on an analysis of the current workforce compared to the availability in the general labor pool. Supporters of affirmative action argue that it benefits society as a whole, given that affirmative action is effective, since creating a diverse culture increases the quality of the society.

From its outset, affirmative action was seen as a transitional strategy, with the intent that in a period, variously estimated from a generation to a century, the effects of past discrimination would be sufficiently countered that such a strategy would no longer be necessary: the power elite would reflect the demographics of society at large. Opponents of affirmative action regard it as demeaning to members of disadvantaged groups, in that affirmative action wrongly sends a condescending message that they are not capable enough to be considered on their own merits. Critics often object to the use of quotas in affirmative action. There is dispute over whether this *de jure* illegality prevents *de facto* quotas, and attempts have been made to show that these goals are not quotas. However, some believe eradicating affirmative action will further deepen economic disparity between groups.

Free market libertarians believe any form of unjustified discrimination is likely to lead to inefficiencies, and that a rational person would therefore be unlikely to seek to discriminate one way or another and should therefore be free to decide who to select. Therefore, libertarians generally do not advocate anti-discrimination laws, as they reportedly distort the situation. They believe that inefficient, overregulated, non-competitive industries enable unjustified discrimination, as said industries need not compete and hire on credentials relevant to the job. In terms of policy, libertarians favor repealing all affirmative action legislation and regulation, so that the government has no official stance on the practice, leaving the decision to uphold and maintain such a policy up to the individual institutions.

Overall, equal opportunity refers to the idea that all people should start out in life from the same platform, in that all should have equal opportunities in life, regardless of where they were born or who their parents were. Egalitarianism is the moral doctrine that equality ought to prevail throughout society and, according to legal egalitarianism, everyone ought to be considered equal under the law. It is important to note that policies, decisions and negotiations that fail to take into account the impact on all members of society may reflect systemic discrimination. Tokenism occurs when a small group is invited to participate in an initiative to demonstrate that a program is progressive or to show someone has consulted the constituency, but in fact has ignored their views, which is discriminatory in itself. Standards or rules of behavior are norms, which help us to predict the behavior of others and, in turn, allow others to know what to expect of us, with our culture defining what is proper and improper behavior, what is right and wrong, and what we are expected to do and not to do.[1]

The concept of minority group has long provided a valuable frame of reference for understanding the experiences of groups of people in society who are singled out, based on some cultural or physical characteristic, for discriminatory treatment.[2] In terms of maternity and culture, they are a cross-cutting determinant within the framework for understanding. Cultural values and traditions determine to a large extent how a given society views maternity. Culture is a key factor in whether or not co-residency with others is the preferred way of living. There is enormous cultural diversity and complexity within countries, and among countries and regions of the world. Policies and programs need to respect current cultures and traditions, while de-bunking outdated stereotypes and misinformation. Moreover, there are critical universal values that transcend culture, such as ethics and human rights. While the significance of national and regional particularities, and various historical, cultural and religious backgrounds must be borne in mind, it is the duty of States, regardless of their political, economic and cultural systems, to promote and protect human rights and fundamental freedoms of all people. The implementation of these principles of equality, including through national laws, strategies, policies, programs and development priorities, is the sovereign responsibility of each State, in conformity with human rights and fundamental freedoms. The significance of and full respect for various philosophical and ethical values, and for cultural and racial backgrounds of individuals and communities should contribute to the full enjoyment of human rights, in order to achieve equality, development and peace.

There must be immediate and concerted action by all to create a peaceful, just and humane world based on human rights and fundamental freedoms, including the principle of equality for people and from all walks of life, and to this end, broad-based and sustained economic growth in the context of sustainable development is necessary to sustain social development and social justice. Success will require a strong commitment on the part of governments, international organizations and institutions at all levels. It will also require adequate mobilization of resources from multilateral, bilateral and private sources for the advancement of all humans for strengthening the capacity of national, sub-regional, regional and international institutions; a commitment to equal rights, equal responsibilities and equal

---

1   Harris, Diana K., 'Age Norms', in Erdman B. Palmore, Laurence Branch, Diana K. Harris, *Encyclopedia of Ageism*, The Haworth Press, Inc., New York, 2005.

2   Wirth, L., 'The Problem of Minority Groups', in R. Linton (ed.), *The Science of Man in the World Crisis* (pp. 347–372), Columbia University Press, New York, 1945.

opportunities for the equal participation of all regardless of maternity issues in all national, regional and international bodies in the policy-making processes; and the establishing or strengthening of mechanisms at all levels for accountability to the world's population in general. As globalization continues to influence economic opportunities worldwide, its effects remain uneven, creating both risks and opportunities for different groups. For many, globalization has intensified existing inequalities and insecurities, often translating into the loss of livelihoods, labor rights and social benefits. Organizations and networks are taking on issues of social justice and equal rights to influence economic policies and decisions at the micro, meso and macro levels.

Even with economic growth, conditions can arise which can aggravate social inequality and marginalization. Hence, it is indispensable to search for new alternatives that ensure that all members of society benefit from economic growth based on a holistic approach to all aspects of development: equality between people, social justice, conservation and protection of the environment, sustainability, solidarity, participation and cooperation, peace and respect for human rights. The rapid process of adjustment due to downsizing in sectors has led to increased unemployment and underemployment. Structural adjustment programs have not been successfully designed to minimize their negative effects on vulnerable and disadvantaged groups, to assure positive effects on those groups by preventing their marginalization in society. Multilateral trade negotiations underscore the increasing interdependence of national economies, as well as the importance of trade liberalization and access to open dynamic markets. Only a new era of international cooperation among peoples based on a spirit of partnership within an equitable international social and economic environment, along with a radical transformation of the relationship to one of full and equal partnership will enable the world to meet the challenges of the twenty-first century. Interestingly, the growing strength of the non-governmental sector has become a driving force for change. Non-governmental organizations (NGOs) have played an important advocacy role in advancing legislation or mechanisms to ensure the promotion of all people, and have become catalysts for new approaches to development.

Actions to be taken at the national and international levels by all governments, the United Nations' system, international and regional organizations, including international financial institutions, the private sector, non-governmental organizations (NGOs) and other actors of civil society, include the creation and maintenance of a non-discriminatory as well as maternity-sensitive legal environment through review of legislation with a view to striving to remove discriminatory provisions. Problems continue to persist in addressing the challenges of equalities, empowerment, poverty eradication, and advancement of all. Political, economic and ecological crises, systematic or *de facto* discrimination, violations of and failure to protect human rights and fundamental freedoms, and ingrained prejudicial attitudes towards different groups are impediments to equality. It will be critical for the international community to demonstrate a new commitment for the future to inspire a new generation to work together for a more just society.

Pregnant Pause Specifically

Globally, it is interesting to note the afforded maternity leave (in weeks):[3]

Afghanistan	13
Albania	52
Algeria	14
Andorra	16
Angola	12
Antigua and Barbuda	13
Argentina	13
Armenia	20
Australia	52
Austria	16
Azerbaijan	18
Bahamas	13
Bahrain	6
Bangladesh	12
Barbados	12
Belarus	18
Belgium	15
Belize	12
Benin	14
Bermuda	12
Bolivia	9
Bosnia & Herzegovina	52
Botswana	12
Brazil	17
British Virgin Islands	13
Bulgaria	19
Burkina Faso	14
Burundi	12
Cambodia	13
Cameroon	14
Canada	17–18
Cape Verde	6
Central African Republic	14
Chad	14
Channel Islands, Guernsey	18
Channel Islands, Jersey	18
Chile	18
China	13
China, Hong Kong SAR	10

---

3   United Nations, Maternity Leave by Country.

Colombia	12
Comoros	14
Congo	15
Costa Rica	16
Cote d'Ivoire	14
Croatia	52+
Cuba	18
Cyprus	16
Czech Republic	28
Democratic Republic of the Congo	14
Denmark	52
Djibouti	14
Dominica	12
Dominican Republic	12
Ecuador	8
Egypt	13
El Salvador	12
Equatorial Guinea	12
Eritrea	8
Estonia	20
Ethiopia	13
Fiji	12
Finland	15
France	16
Gabon	14
Gambia	12
Germany	14
Ghana	12
Greece	17
Grenada	12
Guatemala	12
Guinea	14
Guinea-Bissau	9
Guyana	13
Haiti	12
Honduras	10
Hungary	24
Iceland	12
India	12
Indonesia	12
Iran (Islamic Republic of)	13
Iraq	9
Ireland	18
Isle of Man	26
Israel	12

Italy	20
Jamaica	12
Japan	14
Jordan	10
Kazakhstan	18
Kenya	8
Kiribati	12
Kuwait	10
Kyrgyzstan	18
Lao People's Democratic Rep.	13
Latvia	16
Lebanon	7
Lesotho	12
Libyan Arab Jamahiriya	7
Liechtenstein	20
Lithuania	18
Luxembourg	16
Madagascar	14
Malawi	8
Malaysia	9
Mali	14
Malta	14
Mauritania	14
Mauritius	12
Mexico	12
Monaco	16
Mongolia	17
Morocco	14
Mozambique	8
Myanmar	12
Namibia	12
Nepal	7
Netherlands	16
New Zealand	14
Nicaragua	12
Niger	14
Nigeria	12
Norway	45–52
Pakistan	12
Panama	14
Papua New Guinea	6+
Paraguay	12
Peru	13
Philippines	8
Poland	16

Portugal	17
Qatar	7
Republic of Korea	13
Republic of Moldova	18
Romania	18
Russian Federation	20
Rwanda	12
Saint Kitts and Nevis	13
Saint Lucia	12
Saint Vincent and the Grenadines	13
San Marino	20
Sao Tome and Principe	10
Saudi Arabia	10
Senegal	14
Serbia	52
Seychelles	14
Singapore	16
Slovakia	28
Slovenia	15
Solomon Islands	12
Somalia	14
South Africa	16
Spain	16
Sri Lanka	12
Sudan	8
Swaziland	12
Sweden	68
Switzerland	14
Syrian Arab Republic	7
Tajikistan	20
TFYR of Macedonia	36
Thailand	13
Togo	14
Trinidad and Tobago	13
Tunisia	4–8
Turkey	16
Turkmenistan	16
Uganda	8
Ukraine	18
United Arab Emirates	12
United Kingdom	52
United Republic of Tanzania	12
United States of America	12
Uruguay	12
Uzbekistan	18

Vanuatu	12
Venezuela	18
Viet Nam	16–24
Yemen	9
Zambia	12
Zimbabwe	13

In a study from McGill University's Institute for Health and Social Policy, the United States, Lesotho, Liberia, Swaziland and Papua New Guinea were the only countries out of 173 studied that did not guarantee any paid leave for mothers. Among the 168 countries that do, 98 offer 14 or more weeks of paid leave; at least 145 provide paid sick days for short- and long-term illnesses, with 127 providing for a week or more every year; in addition, 137 countries require its employers to provide paid annual leave. Further, the United States also lags behind in protecting working women's right to breastfeed. At least 107 countries grant women the right to breastfeed, and in 73 of those, the breaks are paid.[4] Paid leave for new mothers improves children's health outcomes by enabling mothers to provide essential care to their children, by facilitating breastfeeding, which reduces the risk of infectious and other diseases, and by increasing the likelihood that children will receive necessary immunizations, all of which contribute to lower infant mortality and morbidity rates. Increased parental leave also facilitates the formation of bonds between parents and infants, which fosters the child's positive emotional development. Paid leave for new mothers increases job and income security and improves families' economic conditions by increasing the long-term employment and earning prospects of working women and eliminating the wage 'child penalty' that mothers often pay. Such workplace supports also benefit employers by reducing staff turnover, improving workers' productivity, increasing job satisfaction, and enhancing employees' commitment to their company's success. Further, in terms of breastfeeding at work, breastfeeding has been demonstrated to markedly reduce the risk of infections, including diarrheal disease, respiratory tract infections, ear infections and meningitis, in infancy and early childhood. Studies have found that breastfed children experience a 1.5- to 5-fold lower relative risk of mortality. In countries with poor sanitation and very low average family incomes, the protective effects of breastfeeding continue after infancy. In addition to these well-established benefits, breastfeeding also results in positive health outcomes for women by decreasing risks of medical problems such as postpartum blood loss and hemorrhaging, ovarian cancer, breast cancer and osteoporosis. Breastfeeding may also enhance mother–child bonding, which is important for children's psychosocial development.[5]

Parental leave laws can support new parents in two complementary ways: by offering job-protected leave and by offering financial support during that

---

4   McGill University Institute for Health and Social Policy, 2009.
5   Ibid.

leave.[6] In examining 21 industrialized countries (Australia, Austria, Belgium, Canada, Denmark, Finland, France, Germany, Greece, Ireland, Italy, Japan, the Netherlands, New Zealand, Norway, Portugal, Spain, Sweden, Switzerland, the United Kingdom, and the United States), in terms of time, all protect at least one parent's job for a period of weeks, months, or years around the birth of a child, which allows parents to take time to care for their infant or young child, secure in the knowledge that they will be able to return to the same or a comparable job at the end of the leave period. Total protected job leave available to couples varies widely, from only 14 weeks in Switzerland to over 300 weeks, about six years, in France and Spain. The United States, with 24 weeks of combined protected job leave for a two-parent family, ranks 20th out of 21.

In terms of money, almost all also provide direct financial support for parents during at least part of the protected leave. Most countries provide between three months and one year of full-time-equivalent paid leave; Sweden, the most generous of the countries examined, provides 47 weeks of full-time-equivalent paid leave. The United States is one of only two countries to offer no paid parental leave; Australia also offers no paid leave, but supports new parents with a substantial financial 'baby bonus' regardless of whether they take parental leave. Most countries provide between three months and one year of full-time-equivalent (FTE) paid leave. Sweden provides the most FTE paid leave: 47 weeks. Eight other countries offer at least six months of FTE paid leave: Norway (44 weeks), Germany (42 weeks), Greece (34 weeks), Finland (32 weeks), France (29 weeks), Canada (28 weeks), New Zealand (28 weeks), Spain (27 weeks), and Japan (26 weeks). Six countries have between four and six months of FTE paid leave: Italy (25 weeks), Portugal (25 weeks), Ireland (21 weeks), Denmark (20 weeks), and Belgium (18 weeks). Four countries guarantee some FTE paid leave, but fewer than four months: Austria and the Netherlands (16 weeks); the United Kingdom (12 weeks); and Switzerland (11 weeks). Finally, Australia and the United States grant no paid leave whatsoever.

In terms of mothers, all countries provide mothers with at least some protected job leave, from a low of 12 weeks in the United States, in the case of mothers who are employed in establishments with 50 or more employees and who have been on the job for at least one year, to a high of 162 weeks, in the case of France. France, Germany (160 weeks) and Spain (156 weeks) provide mothers with at least three years of total parental leave; Austria (112 weeks) grants more than two years; Norway (90 weeks), Sweden (85 weeks), the United Kingdom (65 weeks), Japan (58 weeks), New Zealand (58 weeks), Ireland (56 weeks), Australia (52 weeks) and Canada (52 weeks) require employers to provide mothers at least one year of total leave; Denmark (50 weeks), Italy (48 weeks), Greece (47 weeks), Finland (44 weeks), Portugal (37 weeks), the Netherlands (29 weeks) and Belgium (28 weeks) provide mothers with between six months and one year of total leave. The two least generous countries are Switzerland (14 weeks) and the United States (12 weeks).

---

6 Gornick, Janet C. and Schmitt, John, *Parental Leave Policies in 21 Countries, Assessing Generosity and Gender Equality*, September 2008.

In terms of financing family leave, most of the countries pay for paid leave benefits through payroll taxes, with the overall taxation rates, and the relative shares contributed by employers and employees, varying across countries. In some countries, these programs are financed through contributory funds dedicated solely to family leave benefits. In others, they are financed through health and sickness funds, or through unemployment compensation funds; in some countries, they are financed from social insurance funds that pay for a broad set of contributory programs. The benefits are funded through social insurance schemes, meaning that costs are distributed throughout society, which minimizes the burden on individual employers and, in turn, reduces incentives for employers to discriminate against potential leave-takers. In most countries, these payroll taxes operate at the national level. Canada and Switzerland stand as exceptions: the Canadian province of Quebec and the Swiss canton of Bern administer their own, more generous, benefits apart from their respective national systems.

In terms of scheduling flexibility, the right to take parental leave on a part-time basis, that is to combine leave-taking with part-time employment, can be an important aspect of family leave policy. Drawing a reduced leave while working part-time offers parents the possibility of staying connected to their jobs during parental leave, which in turn has benefits for both parents and employers. Part-time leave can also allow parents to phase out parental leave slowly, such as waiting until the child is older to resume full-time work. Of the countries, 10 allow parental leave to be taken on a part-time basis: Austria, Belgium, Denmark, Finland, Germany, the Netherlands, Norway, Portugal, Spain, and Sweden; Portugal gives parents an incentive to choose part-time over full-time leave, in that parents have three months of full-time parental leave or 12 months of part-time leave; Canada and the United Kingdom give parents the option of being on parental leave and collecting full benefits, while continuing to work for pay on a reduced schedule, with the UK granting mothers up to 10 'Keep in Touch' days to work during maternity leave.

In terms of best practices, there are six countries with policies that are strongest on both generosity and gender equality, which are three Nordic countries – Finland, Norway, and Sweden – plus France, Spain, and Greece. Across these six high-performing systems, five policy practices stand out as the most important:

1. *Generous paid leave:* Paid leave gives lower-wage parents the financial security necessary to take the leave available to them, strengthening a country's support for new parents and their children. In terms of gender equality, generous paid leave allows the higher wage parent, usually the father, to take parental leave without forfeiting the family's larger source of earnings. Among the six high-performing countries identified here, France, Greece, and Spain offer 100% wage replacement for portions of parental leave; Sweden replaces 80% of usual earnings, and Norway allows parents to choose between a longer period of benefits, paid at 80% of usual earnings, and a shorter, fully paid period; Finland utilizes a sliding scale of benefits,

in which low-earning workers receive approximately two-thirds of their usual earnings, and higher earning workers receive progressively less.

2. *Non-transferable quotas of leave for each parent:* Non-transferability helps to counteract social and economic pressures that otherwise encourage fathers to transfer benefits to mothers, thereby reducing fathers' role in caregiving and mothers' attachment to paid work. Finland guarantees fathers four full weeks of paternity leave and Finnish fathers also have an added incentive to take parental leave: if they take the last two weeks to which they are entitled, they receive an extra two weeks thereafter, paid at a higher wage-replacement rate; Spain allows fathers the same paid schedule reductions as those for breastfeeding mothers, independently of whether the mothers take their allotments, until their child is nine months old; Norway and Sweden each reserve a portion of families' financial benefits for fathers' leave, six weeks and two months, respectively, referred to as 'daddy days'.

3. *Universal coverage combined with modest eligibility restrictions:* The best-practice systems are all essentially universal, in that nearly all workplaces are covered, regardless of employer size, industry, geographic location or other criteria, and that individual eligibility restrictions are limited. While the best-practice systems require a recent employment history to qualify for earnings-related benefits, these systems typically offer some, usually flat-rate, benefits to new parents who do not meet the work requirements, because they fall short in terms of tenure or earnings. Norway requires that parents work for at least six of the ten months preceding their leave and meet a minimum earnings requirement; Spain requires parents to be employed and to have made Social Security contributions for 180 days. In each country, parents who do not qualify are entitled to a less generous form of paid leave. Greece limits longer-term parental leave to employees with at least one year with their current employer, but has no job tenure requirement for short-term parental leave; in France, to be eligible for the main parental leave program, parents must have worked at least one year for their employer, two years for the first child, but parents who do not meet the tenure requirement are entitled to a flat-rate payment if their income is below a certain level, in practice, about 90% of families are eligible; in Finland, all parents regardless of employment status are eligible for a minimum flat-rate benefit; to participate in the more generous parental leave program, parents must enroll at least 30 weeks prior to the expected date of birth; in Sweden, to receive the 80% benefit, parents must have earned a minimum specified daily wage for 240 days before the expected date of delivery, but those who do not meet that minimum, or have no recent employment, receive a flat-rate benefit.

4. *Financing structures that pool risk among many employers:* Collective financing allows risk to be shared across all employers, greatly reducing the financial burden for individual employers. Administering contributions and benefit payment at the national or regional level ensures that individual

employers do not bear the burden of directly paying benefits to each employee on parental leave. The centralized financing structure also reduces incentive for discrimination against women of child-bearing age. In France, employee contributions finance parental leave through local Sickness Insurance Funds; Finland, Norway, Spain and Sweden also finance and administer parental benefits through social insurance programs at the national level.

5. *Scheduling flexibility:* Scheduling flexibility allows families to find an arrangement that fits their needs, and to combine leave with part-time work over several years. Parents who can take parental leave on a part-time basis can care for their children without severing their relationship with their employer, which allows professional parents, more likely to be fathers, to take leave without jeopardizing their seniority and career prospects. In Finland, parents can take paid leave until their child's third birthday, and parents who work part-time can extend this benefit until their child's seventh birthday. In France, there are four levels of parental benefits: for parents who work full-time; for those who work between 50% and 80% of their usual schedule; for those who work no more than half of their usual schedule; and for those who take full-time leave. In Greece, private-sector workers can choose between taking parental leave by reducing their schedule by one hour per day for 30 months, at no loss of pay, or taking the same number of paid leave hours in a more condensed fashion, including one continuous leave period of almost four months. Spain, Sweden and Norway all allow leave to be taken on a part-time basis, with Spanish parents allowed to request part-time schedules until their child's eighth birthday and Norwegian parents having an added accommodation that permits both parents to take leave simultaneously if both take part-time leave.

In terms of parental leave and gender equality, in the absence of paid parental leave policies, traditional gender roles that involve women as 'caregivers' and men as 'providers', and the typically lower earnings of mothers, relative to fathers, in the labor market, create strong incentives for women to reduce their employment and take on a large majority of child care responsibilities. The most obvious problems associated with such outcomes are that women bear a disproportionate burden of child care responsibilities and pay both a short- and a long-term penalty in the labor market. A related issue is that traditional gender roles and labor-market outcomes work together to deprive men of the opportunity to participate actively in providing infant and child care. Even generous parental leave policy can act to undermine gender equality. Policies that allow families to allocate paid and unpaid leave heavily or even exclusively for mothers can reinforce traditional gender roles and women's disadvantage in the labor market. The generosity of paid leave is a factor in assessing the gender equality of parental leave policies. Because fathers' earnings are generally higher than mothers' earnings, unpaid or poorly paid parental leave can reinforce social and economic pressures against gender equality. If parental leave does not replace a substantial portion of fathers' earnings, families will bear a greater financial burden when fathers take leave than when mothers take leave. Spain has the second-longest total parental leave policy, 312 weeks per couple, but offers a relatively small number of FTE paid weeks of leave, 18 weeks per couple, so that the benefit level is low, which does little to counteract the effects of traditional gender roles and gender-wage differentials that push women out of the labor market and push fathers out of child care. Finland grants far less total leave, 48 weeks per couple, but a large portion of the leave is paid, 32 weeks, and only one-third of this is earmarked for mothers, giving Finnish families greater latitude for higher-earning fathers to take time to care for infants. Finland paired a recently enacted incentive for fathers to take parental leave with a billboard campaign asking, 'How many men, upon dying, wish they had spent more time with their bosses?' Experience suggests that providing paid parental leave can go some distance toward encouraging fathers to take leave. In Portugal, in the last year that parental leave was unpaid, that is 2000, fewer than 150 men took parental leave; three years later, after Portuguese law was changed to give fathers two weeks of paid family leave, 'daddy days', the number of men who took up the leave rose to 27,000.

Depending on the details, parental leave policy can either reinforce or counteract the factors that work to exclude fathers from child care. Increasing the generosity of parental leave policies can have the effect of reducing gender equality. Parental leave policies can have an important impact on gender equality, both in the workplace and with respect to sharing child care responsibilities. In the absence of paid parental leave policies, traditional gender roles, and the typically lower earnings of mothers relative to fathers in the labor market, create strong incentives for women to reduce their employment and take on a large majority of child care responsibilities. The most obvious problems associated with such outcomes are that women bear a disproportionate burden of child care responsibilities and pay both a short- and a long-term penalty in the labor market. A related issue is that traditional gender roles and labor market outcomes work together to deprive men of the opportunity to participate actively in providing infant and child care. Poorly designed parental leave policies can actually reinforce these tendencies toward gender inequality. At first glance, providing mothers, but not fathers, with leave that is both long and generous may seem to benefit mothers relative to fathers. In practice, however, such a policy would more than likely increase the child care responsibilities for mothers while, at the same time, reducing their long-term earnings relative to fathers. Mothers would have job security and financial support, but would also have the expectation that fathers would provide a substantial portion of child care. Mothers would also spend less time outside of the labor force, doing less damage to their long-term labor market prospects and lifetime earnings, especially relative to fathers, if fathers are also taking time out for child care. Limiting the total time outside of paid work is an especially important consideration given the possibility of divorce, which underscores the advantage for women of maintaining active ties to the labor market. Meanwhile, fathers would be given permission and financial support to care for their young children.

A generous, universal, gender-egalitarian, and flexible parental leave policy, financed through social insurance would go a long way toward spreading the costs of caring for children more equitably across mothers and fathers, parents and non-parents, and employers and employees. The governments of every high-income economy in the world take measures to support parents in their efforts to care for newborn children. These policies reflect the national interest in promoting the health and well-being of infants and young children as well as society's recognition that the first months and years of a child's life require substantial and sustained attention from parents. Governments generally provide two kinds of support for parents of infants and young children: protected job leave and financial support. Job protection allows parents to take time to care for their infant or young child secure in the knowledge that they will be able to return to the same or a comparable job at the end of the leave period. Most of the countries, though not the United States, also provide direct financial support for parents during at least part of the protected leave. How the available time and money for parental leave are allocated between mothers and fathers has a significant influence on how time for child care is shared among adults in families. Family leave policies operate in a broader social context with strong tendencies against equality in the distribution of child care responsibilities. Traditionally, social expectations have been that women will take on most, if not all, child care responsibilities. This traditional view has been reinforced by the reality that mothers tend to earn less at paid work than fathers do. Women's traditional gender roles and their disadvantage relative to men in the labor market work together to shift the responsibility of care for infants and young children heavily toward mothers.

All members of society have a profound interest in the health and well-being of young children and the caregiving parents. All of us benefit from the existence of happy and healthy children who can grow on to become productive members of society. Unfortunately, current U.S. labor law and social policy places almost the entire responsibility for caring for young children, and for combining that care with employment responsibilities, on individual parents. A generous, universal, gender-egalitarian, and flexible parental leave policy, financed through social insurance, would go a long way toward spreading the costs of caring for children more equitably across mothers and fathers, parents and non-parents, and employers and employees.[7]

Conclusion

Fairness at work and good job performance go hand in hand. Tackling maternity discrimination helps to attract, motivate, and retain staff and enhances an organization's reputation as an employer. Eliminating discrimination helps everyone to have an equal opportunity to work and to develop their skills. In order

---

7   Ibid.

to protect human rights, it is necessary for States to avoid, as far as possible, resorting to reservations of international agreements, and to ensure that no reservation is incompatible with the object and purpose of the Convention or is otherwise incompatible with international treaty law. The full enjoyment of equal rights is undermined by the discrepancies between some national legislation, and international law and international instruments on human rights. Overly complex administrative procedures, lack of awareness within the judicial process and inadequate monitoring of the violation of human rights, coupled with the underrepresentation of disabled groups in justice systems, insufficient information on existing rights, and persistent attitudes and practices perpetuate *de facto* and *de jure* inequality, which is also exacerbated by the lack of enforcement of civil, penal, labor and commercial laws or codes, or administrative rules and regulations intended to ensure the full enjoyment of human rights and fundamental freedoms, in the pursuit of *Pregnant Pause*.

Chapter 3

Pregnant Pause in the United Nations

Introduction

In the quest for appreciation of maternity issues in *Pregnant Pause*, this chapter will examine efforts against maternity discrimination in the United Nations. It will look at the important United Nations legislation dealing with maternity discrimination in the fight for maternity rights, namely: the Charter of the United Nations; the Statute of the International Court of Justice; the Universal Declaration of Human Rights; the International Covenant on Civil and Political Rights; the Optional Protocol to the International Covenant on Civil and Political Rights; the International Covenant on Economic, Social and Cultural Rights; for women in general, the Convention on the Elimination of All Forms of Discrimination against Women and the Optional Protocol to the Convention on the Elimination of All Forms of Discrimination against Women; the Equal Remuneration Convention (ILO C100); the Discrimination (Employment and Occupation) Convention (ILO C111); the Employment Policy Convention (ILO C122); the Maternity Protection Convention (ILO C3), (ILO C103), (ILO C183); and the Beijing Declaration. Through the work of the United Nations, international laws, called treaties or conventions, have been developed that require countries to work towards the elimination of all forms of discrimination, and they operate like a contract, as they apply throughout the world. When a country becomes a Party to a convention, it is bound to act in accordance with the rules contained in that convention. In addition to international treaties and conventions, there are several international declarations. The declarations are statements of principles, which are developed through the United Nations or other international bodies, and express the international community's aspirations to eliminate discrimination. These international declarations differ from treaties, because they do not always impose binding international legal obligations, but they are morally binding and have much influence over countries in setting acceptable standards of human rights protections. Internationally, the fundamental concept of human rights is one which human beings have striven both to suppress and promote.

Charter of the United Nations

The Preamble of the Charter of the United Nations, signed on 26 June 1945, states:

WE THE PEOPLES OF THE UNITED NATIONS DETERMINED

to save succeeding generations from the scourge of war, which twice in our lifetime has brought untold sorrow to mankind, and

to reaffirm faith in fundamental human rights, in the dignity and worth of the human person, in the equal rights of men and women and of nations large and small, and

to establish conditions under which justice and respect for the obligations arising from treaties and other sources of international law can be maintained, and

to promote social progress and better standards of life in larger freedom,

AND FOR THESE ENDS

to practice tolerance and live together in peace with one another as good neighbors, and

to unite our strength to maintain international peace and security, and

to ensure, by the acceptance of principles and the institution of methods, that armed force shall not be used, save in the common interest, and

to employ international machinery for the promotion of the economic and social advancement of all peoples,

HAVE RESOLVED TO COMBINE OUR EFFORTS TO ACCOMPLISH THESE AIMS

Accordingly, our respective Governments, through representatives assembled in the city of San Francisco, who have exhibited their full powers found to be in good and due form, have agreed to the present Charter of the United Nations and do hereby establish an international organization to be known as the United Nations.[1]

The purposes of the United Nations as outlined in Article 1 are to maintain international peace and security, and to that end to take effective collective measures for the prevention and removal of threats to the peace, and for the suppression of acts of aggression or other breaches of the peace, and to bring about by peaceful means, and in conformity with the principles of justice and international law, adjustment or settlement of international disputes or situations which might lead to a breach of the peace; to develop friendly relations among nations based on respect for the principle of equal rights and self-determination of peoples, and to take other appropriate measures to strengthen universal peace; to achieve international cooperation in solving international problems of an economic, social, cultural, or humanitarian character, and in promoting and encouraging respect for human rights and for fundamental freedoms for all without distinction; and to be a center for harmonizing the actions of nations in the attainment of these common ends.[2]

---

1   United Nations, Charter of the United Nations, at the Preamble.
2   Ibid., at Article 1.

In terms of international economic and social cooperation, Article 55 guarantees equal rights in employment without distinction, impacting maternity discrimination:

> 55. With a view to the creation of conditions of stability and well-being which are necessary for peaceful and friendly relations among nations based on respect for the principle of equal rights and self-determination of peoples, the United Nations shall promote:
> a. higher standards of living, full employment, and conditions of economic and social progress and development;
> b. solutions of international economic, social, health, and related problems; and international cultural and educational cooperation; and
> c. universal respect for, and observance of, human rights and fundamental freedoms for all without distinction as to ... sex ....[3]

Importantly, the International Court of Justice (ICJ) is established under Article 92 as the principal judicial organ of the United Nations, functioning in accordance with the Statute of the Permanent Court of International Justice.[4] Further, Article 94 binds Member States in their compliance with the decisions of the ICJ in that each Member of the United Nations undertakes to comply with the decision of the International Court of Justice in any case to which it is a party; and if any party to a case fails to perform the obligations incumbent upon it under a judgment rendered by the Court, the other party may have recourse to the Security Council, which may, if it deems necessary, make recommendations or decide upon measures to be taken to give effect to the judgment.[5] In addition, Article 95 holds that nothing in the present Charter shall prevent Members of the United Nations from entrusting the solution of their differences to other tribunals by virtue of agreements already in existence or which may be concluded in the future.[6]

Statute of the International Court of Justice

Article 1 of the Statute of the International Court of Justice, signed on 26 June 1945, holds that the International Court of Justice (ICJ), established by the Charter of the United Nations as the principal judicial organ of the United Nations, shall be constituted and shall function in accordance with the provisions of the present Statute.[7] By virtue of Article 34, only States may be parties in cases before the Court which, subject to and in conformity with its Rules, may request of public

---

3   Ibid., at Article 55.
4   Ibid., at Article 92.
5   Ibid., at Article 94.
6   Ibid., at Article 95.
7   United Nations, Statute of the International Court of Justice, at Article 1.

international organizations information relevant to cases before it, and shall receive such information presented by such organizations on their own initiative.[8]

Jurisdiction of the Court is established under Article 36 as comprising all cases which the parties refer to it and all matters specially provided for in the Charter of the United Nations or in treaties and conventions in force. Further, the States Parties to the present Statute may at any time declare that they recognize as compulsory *ipso facto* and without special agreement, in relation to any other State accepting the same obligation, the jurisdiction of the Court in all legal disputes concerning the interpretation of a treaty; any question of international law; the existence of any fact which, if established, would constitute a breach of an international obligation; and the nature or extent of the reparation to be made for the breach of an international obligation.[9] As to the application of choice of law, Article 38 maintains that the Court, whose function is to decide in accordance with international law such disputes as are submitted to it, shall apply international conventions, whether general or particular, establishing rules expressly recognized by the contesting States; international custom, as evidence of a general practice accepted as law; the general principles of law recognized by civilized nations; and judicial decisions and the teachings of the most highly qualified publicists of the various nations, as subsidiary means for the determination of rules of law.[10]

Universal Declaration of Human Rights

The Universal Declaration of Human Rights was adopted by the United Nations on 10 December 1948 and is an important legal document for combating discrimination, including maternity discrimination. The Preamble of the Universal Declaration of Human Rights states:

> Whereas recognition of the inherent dignity and of the equal and inalienable rights of all members of the human family is the foundation of freedom, justice and peace in the world,
>
> Whereas disregard and contempt for human rights have resulted in barbarous acts which have outraged the conscience of mankind, and the advent of a world in which human beings shall enjoy freedom of speech and belief and freedom from fear and want has been proclaimed as the highest aspiration of the common people,
>
> Whereas it is essential, if man is not to be compelled to have recourse, as a last resort, to rebellion against tyranny and oppression, that human rights should be protected by the rule of law,

---

8   Ibid., at Article 34.
9   Ibid., at Article 36.
10   Ibid., at Article 38.

Whereas it is essential to promote the development of friendly relations between nations,

Whereas the peoples of the United Nations have in the Charter reaffirmed their faith in fundamental human rights, in the dignity and worth of the human person and in the equal rights of men and women and have determined to promote social progress and better standards of life in larger freedom,

Whereas Member States have pledged themselves to achieve, in co-operation with the United Nations, the promotion of universal respect for and observance of human rights and fundamental freedoms,

Whereas a common understanding of these rights and freedoms is of the greatest importance for the full realization of this pledge.

The General Assembly of the United Nations proclaims:

THIS UNIVERSAL DECLARATION OF HUMAN RIGHTS as a common standard of achievement for all peoples and all nations, to the end that every individual and every organ of society, keeping this Declaration constantly in mind, shall strive by teaching and education to promote respect for these rights and freedoms and by progressive measures, national and international, to secure their universal and effective recognition and observance, both among the peoples of Member States themselves and among the peoples of territories under their jurisdiction.[11]

Article 1 recognizes human beings as free and equal:

1. All human beings are born free and equal in dignity and rights. They are endowed with reason and conscience and should act towards one another in a spirit of brotherhood.[12]

In the fight for equality, Article 2, which includes 'other status', is a helpful tool, since it holds that:

2. Everyone is entitled to all the rights and freedoms set forth in this Declaration, without distinction of any kind, such as ... sex ... or other status.[13]

Equality before the law without discrimination, important for maternity discrimination cases, is guaranteed in Article 7:

---

11   United Nations, Universal Declaration of Human Rights, at the Preamble.

12   Ibid., at Article 1.

13   Ibid., at Article 2.

7. All are equal before the law and are entitled without any discrimination to equal protection of the law. All are entitled to equal protection against any discrimination in violation of this Declaration and against any incitement to such discrimination.[14]

In the effort to redress discriminatory action, Article 8 establishes that everyone has the right to an effective remedy by competent national tribunals for acts violating the fundamental rights granted him by the constitution or by law.[15]

Importantly, employment rights, including equal pay for equal work, are protected under Article 23:

23. 1. Everyone has the right to work, to free choice of employment, to just and favorable conditions of work and to protection against unemployment.
   2. Everyone, without any discrimination, has the right to equal pay for equal work.
   3. Everyone who works has the right to just and favorable remuneration ensuring for himself and his family an existence worthy of human dignity, and supplemented, if necessary, by other means of social protection.
   4. Everyone has the right to form and to join trade unions for the protection of his interests.[16]

The right to education as a means of enhancement and advancement, and as a tool for combating discrimination, is established in Article 26, which holds that everyone has the right to education, in that education shall be free, at least in the elementary and fundamental stages, and elementary education shall be compulsory. Technical and professional education shall be made generally available and higher education shall be equally accessible to all on the basis of merit. Further, education shall be directed to the full development of the human personality and to the strengthening of respect for human rights and fundamental freedoms; it shall promote understanding, tolerance and friendship among all nations, racial or religious groups, and shall further the activities of the United Nations for the maintenance of peace.[17]

The Universal Declaration of Human Rights was codified into two Covenants, which the General Assembly adopted on 16 December 1966; these are the International Covenant on Civil and Political Rights and the International Covenant on Economic, Social and Cultural Rights. Described as the 'International Bill of Human Rights', the Covenants along with the Optional Protocols are landmarks in the efforts of the international community to promote human rights.

---

14   Ibid., at Article 7.
15   Ibid., at Article 8.
16   Ibid., at Article 23.
17   Ibid., at Article 26.

International Covenant on Civil and Political Rights (ICCPR)

The International Covenant on Civil and Political Rights was adopted and opened for signature, ratification and accession by the United Nations General Assembly in Resolution 2200A (XXI) of 16 December 1966, and entered into force on 23 March 1976, and is an important legal document for combating discrimination, including maternity discrimination.[18] In the Preamble of the Covenant on Civil and Political Rights, the States Parties to the present Covenant undertake the agreement:

> Considering that, in accordance with the principles proclaimed in the Charter of the United Nations, recognition of the inherent dignity and of the equal and inalienable rights of all members of the human family is the foundation of freedom, justice and peace in the world,
>
> Recognizing that these rights derive from the inherent dignity of the human person,
>
> Recognizing that, in accordance with the Universal Declaration of Human Rights, the ideal of free human beings enjoying civil and political freedom and freedom from fear and want can only be achieved if conditions are created whereby everyone may enjoy his civil and political rights, as well as his economic, social and cultural rights,
>
> Considering the obligation of States under the Charter of the United Nations to promote universal respect for, and observance of, human rights and freedoms,
>
> Realizing that the individual, having duties to other individuals and to the community to which he belongs, is under a responsibility to strive for the promotion and observance of the rights recognized in the present Covenant.[19]

The obligations of Member States are established in Article 2, which includes 'other status' in Article 2(1):

> 2. 1. Each State Party to the present Covenant undertakes to respect and to ensure to all individuals within its territory and subject to its jurisdiction the rights recognized in the present Covenant, without distinction of any kind, such as … sex … or other status.
>   2. Where not already provided for by existing legislative or other measures, each State Party to the present Covenant undertakes to take the necessary steps, in accordance with its constitutional processes and

---

18   United Nations, International Covenant on Civil and Political Rights.

19   Ibid., at the Preamble.

with the provisions of the present Covenant, to adopt such laws or other measures as may be necessary to give effect to the rights recognized in the present Covenant.

3. Each State Party to the present Covenant undertakes:

   a. To ensure that any person whose rights or freedoms as herein recognized are violated shall have an effective remedy, notwithstanding that the violation has been committed by persons acting in an official capacity;

   b. To ensure that any person claiming such a remedy shall have his right thereto determined by competent judicial, administrative or legislative authorities, or by any other competent authority provided for by the legal system of the State, and to develop the possibilities of judicial remedy;

   c. To ensure that the competent authorities shall enforce such remedies when granted.[20]

Equality before the law, important for maternity discrimination cases, is guaranteed under Article 26, which includes 'other status':

26. All persons are equal before the law and are entitled without any discrimination to the equal protection of the law. In this respect, the law shall prohibit any discrimination and guarantee to all persons equal and effective protection against discrimination on any ground such as ... sex ... or other status.[21]

It prohibits discrimination in law or in fact in any field regulated by public authorities and its scope is not limited to civil and political rights, so that it can be used to challenge discriminatory laws whether or not they relate to civil and political rights.

Importantly, the Human Rights Committee is established under Article 28 and consists of 18 members, carrying out the functions provided.[22] Other procedures of recourse are permitted under Article 44, which states that the provisions for the implementation of the present Covenant shall apply without prejudice to the procedures prescribed in the field of human rights by or under the constituent instruments and the conventions of the United Nations and of the specialized agencies and shall not prevent the States Parties to the present Covenant from having recourse to other procedures for settling a dispute in accordance with general or special international agreements in force between them.[23]

---

20 Ibid., at Article 2.
21 Ibid., at Article 26.
22 Ibid., at Article 28.
23 Ibid., at Article 44.

Optional Protocol to the International Covenant on Civil and Political Rights

The Optional Protocol to the International Covenant on Civil and Political Rights (ICCPR) of 16 December 1966 allows individuals, whose countries are party to the ICCPR and the protocol, who claim their rights under the ICCPR have been violated, and who have exhausted all domestic remedies, to submit written communications to the United Nations Human Rights Committee. States Parties to the ICCPR undertake to ensure that all enjoy all the civil and political rights in the Covenant on a basis of equality. The Preamble of the Optional Protocol to the International Covenant on Civil and Political Rights states:

> The States Parties to the present Protocol,
>
> Considering that in order further to achieve the purposes of the International Covenant on Civil and Political Rights (hereinafter referred to as the Covenant) and the implementation of its provisions it would be appropriate to enable the Human Rights Committee set up in part IV of the Covenant (hereinafter referred to as the Committee) to receive and consider, as provided in the present Protocol, communications from individuals claiming to be victims of violations of any of the rights set forth in the Covenant.[24]

Article 1 empowers the Committee to hear claims of violations:

> 1. A State Party to the Covenant that becomes a Party to the present Protocol recognizes the competence of the Committee to receive and consider communications from individuals subject to its jurisdiction who claim to be victims of a violation by that State Party of any of the rights set forth in the Covenant. No communication shall be received by the Committee if it concerns a State Party to the Covenant which is not a Party to the present Protocol.[25]

Finally, Article 2 preserves a person's right to redress:

> 2. Subject to the provisions of article 1, individuals who claim that any of their rights enumerated in the Covenant have been violated and who have exhausted all available domestic remedies may submit a written communication to the Committee for consideration.[26]

---

24 United Nations, Optional Protocol to the International Covenant on Civil and Political Rights, at the Preamble.

25 Ibid., at Article 1.

26 Ibid., at Article 2.

International Covenant on Economic, Social and Cultural Rights (ICESCR)

The International Covenant on Economic, Social and Cultural Rights, which was adopted and opened for signature, ratification and accession by General Assembly resolution 2200A (XXI) of 16 December 1966, and entered into force 16 January 1976, is an important legal document for combating discrimination, including maternity discrimination.[27] In a world where, according to the United Nations Development Program (UNDP), 'a fifth of the developing world's population goes hungry every night, a quarter lacks access to even a basic necessity like safe drinking water, and a third lives in a state of abject poverty at such a margin of human existence that words simply fail to describe it',[28] the importance of renewed attention and commitment to the full realization of economic, social and cultural rights is self-evident with such marginalization. Economic, social and cultural rights are designed to ensure the protection of people as full persons, based on a perspective in which people can enjoy rights, freedoms and social justice. In the Preamble of the International Covenant on Economic, Social and Cultural Rights, the States Parties to the present Covenant undertake the agreement:

> Considering that, in accordance with the principles proclaimed in the Charter of the United Nations, recognition of the inherent dignity and of the equal and inalienable rights of all the members of the human family is the foundation of freedom, justice and peace in the world,
>
> Recognizing that these rights derive from the inherent dignity of the human person,
>
> Recognizing that, in accordance with the Universal Declaration of Human Rights, the ideal of free human beings enjoying freedom from fear and want can only be achieved if conditions are created whereby everyone may enjoy his economic, social and cultural rights, as well as his civil and political rights and freedom,
>
> Realizing that the individual, having duties to other individuals and to the community to which he belongs, is under a responsibility to strive for the promotion and observance of the rights recognized in the present Covenant.[29]

Article 2 specifically guarantees the right to be free from discrimination, which includes 'other status':

---

27   United Nations, International Covenant on Economic, Social and Cultural Rights.

28   United Nations Development Program, *Human Development Report*, Oxford University Press, Oxford, p.2.

29   United Nations, International Covenant on Economic, Social and Cultural Rights, at the Preamble.

> 2. 1. Each State Party to the present Covenant undertakes to take steps, individually and through international assistance and co-operation, especially economic and technical, to the maximum of its available resources, with a view to achieving progressively the full realization of the rights recognized in the present Covenant by all appropriate means, including particularly the adoption of legislative measures.
>   2. The States Parties to the present Covenant undertake to guarantee that the rights enunciated in the present Covenant will be exercised without discrimination of any kind as to ... sex ... or other status.[30]

Importantly, employment rights under Article 6 establishes:

> 6. 1. The States Parties to the present Covenant recognize the right to work, which includes the right of everyone to the opportunity to gain his living by work which he freely chooses or accepts, and will take appropriate steps to safeguard this right.
>   2. The steps to be taken by a State Party to the present Covenant to achieve the full realization of this right shall include technical and vocational guidance and training programs, policies and techniques to achieve steady economic, social and cultural development and full and productive employment under conditions safeguarding fundamental political and economic freedoms to the individual.[31]

Further, Article 7 is a guarantee for equal rights in terms of equal pay and access to employment:

> 7. The States to the present Covenant recognize the right of everyone to the enjoyment of just and favorable conditions of work which ensure, in particular:
>   1. Remuneration which provides all workers, as a minimum, with:
>   1. Fair wages and equal remuneration for work of equal value without distinction of any kind, ... with equal pay for equal work;
>   2. A decent living for themselves and their families in accordance with the provisions of the present Covenant;
>   2. Safe and healthy working conditions;
>   3. Equal opportunity for everyone to be promoted in his employment to an appropriate higher level, subject to no considerations other than those of seniority and competence;
>   4. Rest, leisure and reasonable limitation of working hours and periodic holidays with pay, as well as remuneration for public holidays.[32]

---

30 Ibid., at Article 2.
31 Ibid., at Article 6.
32 Ibid., at Article 7.

State Parties to the Covenant recognize the right of everyone to education for the enhancement of the person, as guaranteed in Article 13, an important tool for combating discrimination. Education shall be directed to the full development of the human personality and the sense of its dignity, shall strengthen the respect for human rights and fundamental freedoms, shall enable all persons to participate effectively in a free society, promote understanding, tolerance and friendship among all nations and all racial, ethnic or religious groups, and further the activities of the United Nations for the maintenance of peace.[33] Compliance by States Parties with their obligations under the Covenant and the level of implementation of the rights and duties in question is monitored by the Committee on Economic, Social and Cultural Rights. The Covenant contains significant international legal provisions establishing economic, social and cultural rights, including rights relating to work in just and favorable conditions, social protection, an adequate standard of living, the highest attainable standards of physical and mental health, education, and enjoyment of the benefits of cultural freedom and scientific progress. In the fight against discrimination, it also provides for the right of self-determination; the right to work; the right to just and favorable conditions of work; the right to form and join trade unions; the right to social security and social insurance; protection and assistance to the family; the right to an adequate standard of living; the right to the highest attainable standard of physical and mental health; the right to education; the right to take part in cultural life; and the right to enjoy the benefits of scientific progress.

Convention on the Elimination of All Forms of Discrimination against Women (CEDAW)

Important for women, the Convention on the Elimination of All Forms of Discrimination against Women (CEDAW) was adopted on 18 December 1979.[34] It is the most comprehensive treaty specifically on the human rights of women, establishing legally binding obligations to end discrimination, and is especially important for women, who can suffer several layers of discrimination due to gender and maternity discrimination. Described as the 'International Bill of Rights for Women', the Convention provides for equality between women and men in the enjoyment of civil, political, economic, social and cultural rights. Discrimination against women is to be eliminated through legal, policy and programmatic measures, and through temporary special measures to accelerate women's equality, which are defined as non-discriminatory. The Convention obliges States Parties to modify the social and cultural patterns of conduct of men and women, in order to eliminate prejudices and customs, which are based on the idea of the inferiority or superiority of either of the sexes or on stereotyped roles for men and women.

---

33   Ibid., at Article 13.

34   United Nations, Convention on the Elimination of All Forms of Discrimination against Women.

As of September 2003, the Convention, which entered into force on 3 September 1981, had 185 signatory States Parties to the Convention, which represents over 90% of the members of the United Nations. In the Preamble of the Convention on the Elimination of All Forms of Discrimination against Women, the State Parties undertake the agreement:

> Noting that the Charter of the United Nations reaffirms faith in fundamental human rights, in the dignity and worth of the human person and in the equal rights of men and women,
>
> Noting that the Universal Declaration of Human Rights affirms the principle of the inadmissibility of discrimination and proclaims that all human beings are born free and equal in dignity and rights and that everyone is entitled to all the rights and freedoms set forth therein, without distinction of any kind, including distinction based on sex,
>
> Noting that the States Parties to the International Covenants on Human Rights have the obligation to ensure the equal rights of men and women to enjoy all economic, social, cultural, civil and political rights,
>
> Considering the international conventions concluded under the auspices of the United Nations and the specialized agencies promoting equality of rights of men and women,
>
> Noting also the resolutions, declarations and recommendations adopted by the United Nations and the specialized agencies promoting equality of rights of men and women,
>
> Concerned, however, that despite these various instruments extensive discrimination against women continues to exist,
>
> Recalling that discrimination against women violates the principles of equality of rights and respect for human dignity, is an obstacle to the participation of women, on equal terms with men, in the political, social, economic and cultural life of their countries, hampers the growth of the prosperity of society and the family and makes more difficult the full development of the potentialities of women in the service of their countries and of humanity,
>
> Concerned that in situations of poverty women have the least access to food, health, education, training and opportunities for employment and other needs,
>
> Convinced that the establishment of the new international economic order based on equity and justice will contribute significantly towards the promotion of equality between men and women,

Emphasizing that the eradication of apartheid, all forms of racism, racial discrimination, colonialism, neo-colonialism, aggression, foreign occupation and domination and interference in the internal affairs of States is essential to the full enjoyment of the rights of men and women,

Affirming that the strengthening of international peace and security, the relaxation of international tension, mutual co-operation among all States irrespective of their social and economic systems, general and complete disarmament, in particular nuclear disarmament under strict and effective international control, the affirmation of the principles of justice, equality and mutual benefit in relations among countries and the realization of the right of peoples under alien and colonial domination and foreign occupation to self-determination and independence, as well as respect for national sovereignty and territorial integrity, will promote social progress and development and as a consequence will contribute to the attainment of full equality between men and women,

Convinced that the full and complete development of a country, the welfare of the world and the cause of peace require the maximum participation of women on equal terms with men in all fields,

Bearing in mind the great contribution of women to the welfare of the family and to the development of society, so far not fully recognized, the social significance of maternity and the role of both parents in the family and in the upbringing of children, and aware that the role of women in procreation should not be a basis for discrimination but that the upbringing of children requires a sharing of responsibility between men and women and society as a whole,

Aware that a change in the traditional role of men as well as the role of women in society and in the family is needed to achieve full equality between men and women,

Determined to implement the principles set forth in the Declaration on the Elimination of Discrimination against Women and, for that purpose, to adopt the measures required for the elimination of such discrimination in all its forms and manifestations.[35]

Importantly, discrimination against women is defined in Article 1:

1. For the purposes of the present Convention, the term 'discrimination against women' shall mean any distinction, exclusion or restriction made on the basis of sex which has the effect or purpose of impairing or nullifying the recognition, enjoyment or exercise by women, irrespective of their marital

---

35   Ibid., at Preamble.

status, on a basis of equality of men and women, of human rights and fundamental freedoms in the political, economic, social, cultural, civil or any other field.[36]

States are expected to stand firm against discrimination and commit to implement a policy to eliminate discrimination against women in Article 2:

2. States Parties condemn discrimination against women in all its forms, agree to pursue by all appropriate means and without delay a policy of eliminating discrimination against women and, to this end, undertake:
   a. To embody the principle of the equality of men and women in their national constitutions or other appropriate legislation if not yet incorporated therein and to ensure, through law and other appropriate means, the practical realization of this principle;
   b. To adopt appropriate legislative and other measures, including sanctions where appropriate, prohibiting all discrimination against women;
   c. To establish legal protection of the rights of women on an equal basis with men and to ensure through competent national tribunals and other public institutions the effective protection of women against any act of discrimination;
   d. To refrain from engaging in any act or practice of discrimination against women and to ensure that public authorities and institutions shall act in conformity with this obligation;
   e. To take all appropriate measures to eliminate discrimination against women by any person, organization or enterprise;
   f. To take all appropriate measures, including legislation, to modify or abolish existing laws, regulations, customs and practices which constitute discrimination against women;
   g. To repeal all national penal provisions which constitute discrimination against women.[37]

Further, Article 3 states:

3. States Parties shall take in all fields, in particular in the political, social, economic and cultural fields, all appropriate measures, including legislation, to ensure the full development and advancement of women, for the purpose of guaranteeing them the exercise and enjoyment of human rights and fundamental freedoms on a basis of equality with men.[38]

Article 4 contains an affirmative action strategy, including maternity rights:

---

36 Ibid., at Article 1.
37 Ibid., at Article 2.
38 Ibid., at Article 3.

4. 1. Adoption by States Parties of temporary special measures aimed at accelerating de facto equality between men and women shall not be considered discrimination as defined in the present Convention, but shall in no way entail as a consequence the maintenance of unequal or separate standards; these measures shall be discontinued when the objectives of equality of opportunity and treatment have been achieved.
    2. Adoption by States Parties of special measures, including those measures contained in the present Convention, aimed at protecting maternity shall not be considered discriminatory.[39]

In order to eliminate prejudices and customary practices, Article 5 establishes:

5. States Parties shall take all appropriate measures:
    a. To modify the social and cultural patterns of conduct of men and women, with a view to achieving the elimination of prejudices and customary and all other practices which are based on the idea of the inferiority or the superiority of either of the sexes or on stereotyped roles for men and women;
    b. To ensure that family education includes a proper understanding of maternity as a social function and the recognition of the common responsibility of men and women in the upbringing and development of their children, it being understood that the interest of the children is the primordial consideration in all cases.[40]

The public life stream is protected under Article 7:

7. States Parties shall take all appropriate measures to eliminate discrimination against women in the political and public life of the country and, in particular, shall ensure to women, on equal terms with men, the right:
    b. To participate in the formulation of government policy and the implementation thereof and to hold public office and perform all public functions at all levels of government;
    c. To participate in non-governmental organizations and associations concerned with the public and political life of the country.[41]

In addition, Article 8 protects equality:

8. States Parties shall take all appropriate measures to ensure to women, on equal terms with men and without any discrimination, the opportunity to

---

39   Ibid., at Article 4.
40   Ibid., at Article 5.
41   Ibid., at Article 7.

represent their Governments at the international level and to participate in the work of international organizations.[42]

The importance of education for the advancement and the enhancement of women are emphasized in Article 10:

10. States Parties shall take all appropriate measures to eliminate discrimination against women in order to ensure to them equal rights with men in the field of education and in particular to ensure, on a basis of equality of men and women:
    a. The same conditions for career and vocational guidance, for access to studies and for the achievement of diplomas in educational establishments of all categories in rural as well as in urban areas; this equality shall be ensured in pre-school, general, technical, professional and higher technical education, as well as in all types of vocational training;
    b. Access to the same curricula, the same examinations, teaching staff with qualifications of the same standard and school premises and equipment of the same quality;
    c. The elimination of any stereotyped concept of the roles of men and women at all levels and in all forms of education by encouraging coeducation and other types of education which will help to achieve this aim and, in particular, by the revision of textbooks and school programs and the adaptation of teaching methods;
    d. The same opportunities to benefit from scholarships and other study grants;
    e. The same opportunities for access to programs of continuing education, including adult and functional literacy programs, particularly those aimed at reducing, at the earliest possible time, any gap in education existing between men and women;
    f. The reduction of female student drop-out rates and the organization of programs for girls and women who have left school prematurely;
    g. The same opportunities to participate actively in sports and physical education;
    h. Access to specific educational information to help to ensure the health and well-being of families, including information and advice on family planning.[43]

Crucially, Article 11(1) guarantees employment rights for women in terms of access to employment and equal pay:

---

42 Ibid., at Article 8.
43 Ibid., at Article 10.

11. 1.	States Parties shall take all appropriate measures to eliminate discrimination against women in the field of employment in order to ensure, on a basis of equality of men and women, the same rights, in particular:

a.	The right to work as an inalienable right of all human beings;

b.	The right to the same employment opportunities, including the application of the same criteria for selection in matters of employment;

c.	The right to free choice of profession and employment, the right to promotion, job security and all benefits and conditions of service and the right to receive vocational training and retraining, including apprenticeships, advanced vocational training and recurrent training;

d.	The right to equal remuneration, including benefits, and to equal treatment in respect of work of equal value, as well as equality of treatment in the evaluation of the quality of work;

e.	The right to social security, particularly in cases of retirement, unemployment, sickness, invalidity and old age and other incapacity to work, as well as the right to paid leave;

f.	The right to protection of health and to safety in working conditions, including the safeguarding of the function of reproduction.[44]

Further, women are protected in the employment area by Article 11(2) as to issues of marriage and maternity:

11. 2.	In order to prevent discrimination against women on the grounds of marriage or maternity and to ensure their effective right to work, States Parties shall take appropriate measures:

a.	To prohibit, subject to the imposition of sanctions, dismissal on the grounds of pregnancy or of maternity leave and discrimination in dismissals on the basis of marital status;

b.	To introduce maternity leave with pay or with comparable social benefits without loss of former employment, seniority or social allowances;

c.	To encourage the provision of the necessary supporting social services to enable parents to combine family obligations with work responsibilities and participation in public life, in particular through promoting the establishment and development of a network of child-care facilities;

d.	To provide special protection to women during pregnancy in types of work proved to be harmful to them.[45]

44	Ibid., at Article 11(1).
45	Ibid., at Article 11(2).

In addition, economic and social life is emphasized in Article 13, including family benefits:

> 13. States Parties shall take all appropriate measures to eliminate discrimination against women in other areas of economic and social life in order to ensure, on a basis of equality of men and women, the same rights, in particular:
>   a. The right to family benefits.[46]

The important concept of equality before the law is guaranteed in Article 15:

> 15. 1. States Parties shall accord to women equality with men before the law.
>   2. States Parties shall accord to women, in civil matters, a legal capacity identical to that of men and the same opportunities to exercise that capacity. In particular, they shall give women equal rights to conclude contracts and to administer property and shall treat them equally in all stages of procedure in courts and tribunals.
>   3. States Parties agree that all contracts and all other private instruments of any kind with a legal effect which is directed at restricting the legal capacity of women shall be deemed null and void.[47]

In view of the issue of marital responsibility, Article 16 enunciates the concept of equality of women and men in marriage:

> 16. 1. States Parties shall take all appropriate measures to eliminate discrimination against women in all matters relating to marriage and family relations and in particular shall ensure, on a basis of equality of men and women:
>   a. The same right to enter into marriage;
>   b. The same right freely to choose a spouse and to enter into marriage only with their free and full consent;
>   c. The same rights and responsibilities during marriage and at its dissolution;
>   d. The same rights and responsibilities as parents, irrespective of their marital status, in matters relating to their children; in all cases the interests of the children shall be paramount;
>   e. The same rights to decide freely and responsibly on the number and spacing of their children and to have access to the information, education and means to enable them to exercise these rights;
>   f. The same rights and responsibilities with regard to guardianship, wardship, trusteeship and adoption of children, or similar institutions

---

46 Ibid., at Article 13.
47 Ibid., at Article 15.

where these concepts exist in national legislation; in all cases the interests of the children shall be paramount;

g. The same personal rights as husband and wife, including the right to choose a family name, a profession and an occupation;

h. The same rights for both spouses in respect of the ownership, acquisition, management, administration, enjoyment and disposition of property, whether free of charge or for a valuable consideration.[48]

Under Article 17, a Committee on the Elimination of Discrimination against Women is established:

17. 1. For the purpose of considering the progress made in the implementation of the present Convention, there shall be established a Committee on the Elimination of Discrimination against Women (hereinafter referred to as the Committee) consisting, at the time of entry into force of the Convention, of eighteen and, after ratification of or accession to the Convention by the thirty-fifth State Party, of twenty-three experts of high moral standing and competence in the field covered by the Convention. The experts shall be elected by States Parties from among their nationals and shall serve in their personal capacity, consideration being given to equitable geographical distribution and to the representation of the different forms of civilization as well as the principal legal systems.[49]

As for greater measures as well as the necessary measures taken by State Parties to combat discrimination, Article 23 states:

23. Nothing in the present Convention shall affect any provisions that are more conducive to the achievement of equality between men and women which may be contained:

a. In the legislation of a State Party; or

b. In any other international convention, treaty or agreement in force for that State.[50]

Finally, Article 24 calls for all necessary measures of implementation:

24. States Parties undertake to adopt all necessary measures at the national level aimed at achieving the full realization of the rights recognized in the present Convention.[51]

---

48   Ibid., at Article 16.
49   Ibid., at Article 17.
50   Ibid., at Article 23.
51   Ibid., at Article 24.

Optional Protocol to the Convention on the Elimination of All Forms of Discrimination against Women

Also important for women, the Optional Protocol to the Convention on the Elimination of All Forms of Discrimination Against Women (CEDAW) was adopted by the United Nations Commission on the Status of Women on 2 March 1999.[52] Essentially, an optional protocol is an additional enforcement mechanism for the original convention. The motivation behind the development of an Optional Protocol for CEDAW was to bring CEDAW itself on an equal footing with other international human rights instruments, enhancing its enforcement mechanisms. As the principal document enunciating women's rights, CEDAW is an important instrument for half of the world's population. The significance of CEDAW, however, is not matched by its lack of implementation strength, since human rights are only as effective as their ability to be implemented. Although CEDAW represents a strong and valuable statement of women's human rights, it is essentially a weak and often ignored instrument among the States party to it, since signatories to CEDAW have made more reservations to its provisions than any other UN convention. However, the Optional Protocol gives individual women and groups of women the ability to make a direct complaint to the CEDAW Committee, which only considers complaints related to incidents within the domestic jurisdiction of State Parties to the Optional Protocol and only when the complainant has demonstrated that available domestic remedies have been exhausted; this latter requirement will be lifted if it can be shown that the application of domestic remedies is unreasonably prolonged or unlikely to bring effective relief.

The Optional Protocol provides a 'backup' for domestic enforcement mechanisms to ensure that they are adequate and effective. In States with a federalist system, regional and federal governments may have separate and independent legislative power, with the actions of one level of government perhaps being contrary to CEDAW, and the Optional Protocol would help to ensure that all levels of government find domestic methods to set uniform standards in accordance with CEDAW. The Committee's views on communications would amount to jurisprudence, case law used for guidance in interpreting laws, providing clarification and guidance for States and for individuals about States' obligations under CEDAW. In order to enhance existing mechanisms for the implementation of human rights within the United Nations system, the Optional Protocol to CEDAW is effectively the first gender-specific international complaints procedure. As well as putting CEDAW on a par with human rights treaties which have a complaints process, it enhances existing mechanisms by specifically incorporating practices and procedures that have been developed under other international complaints procedures, such as the International Covenant on Civil and Political Rights (ICCPR) and its Protocol; the Convention on the Elimination of All Forms of

---

52 Optional Protocol to the Convention on the Elimination of All Forms of Discrimination against Women.

Racial Discrimination; and the Convention Against Torture and Other Cruel, Inhuman or Degrading Treatment or Punishment.

In the Preamble of the Optional Protocol to the Convention on the Elimination of All Forms of Discrimination against Women, the State Parties undertake the agreement:

> Noting that the Charter of the United Nations reaffirms faith in fundamental human rights, in the dignity and worth of the human person and in the equal rights of men and women,
>
> Also noting that the Universal Declaration of Human Rights proclaims that all human beings are born free and equal in dignity and rights and that everyone is entitled to all the rights and freedoms set forth therein, without distinction of any kind, including distinction based on sex,
>
> Recalling that the International Covenants on Human Rights and other international human rights instruments prohibit discrimination on the basis of sex,
>
> Also recalling the Convention on the Elimination of All Forms of Discrimination against Women ('the Convention'), in which the States Parties thereto condemn discrimination against women in all its forms and agree to pursue by all appropriate means and without delay a policy of eliminating discrimination against women,
>
> Reaffirming their determination to ensure the full and equal enjoyment by women of all human rights and fundamental freedoms and to take effective action to prevent violations of these rights and freedoms.[53]

Article 1 establishes that States who become Parties to the Optional Protocol recognize the competence of the Committee to receive and consider communications under the Protocol.[54] In addition, Article 2 provides a communications procedure, which allows either individuals or groups of individuals to submit individual complaints to the Committee, and communications may also be submitted on behalf of individuals or groups of individuals, with their consent, unless it can be shown why that consent was not received.[55] However, Article 4 stipulates the admissibility criteria of communications in that before a complaint is considered, the Committee must determine that all available domestic remedies have been exhausted and the complaint is not, nor has been examined by the Committee or has been or is being examined under another procedure of international

---

53   Ibid., at Preamble.
54   Ibid., at Article 1.
55   Ibid., at Article 2.

investigation or settlement. In addition, a complaint will only be admissible provided the complaint is compatible with the provisions of the Convention, is not an abuse of the right to submit a communication, the claimants' allegations can be substantiated, and the facts presented occurred after the State party ratified the Protocol.[56] Further, Article 5 holds that, after receipt of a communication and prior to its final decision, the Committee has the option of contacting the State Party with an urgent request that the State Party take steps to protect the alleged victim or victims from irreparable harm.[57]

Article 7 outlines the process of complaint consideration in that the Committee will examine and consider all information provided by a complaint in closed meetings, and the Committee's views and recommendations will be transmitted to the parties concerned; the State Party has six months to consider the views of the Committee and provide a written response, including remedial steps taken, and the Committee may request additional information from the State Party, including in subsequent reports.[58] Further, Article 8 establishes an inquiry procedure that allows the Committee to initiate a confidential investigation by one or more of its members where it has received reliable information of grave or systematic violations by a State Party of rights established in the Convention, and any findings, comments or recommendations will be transmitted to the State Party concerned, to which it may respond within six months.[59] As well, Article 9 provides for a follow-up procedure in that the State Party may be invited to provide the Committee with details of any remedial efforts taken following an inquiry.[60]

Article 10 provides an opt-out clause, since ratification of the Optional Protocol, a State Party has the option of refusing to recognize the competence of the Committee to initiate and conduct an inquiry as established under articles 8 and 9; however, this declaration may be withdrawn at a later time.[61] Further, under Article 11, a State Party shall take all appropriate steps to ensure that individuals under its jurisdiction are not subjected to ill treatment or intimidation as a consequence of communicating with the Committee pursuant to the present Protocol.[62]

There are currently two ways CEDAW is enforced: The Reporting Procedure, in that State Parties have to submit a national report to the Committee within one year of accession or ratification of CEDAW and thereafter every four years or when the Committee requests, and in the reports, States must indicate the measures they have adopted to give effect to the provisions of CEDAW, and the Committee discusses these reports with government representatives and explores areas for further action by the specific country; and The Interstate Procedure, in

---

56   Ibid., at Article 4.
57   Ibid., at Article 5.
58   Ibid., at Article 7.
59   Ibid., at Article 8.
60   Ibid., at Article 9.
61   Ibid., at Article 10.
62   Ibid., at Article 11.

that under article 29 of CEDAW, two or more State Parties can refer disputes about the interpretation and implementation of CEDAW to arbitration, and if the dispute is not settled, it can be referred to the International Court of Justice.

Equal Remuneration Convention (ILO C100)

Important for workers who suffer maternity discrimination in the workplace, the General Conference of the International Labour Organization adopted the Equal Remuneration Convention (ILO C100) in 1951. The Preamble of the Equal Remuneration Convention states:

> The General Conference of the International Labour Organization,
>
> Having been convened at Geneva by the Governing Body of the International Labour Office, and having met in its thirty-fourth session on 6 June 1951, and
>
> Having decided upon the adoption of certain proposals with regard to the principle of equal remuneration for men and women workers for work of equal value, which is the seventh item on the agenda of the session, and
>
> Having determined that these proposals shall take the form of an international Convention, Adopts this twenty-ninth day of June of the year one thousand nine hundred and fifty-one the following Convention, which may be cited as the Equal Remuneration Convention, 1951.[63]

The term remuneration is defined in Article 1:

1. For the purpose of this Convention:
    a. The term 'remuneration' includes the ordinary, basic or minimum wage or salary and any additional emoluments whatsoever payable directly or indirectly, whether in cash or in kind, by the employer to the worker and arising out of the worker's employment;
    b. The term 'equal remuneration for men and women workers for work of equal value' refers to rates of remuneration established without discrimination based on sex.[64]

Different methods for equality are envisioned in Article 2:

---

63   United Nations, Equal Remuneration Convention (ILO C100), at the Preamble.
64   Ibid., at Article 1.

2. 1. Each Member shall, by means appropriate to the methods in operation for determining rates of remuneration, promote and, in so far as is consistent with such methods, ensure the application to all workers of the principle of equal remuneration for ... workers for work of equal value.
   2. This principle may be applied by means of:
      a. National laws or regulations;
      b. Legally established or recognized machinery for wage determination;
      c. Collective agreements between employers and workers; or
      d. A combination of these various means.[65]

Finally, objective methods of appraisal are ensured in Article 3:

3. 1. Where such action will assist in giving effect to the provisions of this Convention, measures shall be taken to promote objective appraisal of jobs on the basis of the work to be performed.[66]

Discrimination (Employment and Occupation) Convention (ILO C111)

Important for workers who suffer maternity discrimination in the workplace, the General Conference of the International Labour Organization, adopted the Discrimination (Employment and Occupation) Convention (ILO C111), which entered into force in 1960. The Preamble of the Discrimination (Employment and Occupation) Convention states:

Having decided upon the adoption of certain proposals with regard to discrimination in the field of employment and occupation, and

Having determined that these proposals shall take the form of an international Convention, and Considering that the Declaration of Philadelphia affirms that all human beings, irrespective of race, creed or sex, have the right to pursue both their material well-being and their spiritual development in conditions of freedom and dignity, of economic security and equal opportunity, and

Considering further that discrimination constitutes a violation of rights enunciated by the Universal Declaration of Human Rights.[67]

The word discrimination is defined in Article 1:

---

65 Ibid., at Article 2.
66 Ibid., at Article 3.
67 United Nations, Discrimination (Employment and Occupation) Convention (ILO C111), at the Preamble.

1. 1. For the purpose of this Convention the term 'discrimination' includes:
    a. any distinction, exclusion or preference made on the basis of race, color, sex, religion, political opinion, national extraction or social origin, which has the effect of nullifying or impairing equality of opportunity or treatment in employment or occupation;
    b. such other distinction, exclusion or preference which has the effect of nullifying or impairing equality of opportunity or treatment in employment or occupation as may be determined by the Member concerned after consultation with representative employer's and worker's organizations, where such exist, and with other appropriate bodies.
   2. Any distinction, exclusion or preference in respect of a particular job based on the inherent requirements thereof shall not be deemed to be discrimination.
   3. For the purpose of this Convention the terms 'employment' and 'occupation' include access to vocational training, access to employment and to particular occupations, and terms and conditions of employment.[68]

Member commitment to equality of opportunity and treatment is contained in Article 2:

   2. Each Member for which this Convention is in force undertakes to declare and pursue a national policy designed to promote, by methods appropriate to national conditions and practice, equality of opportunity and treatment in respect of employment and occupation, with a view to eliminating any discrimination in respect thereof.[69]

Further, Article 3 specifically enunciates Member responsibilities:

   3. Each Member for which this Convention is in force undertakes, by methods appropriate to national conditions and practice:
    a. To seek the co-operation of employers' and workers' organizations and other appropriate bodies in promoting the acceptance and observance of this policy;
    b. To enact such legislation and to promote such educational programs as may be calculated to secure the acceptance and observance of the policy;
    c. To repeal any statutory provisions and modify any administrative instructions or practices which are inconsistent with the policy;

---

68   Ibid., at Article 1.
69   Ibid., at Article 2.

    d.   To pursue the policy in respect of employment under the direct control of a national authority;

    e.   To ensure observance of the policy in activities of vocational guidance, vocational training and placement services under the direction of a national authority;

    f.   To indicate in its annual reports on the application of the Convention the action taken in pursuance of the policy and the results secured by such action.[70]

Finally, special measures are provided for in Article 5:

5. 1.   Special measures of protection or assistance provided in other Conventions or Recommendations adopted by the International Labour Conference shall not be deemed to be discrimination.

    2.   Any Member may, after consultation with representative employers' and workers' organizations, where such exist, determine that other special measures designed to meet the particular requirements of persons who, for reasons such as sex, age, disablement, family responsibilities or social or cultural status, are generally recognized to require special protection or assistance, shall not be deemed to be discrimination.[71]

Employment Policy Convention (ILO C122)

Important for workers who suffer maternity discrimination in the workplace, the General Conference of the International Labour Organization, adopted the Employment Policy Convention (ILO C122), which entered into force in 1965. The Preamble of the Employment Policy Convention states:

Considering that the Declaration of Philadelphia recognizes the solemn obligation of the International Labour Organization to further among the nations of the world programs which will achieve full employment and the raising of standards of living, and that the Preamble to the Constitution of the International Labour Organization provides for the prevention of unemployment and the provision of an adequate living wage, and

Considering further that under the terms of the Declaration of Philadelphia it is the responsibility of the International Labour Organization to examine and consider the bearing of economic and financial policies upon employment policy in the light of the fundamental objective that 'all human beings, irrespective of race, creed or sex, have the right to pursue both their material well-being and

---

70   Ibid., at Article 3.
71   Ibid., at Article 5.

their spiritual development in conditions of freedom and dignity, of economic security and equal opportunity', and

Considering that the Universal Declaration of Human Rights provides that 'everyone has the right to work, to free choice of employment, to just and favorable conditions of work and to protection against unemployment'.[72]

A commitment to full, productive and freely chosen employment is envisioned in Article 1:

1. 1. With a view to stimulating economic growth and development, raising levels of living, meeting manpower requirements and overcoming unemployment and under-employment, each Member shall declare and pursue, as a major goal, an active policy designed to promote full, productive and freely chosen employment.
    2. The said policy shall aim at ensuring that:
        a. There is work for all who are available for and seeking work;
        b. Such work is as productive as possible;
        c. There is freedom of choice of employment and the fullest possible opportunity for each worker to qualify for, and to use his skills and endowments in, a job for which he is well suited, irrespective of race, color, sex, religion, political opinion, national extraction or social origin.
    3. The said policy shall take due account of the stage and level of economic development and the mutual relationships between employment objectives and other economic and social objectives, and shall be pursued by methods that are appropriate to national conditions and practices.[73]

Maternity Protection Convention (ILO C3), (ILO C103), (ILO C183)

Important for maternity rights and the fight against maternity discrimination, the General Conference of the International Labour Organization adopted the Maternity Protection Convention (ILO C3), which entered into force in 1921. The Preamble of the Maternity Protection Convention states:

The General Conference of the International Labour Organization,

Having been convened at Washington by the Government of the United States of America on the 29th day of October 1919, and

---

72   United Nations, Employment Policy Convention (ILO C122), at the Preamble.
73   Ibid., at Article 1.

Having decided upon the adoption of certain proposals with regard to 'women's employment, before and after childbirth, including the question of maternity benefit', which is part of the third item in the agenda for the Washington meeting of the Conference, and

Having determined that these proposals shall take the form of an international Convention,

adopts the following Convention, which may be cited as the Maternity Protection Convention, 1919, for ratification by the Members of the International Labour Organization in accordance with the provisions of the Constitution of the International Labour Organization.[74]

Maternity protection and breastfeeding are provided under Article 3:

3. In any public or private industrial or commercial undertaking, or in any branch thereof, other than an undertaking in which only members of the same family are employed, a woman
   a. shall not be permitted to work during the six weeks following her confinement;
   b. shall have the right to leave her work if she produces a medical certificate stating that her confinement will probably take place within six weeks;
   c. shall, while she is absent from her work in pursuance of paragraphs (a) and (b), be paid benefits sufficient for the full and healthy maintenance of herself and her child, provided either out of public funds or by means of a system of insurance, the exact amount of which shall be determined by the competent authority in each country, and as an additional benefit shall be entitled to free attendance by a doctor or certified midwife; no mistake of the medical adviser in estimating the date of confinement shall preclude a woman from receiving these benefits from the date of the medical certificate up to the date on which the confinement actually takes place;
   d. shall in any case, if she is nursing her child, be allowed half an hour twice a day during her working hours for this purpose.[75]

Finally, Article 4:

4. Where a woman is absent from her work in accordance with paragraph (a) or (b) of Article 3 of this Convention, or remains absent from her work for a longer period as a result of illness medically certified to arise out of pregnancy or confinement and rendering her unfit for work, it shall not be

---

74 Maternity Protection Convention (ILO C3), at the Preamble.
75 Ibid., at Article 3.

lawful, until her absence shall have exceeded a maximum period to be fixed by the competent authority in each country, for her employer to give her notice of dismissal during such absence, nor to give her notice of dismissal at such a time that the notice would expire during such absence.[76]

Further, the General Conference of the International Labour Organization revised the Maternity Protection Convention (ILO C103), which entered into force in 1955. The Preamble of the Maternity Protection Convention states:

> The General Conference of the International Labour Organization,
>
> Having been convened at Geneva by the Governing Body of the International Labour Office, and having met in its Thirty-fifth Session on 4 June 1952, and
>
> Having decided upon the adoption of certain proposals with regard to maternity protection, which is the seventh item on the agenda of the session, and
>
> Having determined that these proposals shall take the form of an international Convention,
>
> adopts this twenty-eighth day of June of the year one thousand nine hundred and fifty-two the following Convention, which may be cited as the Maternity Protection Convention (Revised), 1952.[77]

Article 1 deals with the application of the Convention:

1. 1. This Convention applies to women employed in industrial undertakings and in non-industrial and agricultural occupations, including women wage earners working at home.[78]

Crucially, Article 3 provides for maternity leave:

3. 1. A woman to whom this Convention applies shall, on the production of a medical certificate stating the presumed date of her confinement, be entitled to a period of maternity leave.
   2. The period of maternity leave shall be at least twelve weeks, and shall include a period of compulsory leave after confinement.
   3. The period of compulsory leave after confinement shall be prescribed by national laws or regulations, but shall in no case be less than six weeks; the remainder of the total period of maternity leave may be provided

---

76 Ibid., at Article 4.
77 Maternity Protection Convention (ILO C103), at the Preamble.
78 Ibid., at Article 1.

before the presumed date of confinement or following expiration of the compulsory leave period or partly before the presumed date of confinement and partly following the expiration of the compulsory leave period as may be prescribed by national laws or regulations.

4. The leave before the presumed date of confinement shall be extended by any period elapsing between the presumed date of confinement and the actual date of confinement and the period of compulsory leave to be taken after confinement shall not be reduced on that account.

5. In case of illness medically certified arising out of pregnancy, national laws or regulations shall provide for additional leave before confinement, the maximum duration of which may be fixed by the competent authority.

6. In case of illness medically certified arising out of confinement, the woman shall be entitled to an extension of the leave after confinement, the maximum duration of which may be fixed by the competent authority.[79]

Further, Article 4 deals with maternity benefits:

4. 1. While absent from work on maternity leave in accordance with the provisions of Article 3, the woman shall be entitled to receive cash and medical benefits.

2. The rates of cash benefit shall be fixed by national laws or regulations so as to ensure benefits sufficient for the full and healthy maintenance of herself and her child in accordance with a suitable standard of living.

3. Medical benefits shall include pre-natal, confinement and post-natal care by qualified midwives or medical practitioners as well as hospitalization care where necessary; freedom of choice of doctor and freedom of choice between a public and private hospital shall be respected.

4. The cash and medical benefits shall be provided either by means of compulsory social insurance or by means of public funds; in either case they shall be provided as a matter of right to all women who comply with the prescribed conditions.

5. Women who fail to qualify for benefits provided as a matter of right shall be entitled, subject to the means test required for social assistance, to adequate benefits out of social assistance funds.

6. Where cash benefits provided under compulsory social insurance are based on previous earnings, they shall be at a rate of not less than two-thirds of the woman's previous earnings taken into account for the purpose of computing benefits.

7. Any contribution due under a compulsory social insurance scheme providing maternity benefits and any tax based upon payrolls which is raised for the purpose of providing such benefits shall, whether paid

---

79 Ibid., at Article 3.

both by the employer and the employees or by the employer, be paid in respect of the total number of men and women employed by the undertakings concerned, without distinction of sex.

8. In no case shall the employer be individually liable for the cost of such benefits due to women employed by him.[80]

In addition, Article 5 provides for breastfeeding:

5. 1. If a woman is nursing her child she shall be entitled to interrupt her work for this purpose at a time or times to be prescribed by national laws or regulations.

2. Interruptions of work for the purpose of nursing are to be counted as working hours and remunerated accordingly in cases in which the matter is governed by or in accordance with laws and regulations; in cases in which the matter is governed by collective agreement, the position shall be as determined by the relevant agreement.[81]

Article 6 protects against unlawful dismissal:

6. While a woman is absent from work on maternity leave in accordance with the provisions of Article 3 of this Convention, it shall not be lawful for her employer to give her notice of dismissal during such absence, or to give her notice of dismissal at such a time that the notice would expire during such absence.[82]

Finally, Article 7 provides for exceptions:

7. 1. Any Member of the International Labour Organization which ratifies this Convention may, by a declaration accompanying its ratification, provide for exceptions from the application of the Convention in respect of
   a. certain categories of non-industrial occupations;
   b. occupations carried on in agricultural undertakings, other than plantations;
   c. domestic work for wages in private households;
   d. women wage earners working at home;
   e. undertakings engaged in the transport of passengers or goods by sea.[83]

---

80 Ibid., at Article 4.
81 Ibid., at Article 5.
82 Ibid., at Article 6.
83 Ibid., at Article 7.

Finally, the General Conference of the International Labour Organization further revised the Maternity Protection Convention (ILO C183), which entered into force in 2002. The Preamble of the Maternity Protection Convention states:

> The General Conference of the International Labour Organization,
>
> Having been convened at Geneva by the Governing Body of the International Labour Office, and having met in its 88th Session on 30 May 2000, and
>
> Noting the need to revise the Maternity Protection Convention (Revised), 1952, and the Maternity Protection Recommendation, 1952, in order to further promote equality of all women in the workforce and the health and safety of the mother and child, and in order to recognize the diversity in economic and social development of Members, as well as the diversity of enterprises, and the development of the protection of maternity in national law and practice, and
>
> Noting the provisions of the Universal Declaration of Human Rights (1948), the United Nations Convention on the Elimination of All Forms of Discrimination Against Women (1979), the United Nations Convention on the Rights of the Child (1989), the Beijing Declaration and Platform for Action (1995), the International Labour Organization's Declaration on Equality of Opportunity and Treatment for Women Workers (1975), the International Labour Organization's Declaration on Fundamental Principles and Rights at Work and its Follow-up (1998), as well as the international labor Conventions and Recommendations aimed at ensuring equality of opportunity and treatment for men and women workers, in particular the Convention concerning Workers with Family Responsibilities, 1981, and
>
> Taking into account the circumstances of women workers and the need to provide protection for pregnancy, which are the shared responsibility of government and society, and
>
> Having decided upon the adoption of certain proposals with regard to the revision of the Maternity Protection Convention (Revised), 1952, and Recommendation, 1952, which is the fourth item on the agenda of the session, and
>
> Having determined that these proposals shall take the form of an international Convention;
>
> adopts this fifteenth day of June of the year two thousand the following Convention, which may be cited as the Maternity Protection Convention, 2000.[84]

---

84   Maternity Protection Convention (ILO C183), at the Preamble.

Article 2 deals with the application of the Convention:

2. 1. This Convention applies to all employed women, including those in atypical forms of dependent work.
    2. However, each Member which ratifies this Convention may, after consulting the representative organizations of employers and workers concerned, exclude wholly or partly from the scope of the Convention limited categories of workers when its application to them would raise special problems of a substantial nature.
    3. Each Member which avails itself of the possibility afforded in the preceding paragraph shall, in its first report on the application of the Convention under article 22 of the Constitution of the International Labour Organization, list the categories of workers thus excluded and the reasons for their exclusion. In its subsequent reports, the Member shall describe the measures taken with a view to progressively extending the provisions of the Convention to these categories.[85]

Health protection is covered under Article 3:

3. Each Member shall, after consulting the representative organizations of employers and workers, adopt appropriate measures to ensure that pregnant or breastfeeding women are not obliged to perform work which has been determined by the competent authority to be prejudicial to the health of the mother or the child, or where an assessment has established a significant risk to the mother's health or that of her child.[86]

Crucially, in terms of maternity leave, Article 4 guarantees:

4. 1. On production of a medical certificate or other appropriate certification, as determined by national law and practice, stating the presumed date of childbirth, a woman to whom this Convention applies shall be entitled to a period of maternity leave of not less than 14 weeks.
    2. The length of the period of leave referred to above shall be specified by each Member in a declaration accompanying its ratification of this Convention.
    3. Each Member may subsequently deposit with the Director-General of the International Labour Office a further declaration extending the period of maternity leave.
    4. With due regard to the protection of the health of the mother and that of the child, maternity leave shall include a period of six weeks' compulsory leave after childbirth, unless otherwise agreed at the national level by

---

85   Ibid., at Article 2.
86   Ibid., at Article 3.

the government and the representative organizations of employers and workers.

5. The prenatal portion of maternity leave shall be extended by any period elapsing between the presumed date of childbirth and the actual date of childbirth, without reduction in any compulsory portion of postnatal leave.[87]

In terms of leave in case of illness or complications, Article 5 states:

5. On production of a medical certificate, leave shall be provided before or after the maternity leave period in the case of illness, complications or risk of complications arising out of pregnancy or childbirth. The nature and the maximum duration of such leave may be specified in accordance with national law and practice.[88]

In terms of maternity benefits, Article 6 provides:

6. 1. Cash benefits shall be provided, in accordance with national laws and regulations, or in any other manner consistent with national practice, to women who are absent from work on leave referred to in Articles 4 or 5.

2. Cash benefits shall be at a level which ensures that the woman can maintain herself and her child in proper conditions of health and with a suitable standard of living.

3. Where, under national law or practice, cash benefits paid with respect to leave referred to in Article 4 are based on previous earnings, the amount of such benefits shall not be less than two-thirds of the woman's previous earnings or of such of those earnings as are taken into account for the purpose of computing benefits.

4. Where, under national law or practice, other methods are used to determine the cash benefits paid with respect to leave referred to in Article 4, the amount of such benefits shall be comparable to the amount resulting on average from the application of the preceding paragraph.

5. Each Member shall ensure that the conditions to qualify for cash benefits can be satisfied by a large majority of the women to whom this Convention applies.

6. Where a woman does not meet the conditions to qualify for cash benefits under national laws and regulations or in any other manner consistent with national practice, she shall be entitled to adequate benefits out of social assistance funds, subject to the means test required for such assistance.

---

87 Ibid., at Article 4.
88 Ibid., at Article 5.

7. Medical benefits shall be provided for the woman and her child in accordance with national laws and regulations or in any other manner consistent with national practice. Medical benefits shall include prenatal, childbirth and postnatal care, as well as hospitalization care when necessary.

8. In order to protect the situation of women in the labour market, benefits in respect of the leave referred to in Articles 4 and 5 shall be provided through compulsory social insurance or public funds, or in a manner determined by national law and practice. An employer shall not be individually liable for the direct cost of any such monetary benefit to a woman employed by him or her without that employer's specific agreement except where:

    a. such is provided for in national law or practice in a member State prior to the date of adoption of this Convention by the International Labour Conference; or

    b. it is subsequently agreed at the national level by the government and the representative organizations of employers and workers.[89]

Further, Article 7 deals with maternity benefits:

7. 1. A Member whose economy and social security system are insufficiently developed shall be deemed to be in compliance with Article 6, paragraphs 3 and 4, if cash benefits are provided at a rate no lower than a rate payable for sickness or temporary disability in accordance with national laws and regulations.

    2. A Member which avails itself of the possibility afforded in the preceding paragraph shall, in its first report on the application of this Convention under article 22 of the Constitution of the International Labour Organization, explain the reasons therefore and indicate the rate at which cash benefits are provided. In its subsequent reports, the Member shall describe the measures taken with a view to progressively raising the rate of benefits.[90]

Article 10 deals with the right to breastfeed:

10. 1. A woman shall be provided with the right to one or more daily breaks or a daily reduction of hours of work to breastfeed her child.

    2. The period during which nursing breaks or the reduction of daily hours of work are allowed, their number, the duration of nursing breaks and the procedures for the reduction of daily hours of work shall be determined by national law and practice. These breaks or the reduction

---

89   Ibid., at Article 6.
90   Ibid., at Article 7.

of daily hours of work shall be counted as working time and remunerated accordingly.[91]

Importantly, in terms of employment protection and non-discrimination, Article 8 states:

8. 1. It shall be unlawful for an employer to terminate the employment of a woman during her pregnancy or absence on leave referred to in Articles 4 or 5 or during a period following her return to work to be prescribed by national laws or regulations, except on grounds unrelated to the pregnancy or birth of the child and its consequences or nursing. The burden of proving that the reasons for dismissal are unrelated to pregnancy or childbirth and its consequences or nursing shall rest on the employer.
   2. A woman is guaranteed the right to return to the same position or an equivalent position paid at the same rate at the end of her maternity leave.[92]

Finally, Article 9 combats maternity discrimination:

9. 1. Each Member shall adopt appropriate measures to ensure that maternity does not constitute a source of discrimination in employment, including … access to employment.
   2. Measures referred to in the preceding paragraph shall include a prohibition from requiring a test for pregnancy or a certificate of such a test when a woman is applying for employment, except where required by national laws or regulations in respect of work that is:
      a. prohibited or restricted for pregnant or nursing women under national laws or regulations; or
      b. where there is a recognized or significant risk to the health of the woman and child.[93]

The Beijing Declaration and the Platform for Action

The Beijing Declaration, the Fourth World Conference on Women, states:

1. We, the Governments participating in the Fourth World Conference on Women,
2. Gathered here in Beijing in September 1995, the year of the fiftieth anniversary of the founding of the United Nations,

---

91   Ibid., at Article 10.
92   Ibid., at Article 8.
93   Ibid., at Article 9.

3. Determined to advance the goals of equality, development and peace for all women everywhere in the interest of all humanity,

4. Acknowledging the voices of all women everywhere and taking note of the diversity of women and their roles and circumstances, honoring the women who paved the way and inspired by the hope present in the world's youth,

5. Recognize that the status of women has advanced in some important respects in the past decade but that progress has been uneven, inequalities between women and men have persisted and major obstacles remain, with serious consequences for the well-being of all people,

6. Also recognize that this situation is exacerbated by the increasing poverty that is affecting the lives of the majority of the world's people, in particular women and children, with origins in both the national and international domains,

7. Dedicate ourselves unreservedly to addressing these constraints and obstacles and thus enhancing further the advancement and empowerment of women all over the world, and agree that this requires urgent action in the spirit of determination, hope, cooperation and solidarity, now and to carry us forward into the next century.

The States reaffirm a commitment to:

8. The equal rights and inherent human dignity of women and men and other purposes and principles enshrined in the Charter of the United Nations, to the Universal Declaration of Human Rights and other international human rights instruments, in particular the Convention on the Elimination of All Forms of Discrimination against Women and the Convention on the Rights of the Child, as well as the Declaration on the Elimination of Violence against Women and the Declaration on the Right to Development;

9. Ensure the full implementation of the human rights of women and of the girl child as an inalienable, integral and indivisible part of all human rights and fundamental freedoms;

10. Build on consensus and progress made at previous United Nations conferences and summits – on women in Nairobi in 1985, on children in New York in 1990, on environment and development in Rio de Janeiro in 1992, on human rights in Vienna in 1993, on population and development in Cairo in 1994 and on social development in Copenhagen in 1995 with the objective of achieving equality, development and peace;

11. Achieve the full and effective implementation of the Nairobi Forward-looking Strategies for the Advancement of Women;

12. The empowerment and advancement of women, including the right to freedom of thought, conscience, religion and belief, thus contributing to the moral, ethical, spiritual and intellectual needs of women and men, individually or in community with others and thereby guaranteeing them the possibility of realizing their full potential in society and shaping their lives in accordance with their own aspirations.

The States are convinced that:

13. Women's empowerment and their full participation on the basis of equality in all spheres of society, including participation in the decision-making process and access to power, are fundamental for the achievement of equality, development and peace;
14. Women's rights are human rights;
15. Equal rights, opportunities and access to resources, equal sharing of responsibilities for the family by men and women, and a harmonious partnership between them are critical to their well-being and that of their families as well as to the consolidation of democracy;
16. Eradication of poverty based on sustained economic growth, social development, environmental protection and social justice requires the involvement of women in economic and social development, equal opportunities and the full and equal participation of women and men as agents and beneficiaries of people-centered sustainable development;
17. The explicit recognition and reaffirmation of the right of all women to control all aspects of their health, in particular their own fertility, is basic to their empowerment;
18. Local, national, regional and global peace is attainable and is inextricably linked with the advancement of women, who are a fundamental force for leadership, conflict resolution and the promotion of lasting peace at all levels;
19. It is essential to design, implement and monitor, with the full participation of women, effective, efficient and mutually reinforcing gender-sensitive policies and programs, including development policies and programs, at all levels that will foster the empowerment and advancement of women;
20. The participation and contribution of all actors of civil society, particularly women's groups and networks and other non-governmental organizations and community-based organizations, with full respect for their autonomy, in cooperation with Governments, are important to the effective implementation and follow-up of the Platform for Action;
21. The implementation of the Platform for Action requires commitment from Governments and the international community. By making national and international commitments for action, including those made at the Conference, Governments and the international community recognize the need to take priority action for the empowerment and advancement of women.

The States are determined to:

22. Intensify efforts and actions to achieve the goals of the Nairobi Forward-looking Strategies for the Advancement of Women by the end of this century;

23. Ensure the full enjoyment by women and the girl child of all human rights and fundamental freedoms and take effective action against violations of these rights and freedoms;

24. Take all necessary measures to eliminate all forms of discrimination against women and the girl child and remove all obstacles to gender equality and the advancement and empowerment of women;

25. Encourage men to participate fully in all actions towards equality;

26. Promote women's economic independence, including employment, and eradicate the persistent and increasing burden of poverty on women by addressing the structural causes of poverty through changes in economic structures, ensuring equal access for all women, including those in rural areas, as vital development agents, to productive resources, opportunities and public services;

27. Promote people-centered sustainable development, including sustained economic growth, through the provision of basic education, life-long education, literacy and training, and primary health care for girls and women;

28. Take positive steps to ensure peace for the advancement of women and, recognizing the leading role that women have played in the peace movement, work actively towards general and complete disarmament under strict and effective international control, and support negotiations on the conclusion, without delay, of a universal and multilaterally and effectively verifiable comprehensive nuclear-test-ban treaty which contributes to nuclear disarmament and the prevention of the proliferation of nuclear weapons in all its aspects;

29. Prevent and eliminate all forms of violence against women and girls;

30. Ensure equal access to and equal treatment of women and men in education and health care and enhance women's sexual and reproductive health as well as education;

31. Promote and protect all human rights of women and girls;

32. Intensify efforts to ensure equal enjoyment of all human rights and fundamental freedoms for all women and girls who face multiple barriers to their empowerment and advancement because of such factors as their race, age, language, ethnicity, culture, religion, or disability, or because they are indigenous people;

33. Ensure respect for international law, including humanitarian law, in order to protect women and girls in particular;

34. Develop the fullest potential of girls and women of all ages, ensure their full and equal participation in building a better world for all and enhance their role in the development process.

The States are determined to:

35. Ensure women's equal access to economic resources, including land, credit, science and technology, vocational training, information, communication

and markets, as a means to further the advancement and empowerment of women and girls, including through the enhancement of their capacities to enjoy the benefits of equal access to these resources, inter alia, by means of international cooperation;

36. Ensure the success of the Platform for Action, which will require a strong commitment on the part of Governments, international organizations and institutions at all levels. We are deeply convinced that economic development, social development and environmental protection are interdependent and mutually reinforcing components of sustainable development, which is the framework for our efforts to achieve a higher quality of life for all people. Equitable social development that recognizes empowering the poor, particularly women living in poverty, to utilize environmental resources sustainably is a necessary foundation for sustainable development. We also recognize that broad-based and sustained economic growth in the context of sustainable development is necessary to sustain social development and social justice. The success of the Platform for Action will also require adequate mobilization of resources at the national and international levels as well as new and additional resources to the developing countries from all available funding mechanisms, including multilateral, bilateral and private sources for the advancement of women; financial resources to strengthen the capacity of national, subregional, regional and international institutions; a commitment to equal rights, equal responsibilities and equal opportunities and to the equal participation of women and men in all national, regional and international bodies and policy-making processes; and the establishment or strengthening of mechanisms at all levels for accountability to the world's women;

37. Ensure also the success of the Platform for Action in countries with economies in transition, which will require continued international cooperation and assistance;

38. We hereby adopt and commit ourselves as Governments to implement the following Platform for Action, ensuring that a gender perspective is reflected in all our policies and programs. We urge the United Nations system, regional and international financial institutions, other relevant regional and international institutions and all women and men, as well as non-governmental organizations, with full respect for their autonomy, and all sectors of civil society, in cooperation with Governments, to fully commit themselves and contribute to the implementation of this Platform for Action.[94]

According to the Fourth World Conference on Women's Platform for Action, governments, the international community and civil society, including non-governmental organizations (NGOs) and the private sector, are called upon to

---

94 United Nations, *Beijing Declaration and Platform for Action, Fourth World Conference on Women*..

Pregnant Pause

take strategic action: Strategic Objective: Eliminate occupational segregation and all forms of employment discrimination – actions to be taken by governments, employers, employees, trade unions and women's organizations include:

a. Implement and enforce laws and regulations and encourage voluntary codes of conduct that ensure that international labor standards, such as International Labour Organization Convention No. 100 on equal pay and workers' rights, apply equally to female and male workers;

b. Enact and enforce laws and introduce implementing measures, including means of redress and access to justice in cases of non-compliance, to prohibit direct and indirect discrimination on grounds of gender, including by reference to marital or family status, in relation to access to employment, conditions of employment, including training, promotion, health and safety, as well as termination of employment and social security of workers, including legal protection against sexual and racial harassment;

c. Enact and enforce laws and develop workplace policies against gender discrimination in the labor market, especially considering older women workers, in hiring and promotion, and in the extension of employment benefits and social security, as well as regarding discriminatory working conditions and sexual harassment; mechanisms should be developed for the regular review and monitoring of such laws;

d. Eliminate discriminatory practices by employers on the basis of women's reproductive roles and functions, including refusal of employment and dismissal of women due to pregnancy and breastfeeding responsibilities;

e. Develop and promote employment programs and services for women entering and re-entering the labor market, especially poor urban, rural and young women, the self-employed and those negatively affected by structural adjustment;

f. Implement and monitor positive public and private-sector employment, equity and positive action programs to address systemic discrimination against women in the labor force, in particular women with disabilities and women belonging to other disadvantaged groups, with respect to hiring, retention and promotion, and vocational training of women in all sectors;

g. Eliminate occupational segregation, especially by promoting the equal participation of women in highly skilled jobs and senior management positions, and through other measures, such as counseling and placement, that stimulate their on-the-job career development and upward mobility in the labor market, and by stimulating the diversification of occupational choices by both women and men; encourage women to take up non-traditional jobs, especially in science and technology, and encourage men to seek employment in the social sector;

h. Recognize collective bargaining as a right and as an important mechanism for eliminating wage inequality for women and to improve working conditions;

i. Promote the election of women trade union officials and ensure that trade union officials elected to represent women are given job protection and physical security in connection with the discharge of their functions;

j. Ensure access to and develop special programs to enable women with disabilities to obtain and retain employment, and ensure access to education and training at all proper levels, in accordance with the Standard Rules on the Equalization of Opportunities for Persons with Disabilities; adjust working conditions, to the extent possible, in order to suit the needs of women with disabilities, who should be assured legal protection against unfounded job loss on account of their disabilities;

k. Increase efforts to close the gap between women's and men's pay, take steps to implement the principle of equal remuneration for equal work of equal value by strengthening legislation, including compliance with international labor laws and standards, and encourage job evaluation schemes with gender-neutral criteria;

l. Establish and strengthen mechanisms to adjudicate matters relating to wage discrimination;

m. Set specific target dates for eliminating all forms of child labor that are contrary to accepted international standards and ensure the full enforcement of relevant existing laws and, where appropriate, enact the legislation necessary to implement the Convention on the Rights of the Child and International Labour Organization standards, ensuring the protection of working children, in particular, street children, through the provision of appropriate health, education and other social services;

n. Ensure that strategies to eliminate child labor also address the excessive demands made on some girls for unpaid work in their household and other households, where applicable;

o. Review, analyze and, where appropriate, reformulate the wage structures in female-dominated professions, such as teaching, nursing and childcare, with a view to raising their low status and earnings;

p. Facilitate the productive employment of documented migrant women, including women who have been determined refugees according to the 1951 Convention relating to the Status of Refugees, through greater recognition of foreign education and credentials, and by adopting an integrated approach to labor market training that incorporates language training.[95]

Strategic Objective: Promote harmonization of work and family responsibilities for women and men, important in the fight against maternity discrimination – actions to be taken by governments include:

a. Adopt policies to ensure the appropriate protection of labor laws and social security benefits for part-time, temporary, seasonal and home-based

---

95   Ibid., at Strategic Objective F5.

workers; promote career development based on work conditions that harmonize work and family responsibilities;

b. Ensure that full- and part-time work can be freely chosen by women and men on an equal basis, and consider appropriate protection for atypical workers in terms of access to employment, working conditions and social security;

c. Ensure, through legislation, incentives and encouragement, opportunities for women and men to take job-protected parental leave and to have parental benefits; promote the equal sharing of responsibilities for the family by men and women, including through appropriate legislation, incentives and encouragement, and also promote the facilitation of breast-feeding for working mothers;

d. Develop policies in education to change attitudes that reinforce the division of labor based on gender in order to promote the concept of shared family responsibility for work in the home, particularly in relation to children and elder care;

e. Improve the development of, and access to, technologies that facilitate occupational as well as domestic work, encourage self-support, generate income, transform gender-prescribed roles within the productive process and enable women to move out of low-paying jobs;

f. Examine a range of policies and programs, including social security legislation and taxation systems, in accordance with national priorities and policies, to determine how to promote gender equality and flexibility in the way people divide their time between and derive benefits from education and training, paid employment, family responsibilities, volunteer activity, and other socially useful forms of work, rest and leisure.[96]

Actions to be taken by governments, the private sector and non-governmental organizations (NGOs), trade unions and the United Nations include:

a. Adopt appropriate measures involving relevant governmental bodies and employers' and employees' associations so that women and men are able to take temporary leave from employment, have transferable employment and retirement benefits and make arrangements to modify work hours without sacrificing their prospects for development and advancement at work and in their careers;

b. Design and provide educational programs through innovative media campaigns, and school and community education programs to raise awareness on gender equality and non-stereotyped gender roles of women and men within the family; provide support services and facilities, such as on-site child care at workplaces and flexible working arrangements;

---

96   Ibid., at Strategic Objective F6.

c. Enact and enforce laws against sexual and other forms of harassment in all workplaces.[97]

Strategic Objective: Integrate gender perspectives in legislation, public policies, programs and projects – actions to be taken by governments include:

a. Seek to ensure that before policy decisions are taken, an analysis of their impact on women and men, respectively, is carried out;
b. Regularly review national policies, programs and projects, as well as their implementation, evaluating the impact of employment and income policies in order to guarantee that women are direct beneficiaries of development and that their full contribution to development, both remunerated and unremunerated, is considered in economic policy and planning;
c. Promote national strategies and aims on equality between women and men in order to eliminate obstacles to the exercise of women's rights and eradicate all forms of discrimination against women;
d. Work with members of legislative bodies, as appropriate, to promote a gender perspective in all legislation and policies;
e. Give all ministries the mandate to review policies and programs from a gender perspective and in the light of the Platform for Action. Locate the responsibility for the implementation of that mandate at the highest possible level. Establish and strengthen an inter-ministerial coordination structure to carry out this mandate and monitor progress and to network with relevant machineries.[98]

Actions to be taken by national machinery:

a. Facilitate the formulation and implementation of government policies on equality between women and men, develop appropriate strategies and methodologies, and promote coordination and cooperation within the central government in order to ensure mainstreaming of a gender perspective in all policy-making processes;
b. Promote and establish cooperative relationships with relevant branches of government, centers for women's studies and research, academic and educational institutions, the private sector, the media, Non- governmental organizations (NGOs), especially women's organizations, and all other actors of civil society;
c.&d. Undertake activities focusing on legal reform with regard, to the family, conditions of employment, social security, income tax, equal opportunity in education, positive measures to promote the advancement of women, and

---

97 Ibid., at Strategic Objective F6.
98 Ibid., at Strategic Objective H2.

the perception of attitudes and a culture favorable to equality, as well as promote a gender perspective in legal policy and programming reforms;

e. Promote the increased participation of women as both active agents and beneficiaries of the development process, which would result in an improvement of quality of life for all;

f. Establish direct links with national, regional and international bodies dealing with the advancement of women;

g. Provide training and advisory assistance to government agencies in order to integrate a gender perspective in their policies and programs.[99]

Strategic Objective: Ensure equality and non-discrimination under the law and in practice – actions to be taken by governments:

a. Give priority to promoting and protecting the full and equal enjoyment by women and men of all human rights and fundamental freedoms without distinction of any kind as to race, color, sex, language, religion, political or other opinions, national or social origins, property, birth or other status;

b. Provide constitutional guarantees and enact appropriate legislation to prohibit discrimination on the basis of sex for all women and girls of all ages and assure women of all ages equal rights and their full enjoyment;

c. Embody the principle of the equality of men and women in their legislation and ensure, through law and other appropriate means, the practical realization of this principle;

d. Review national laws, including customary laws and legal practices in the areas of family, civil, penal, labor and commercial law in order to ensure the implementation of the principles and procedures of all relevant international human rights instruments by means of national legislation, and revoke any remaining laws that discriminate on the basis of sex and remove gender bias in the administration of justice;

e. Strengthen and encourage the development of programs to protect the human rights of women in the national institutions on human rights that carry out programs, such as human rights commissions or ombudspersons, according them appropriate status, resources and access to the Government to assist individuals, in particular women, and ensure that these institutions pay adequate attention to problems involving the violation of the human rights of women;

f. Take action to ensure that the human rights of women are fully respected and protected;

g. Take urgent action to combat and eliminate violence against women, which is a human rights violation, resulting from harmful traditional or customary practices, cultural prejudices and extremism;

---

99 Ibid., at Strategic Objective H2.

h. Prohibit female genital mutilation wherever it exists and give vigorous support to efforts among non-governmental and community organizations and religious institutions to eliminate such practices;

i. Provide gender-sensitive human rights education and training to public officials, including police and military personnel, corrections officers, health and medical personnel, and social workers, including people who deal with migration and refugee issues, and teachers at all levels of the educational system, and make available such education and training also to the judiciary and members of parliament in order to enable them to better exercise their public responsibilities;

j. Promote the equal right of women to be members of trade unions and other professional and social organizations;

k. Establish effective mechanisms for investigating violations of the human rights of women perpetrated by any public official and take the necessary punitive legal measures in accordance with national laws;

l. Review and amend criminal laws and procedures, as necessary, to eliminate any discrimination against women in order to ensure that criminal law and procedures guarantee women effective protection against, and prosecution of, crimes directed at or disproportionately affecting women, regardless of the relationship between the perpetrator and the victim, and ensure that women defendants, victims and witnesses are not revictimized or discriminated against in the investigation and prosecution of crimes;

m. Ensure that women have the same right as men to be judges, advocates or other officers of the court, as well as police officers and prison and detention officers, among other things;

n. Strengthen existing or establish readily available and free or affordable alternative administrative mechanisms and legal aid programs to assist disadvantaged women seeking redress for violations of their rights;

o. Ensure that all women and non-governmental organizations (NGOs) and their members in the field of protection and promotion of all human rights, civil, cultural, economic, political and social rights, including the right to development, enjoy fully all human rights and freedoms in accordance with the Universal Declaration of Human Rights and all other human rights instruments and the protection of national laws;

p. Strengthen and encourage the implementation of the recommendations contained in the Standard Rules on the Equalization of Opportunities for Persons with Disabilities, paying special attention to ensure non-discrimination and equal enjoyment of all human rights and fundamental freedoms by women and girls with disabilities, including their access to information and services in the field of violence against women, as well as their active participation in and economic contribution to all aspects of society;

q. Encourage the development of gender-sensitive human rights programs.[100]

---

100   Ibid., at Strategic Objective I1.

All human rights, civil, cultural, economic, political and social, including the right to development, are universal, indivisible, interdependent and interrelated. Governments and others must not only refrain from violating the human rights of all women, but must work actively to promote and protect these rights. Recognition of the importance of the human rights of women is reflected in the fact that three-quarters of the States Members of the United Nations have become parties to the Convention on the Elimination of All Forms of Discrimination against Women. In order to protect the human rights of women, it is necessary to avoid, as far as possible, resorting to reservations and to ensure that no reservation is incompatible with the object and purpose of the Convention or is otherwise incompatible with international treaty law. Further, women's full enjoyment of equal rights is undermined by the discrepancies between some national legislation and international law and international instruments on human rights. Overly complex administrative procedures, lack of awareness within the judicial process and inadequate monitoring of the violation of the human rights of all women, coupled with the underrepresentation of women in justice systems, insufficient information on existing rights and persistent attitudes and practices perpetuate women's *de facto* inequality, which is also perpetuated by the lack of enforcement of family, civil, penal, labor and commercial laws or codes, or administrative rules and regulations intended to ensure women's full enjoyment of human rights and fundamental freedoms.[101]

The full and equal participation of women in political, civil, economic, social and cultural life at the national, regional and international levels, and the eradication of all forms of discrimination on the grounds of gender are priority objectives of the international community. The Platform for Action is an agenda for women's empowerment, which aims at removing all the obstacles to women's active participation in all spheres of public and private life through a full and equal share in economic, social, cultural and political decision-making. The principle of shared power and responsibility should be established between women and men at home, in the workplace, and in the wider national and international communities. Equality between men and women is a matter of human rights and a condition for social justice, and is also a necessary and fundamental prerequisite for equality, development and peace. A transformed partnership based on equality between men and women is a condition for people-centered sustainable development, and a long-term commitment is essential, so that women and men can work together for themselves, for their children and for society to meet the challenges of the twenty-first century. The general objective of the Platform for Action, which is in full conformity with the purposes and principles of the Charter of the United Nations and international law, is the complete realization of human rights and fundamental freedoms of all women, essential for the empowerment of women.[102]

---

101   Ibid., at Strategic Objective I.
102   United Nations Women Watch, *Commitments of Governments to Implement the Beijing Platform for Action.*

While the significance of national and regional particularities and various historical, cultural and religious backgrounds must be borne in mind, it is the duty of States, regardless of their political, economic and cultural systems, to promote and protect human rights and fundamental freedoms of all people. Women share common concerns that can be addressed only by working together and in partnership with men towards the common goal of gender equality around the world. It will also require adequate mobilization of resources from multilateral, bilateral and private sources for the advancement of women for strengthening the capacity of national, sub-regional, regional and international institutions; a commitment to equal rights, equal responsibilities and equal opportunities for the equal participation of women and men in all national, regional and international bodies in the policy-making processes; and the establishing or strengthening of mechanisms at all levels for accountability to the world's women.

In looking at the economic stream which affects labor market conditions, recent international economic developments have had a disproportionate impact on women and children. Economic recession in many 'developed' and 'developing' countries, as well as ongoing restructuring in countries with economies in transition, have had a disproportionately negative impact on women's employment. Women often have no choice but to take employment that lacks long-term job security or involves dangerous working conditions, or to be unemployed. Many women enter the labor market in under-remunerated and undervalued jobs, seeking to improve their household income. This has increased the total burden of work for women. Macro- and micro-economic policies and programs, including structural adjustment, have not always been designed to take account of their impact on women, especially those living in poverty, in both urban and remote rural areas. Importantly, women are key contributors to the economy and to combating poverty through both remunerated and unremunerated work at home, in the community and in the workplace. Growing numbers of women have achieved economic independence through gainful employment. One-fourth of all households worldwide are headed by women, and many other households are dependent on female income even where men are present. Unfortunately, female-maintained households are very often among the poorest, because of wage discrimination, occupational segregation patterns in the labor market and other gender-based barriers.

As globalization continues to influence economic opportunities worldwide, its effects remain uneven, creating both risks and opportunities for different groups. For many women, globalization has intensified existing inequalities and insecurities, often translating into the loss of livelihoods, labor rights, and social benefits.[103] Member States of the United Nations have endorsed the Millennium Development Goals of halving extreme poverty by 2015 and of achieving gender equality. Social movements are fueling increased global networking, civil society activism, and consumer awareness. Women's organizations and networks are taking on issues of social justice and equal rights to influence economic policies and decisions at the

---

103   United Nations Women Watch, *Progress of the World's Women*, 2000.

micro, meso and macro levels. Women's economic security and rights means more than helping women find employment. It means improving the power relationships in a woman's home, in her community and in the marketplace, so that she can take advantage of growing international markets. Ultimately, it means helping women lift themselves and their families out of poverty for a better future.

Of the more than 1 billion people living in abject poverty, women are an overwhelming majority. The rapid process of adjustment due to downsizing in sectors has also led to increased unemployment and underemployment, having a particular impact on women. Structural adjustment programs have not been successfully designed to minimize their negative effects on vulnerable and disadvantaged groups, such as women, or to assure positive effects on those groups by preventing their marginalization in society. The Final Act of the Uruguay Round of multilateral trade negotiations underscored the increasing interdependence of national economies, as well as the importance of trade liberalization and access to open dynamic markets. The feminization of unemployment, poverty, the increasing fragility of the environment, continued violence against women, and the widespread exclusion of half of humanity from institutions of power and governance underscore the need to continue the search for development, peace and security, and for ways of assuring people-centered sustainable development. The participation and leadership of the half of humanity that is female is essential. Therefore, only a new era of international cooperation among peoples based on a spirit of partnership within an equitable international social and economic environment, along with a radical transformation of the relationship between men and women to one of full and equal partnership will enable the world to meet the challenges of the twenty-first century.

However, equality between men and women has still not been achieved. In leadership roles, women represent a mere 10% of all elected legislators worldwide, and in most national and international administrative structures, both public and private, including the United Nations, they remain underrepresented. In examining the policy stream, a worldwide movement towards democratization has opened up the political process in many nations, but the popular participation of women in key decision-making arenas as full and equal partners with men has not yet been achieved.

Further, in examining the family, women play a critical role, as the family is the basic unit of society. Today, in different cultural, political and social systems, various forms of the family exist. Women make a crucial contribution to the welfare of the family and hence to the development of society, which is still not recognized for its full importance. The social significance of the role of parents and society as a whole in the upbringing of children should be acknowledged. Further, recognition should also be given to the important role often played by women in caring for other members of their family. Major demographic trends have had profound repercussions on the dependency ratio within families. Care of children, the sick and the elderly is a responsibility that falls disproportionately on women, owing to the lack of equality and the unbalanced distribution of remunerated and unremunerated work between women and men.

Actions to be taken at the national and international levels by governments, the United Nations system, international and regional organizations, including international financial institutions, the private sector, non-governmental organizations (NGOs) and other actors of civil society, include the creation and maintenance of a non-discriminatory, as well as a gender-sensitive legal environment through review of legislation with a view to striving to remove discriminatory provisions. Problems continue to persist in addressing the challenges of gender inequalities, empowerment, and advancement of women in employment.[104]

The boundaries of the gender division of labor between productive and reproductive roles are gradually being crossed, as women have entered formerly male-dominated areas of work, and men have started to accept greater responsibility for domestic tasks and child care. However, changes in women's roles have been greater and much more rapid than changes in men's roles. In many countries, the differences between women's and men's achievements and activities are still not recognized as the consequences of false socially constructed gender roles, rather than immutable biological differences. Unfortunately, most of the goals set out in the Nairobi Forward-looking Strategies for the Advancement of Women have not yet been achieved. Barriers to women's empowerment remain, despite the efforts of women and men everywhere. Vast political, economic and ecological crises, systematic or *de facto* discrimination, violations of and failure to protect human rights and fundamental freedoms, and ingrained prejudicial attitudes towards women are impediments to equality.

International human rights experts have called for greater attention to the intersections of gender-based discrimination, and other forms of discrimination, such as racism and intolerance. Overall, the promotion and protection of all human rights and fundamental freedoms is essential for the creation of an inclusive society for all. Specifically, appreciation for maternity issues requires a political, economic, ethical and spiritual vision for social development based on human dignity, human rights, equality, respect, peace, democracy, mutual responsibility and cooperation, and full respect for the various religious and ethical values, and cultural backgrounds of people. On the national level, innovation, mobilization of financial resources and the development of necessary human resources should be undertaken simultaneously. Progress should be contingent upon effective partnership among governments, all parts of civil society and the private sector, as well as an enabling environment based on democracy, the rule of law, respect for all human rights, fundamental freedoms and good governance at all levels, including national and international levels. Other crucial elements include: effective organizations of all people; educational, training and research activities on tolerance; and national data collection and analysis, such as the compilation of specific information for policy planning, monitoring and evaluation. Independent impartial monitoring of

---

104   United Nations Women Watch, *Beijing+5 Process and Beyond.*

progress in implementation is valuable. On the international level, globalization and interdependence are opening new opportunities through trade, investment and capital flows, and advances in technology, including information technology, for the growth of the world economy and the development.

However, there remain serious challenges, including serious financial crises, insecurity, poverty, exclusion and inequality within and among societies. Considerable obstacles to further integration and full participation in the global economy remain. Unless the benefits of social and economic development are extended to all countries, a growing number of people in all countries and even entire regions will remain marginalized from the global economy. Obstacles affecting peoples and countries must be overcome in order to realize the full potential of opportunities presented for the benefit of all. Thus, globalization offers opportunities and challenges, but the developing countries and countries with economies in transition face special difficulties in responding to those challenges and opportunities. Globalization should be fully inclusive and equitable, with a strong need for policies and measures at the national and international levels, formulated and implemented with the full and effective participation of developing countries and countries with economies in transition to help them respond effectively to those challenges and opportunities.

Throughout the entire life cycle, women's daily existence and long-term aspirations are restricted by discriminatory attitudes, unjust social and economic structures, and a lack of resources in most countries that prevent their full and equal participation. Discrimination against women begins at the earliest stages of life. The girl child of today is the woman of tomorrow. Women should be equal partners with men, in every aspect of life and development. Special measures must be taken to ensure that young women have the life skills necessary for active and effective participation in all facets of society. It will be critical for the international community to demonstrate a new commitment for the future to inspire a new generation of women and men to work together for a more just society. In the fight against maternity discrimination, the advancement of women and the achievement of equality between men and women are a matter of human rights and a condition for social justice, and should not be seen in isolation as women's issues.

Conclusion

Much needs to be done inside and outside the United Nations, in order to specifically outlaw maternity discrimination. Awareness and information about the situation of those who are suffering discrimination is critical if full participation and equality are to be achieved. The media is a key partner in the process of empowering people, in addressing discrimination, prejudice and ignorance, and in ending stereotypical portrayals. Non-governmental organizations also have a vital role to play in building understanding among society as a whole, with a need to utilize information and communications technologies to empower all people.

On the international level, attempts have been made to provide legislatively for equality to end maternity discrimination. In recycling discrimination, 'the stream always tries to return to its habitual course'.[105] However, international law has made great strides to work toward overcoming maternity discrimination, in the pursuit of *Pregnant Pause*.

---

105 Canadian Advisory Council on the Status of Women, *Feminist Guide to the Canadian Constitution*, Ottawa, at p. 57.

Chapter 4

Pregnant Pause in Australia and New Zealand

Introduction

In the quest for appreciation for maternity issues in *Pregnant Pause*, this chapter will examine efforts against maternity discrimination in Australia and New Zealand. It will examine important legislation impacting maternity rights, first in Australia, namely: the Sex Discrimination Act, the Discrimination Act and the Anti-Discrimination Act, the Human Rights and Equal Opportunity Commission Act, the Human Rights Act, and the Workplace Relations Act; and then in New Zealand, namely: the Treaty of Waitangi, the Bill of Rights Act, the Human Rights Act and the Human Rights Amendment Act, and the Employment Contracts Act and the Employment Relations Act.

Australia

The Role of Women in Australia

In the 100 years since the Commonwealth Franchise Act granted most Australian women the right to vote and stand in Commonwealth elections, female dynamics have changed greatly.[1] Australia has a total population of 21,374,000.[2] In 1902, there were 1,831,787 women living in Australia, making up 47.6% of the population, and by the twenty-first century there were 9,731,241 women, comprising 50.2% of the population. In terms of employment, the representation of women in the workplace has more than doubled in the last century; the labor force participation rate of women aged 15 and over was 25% in 1911, compared to 55% today. Over the century, women's labor force participation rates have increased in every age group up to 64 years of age, and women continue to make significant contributions to the Australian workforce. There are 4,108,700 women in employment, and the labor force participation rate of women of workforce age, that is, 15–64, is 66.2%; further, women's unemployment rate is 5.8%. In the private sector, the proportion of women occupying board positions has doubled in recent years, and the number of women in private sector managerial positions has risen to 24.7%.

---

1 Commonwealth of Australia, *Women*.
2 Australian Census.

In terms of salaries, the gap between men and women's earnings has fallen over time. Today, the ratio of female-to-male full-time average weekly ordinary time earnings stands at 84.6%. The gap has also narrowed when comparing average hourly pay rates, which takes account of the large proportion of women who work on a part-time basis. The ratio of female to male average hourly time earnings stands at 92.6%. Pay equity is about providing equal remuneration for work of equal value. For employers, that means: paying men and women equally for work that is of equal skill and responsibility, and is performed under comparable conditions; and ensuring that all workers have the same access to benefits, superannuation, allowances and other discretionary payments. Women currently earn on average roughly 84% of what men earn, and thus a significant pay gap between men and women still exists. Women in full-time employment earn just 84.3% of male earnings, and women in all types of employment, that is full-time, part-time and overtime employment, earn just 66.3% of male earnings. The gap between men's and women's earnings is caused by many contributing factors, most notably equal pay factors and equal opportunity factors. Equal pay factors include: undervaluation of women's work and skills; undervaluation of women's occupations; and unequal remuneration structures. Equal opportunity factors include: occupational segregation; unequal workforce participation; and unequal distribution of carer responsibility.

In terms of education, each year sees new records in access to education and training for women. Women make up 57% of the higher education students commencing an undergraduate qualification, and 50.5% of postgraduate commencements. In addition, 18% of the total female student population is undertaking postgraduate work, almost matching the 20% of the total male population. Now more than ever, not only do women have increased access to education but they are also forming an increasing majority of the teaching profession. Educational opportunities and outcomes have continued to grow strongly for women. Women make up more than half of all higher education students in Australia since 1987, and the proportion of female students has increased steadily. Women have also made significant inroads into several traditional male areas of study, such as science, engineering and medicine, and more women today are studying mathematics and technology-based subjects than ever before.[3]

It is important to create a workplace environment that helps parents meet the challenges they face in juggling their work and family commitments for increased family-friendly employment conditions. Australian laws do impose an obligation on everyone to be vigilant about discrimination and to take action when incidents of prejudice occur, particularly where those incidents might be unlawful. When Australia becomes a party to an international convention, the terms of the convention create binding obligations in international law. However, international laws do not automatically become a part of Australian law. The Australian Government can choose to give effect to its international obligations in various forms, legislative, policy or symbolic. In Australia, they are reflected in a range of

---

3   Government of Australia, *Implementation of the Beijing Platform for Action*.

government policies and programs, and some are also incorporated in law. Australia has taken practical steps to improve access to justice and protection under the law in the pursuit of equality, and is committed to providing more accessible, low-cost alternative dispute resolution options. Australia has a regime of legislation and institutional mechanisms to protect against maternity discrimination, and is committed to promoting, supporting and protecting human rights.

Legislation

Sex Discrimination Act   The Sex Discrimination Act 1984 prohibits discrimination on the grounds of gender, marital status, pregnancy, and potential pregnancy and family responsibilities, and is administered by the Sex Discrimination Commissioner under the auspices of the Human Rights & Equal Opportunity Commission. Section 3 outlines the objects of the Act:

3. a. to give effect to certain provisions of the Convention on the Elimination of All Forms of Discrimination Against Women; and
   b. to eliminate, so far as is possible, discrimination against persons on the ground of sex, marital status, pregnancy or potential pregnancy in the areas of work, accommodation, education, the provision of goods, facilities and services, the disposal of land, the activities of clubs and the administration of Commonwealth laws and programs; and
   ba. to eliminate, so far as is possible, discrimination involving dismissal of employees on the ground of family responsibilities; and
   c. to eliminate, so far as is possible, discrimination involving sexual harassment in the workplace, in educational institutions and in other areas of public activity; and
   d. to promote recognition and acceptance within the community of the principle of the equality of men and women.[4]

Importantly, Section 5 deals directly with the definition of gender discrimination:

5. 1. For the purposes of this Act, a person (in this subsection referred to as the discriminator) discriminates against another person (in this subsection referred to as the aggrieved person) on the ground of the sex of the aggrieved person if, by reason of:
   a. the sex of the aggrieved person;
   b. a characteristic that appertains generally to persons of the sex of the aggrieved person; or
   c. a characteristic that is generally imputed to persons of the sex of the aggrieved person; the discriminator treats the aggrieved person less favourably than, in circumstances that are the same or are not

---

4   Sex Discrimination Act, Australia, at Section 3.

        materially different, the discriminator treats or would treat a person of the opposite sex.

2. For the purposes of this Act, a person (the discriminator) discriminates against another person (the aggrieved person) on the ground of the sex of the aggrieved person if the discriminator imposes, or proposes to impose, a condition, requirement or practice that has, or is likely to have, the effect of disadvantaging persons of the same sex as the aggrieved person. [5]

Indirect discrimination and the reasonableness test are dealt with under Section 7B, which holds that a person does not discriminate against another person by imposing, or proposing to impose, a condition, requirement or practice that has, or is likely to have, the disadvantaging effect mentioned in subsection 5(2) if the condition, requirement or practice is reasonable in the circumstances. The matters to be taken into account in deciding whether a condition, requirement or practice is reasonable in the circumstances include the nature and extent of the disadvantage resulting from the imposition, or proposed imposition, of the condition, requirement or practice; and the feasibility of overcoming or mitigating the disadvantage; and whether the disadvantage is proportionate to the result sought by the person who imposes, or proposes to impose, the condition, requirement or practice.[6] Further, Section 7C states that the burden of proving that an act does not constitute discrimination, because of section 7B, lies on the person who did the act.[7]

In terms of affirmative action, Section 7D stipulates that a person may take special measures for the purpose of achieving substantive equality between men and women; or people of different marital status; or women who are pregnant and people who are not pregnant; or women who are potentially pregnant and people who are not potentially pregnant.[8]

Importantly, in terms of equality in access to employment, Section 14 establishes that it is unlawful for an employer to discriminate against a person on the ground of the person's sex, marital status, pregnancy or potential pregnancy in the arrangements made for the purpose of determining who should be offered employment; in determining who should be offered employment; or in the terms or conditions on which employment is offered; in the terms or conditions of employment that the employer affords the employee; by denying the employee access, or limiting the employee's access, to opportunities for promotion, transfer or training, or to any other benefits associated with employment; by dismissing the employee; or by subjecting the employee to any other detriment. Further, it is unlawful for an employer to discriminate against an employee on the ground of the employee's family responsibilities by dismissing the employee.[9]

---

5   Ibid., at Section 5.
6   Ibid., at Section 7B.
7   Ibid., at Section 7C.
8   Ibid., at Section 7D.
9   Ibid., at Section 14.

However, in terms of genuine occupational qualification, Section 30 holds that it is not unlawful for a person to discriminate against another person, on the ground of the other person's sex, in connection with a position as an employee, commission agent or contract worker, being a position in relation to which it is a genuine occupational qualification to be a person of the opposite sex to the sex of the other person. It is considered a genuine occupational qualification, in relation to a particular position, to be a person of a particular sex if, among other things, the duties of the position can be performed only by a person having particular physical attributes other than attributes of strength or stamina that are not possessed by persons of the opposite sex to the relevant sex; and the position is declared to be a position in relation to which it is a genuine occupational qualification to be a person of a particular sex.[10]

The Act provides an important role for the Human Rights and Equal Opportunity Commission in addressing the issue of gender discrimination. Its functions are defined under Section 48, namely to promote an understanding and acceptance of, and compliance with, this Act; to undertake research and educational programs, and other programs, on behalf of the Commonwealth for the purpose of promoting the objects of this Act; to examine enactments, and proposed enactments, for the purpose of ascertaining whether they are or would be inconsistent with or contrary to the objects of this Act, and to report to the Minister the results of any such examination. Further, on issues of discrimination on the ground of gender, marital status, pregnancy or potential pregnancy or discrimination involving sexual harassment, the Human Rights and Equal Opportunity Commission is to report to the Minister as to the laws that should be made by the Parliament, or action that should be taken by the Commonwealth; to prepare, and to publish in such manner as the Commission considers appropriate, guidelines for the avoidance of discrimination; and where the Commission considers it appropriate to do so, with the leave of the court and subject to any conditions imposed by the court, to intervene in proceedings.[11]

Discrimination Act and Anti-Discrimination Act   Important for appreciation for maternity issues, the Australian Discrimination Act 1991 (Act No. 81 of 1991) provides against discrimination. Section 7 enumerates the grounds, which include status as a parent, pregnancy and breastfeeding under (e), (f) and (g) respectively:

7. 1. This Act applies to discrimination on the ground of any of the following attributes:
    a. sex;
    e. status as a parent or carer;
    f. pregnancy;
    g. breastfeeding.

---

10   Ibid., at Section 30.
11   Racial Discrimination Act, Australia, at Section 48.

2. In this Act, a reference to an attribute mentioned in subsection (1) includes
   a. a characteristic that people with that attribute generally have; and
   b. a characteristic that people with that attribute are generally presumed to have; and
   c. such an attribute that a person is presumed to have; and
   d. such an attribute that the person had in the past but no longer has.[12]

Discrimination is defined under Section 8:

8. 1. For this Act, a person *discriminates* against another person if
   a. the person treats or proposes to treat the other person unfavourably because the other person has an attribute referred to in section 7; or
   b. the person imposes or proposes to impose a condition or requirement that has, or is likely to have, the effect of disadvantaging people because they have an attribute referred to in section 7.
   2. Subsection (1) (b) does not apply to a condition or requirement that is reasonable in the circumstances.
   3. In deciding whether a condition or requirement is reasonable in the circumstances, the matters to be taken into account include
   a. the nature and extent of the resultant disadvantage; and
   b. the feasibility of overcoming or mitigating the disadvantage; and
   c. whether the disadvantage is disproportionate to the result sought by the person who imposes or proposes to impose the condition or requirement.[13]

With regard to employees, Section 10 states:

10. 1. It is unlawful for an employer to discriminate against a person
   a. in the arrangements made for the purpose of deciding who should be offered employment; or
   b. in deciding who should be offered employment; or
   c. in the terms or conditions on which employment is offered.
   2. It is unlawful for an employer to discriminate against an employee
   a. in the terms or conditions of employment that the employer affords the employee; or
   b. by denying the employee access, or limiting the employee's access, to opportunities for promotion, transfer or training or to any other benefit associated with employment; or
   c. by dismissing the employee; or
   d. by subjecting the employee to any other detriment.[14]

---

12   Discrimination Act, Australia, at Section 7.
13   Ibid., at Section 8.
14   Ibid., at Section 10.

Finally, the Australian Anti-Discrimination Act 1991 (Act No. 85 of 1991) provides for the protection of an employee under Section 7, prohibiting discrimination on the grounds of pregnancy, parental status and breastfeeding under (c), (d) and (e) respectively:

> 7. 1. The Act prohibits discrimination on the basis of the following attributes
>   a. sex;
>   c. pregnancy;
>   d. parental status;
>   e. breast feeding.[15]

Human Rights and Equal Opportunity Commission Act (HREOCA)   Important for equal rights and appreciation for maternity issues, the Human Rights and Equal Opportunity Commission Act 1986 (HREOCA) gives effect to such relevant international conventions and declarations as the International Covenant on Civil and Political Rights, and for employment discrimination the International Labour Organization Convention on Discrimination in Employment and Occupation. The Human Rights and Equal Opportunity Commission (HREOC) inquires into complaints under federal anti-discrimination law and educates the community about obligations under domestic legislation. The HREOCA enables the HREOC to investigate complaints of breaches of conventions by Commonwealth Government agencies and may also investigate complaints of discrimination in employment by any employer. Discrimination is defined in Section 3:

> 3. discrimination, except in Part IIB, means:
>   a. any distinction, exclusion or preference made on the basis of race, colour, sex, religion, political opinion, national extraction or social origin that has the effect of nullifying or impairing equality of opportunity or treatment in employment or occupation; and
>   b. any other distinction, exclusion or preference that:
>   i. has the effect of nullifying or impairing equality of opportunity or treatment in employment or occupation; and
>   ii. has been declared by the regulations to constitute discrimination for the purposes of this Act;
>   but does not include any distinction, exclusion or preference;
>   c. in respect of a particular job based on the inherent requirements of the job.[16]

Further, the duties of the Commission are outlined in Section 10A:

---

15 Anti-Discrimination Act, Australia, at Section 7.
16 Human Rights and Equal Opportunity Commission Act, Australia, at Section 3.

10A.1. It is the duty of the Commission to ensure that the functions of the Commission under this or any other Act are performed:
  a. with regard for:
      i.   the indivisibility and universality of human rights; and
      ii. the principle that every person is free and equal in dignity and rights; and
  b. efficiently and with the greatest possible benefit to the people of Australia.
   2. Nothing in this section imposes a duty on the Commission that is enforceable by proceedings in a court.[17]

In addition, the functions of Commission are outlined in Section 11:

11. 1. The functions of the Commission are:
        aa. to inquire into, and attempt to conciliate, complaints of unlawful discrimination.[18]

Finally, written complaints are contained in Section 46P:

46P.1. A written complaint may be lodged with the Commission, alleging unlawful discrimination.
   2. The complaint may be lodged:
       a. by a person aggrieved by the alleged unlawful discrimination:
           i.   on that person's own behalf; or
           ii. on behalf of that person and one or more other persons who are also aggrieved by the alleged unlawful discrimination; or
       b. by 2 or more persons aggrieved by the alleged unlawful discrimination:
           i.   on their own behalf; or
           ii. on behalf of themselves and one or more other persons who are also aggrieved by the alleged unlawful discrimination; or
       c. by a person or trade union on behalf of one or more other persons aggrieved by the alleged unlawful discrimination.
   3. A person who is a class member for a representative complaint is not entitled to lodge a separate complaint in respect of the same subject matter.[19]

Human Rights Act Important for appreciation for maternity issues, the Human Rights Act, also known as An Act to Respect, Protect and Promote Human Rights, is the first Bill of Rights in Australia. The Preamble of the Human Rights Act states:

---

17 Ibid., at Section 10A.
18 Ibid., at Section 11.
19 Ibid., at Section 46P.

1. Human rights are necessary for individuals to live lives of dignity and value.
2. Respecting, protecting and promoting the rights of individuals improves the welfare of the whole community.
3. Human rights are set out in this Act so that individuals know what their rights are.
4. Setting out these human rights also makes it easier for them to be taken into consideration in the development and interpretation of legislation.
5. This Act encourages individuals to see themselves, and each other, as the holders of rights, and as responsible for upholding the human rights of others.
6. Few rights are absolute. Human rights may be subject only to the reasonable limits in law that can be demonstrably justified in a free and democratic society. One individual's rights may also need to be weighed against another individual's rights.
7. Although human rights belong to all individuals, they have special significance for Indigenous people – the first owners of this land, members of its most enduring cultures, and individuals for whom the issue of rights protection has great and continuing importance.[20]

In the legislation are included examples of discrimination such as discrimination because of race, color, sex, sexual orientation, language, religion, political or other opinion, national or social origin, property, birth, disability or other status. However, it is important to note that an example as part of the Act is not exhaustive and may extend, but does not limit, the meaning of the provision in which it appears. Further, Section 5 defines human rights and Section 6 defines who possesses human rights:

5. In this Act:
   human rights means the civil and political rights.[21]
6. Only individuals have human rights.[22]

Importantly, Section 7 notes that the Act is not exhaustive:

7. This Act is not exhaustive of the rights an individual may have under domestic or international law.[23]

Equality before the law is recognized in Section 8:

---

20 Human Rights Act, Australia, at the Preamble.
21 Ibid., at Section 5.
22 Ibid., at Section 6.
23 Ibid., at Section 7.

8. Recognition and equality before the law
    1. Everyone has the right to recognition as a person before the law.
    2. Everyone has the right to enjoy his or her human rights without distinction or discrimination of any kind.
    3. Everyone is equal before the law and is entitled to the equal protection of the law without discrimination. In particular, everyone has the right to equal and effective protection against discrimination on any ground.[24]

However, Section 28 is a limiting clause:

28. 1. Human rights may be subject only to reasonable limits set by Territory laws that can be demonstrably justified in a free and democratic society.
    2. In deciding whether a limit is reasonable, all relevant factors must be considered, including the following:
        a. the nature of the right affected;
        b. the importance of the purpose of the limitation;
        c. the nature and extent of the limitation;
        d. the relationship between the limitation and its purpose;
        e. any less restrictive means reasonably available to achieve the purpose the limitation seeks to achieve.[25]

Section 31 deals with interpretation of human rights:

31. 1. International law, and the judgments of foreign and international courts and tribunals, relevant to a human right may be considered in interpreting the human right.
    2. In deciding whether material mentioned in subsection (1) or any other material should be considered, and the weight to be given to the material, the following matters must be taken into account:
        a. the desirability of being able to rely on the ordinary meaning of this Act, having regard to its purpose and its provisions read in the context of the Act as a whole;
        b. the undesirability of prolonging proceedings without compensating advantage;
        c. the accessibility of the material to the public.[26]

Further, Section 32 covers a declaration of incompatibility with the Act:

32. 1. This section applies if

---

24 Ibid., at Section 8.
25 Ibid., at Section 28.
26 Ibid., at Section 31.

      a. a proceeding is being heard by the Supreme Court; and

      b. an issue arises in the proceeding about whether a Territory law is consistent with a human right.

2. If the Supreme Court is satisfied that the Territory law is not consistent with the human right, the court may declare that the law is not consistent with the human right (the *declaration of incompatibility*).

3. The declaration of incompatibility does not affect

      a. the validity, operation or enforcement of the law; or

      b. the rights or obligations of anyone.

4. The registrar of the Supreme Court must promptly give a copy of the declaration of incompatibility to the Attorney-General.[27]

The Human Rights Commissioner's special role is noted in Section 36:

36. 1. The human rights commissioner may intervene in a proceeding before a court that involves the application of this Act with the leave of the court.

     2. The court may give leave subject to conditions.[28]

Finally, it is stressed in Section 40B that Public Authorities are held to a higher standard in terms of respect for the Act:

40B. Public authorities must act consistently with human rights

1. It is unlawful for a public authority

      a. to act in a way that is incompatible with a human right; or

      b. in making a decision, to fail to give proper consideration to a relevant human right.

2. Subsection (1) does not apply if the act is done or decision made under a law in force in the Territory and

      a. the law expressly requires the act to be done or decision made in a particular way and that way is inconsistent with a human right; or

      b. the law cannot be interpreted in a way that is consistent with a human right.[29]

Workplace Relations Act   Important for employment rights and maternity issues in the workplace, the Workplace Relations Act 1996 has provisions to safeguard groups of workers. The Act provides for equal remuneration for work of equal value without discrimination. Section 3 enunciates the principal objectives, which mentions family responsibilities and pregnancy specifically:

---

27   Ibid., at Section 32.

28   Ibid., at Section 36.

29   Ibid., at Section 40B.

3. The principal object of this Act is to provide a framework for cooperative workplace relations which promotes the economic prosperity and welfare of the people of Australia by:
    m. respecting and valuing the diversity of the work force by helping to prevent and eliminate discrimination on the basis of ... family responsibilities, pregnancy....[30]

Employment is not to be terminated on certain grounds, which mentions family responsibilities and pregnancy specifically:

659.2. Except as provided by subsection (3) or (4), an employer must not terminate an employee's employment for any one or more of the following reasons, or for reasons including any one or more of the following reasons:
    f. ... family responsibilities, pregnancy....[31]

The Commission is to take into account discrimination issues under Section 104, which mentions family responsibilities and pregnancy specifically:

104. In the performance of its functions, the Commission must take into account the following:
    a. the need to apply the principle of equal pay for work of equal value;
    b. the need to prevent and eliminate discrimination because of, or for reasons including ... sex ... family responsibilities, pregnancy....[32]

Finally, the functions of the Workplace Authority Director are enumerated under Section 150B, which mentions the need to prevent and eliminate discrimination based on family responsibilities and pregnancy specifically:

150B.2. In performing his or her functions relating to workplace agreements, the Workplace Authority Director must have particular regard to:
    d. the need to prevent and eliminate discrimination because of, or for reasons including ... sex ... family responsibilities, pregnancy....[33]

Workplace Relations Amendment (Paid Maternity Leave) Bill The Workplace Relations Amendment (Paid Maternity Leave) Bill 2002, entitled A Bill for an Act to provide paid maternity leave, and for related purposes, was proposed specifically to afford paid maternity leave and combat maternity discrimination. The Bill's application is:

---

30 Workplace Relations Act, Australia, at Section 3.
31 Ibid., at Section 659(2).
32 Ibid., at Section 104.
33 Ibid., at Section 150B.

This Act applies to an employee who takes parental leave from his or her employment in respect of a child, if:

a.   the child is born on or after 1 September 2002; or
b.   in the case of an adoption, the date on which the employee, with a view to adoption, first assumes the care of the child is on or after 1 September 2002.[34]

Section 170KD outlines the effect of the Bill:

170KD.1. The object of this Division and Schedule 15 is to give effect, or further effect, to:

a.   Article 11.2(b), Convention on the Elimination of All Forms of Discrimination Against Women, 1979; and
b.   the Family Responsibilities Convention; and
c.   the Workers with Family Responsibilities Recommendation, 1981, which the General Conference of the International Labour Organization adopted on 23 June 1981 and is also known as Recommendation No. 165; by providing for a system of government-funded paid maternity leave that will help employees who take maternity leave from their employment in respect of a child.

2.   In particular, Schedule 15 gives effect, or further effect, to the Article, Convention and Recommendation by entitling certain employees up to 14 weeks of maternity payments out of public money when they take maternity leave from their employment in respect of a child.

3.   This provision is to be implemented in conjunction with Division 5 of this Part and its provision of unpaid parental (defined to include maternity and paternity) leave, so that employees entitled to paid maternity leave receive a maternity payment for 14 weeks of their maternity leave at and around the birth of a child.

4.   This maternity payment is payable to eligible employees by means of a payment by the Commonwealth to the employers of eligible employees. Employers then make the payment directly to their employees through established payment systems.

5.   This maternity payment does not affect or reduce any other entitlement that the employee may have under the terms of any other employment agreement, award or law.

6.   However, this maternity payment is not paid to Commonwealth, State or Territory government employees (who receive other government funded payments). It is payable to other employees who meet the eligibility requirements.

7.   The maternity payment is for mothers in recognition of the physical demands of the later stages of pregnancy, birth, recovery from birth,

---

34   Workplace Relations Amendment (Paid Maternity Leave) Bill.

and establishment, where possible, of breast feeding. It is not intended as a transferable payment between employee and spouse except in exceptional circumstances.

8. If a person is eligible to receive a maternity payment under this Act and either or both the maternity allowance and the maternity immunisation allowance under the *A New Tax System (Family Assistance) (Administration) Act 1999*, the person must elect to receive either the payment, or the allowance or allowances, as the case may be.

9. A person is not entitled to a maternity payment if the person claims and is paid either or both the maternity allowance and the maternity immunisation allowance under the *A New Tax System (Family Assistance) (Administration) Act 1999*.

10. Schedule 15 establishes minimum entitlements and so is intended to supplement, and not to override, entitlements under other Commonwealth, State and Territory legislation, awards and agreements.

11. This maternity payment is to be treated as wage and salary income for the purposes of taxation, superannuation and other relevant laws and agreements.

12. The regulations may provide for an analogous system of paid adoption leave.[35]

The Purpose of Schedule 15 Paid Maternity Leave is outlined in Clause 1:

1. The purpose of this Part is to entitle certain employees, particularly mothers, to up to 14 weeks of maternity payments out of public money when they take parental leave from their employment in respect of a child.[36]

Clause 3 defines maternity leave:

3. *maternity leave* means Schedule 14 maternity leave or any other leave (however described):

   a. to which an employee is entitled, or that has been applied for by or granted to an employee, in respect of her pregnancy or the birth of her child, otherwise than under Schedule 14 (for example, under another law of the Commonwealth or of a State or Territory, or under an award, order or agreement);

   and

   b. that is of a kind analogous to Schedule 14 maternity leave, or would be of such a kind but for one or more of the following:
      i. it is paid leave;
      ii. it can begin before the estimated date of birth;

---

35 Ibid., at Section 170KD.
36 Ibid., at Schedule 15, Clause 1.

iii. differences in the rules governing eligibility for it;

iv. differences in the period or periods for which it can be taken.[37]

Clause 4 deals with entitlement to maternity payment:

4. 1. An employee is entitled to a maternity payment under this Schedule if the employee applies in the approved form and:
   a. is an eligible employee; or
   b. is an eligible spouse.

2. An *eligible employee* is a female employee:
   a. who is granted maternity leave for the child under section 170KB; and
   b. is not employed by a Commonwealth, State or Territory government (including government departments, non-market non-profit institutions that are controlled and mainly financed by government, and corporations and quasi-corporations that are controlled by government).

3. An *eligible spouse* is an employee:
   a. to whom all or part of an entitlement to a maternity payment is transferred under subclause 5(1); or
   b. who succeeds to a maternity payment under subclause 5(3).[38]

According to Clause 5, entitlements may be transferred to an eligible spouse:

5. 1. An eligible employee (within the meaning of subclause 4(2)) may transfer all or part of her entitlement to a maternity payment in respect of a child to her spouse if:
   a. the spouse has been granted parental leave; and
   b. the spouse takes parental leave from his or her employment in respect of the child; and
   c. exceptional circumstances, as defined by the regulations, make such a transfer necessary (such as the spouse becoming sole guardian of the child to the exclusion of the employee).

   Note: As maternity leave recognises the physical demands of the later stages of pregnancy, birth, recovery from birth and establishment, where possible, of breast feeding, the payment is intended for the mother, and is not intended, under normal circumstances, to be transferable from the biological mother to the spouse.

2. To the extent that an eligible employee transfers all or part of her entitlement to a maternity payment to her spouse under this clause:

---

37   Ibid., at Schedule 15, Clause 3.
38   Ibid., at Schedule 15, Clause 4.

a. references in this Schedule to the employee's entitlement to a maternity payment are references to the eligible spouse's entitlement to a maternity payment; and

b. references in this Schedule to the period of maternity leave are references to the period of parental leave taken by the eligible spouse; and

c. the amount of the maternity payment is calculated according to the work circumstances of the eligible spouse; and

d. the entitlement that is transferred is deducted from the transferring employee's entitlement to a maternity payment.

3. An eligible spouse succeeds to the maternity leave entitlements of an eligible employee under this clause on the later of:

a. the date of the eligible employee's death or the date when the spouse becomes sole guardian, as the case may be; or

b. the date on which the eligible spouse's bereavement leave in respect of the eligible spouse expires (if any).[39]

Clause 6 deals with applications for maternity payments:

6. 1. An eligible employee is not entitled to a maternity payment, and an employer is not entitled to a maternity advance, unless the employee makes an application for payment in accordance with this clause.

2. The application must:

a. be made before the date on which the employee returns to work or the parental leave otherwise ends; and

b. be made in the manner prescribed in regulations; and

c. specify the matters, and be accompanied by the documents, prescribed in regulations.

3. An employer and an employee must comply with any provision in the regulations that requires them to specify matters in, or attach documents to, or sign, an application under this clause or the regulations.[40]

The duration of the maternity payment is established under Clause 7:

7. A maternity payment is payable by an employer to an entitled employee:

a. for one continuous period not exceeding 14 weeks; or

b. if part of the entitlement is transferred under clause 5, for one continuous period per employee, so long as the two continuous periods do not together exceed 14 weeks.[41]

---

39 Ibid., at Schedule 15, Clause 5.
40 Ibid., at Schedule 15, Clause 6.
41 Ibid., at Schedule 15, Clause 7.

The start of maternity payment is outlined under Clause 8:

8. A maternity payment is payable by an employer to an entitled employee who is:
    a. an eligible employee, for a period that begins on the date of commencement of her maternity leave; or
    b. an eligible spouse, for a period that begins on the date the entitlement is transferred under clause 5.[42]

The end of maternity payment is outlined under Clause 10:

10. 1. Subject to clause 7 (duration of maternity payment), a maternity payment is payable by an employer to an employee for a period that ends on the earlier of:
        a. 14 weeks after the date of start of his or her maternity payment; or
        b. the date on which that employee returns to work or resigns from his or her employment.
    2. Subclause (1) applies despite the fact that the employee's parental leave may end before that date if:
        a. the employee's employment is terminated due to redundancy or dismissal for cause; or
        b. the employee has a miscarriage or ceases to have the care of the child; or
        c. the employee or the child dies.
    3. However, the period for which a maternity payment is payable to an employee terminates earlier than the date referred to in subclause (1):
        a. if the employee takes parental leave only from fixed term employment, in which case the payment stops on the date on which fixed term employment ends; or
        b. if the employee's spouse succeeds to the maternity payment under subclause 5(3), in which case the payment to the employee stops on the date of succession.[43]

Clause 11 deals with the amount of the maternity payment:

11. 1. The rate of maternity payment payable to any employee is the lesser of:
        a. the Federal minimum wage as ordered, from time to time, by the Australian Industrial Relations Commission; or
        b. 100% of the employee's average weekly earnings (averaged over the 12 months preceding the commencement of parental leave).

---

42   Ibid., at Schedule 15, Clause 8.
43   Ibid., at Schedule 15, Clause 10.

2. If an employee is entitled to receive a maternity payment from more than
    one employer in respect of a child, the total of those payments cannot
    exceed the amount mentioned in paragraph (1)(a).
3. This maternity payment is to be treated as wage and salary income
    received by the eligible employee, or eligible spouse as the case may
    be, for the purposes of taxation, superannuation and other relevant laws
    and agreements.[44]

The obligation to notify early return to work is covered under Clause 16:

16. 1. An employee must give notice if, during the period for which the
        employee is receiving a maternity payment under this Schedule:
        a. the employee returns to work; or
        b. the employee's fixed term employment ends; or
        c. the employee resigns from his or her employment.
    2. The notification must be made in the manner prescribed in the regulations
        and specify the matters, and be accompanied by the documents,
        prescribed in the regulations.[45]

Finally, the failure to return to work does not affect payment and is protected under
Clause 17:

17. An employee is not required to refund any maternity payment under this
    Schedule because the employee does not return to work at the end of his or
    her parental leave.[46]

In terms of maternity/parental leave milestones in Australia, the Federal Childcare
Act 1972 was enacted which provided the first direct Federal Government
participation in childcare. In 1973, Paid Maternity Leave was granted for the
Commonwealth Public Service, 12 weeks plus 40 weeks' unpaid leave, under the
Maternity Leave (Commonwealth Employees) Act 1973, which was intended to
be a 'pace-setter' to be emulated by the private sector. In 1975, the Federal Family
Law Act, subsequently amended in 1983, introduced a no-fault divorce system,
and irretrievable breakdown of marriage became the only ground for divorce,
and legislative recognition of the economic value of women's traditional work in
the home was given in the division of assets on divorce. In 1977, the Maternity
Leave Test Case decision of the then Australian Conciliation and Arbitration
Commission granted a 12-month maternity leave entitlement to all permanent
workers, guaranteeing continuity of employment following leave for the birth of
a child. In 1979, the Australian Conciliation and Arbitration Commission handed

---

44   Ibid., at Schedule 15, Clause 11.
45   Ibid., at Schedule 15, Clause 16.
46   Ibid., at Schedule 15, Clause 17.

down the Maternity Leave Test Case providing Australian employees with the right to 52 weeks' unpaid maternity leave. In 1983, the National Wage Case was held, in which the Australian Conciliation and Arbitration Commission (ACAC) acknowledged women's work as undervalued and underpaid, but it was stressed that the economy could not afford to pay commensurate women's wages.[47]

In 2002, unpaid parental leave in Australia was extended to cover casual employees, previously legislated in NSW and Queensland. In 2004, the Australian Government introduced the one-off Maternity Payment of $3,000 to replace Maternity Allowance and the Baby Bonus, and in 2006, the Maternity Payment was increased to $4,000, and then again in 2008 to $5,000. In 2007, HREOC recommended a national paid maternity leave scheme be funded by the federal Government.[48]

Australian law entitles women to 12 months' unpaid leave. However, about two-thirds of women in the workforce are not entitled to paid maternity leave and many working women are ineligible for unpaid leave because they are casual employees. Factors such as company culture, lack of information, and limited child care on return to work impede women's use of paid maternity leave, even where it is available. Further, Australia's female workforce is highly segmented, heavily casualized, or in part-time employment, all of which are known to reduce a female employee's entitlement to paid maternity leave. The duration of paid maternity leave currently available in Australian enterprise agreements varies, and in some cases, the pay is contingent on return to work.[49] Based on the fundamental principles of providing equal economic opportunity for women and the social importance of maternity, paid maternity leave should be a right for all working women.

According to the Parental Leave in Australia Survey done in December 2006, in terms of employment and eligibility for unpaid parental leave, around 70% of mothers were in paid employment during the 12 months prior to the birth of their child; among the remainder, the majority reported that they were not in paid employment because they were at home looking after their family. Among fathers, 96% were in paid employment in the 12 months prior to the birth.[50] Among parents who were in paid employment during the 12 months prior to the birth, around 30% of mothers and 35% of fathers did not meet criteria for eligibility for Australia's statutory 52 weeks' unpaid parental leave. Reasons for non-eligibility included: self-employment; not being with the same employer for 12 months prior to the birth; not working for an employer for the full 12 months. At least another 10% of mothers, and around 5% of fathers, were casuals who had been with one employer for 12 months.

---

47   Commonwealth Office of the Status of Women, Australia.

48   National Foundation for Australian Women.

49   Baird, Marian, University of Sydney, Valuing Parenthood, Options for Paid Maternity Leave, *Australia Review of Public Affairs*, 14 June 2002.

50   Whitehouse, G., M. Baird and C. Diamond, *Highlights from the Parental Leave in Australia Survey*, December 2006.

Overall, 14% of employed mothers opted to leave the labor market around the time of the birth; this included 8% of those meeting basic eligibility criteria for unpaid parental leave. The most common reason identified for leaving was to look after family full-time, but around 20% cited lack of paid maternity leave as a reason why they quit work. Mothers who quit work around the time of the birth were less likely than all employed mothers to be in full-time jobs, permanent jobs or in the public sector. First-time mothers were much more likely than mothers with other children to be in full-time jobs prior to the birth, 73% compared with 28%; they were also more likely to be in permanent jobs, 76% compared with 66%, and less likely to be in public sector jobs, 31% compared with 37%.

In terms of patterns of leave taken by mothers, around one-third of mothers who were employed in the period leading up to the birth accessed some paid maternity leave, but only 4% of leave-takers used paid maternity leave only. Among those who used some paid maternity leave, 18% used it at half-pay to double the duration. Over 50% of mothers who were employed in the period leading up to the birth used some unpaid maternity leave; but only around one-quarter of leave-takers used unpaid maternity leave only. Among mothers who took leave, around 50% took combinations of maternity and other types of leave, such as annual leave. Less than 15% of mothers who took leave used paid leave only; while more than half used combinations of paid and unpaid leave. The average duration of leave among mothers was around 40 weeks. Mothers working in the public sector, in very large workplaces, fewer than 500 employees and earning high salaries were more likely to use paid maternity leave, while those working part-time, or on casual or fixed-term contracts were considerably less likely to utilize this form of leave.

In terms of patterns of leave taken by fathers, less than one-quarter of fathers who were employed in the period leading up to the birth used some paid paternity leave; and less than 15% of leave-takers used paid paternity leave only. Less than 10% of fathers who were employed in the 12 months prior to the birth used any unpaid paternity leave; and only 5% of leave-takers used unpaid paternity leave only. Fathers were much more likely than mothers to rely on forms of leave other than formally designated 'parental' leave, with over 60% of leave-takers using 'other', that is non-parental forms of leave only, with the comparable figure for mothers being around 10%. A relatively small proportion of fathers who took leave used combinations of paternity and 'other' forms of leave, less than 20%, compared with around 50% of mothers. Over 80% of fathers who took leave used paid leave only, compared with less than 15% of mothers. The most frequently used form of paid leave taken by fathers was annual leave. The average duration of leave among fathers was around 14 days. Fathers working in the public sector and those with relatively high wages were more likely to use paternity leave.

In terms of mothers' return to paid employment, among mothers who were employed prior to the birth of their child and took leave from employment, one-quarter returned within six months, around 60% returned within 12 months, and 70% returned within 15 months, the age of the youngest children at the time of the survey. A significant proportion, 46%, of Australian mothers who took leave and returned to work within 15 months reported that they would have taken longer if they had access to some or more paid maternity leave. Only 7%, however, reported that improved access to unpaid parental leave would lead them to take a longer break. Among this group of mothers, 45% said they had returned earlier than they would have liked because they needed the money.

Two-thirds of women who were employed prior to the birth of their child, took leave and returned to work within 15 months reported that they returned to the same employer and the same job. Almost one-fifth reported returning to the same employer but a different job. Another 9% changed employer, with around half of these also changing occupation. The balance either continued in, or changed to, self-employment. Almost 70% of mothers who had worked full-time prior to the birth returned to work part-time; overall 83% of mothers were working part-time on their return to work. Among those who were in permanent positions prior to the birth, 87% returned to permanent positions, and among those who were in casual jobs prior to the birth, over 90% returned to casual positions. Those who were in fixed-term positions prior to the birth were more likely to experience change, 20% returning to casual jobs and 16% to permanent positions. Interestingly, around one-quarter of mothers thought that their career opportunities were worse on their return to work, while less than 10% thought they had improved. The perception of declining career opportunities was higher among those who changed from full-time to part-time employment, over one-third.

Finally, in terms of policy preferences, close to 50% of families identified better parental leave provisions as policies that would have improved things most for them in the period since the birth of their child. A national paid maternity leave scheme would go some way to addressing the male/female wage disadvantage and compensate for the period of childbirth and time shortly after when women take time off work or reduce their labor force activity. Striking a balance between affordable policies and meeting the needs of families is challenging. The roles of bearing and caring for children still fall primarily to women, yet a social revolution has seen women confronting many additional life transitions and challenges, including education, paid work, travel and housing. Paid maternity leave, it is argued, is one way of assisting women to combine these roles and meet these challenges. Other objectives of paid maternity leave include addressing declining birth rates, providing the time and means to ensure the health and well-being of women and babies at the time of birth, and delivering economic security for women at a crucial stage in their lives and careers. Supporters of a comprehensive paid maternity leave say motherhood means a substantial loss of earnings, demotion and insecurity in the workplace for many women. Providing financial and job security for women, as well as helping businesses retain skilled employees, makes good financial sense.[51]

Most women's life patterns continue to be different from those of men. Many women have primary responsibility for caring for children, the elderly

---

51   Ibid.

and the sick. This means that significantly more women than men have disrupted work patterns and have taken on part-time and casual jobs. Women's capacity to achieve financial security depends on access to education and training, jobs, superannuation, affordable child care, equal pay, a fair division of family responsibility, and adequate income security. The critical area of concern is the inequality in economic structures and policies, in all forms of productive activities and in access to resources, with corrective action to promote women's economic rights and independence, including access to employment, appropriate working conditions and control over economic resources; facilitate women's equal access to resources, employment, markets and trade; provide business services, training and access to markets, information and technology, particularly to low-income women; strengthen women's economic capacity and commercial networks; eliminate occupational segregation and all forms of employment discrimination; and promote harmonization of work and family responsibilities for women and men. Policies to improve opportunities and choices for women are essential whether participating in the paid workforce or full-time parents or carers. Reforms to workplace relations are providing greater flexibility for women and men to combine work and family responsibilities, while maintaining a safety net of fair minimum wages and conditions of employment, as well as opening up a far wider range of employment options for women. Further, there are more opportunities for women to participate in part-time jobs, job-sharing and home-based work, and more women are entering non-traditional areas of the labor force.

New Zealand

The Role of Women in New Zealand

New Zealand is an island nation of 103,000 square miles and a population of 4,268,600. New Zealand has ratified several international covenants, which obligate governments to ensure equality to enjoy all economic, social, cultural, civil and political rights. Although international agreements do not automatically become part of New Zealand domestic law upon ratification but must be enacted into law by Parliament, jurisprudence has developed in New Zealand that recognizes the value of international agreements as tools for interpreting the legislative provisions which implement them into domestic law. New Zealand has a total population of 4,268,600 people.[52] While half the resident population is under the age of 33 years, one-quarter of the population is aged 50 years or over, reflecting the fact that New Zealand's population is ageing, with women accounting for 53.3% of the population aged over 50 years and 56.9% of the population aged 65 years and over.[53]

---

52   New Zealand Census.
53   Ministry of Women's Affairs, New Zealand.

Over the years, there has been an increase in the percentage of working age women joining the labor force and an increase in the numbers of women in self-employment. The percentage of working age women – that is, 15 years and over – joining the labor force continues to increase, since women comprise 51.2% of the working age population and 44.7% of the labor force. While 52% of working age women are in the labor force, 62% of employed women are working full-time and 38% are working part-time. Ethnicity plays a factor in gender discrimination. In New Zealand, although participation rates for Māori and Pacific women have risen over the past six years, Māori, Pacific and women from 'other' ethnic groups are currently less likely to participate in the labor force than European/Pakeha women. The decrease in participation by women from 'other' ethnic groups is likely to be influenced by the high level of immigration. While Māori and Pacific women, and women from 'other' ethnic groups, face higher rates of unemployment than European/Pakeha women, there has been a significant improvement in the unemployment rates for Māori and Pacific women in the last six years.

A major difference between men and women is in hours of work. Although an increasing proportion of men and women are working part-time, women are more than twice as likely to work part-time than men, as 38% of women employed were in part-time work compared to 12% of men employed. Women comprise 73% of all part-time workers. Many women work part-time to allow them to combine paid work and family responsibilities. However, many part-timers are working fewer hours than they would like, since 35% of men and 27% of women working part-time would prefer more hours. Of all part-time workers wanting more hours, 67% are women, since women working part-time also work shorter hours than their male counterparts.

In terms of occupation, women continue to work in different occupations from men and are concentrated in a narrower range of occupations. Over 90% of early childhood workers are women, and approximately 80% of primary teachers are women. However, there has been an increase over the years in the proportion of women working as legislators, administrators and managers, from 8.1% in 1991 to 9.3% in 1997; and working as technicians from 11.1% in 1991 to 13.2% in 1997. Occupation is also a major factor influencing earning capacity. A higher proportion of women work in lower-paid clerical, sales and service occupations. However, within every occupation, male full-time employees receive higher incomes than female full-time employees. In percentage terms, the largest income gap is among service and sales workers, and the smallest income gap is among clerical workers.

In looking at women in self-employment and small business, women's self-employment grew by 31.5% in recent years, with the largest increases in community, social and personal services, in finance, insurance, real estate and business industries, and in manufacturing. As well, almost twice as many women as men of working age are not in the labor force, with the reason being the doing of unpaid work at home, caring for children and dependent older relatives. In looking at women in self-employment, 40% of new businesses are started up by women, and this is predicted to increase to 50% within the next few years, since the numbers of women going into self-employment are increasing at a rate of 20 per working day. Further, women setting up their own businesses are increasing at a faster rate than men, with women considered to be 49% more successful than men in such ventures. Of women with their own business, 55% were under 40 when they set up in business.

In examining earnings, the average ordinary time weekly earnings for females is $537.65, that is 76.8% of males' average ordinary time weekly pay of $700.02. Women's average hourly earnings are 81.2% of men's. Part of the difference in men's and women's average weekly earnings is attributable to differences in the hours spent in paid employment, since male employees tend to work longer hours and receive more paid overtime than women. The gap between female and male average ordinary time hourly earnings in the public sector is wider than that in the private sector, since the average ordinary time hourly earnings for female employees in the public sector is at 76.2%, and in the private sector at 80.2% of that for males. Other significant factors affecting earnings are the level of seniority, the level of skills, experience and job-related training, and the duration and continuity of employment.

In looking at the distribution of family/household income, it was found that the more a woman contributes to household income, the more she is likely to have some say in household financial decisions. Men exert various forms of direct and indirect control over money that inhibits women spending on themselves for things unrelated to the role of housewife and mother, such as health care, dentistry, and further education or retraining to enhance employment prospects. Women in all ethnic groups prioritize their children's needs over their own. In terms of the economic consequences of marriage breakdown, women's income and standard of living drop significantly after divorce and often never fully recover. This is largely due to the fact that women still retain primary care of children after marriage breakdown, and may, as a result, have a weakened attachment to the labor market. This is known as the 'equality is not equity' phenomenon, which is a barrier to equality of outcomes following marriage breakdown. In looking at family responsibilities, there have been changes over the years to family composition, which affect women. There is a significant increase in the number of sole-parent families – that is, 28.3% of all families with children in New Zealand – the majority headed by women.

Overall, as a result of social attitudes to and distinctions made on the basis of gender, women experience particularly daunting barriers when seeking access to legal services, and consequently to courts and tribunals. The evidence suggests that women usually become involved in legal proceedings when the circumstances are such that, effectively, they have no choice but to become involved. This is the case in family matters and in criminal matters. Women find it especially problematic to obtain information about legal rights and processes; experience difficulties finding an appropriate legal advisor as most lawyers are men, and have limited opportunities during their education and training to become informed about the effects of gender; and find the cost of legal services too high, deterring women from proceeding to protect and enforce their legal rights. For a great many women, 'access to justice' means ready access to quality legal services and procedures, measured to a significant extent by the responsiveness of legal services to clients' social and economic situation and cultural background.[54]

Legislation

Treaty of Waitangi   In the late 1830s, there were approximately 125,000 Māori and about 2,000 settlers in New Zealand. More immigrants were arriving all the time, though, and Captain William Hobson was sent to act for the British Crown in the negotiation of a treaty between the Crown and Māori. The Colonial Secretary, Lord Normanby, instructed Hobson:

> All dealings with the Aborigines for their Lands must be conducted on the same principles of sincerity, justice, and good faith as must govern your transactions with them for the recognition of Her Majesty's Sovereignty in the Islands. Nor is this all. They must not be permitted to enter into any Contracts in which they might be the ignorant and unintentional authors of injuries to themselves. You will not, for example, purchase from them any Territory the retention of which by them would be essential, or highly conducive, to their own comfort, safety or subsistence. The acquisition of Land by the Crown for the future Settlement of British Subjects must be confined to such Districts as the Natives can alienate without distress or serious inconvenience to themselves. To secure the observance of this rule will be one of the first duties of their official protector.

The Treaty of Waitangi is an important legislative instrument. The Preamble of the English version of the Treaty of Waitangi, which came into effect on 6 February 1840, states:

> HER MAJESTY VICTORIA Queen of the United Kingdom of Great Britain and Ireland regarding with Her Royal favor the Native Chiefs and Tribes of New Zealand and anxious to protect their just Rights and Property and to secure to them the enjoyment of Peace and Good Order has deemed it necessary in consequence of the great number of Her Majesty's Subjects who have already settled in New Zealand and the rapid extension of Emigration both from Europe and Australia which is still in progress to constitute and appoint a functionary properly authorized to treat with the Aborigines of New Zealand for the recognition of Her Majesty's Sovereign authority over the whole or any part of those islands, Her Majesty therefore being desirous to establish a settled form of Civil Government with a view to avert the evil consequences which must result from the absence of the necessary Laws and Institutions alike to the native

---

54   Ibid.

population and to Her subjects has been graciously pleased to empower and to authorize me William Hobson a Captain in Her Majesty's Royal Navy Consul and Lieutenant Governor of such parts of New Zealand as may be or hereafter shall be ceded to her Majesty to invite the confederated and independent Chiefs of New Zealand to concur in the following Articles and Conditions.[55]

In terms of the meaning of the Treaty, the Preamble of the English text states that the British intentions were to protect Māori interests from the encroaching British settlement, provide for British settlement and establish a government to maintain peace and order. The Māori text has a different emphasis, suggesting that the Queen's main promises to Māori were to secure tribal *rangatiratanga* and secure Māori land ownership.

Article 1 states:

> The Chiefs of the Confederation of the United Tribes of New Zealand and the separate and independent Chiefs who have not become members of the Confederation cede to Her Majesty the Queen of England absolutely and without reservation all the rights and powers of Sovereignty which the said Confederation or Individual Chiefs respectively exercise or possess, or may be supposed to exercise or to possess over their respective Territories as the sole Sovereigns thereof.[56]

In terms of the meaning of the Treaty, in the Māori text of Article 1, the Māori gave the British a right of governance, *kawanatanga*, whereas in the English text, the Māori ceded 'sovereignty'. One of the problems that faced the original translators of the English draft of the Treaty was that 'sovereignty' in the British understanding of the word had no direct translation in the context of Māori society. *Rangatira*, the chiefs, held *rangatiratanga*, the autonomy and authority, over their own domains but there was no supreme ruler of the whole country. In the Māori text, the translators used the inadequate term *kawanatanga*, a transliteration of the word 'governance', which was then in current use. The Māori understanding of this word came from familiar use in the New Testament of the Bible when referring to the likes of Pontious Pilate, and from their knowledge of the role of the *Kawana*, the Governor of New South Wales, whose jurisdiction then extended to British subjects in New Zealand. As a result, in Article 1, the Māori believe they ceded to the Queen a right of governance in return for the promise of protection, while retaining the authority to manage their own affairs.

Article 2 states:

> Her Majesty the Queen of England confirms and guarantees to the Chiefs and Tribes of New Zealand and to the respective families and individuals thereof the full

---

55   Treaty of Waitangi, New Zealand, at the Preamble.
56   Ibid., at Article 1.

exclusive and undisturbed possession of their Lands and Estates Forests Fisheries and other properties which they may collectively or individually possess so long as it is their wish and desire to retain the same in their possession; but the Chiefs of the United Tribes and the individual Chiefs yield to Her Majesty the exclusive right of Preemption over such lands as the proprietors thereof may be disposed to alienate at such prices as may be agreed upon between the respective Proprietors and persons appointed by Her Majesty to treat with them in that behalf.[57]

In terms of the meaning of the Treaty, the Māori text of Article 2 uses the word *rangatiratanga* in promising to uphold the authority that tribes had always had over their lands and *taonga*. This choice of wording emphasizes status and authority. In the English text, the Queen guaranteed to the Māori the undisturbed possession of their properties, including their lands, forests, and fisheries, for as long as they wished to retain them, emphasizing property and ownership rights. Article 2 provides for land sales to be effected through the Crown, giving the Crown the right of pre-emption in land sales. The Waitangi Tribunal, after reading the instructions for the Treaty provided by Lord Normanby, concluded that the purpose of this provision was not just to regulate settlement but to ensure that each tribe retained sufficient land for its own purposes and needs.

Article 3 states:

In consideration thereof Her Majesty the Queen of England extends to the Natives of New Zealand Her royal protection and imparts to them all the Rights and Privileges of British Subjects.

W HOBSON Lieutenant Governor.

Now therefore We the Chiefs of the Confederation of the United Tribes of New Zealand being assembled in Congress at Victoria in Waitangi and We the Separate and Independent Chiefs of New Zealand claiming authority over the Tribes and Territories which are specified after our respective names, having been made fully to understand the Provisions of the foregoing Treaty, accept and enter into the same in the full spirit and meaning thereof: in witness of which we have attached our signatures or marks at the places and the dates respectively specified.[58]

In terms of the meaning of the Treaty, in Article 3, the Crown promised to the Māori the benefits of royal protection and full citizenship, emphasizing equality. Further, in the epilogue, the signatories acknowledge that they have entered into the full spirit of the Treaty. It is the principles of the Treaty, rather than the meaning of its strict terms, that is important and the Waitangi Tribunal must have regard for

---

57   Ibid., at Article 2.
58   Ibid., at Article 3.

cultural meanings of words, the surrounding circumstances, comments made at the time, and the parties' objectives.

Bill of Rights Act   Important for equal rights and appreciation for maternity issues, according to the Preamble of the Bill of Rights Act 1990, as amended by the Human Rights Act, the Bill of Rights aims to affirm, protect, and promote human rights and fundamental freedoms in New Zealand; and to affirm New Zealand's commitment to the International Covenant on Civil and Political Rights.[59] It applies to acts done by the legislative, executive and judicial branches of the Government, or by any person or body in the performance of any public function, power or duty conferred or imposed on that person or body by or pursuant to law. In addition, freedom from discrimination is guaranteed under Section 19:

19. 1.   Everyone has the right to freedom from discrimination on the grounds of … sex…
    2.   Measures taken in good faith for the purpose of assisting or advancing persons or groups of persons disadvantaged because of … sex … do not constitute discrimination.[60]

Importantly, the right to justice and hence remedies are contained in Section 27:

27. 1.   Every person has the right to the observance of the principles of natural justice by any tribunal or other public authority which has the power to make a determination in respect of that person's right, obligations, or interests protected or recognized by law.
    2.   Every person whose rights, obligations, or interests protected or recognized by law have been affected by a determination of any tribunal or other public authority has the right to apply, in accordance with law, for judicial review of that determination.
    3.   Every person has the right to bring civil proceedings against, and to defend civil proceedings brought by, the Crown, and to have those proceedings heard, according to law, in the same way as civil proceedings between individuals.[61]

Human Rights Act (HRA) and Human Rights Amendment Act   Important for equal rights and appreciation for maternity issues, the Human Rights Act 1993 (HRA), entitled An Act to consolidate and amend the Race Relations Act 19711 and the Human Rights Commission Act 1977 and to provide better protection of human rights in New Zealand in general accordance with the United Nations Covenants or Conventions on Human Rights, protects New Zealanders from unlawful

---

59   Bill of Rights Act, New Zealand, at the Preamble.
60   Ibid., at Section 19.
61   Ibid., at Section 27.

discrimination in a number of areas of life. The Human Rights Commission (HRC) was established by the Human Rights Commission Act 1977 (HRCA), and is empowered under the HRA to protect human rights in accordance with United Nations Covenants and Conventions. The Human Rights Amendment Act 2001 (HRAA) made several significant changes to the HRA, and specifically to the functions and powers of the Commission, and specifically as to the way complaints of unlawful discrimination are received and resolved by the Commission. Some of the key changes to the Commission's functions and powers include: advocating and promoting respect for and appreciation of human rights in New Zealand society, and encouraging the maintenance and development of harmonious relations between individuals and the diverse groups in New Zealand society; advocating and promoting, by education and publicity, respect for, and observance of, human rights; making public statements promoting an understanding of, and compliance with, the New Zealand Bill of Rights Act 1990; developing a national plan of action, in consultation with interested parties, for the promotion and protection of human rights in New Zealand; promoting, by research, education and discussion, a better understanding of the human rights dimensions of the Treaty of Waitangi and their relationship with domestic and international human rights law; bringing civil proceedings for any breach of the Act arising out of any inquiry conducted by the Commission; and applying to a court or tribunal to be appointed as intervener or as counsel, assisting the Court or Tribunal, in facilitating the performance of the Commission's functions relating to advocacy for, or promotion of, human rights.

Further, the functions and powers of the HRC include to encourage, by education and publicity, respect for and observance of human rights; to encourage and coordinate programs and activities in the field of human rights; to make public statements in relation to any matter affecting human rights, including statements promoting an understanding of, and compliance with, the Act; to prepare and publish guidelines for the avoidance of acts or practices that may be inconsistent with the provisions of this Act; to receive representations from members of the public on any matter affecting human rights; to consult and cooperate with other people and bodies concerned with the protection of human rights; to inquire into any matter, including any enactment or law, or any practice, or any procedure, whether governmental or non-governmental, if it appears to the Commission that human rights are, or may be, infringed thereby; and to report to the Prime Minister from time to time on any matter affecting human rights, including the desirability of legislative, administrative, or other action to give better protection to human rights and to ensure better compliance with standards laid down in international instruments on human rights, the desirability of New Zealand becoming bound by any international instrument on human rights, and the implications of any proposed legislation or proposed policy of the Government that the Commission considers may affect human rights.[62] Employment remains the largest area of complaints at about 60%.

---

62 Human Rights Act, New Zealand, at Section 5(1).

Prohibited grounds are personal characteristics and discrimination because of these characteristics is unlawful. Important for equal rights, Section 21 defines discrimination under prohibited grounds for discrimination, which mentions sex including pregnancy and childbirth, and family status under Section 21(1)(a) and (l) respectively:

21. 1. For the purposes of this Act, the prohibited grounds of discrimination are:
    a. sex, which includes pregnancy and childbirth;
    l. family status, which means:
        i. having the responsibility for parttime care or fulltime care of children or other dependants; or
        ii. having no responsibility for the care of children or other dependants; or
        iii. being married to, or being in a relationship in the nature of a marriage with, a particular person; or
        iv. being a relative of a particular person.
    2. Each of the grounds specified in subsection (1) of this section is a prohibited ground of discrimination, for the purposes of this Act, if:
        a. it pertains to a person or to a relative or associate of a person; and
        b. it either:
            i. currently exists or has in the past existed; or
            ii. is suspected or assumed or believed to exist or to have existed by the person alleged to have discriminated.[63]

Indirect discrimination is defined in Section 65:

65. Where any conduct, practice, requirement, or condition that is not apparently in contravention of any provision of this Part of this Act has the effect of treating a person or group of persons differently on one of the prohibited grounds of discrimination in a situation where such treatment would be unlawful under any provision of this Part of this Act other than this section, that conduct, practice, condition, or requirement shall be unlawful under that provision unless the person whose conduct or practice is in issue, or who imposes the condition or requirement, establishes good reason for it.[64]

Further, as regards discrimination in employment, Section 22(1) states:

22. 1. Where an applicant for employment or an employee is qualified for work of any description, it shall be unlawful for an employer, or any person acting or purporting to act on behalf of an employer:

---

63   Ibid., at Section 21.
64   Ibid., at Section 65.

    a. to refuse or omit to employ the applicant on work of that description which is available; or

    b. to offer or afford the applicant or the employee less favourable terms of employment, conditions of work, superannuation or other fringe benefits, and opportunities for training, promotion, and transfer than are made available to applicants or employees of the same or substantially similar capabilities employed in the same or substantially similar circumstances on work of that description; or

    c. to terminate the employment of the employee, or subject the employee to any detriment, in circumstances in which the employment of other employees employed on work of that description would not be terminated, or in which other employees employed on work of that description would not be subjected to such detriment; or

    d. to retire the employee, or to require or cause the employee to retire or resign (applies to all (a), (b), (c) and (d)), by reason of any of the prohibited grounds of discrimination.[65]

Section 35 outlines the general qualification on exceptions:

35. No employer shall be entitled … to accord to any person in respect of any position different treatment based on a prohibited ground of discrimination even though some of the duties of that position would fall within any of those exceptions if, with some adjustment of the activities of the employer (not being an adjustment involving unreasonable disruption of the activities of the employer), some other employee could carry out those particular duties.[66]

Further, Section 27 includes exceptions in relation to authenticity and privacy:

27. 1. Nothing … shall prevent different treatment based on sex or age where, for reasons of authenticity, being of a particular sex … is a genuine occupational qualification for the position or employment.

   2. Nothing … shall prevent different treatment based on sex … where the position is one of domestic employment in a private household.

   3. Nothing … shall prevent different treatment based on sex where:

      a. the position needs to be held by one sex to preserve reasonable standards of privacy; or

      b. the nature or location of the employment makes it impracticable for the employee to live elsewhere than in premises provided by the employer, and:

---

65 Ibid., at Section 22(1).
66 Ibid., at Section 35.

      i. the only premises available (being premises in which more than one employee is required to sleep) are not equipped with separate sleeping accommodation for each sex; and

     ii. it is not reasonable to expect the employer to equip those premises with separate accommodation, or to provide separate premises, for each sex.

5. Where, as a term or condition of employment, a position ordinarily obliges or qualifies the holder of that position to live in premises provided by the employer, the employer does not commit a breach ... by omitting to apply that term or condition in respect of employees of a particular sex ... if in all the circumstances it is not reasonably practicable for the employer to do so.[67]

Finally, measures to ensure equality are established under Section 73:

73. 1. Anything done or omitted which would otherwise constitute a breach of any of the provisions of this Part of this Act shall not constitute such a breach if:

    a. it is done or omitted in good faith for the purpose of assisting or advancing persons or groups of persons, being in each case persons against whom discrimination is unlawful by virtue of this Part of this Act; and

    b. those persons or groups need or may reasonably be supposed to need assistance or advancement in order to achieve an equal place with other members of the community.[68]

Employment Contracts Act and Employment Relations Act Important for employment rights and appreciation for maternity issues in the workplace, the Employment Contracts Act 1991[69] and the Employment Relations Act 2000 provide people with the right to take discrimination cases to the Employment Court as a personal grievance. Further, Section 3 of the Employment Relations Act establishes the objectives:

3. The object of this Act is

    a. to build productive employment relationships through the promotion of mutual trust and confidence in all aspects of the employment environment and of the employment relationship

      i. by recognising that employment relationships must be built on good faith behaviour; and

---

67 Ibid., at Section 27.

68 Ibid., at Section 73.

69 Employment Contracts Act, New Zealand.

ii. by acknowledging and addressing the inherent inequality of bargaining power in employment relationships; and

iii. by promoting collective bargaining; and

iv. by protecting the integrity of individual choice; and

v.   by promoting mediation as the primary problem-solving mechanism; and

vi. by reducing the need for judicial intervention; and

b. to promote observance in New Zealand of the principles underlying International Labour Organization Convention 87 on Freedom of Association, and Convention 98 on the Right to Organise and Bargain Collectively.[70]

Finally, the jurisdiction of the Employment Court is established under Section 187 of the Employment Relations Act:

187. 1. The Court has exclusive jurisdiction

a. to hear and determine elections under section 179 for a hearing of a matter previously determined by the Authority, whether under this Act or any other Act conferring jurisdiction on the Authority:

b. to hear and determine actions for the recovery of penalties under this Act for a breach of any provision of this Act (being a provision that provides for the penalty to be recovered in the Court):

c. to hear and determine questions of law referred to it by the Authority under section 177:

d. to hear and determine applications for leave to have matters before the Authority removed into the Court under section 178(3):

e. to hear and determine matters removed into the Court under section 178:

f. to hear and determine, under section 6(5), any question whether any person is to be declared to be

i.   an employee within the meaning of this Act; or

ii. a worker or employee within the meaning of any of the Acts referred to in section 223(1):

g. to order compliance under section 139:

h. to hear and determine proceedings founded on tort and resulting from or related to a strike or lockout:

i. to hear and determine any application for an injunction of a type specified in section 100:

j. to hear and determine any application for review of the type referred to in section 194:

k. to issue warrants under section 231:

l. to exercise its powers in respect of any offence against this Act:

---

70 Employment Relations Act, New Zealand, at Section 3.

m. to exercise such other functions and powers as are conferred on it by this or any other Act.

2. The Court does not have jurisdiction to entertain an application for summary judgment.[71]

In examining the Parental Leave Policy (PPL) in New Zealand, important trends are apparent.[72] PPL allows for 14 weeks of job-protected paid parental leave, and to be eligible for PPL, employees must have worked continuously with the same employer for an average of at least 10 hours a week, including at least one hour in every week or 40 hours in every month, in the six or 12 months immediately before the baby's expected due date or the date the employee has assumed the care of a child they intend to adopt. Eligibility for PPL is primarily determined through the birth mother. However, if the spouse/partner, including same-sex couples, fits the eligibility criteria, the mother can transfer part or all of the leave to them, and in the case of joint adoption, the spouse/partner can be nominated as the primary caregiver. In addition, employees who have worked continuously with the same employer for 12 months or more are also entitled to extended leave of up to 52 weeks of employment-protected unpaid parental leave, less any PPL taken. Unpaid leave must be taken continuously and can be shared between parents where they are both eligible. Both parents can take their leave at the same time or consecutively with each other. Further, up to 10 days of unpaid leave is available to a mother before maternity leave for reasons connected with pregnancy, such as antenatal checks.

The rationale underlying the eligibility criteria for both the paid and unpaid parental leave is that to qualify for the job protection that accompanies leave, an employee should have demonstrated workplace attachment with their employer, which helps to strike a balance between an employee's interest in job-protected leave and an employer's interest in maintaining qualified staff. Starting in 2006, to be eligible for parental leave payments, a birth mother/adoptive parent has to establish that they had worked an average of at least 10 hours a week over the six or 12 months immediately before the expected date of delivery or adoption of a child. In terms of partners/paternity leave, unpaid leave of one week is available to spouse/partners with six months' eligible service and two weeks of unpaid leave is available to spouse/partners with 12 months' eligible service.

Overall, there is widespread support among mothers, fathers and employers for paid parental leave, in that it is almost universally recognized that PPL, with its job protection and payment, is important for parents, primarily mothers, to take time out of paid work around the birth or adoption of a child. However, for both biological and social reasons, it is almost solely mothers who take PPL and extended parental leave; recovery from childbirth is seen as being supported by

---

71   Ibid., at Section 187.

72   Department of Labour New Zealand and Research New Zealand, *Parental Leave in New Zealand 2005/2006 Evaluation.*

PPL as is breastfeeding. Fathers rarely take partners/paternity leave under the Act, and most mothers do not transfer any PPL to their spouse/partner, as most commonly fathers use annual leave. After the birth of a child, the majority of fathers feel increased pressure as the main income earner and have greater concern about financial security. Of those mothers who were eligible for PPL, eight in 10 of these women took a period of leave. Overall, this is two-thirds of all women in paid work in the immediate period before giving birth to a baby or adopting a child. Of the remaining third of all mothers in paid work and who did not take PPL, two-thirds take no leave at all and one-third took other types of leave. PPL is typically taken at the end of all other available paid leave and allows eligible mothers to extend the total amount of leave taken.

In terms of mothers, most mothers would like to take longer leave than they actually do; on average, most mothers return to work when their baby is six months old, but would like to return when their baby is 12 months old. Two-thirds of mothers, who took PPL and then returned to work, went back to the same employer. Most returned with the same terms and conditions. Although a little lower, the majority of women who did not take PPL also returned with the same terms and conditions. Most mothers change their working arrangements when returning from leave. A change in working hours is particularly common, with two-thirds working part-time compared to one-third before the birth. Of those who decreased their hours, two-thirds planned for it to be a permanent change. Most mothers prefer the time provided by PPL for themselves, and not for their partners. This is because PPL occurs during the first few months of the baby's life when the baby's health and bonding are critical considerations.

In terms of fathers, most fathers take some sort of leave around the birth or adoption of a child. Very few eligible fathers, however, are taking unpaid partners paternity leave and are more likely to save up and use all other types of paid leave around the birth of a baby. The most common arrangement is for men to take two weeks' annual leave around the birth of the baby. The ideal leave for fathers is four weeks' concurrent leave with the mother. One in two fathers had more involvement in domestic responsibilities around the birth. Where the mother had returned to paid work, all fathers maintained or increased their involvement. Fathers find employers more supportive about changing work patterns around the time of the birth, but not necessarily for longer-term changes.

In terms of employers, the majority of employers, and especially small employers, have very little experience of women taking PPL. Large employers are more likely to have formalized policies and systems in place to manage parental leave, and are more likely to have greater knowledge of their legal obligations. Small employers are more likely to consider parental leave on a case-by-case basis.

Employing someone to cover the position of an employee on parental leave is one of the most difficult aspects to manage for employers. Small and medium enterprises are more likely to find this difficult and prefer to re-allocate work across existing staff rather than try to hire someone to temporarily fill the role. Two-thirds of employers agree that PPL allows them to plan and manage workloads with greater confidence. Typically employers accommodate changes in working patterns on the mother's return to work and on an ongoing basis, particularly changing the number of hours worked and working flexible hours. Small and medium enterprises appear to be more flexible than larger employers. They are more likely to strongly agree that they work around the needs of families where possible and re-evaluate the needs of mothers on a regular basis. Employers are more supportive of changes to working patterns for fathers around the time of the birth, rather than on a long-term basis.

Uptake of leave is limited by a number of factors, including: awareness of leave policies; a conscious choice to exit the workforce and ethical obligation to employers; perceived flexibility of paid work to fit around family; and the type of role in the workplace. Most of those who were ineligible for PPL said that the financial contribution had they been eligible would have been significant. Just under half said a payment would have meant they took more leave. The biggest barrier to taking the full 12 months of parental leave available is financial pressure; mothers acknowledge that PPL lessens money worries, but does not provide financial security. Overall, paid maternity, paternity and parental leave policies available in other countries can have an influence on New Zealand policies in at least two important ways: firstly, when considering the effectiveness of New Zealand's PPL scheme, policy makers often compare New Zealand's policies with those of similar countries, and secondly, the parents themselves may have experienced other countries' systems of parental leave, and so may make comparisons themselves.[73]

Conclusion

Despite strong legislative provisions both in Australia and New Zealand, there is still progress to be made to achieve equal outcomes and opportunities for all. Equality and the rights contained within legislation rely on the overall legal system, as well as cultural attitudes for implementation and enforcement. However, gaps do exist in the coverage of legislation, and in the manner by which it is enforced. Taking concrete action to advance human rights and support opportunity and choice require a concerted effort across the whole of government, in addition to the important ongoing role of specialist human rights monitoring and complaints mechanisms, in the pursuit of *Pregnant Pause*.

---

73   Ibid.

Chapter 5
Pregnant Pause in Africa and South Africa

Introduction

In the quest for appreciation for maternity issues in *Pregnant Pause*, this chapter will examine efforts against maternity discrimination on the continent of Africa, and in South Africa. It will examine important legislation impacting maternity rights, first in Africa, namely: the Charter of the Organization of African Unity, the African Charter on Human and Peoples' Rights and the Protocol of the African Charter on Human and Peoples' Rights, and for women in general, the Protocol on Rights of Women in Africa; and then in South Africa, namely: the Interim Constitution Schedule 4 and the Constitution, the Employment Equity Act, and the Promotion of Equality, Prevention of Unfair Discrimination Act, the Basic Conditions of Employment Act, and the Unemployment Insurance Act.

Africa

The Role of Women in Africa

Women play a key, but often unrecognized, role in all the important aspects of life in Africa, as food producers, carriers of water, collectors of fuel wood, processors of food, caretakers of children and the elderly, and often times the primary earners of cash incomes.[1] The constraints faced by women influence and are influenced by activities relating to population growth, the environment and food security. Women's roles impact directly on Africa's problems of food insufficiency and environmental degradation. The pressure on women's time and the gender-specific constraints that women face, with notable limited access to the productive resources, have serious implications for the environment, agriculture and sustainable development throughout Africa. Africa's challenges and opportunities include: empowering every member of the population, particularly women; reducing poverty; reducing food insecurity; improving social and economic amenities in rural and urban areas; and generating and disseminating information widely.

Africa is not a single uniform entity. Within Africa, there is much diversity, in terms of race, culture, gender relations, disability, age, religion, sexual orientation, society, family, geography, economy, and natural resources. There is not one

---

1 Economic Commission for Africa, *Africa's Population and Development Bulletin*, Addis Ababa.

formula that can be applied in every case, and as such every community has to make its individual needs heard. In addition, Africa is not static. It is a continent in flux and is rapidly undergoing fundamental changes, namely the growth of urban populations, deterioration of the environment and increasing desertification, growing dependency on world markets, increasing numbers of young people and seniors, and civil strife and conflict. Development policies, plans and programs must be flexible to react and respond to these changes. The knowledge, attitudes and practices of the general African population have some components that are historically accumulated, based on the cultural and institutional heritage of the past. This is especially so among populations where a majority live in traditional ways, a lesser proportion are in transition, and a small powerful minority are considered 'modern'. Citizen services during the past several decades seem to have been dominated by the disparate trends and methods of funding from various European countries. Such developments, imported from countries with much stronger economies and longer histories of universal primary and child-centered education, as well as educational research, have seldom been culturally or conceptually appropriate to the countries in which they have taken place. Setting current efforts against a century or more of antiquated foreign development is intended to bring more realistic perspectives.

The current emphases within South Africa on human rights and policy reform go hand in hand with greater empowerment of all people. In terms of international trade, African countries adopted the Dakar/Ngor Declaration as the African common position to the International Conference on Population and Development (ICPD). It was recognized that population and development are inextricably linked, and that empowering and meeting people's needs for education and health are necessary for both individual advancement and balanced development. For population and sustainable development in Africa, a key measure must be the promotion of access to equitable distribution of resources. Further, there needs to be a mix of macroeconomic and structural policies and programs for enhancing investment, growth, poverty reduction and social development; infrastructure improvement and institutional support services policies; and policies aimed at strengthening grassroots institutions and local participation. The ICPD+5 Program of Action recommended a set of interdependent quantitative goals and objectives, which included universal access to primary education, with special attention to closing the gap in primary and secondary school education; universal access to primary health care; universal access to a full range of comprehensive reproductive health care services, including family planning; reductions in infant, child and maternal morbidity and mortality; and increased life expectancy impacting seniors. Overall, in terms of trade and its impact on people in Africa, the United States Congress passed the African Growth and Opportunity Act (AGOA), which eliminated American duties on textile imports from eligible sub-Saharan countries. To ensure long-term benefits from better access to American markets, African countries must diversify their economies, investing in infrastructure and in education to attract higher-tech companies. Africa's main goals are to substantially reduce or eliminate all tariffs on agricultural products, including quota duties; substantially reduce or eliminate tariff escalation; simplify complex tariffs by converting all tariffs to an *ad valorem* or fixed percentage of a product's value; substantially reduce or eliminate market-distorting export subsidies and domestic support; and recognize and meet the special needs of the world's least developed countries.

Importantly, the New Partnership for Africa's Development (NEPAD) is a pledge by all of Africa's leaders to eradicate poverty in which many seniors live and move towards sustainable growth and development. The partnership focuses on African ownership of the development process and seeks to reinvigorate the continent in all areas of human activity. Through cooperation and partnership, African leaders have agreed to promote the role of different groups in social and economic development; promote and protect democracy and human rights by developing standards for accountability, transparency and participatory governance; restore and maintain macroeconomic stability; implement transparent legal and regulatory frameworks; revitalize and extend education, technical training and health care services; and promote the development of infrastructure, agriculture, agroprocessing, and manufacturing to meet the needs of export and domestic markets as well as local employment. NEPAD draws Africa's attention to the seriousness of the continent's economic challenges, the potential for addressing them and the challenge of mobilizing support. The main strategies proposed include pursuing equality in education, business, and public service; developing education and human resources at all levels, and in particular increasing the role of information and communication technology in education and training, inducing a 'brain gain' for Africa and eliminating disparities in education; and increasing domestic resource mobilization and accelerating foreign investment, creating a conducive environment for private sector activities, with an emphasis on domestic entrepreneurs.[2]

Legislation

Charter of the Organization of African Unity   The heads of African States and governments signed the Charter of the Organization of African Unity on 25 May 1963 in Addis Ababa, Ethiopia, and it entered into force on 13 September 1963. The Preamble of the Charter of the Organization of African Unity states:

> Convinced that it is the inalienable right of all people to control their own destiny,

> Conscious of the fact that freedom, equality, justice and dignity are essential objectives for the achievement of the legitimate aspirations of the African peoples,

---

2   Ibid.

Conscious of our responsibility to harness the natural and human resources of our continent for the total advancement of our peoples in all spheres of human endeavor,

Inspired by a common determination to promote understanding among our peoples and cooperation among our states in response to the aspirations of our peoples for brother-hood and solidarity, in a larger unity transcending ethnic and national differences,

Convinced that, in order to translate this determination into a dynamic force in the cause of human progress, conditions for peace and security must be established and maintained,

Determined to safeguard and consolidate the hard-won independence as well as the sovereignty and territorial integrity of our states, and to fight against neo-colonialism in all its forms,

Dedicated to the general progress of Africa,

Persuaded that the Charter of the United Nations and the Universal Declaration of Human Rights, to the Principles of which we reaffirm our adherence, provide a solid foundation for peaceful and positive cooperation among States,

Desirous that all African States should henceforth unite so that the welfare and well-being of their peoples can be assured,

Resolved to reinforce the links between our states by establishing and strengthening common institutions.[3]

Article I establishes the Organization of African Unity:

I. 1. The High Contracting Parties do by the present Charter establish an Organization to be known as the ORGANIZATION OF AFRICAN UNITY.
   2. The Organization shall include the Continental African States, Madagascar and other Islands surrounding Africa.[4]

Its purposes are outlined in Article II:

II. 1. The Organization shall have the following purposes:
   a. To promote the unity and solidarity of the African States;

---

3 Charter of the Organization of African Unity, at the Preamble.
4 Ibid., at Article I.

b. To coordinate and intensify their cooperation and efforts to achieve a better life for the peoples of Africa;

c. To defend their sovereignty, their territorial integrity and independence;

d. To eradicate all forms of colonialism from Africa; and

e. To promote international cooperation, having due regard to the Charter of the United Nations and the Universal Declaration of Human Rights.

2. To these ends, the Member States shall coordinate and harmonize their general policies, especially in the following fields:

a. Political and diplomatic cooperation;

b. Economic cooperation, including transport and communications;

c. Educational and cultural cooperation;

d. Health, sanitation and nutritional cooperation;

e. Scientific and technical cooperation; and

f. Cooperation for defense and security.[5]

The various institutions are outlined in Article VII:

VII. The Organization shall accomplish its purposes through the following principal institutions:

1. The Assembly of Heads of State and Government.

2. The Council of Ministers.

3. The General Secretariat.

4. The Commission of Mediation, Conciliation and Arbitration.[6]

The Assembly of Heads of State and Government is contained in Article VIII:

VIII. The Assembly of Heads of State and Government shall be the supreme organ of the Organization. It shall, subject to the provisions of this Charter, discuss matters of common concern to Africa with a view to coordinating and harmonizing the general policy of the Organization. It may in addition review the structure, functions and acts of all the organs and any specialized agencies which may be created in accordance with the present Charter.[7]

The Council of Ministers is contained in Article XII:

XII. 1. The Council of Ministers shall consist of Foreign Ministers or other Ministers as are designated by the Governments of Member States.

5　Ibid., at Article II.

6　Ibid., at Article VII.

7　Ibid., at Article VIII.

2. The Council of Ministers shall meet at least twice a year. When requested by any Member State and approved by two-thirds of all Member States, it shall meet in extraordinary session.[8]

The General Secretariat is contained in Article XVI:

XVI. There shall be a Secretary-General of the Organization, who shall be appointed by the Assembly of Heads of State and Government. The Secretary-General shall direct the affairs of the Secretariat.[9]

The Commission of Mediation, Conciliation and Arbitration is contained in Article XIX:

XIX. Member States pledge to settle all disputes among themselves by peaceful means and, to this end decide to establish a Commission of Mediation, Conciliation and Arbitration, the composition of which and condition of service shall be defined by a separate Protocol to be approved by the Assembly of Heads of State and Government. Said Protocol shall be regarded as forming an integral part of the present Charter.[10]

The Specialized Commission is contained in Article XX:

XX. The Assembly shall establish such Specialized Commissions as it may, deem necessary, including the following:
1. Economic and Social Commission.
2. Educational, Scientific, Cultural and Health Commission.
3. Defense Commission.[11]

African Charter on Human and Peoples' Rights   The African Charter on Human and Peoples' Rights was adopted by the Eighteenth Assembly of Heads of State and Government on 27 June 1981 in Nairobi, Kenya, and is one the most widely accepted regional human rights instruments, having been ratified by more than 50 countries. The Preamble of the African Charter on Human and Peoples' Rights states:

The African States members of the Organization of African Unity, parties to the present Convention entitled African Charter on Human and Peoples' Rights,

---

8   Ibid., at Article XII.
9   Ibid., at Article XVI.
10   Ibid., at Article XIX.
11   Ibid., at Article XX.

Considering the Charter of the Organization of African Unity, which stipulates that 'freedom, equality, justice and dignity are essential objectives for the achievement of the legitimate aspirations of the African peoples';

Reaffirming the pledge they solemnly made in Article 2 of the said Charter to eradicate all forms of colonialism from Africa, to coordinate and intensify their cooperation and efforts to achieve a better life for the peoples of Africa and to promote international cooperation having due regard to the Charter of the United Nations and the Universal Declaration of Human Rights;

Taking into consideration the virtues of their historical tradition and the values of African civilization which should inspire and characterize their reflection on the concept of human and peoples' rights;

Recognizing on the one hand, that fundamental human rights stem from the attitudes of human beings, which justifies their international protection, and on the other hand that the reality and respect of peoples' rights should necessarily guarantee human rights;

Considering that the enjoyment of rights and freedoms also implies the performance of duties on the part of everyone;

Convinced that it is henceforth essential to pay particular attention to the right to development and that civil and political rights cannot be dissociated from economic, social and cultural rights in their conception as well as universality and that the satisfaction of economic, social and cultural rights is a guarantee for the enjoyment of civil and political rights;

Conscious of their duty to achieve the total liberation of Africa, the peoples of which are still struggling for their dignity and genuine independence, and undertaking to eliminate colonialism, neo-colonialism, apartheid, zionism and to dismantle aggressive foreign military bases and all forms of discrimination, language, religion or political opinions;

Reaffirming their adherence to the principles of human and peoples' rights and freedoms contained in the declarations, conventions and other instruments adopted by the Organization of African Unity, the Movement of Non-Aligned Countries and the United Nations;

Firmly convinced of their duty to promote and protect human and peoples' rights and freedoms and taking into account the importance traditionally attached to these rights and freedoms in Africa.[12]

---

12   African Charter on Human and Peoples' Rights, at the Preamble.

In terms of rights and duties in general, and human and peoples' rights, specifically, Article 1 states:

> 1. The Member States of the Organization of African Unity, parties to the present Charter shall recognize the rights, duties and freedoms enshrined in the Charter and shall undertake to adopt legislative or other measures to give effect to them.[13]

Article 5 upholds the dignity of the human person:

> 5. Every individual shall have the right to the respect of the dignity inherent in a human being and to the recognition of his legal status. All forms of exploitation and degradation of man, particularly slavery, slave trade, torture, cruel, inhuman or degrading punishment and treatment shall be prohibited.[14]

The concept of equality is guaranteed in Article 19:

> 19. All peoples shall be equal; they shall enjoy the same respect and shall have the same rights. Nothing shall justify the domination of a people by another.[15]

Further, important for equal rights and maternity issues, Article 2 protects against discrimination:

> 2. Every individual shall be entitled to the enjoyment of the rights and freedoms recognized and guaranteed in the present Charter without distinction of any kind such as … sex … or any status.[16]

Finally, respect and tolerance without discrimination are espoused in Article 28:

> 28. Every individual shall have the duty to respect and consider his fellow beings without discrimination, and to maintain relations aimed at promoting, safeguarding and reinforcing mutual respect and tolerance.[17]

Article 3 guarantees equal protection of the law, important for maternity discrimination:

---

13 Ibid., at Article 1.
14 Ibid., at Article 5.
15 Ibid., at Article 19.
16 Ibid., at Article 2.
17 Ibid., at Article 28.

3.　Every individual shall be equal before the law.
　　Every individual shall be entitled to equal protection of the law.[18]

Further, important for equal rights and maternity issues in the workplace, employment rights and equal pay for equal work are guaranteed in Article 15:

15.　Every individual shall have the right to work under equitable and satisfactory conditions, and shall receive equal pay for equal work.[19]

The right to education, not only for advancement but as a tool against discrimination, is contained in Article 17:

17.　Every individual shall have the right to education.
　　Every individual may freely take part in the cultural life of his community.
　　The promotion and protection of morals and traditional values recognized by the community shall be the duty of the State.[20]

Article 20 upholds the self-determination of people:

20.　All peoples shall have the right to existence. They shall have the unquestionable and inalienable right to self-determination. They shall freely determine their political status and shall pursue their economic and social development according to the policy they have freely chosen.[21]

Further, cultural development of the heritage of mankind is recognized in Article 22:

22.　All peoples shall have the right to their economic, social and cultural development with due regard to their freedom and identity and in the equal enjoyment of the common heritage of mankind.
　　States shall have the duty, individually or collectively, to ensure the exercise of the right to development.[22]

Importantly, duties of individuals towards one another are established in Article 27:

27.　Every individual shall have duties towards his family and society, the State and other legally recognized communities and the international community.

18　Ibid., at Article 3.
19　Ibid., at Article 15.
20　Ibid., at Article 17.
21　Ibid., at Article 20.
22　Ibid., at Article 22.

The rights and freedoms of each individual shall be exercised with due regard to the rights of others, collective security, morality and common interest.[23]

In Article 29, the individual shall also have the duty, among other things:

29. To serve his national community by placing his physical and intellectual abilities at its service;
To preserve and strengthen positive African cultural values in his relations with other members of the society, in the spirit of tolerance, dialogue and consultation and, in general, to contribute to the promotion of the moral well being of society.[24]

Article 7 stresses the importance of the courts in safeguarding rights:

7. 1. Every individual shall have the right to have his cause heard. This comprises:
   a. the right to an appeal to competent national organs against acts of violating his fundamental rights as recognized and guaranteed by conventions, laws, regulations and customs in force.[25]

Further, the paramount role of the Courts is guaranteed in Article 26:

26. State Parties to the present Charter shall have the duty to guarantee the independence of the Courts and shall allow the establishment and improvement of appropriate national institutions entrusted with the promotion and protection of the rights and freedoms guaranteed by the present Charter.[26]

The African Commission on Human and Peoples' Right is established under Article 30:

30. An African Commission on Human and Peoples' Rights, hereinafter called 'the Commission', shall be established within the Organization of African Unity to promote human and peoples' rights and ensure their protection in Africa.[27]

The mandate of the Commission is contained in Article 45:

---

23 Ibid., at Article 27.
24 Ibid., at Article 29.
25 Ibid., at Article 7.
26 Ibid., at Article 26.
27 Ibid., at Article 30.

45. The functions of the Commission shall be:

    To promote human and peoples' rights and in particular:

        to collect documents, undertake studies and researches on African problems in the field of human and peoples' rights, organize seminars, symposia and conferences, disseminate information, encourage national and local institutions concerned with human and peoples' rights and, should the case arise, give its views or make recommendations to Governments.

        to formulate and lay down principles and rules aimed at solving legal problems relating to human and peoples' rights and fundamental freedoms upon which African Governments may base their legislation.

        cooperate with other African and international institutions concerned with the promotion and protection of human and peoples' rights.

    Ensure the protection of human and peoples' rights under conditions laid down by the present Charter.

    Interpret all the provisions of the present Charter at the request of a State Party, an institution of the OAU or an African Organization recognized by the OAU.[28]

The procedure of the Commission is contained in Article 46:

46. The Commission may resort to any appropriate method of investigation; it may hear from the Secretary General of the Organization of African Unity or any other person capable of enlightening it.[29]

Communications from States are envisioned in Article 47:

47. If a State Party to the present Charter has good reasons to believe that another State Party to this Charter has violated the provisions of the Charter, it may draw, by written communication, the attention of that State to the matter. This Communication shall also be addressed to the Secretary General of the OAU and to the Chairman of the Commission. Within three months of the receipt of the Communication, the State to which the Communication is addressed shall give the enquiring State, written explanation or statement elucidating the matter. This should include as much as possible, relevant information relating to the laws and rules of procedure applied and applicable and the redress already given or course of action available.[30]

Article 48 provides for submissions to the Commission:

---

28   Ibid., at Article 45.
29   Ibid., at Article 46.
30   Ibid., at Article 47.

48. If within three months from the date on which the original communication is received by the State to which it is addressed, the issue is not settled to the satisfaction of the two States involved through bilateral negotiation or by any other peaceful procedure, either State shall have the right to submit the matter to the Commission through the Chairman and shall notify the other States involved.[31]

So too under Article 49:

49. Notwithstanding the provisions of Article 47, if a State Party to the present Charter considers that another State Party has violated the provisions of the Charter, it may refer the matter directly to the Commission by addressing a communication to the Chairman, to the Secretary General of the Organization of African unity and the State concerned.[32]

Exhaustion of remedies is recognized under Article 50:

50. The Commission can only deal with a matter submitted to it after making sure that all local remedies, if they exist, have been exhausted, unless it is obvious to the Commission that the procedure of achieving these remedies would be unduly prolonged.[33]

A report issued by the Commission is entailed in Article 52:

52. After having obtained from the States concerned and from other sources all the information it deems necessary and after having tried all appropriate means to reach an amicable solution based on the respect of human and peoples' rights, the Commission shall prepare, within a reasonable period of time from the notification referred to in Article 48, a report to the States concerned and communicated to the Assembly of Heads of State and Government.[34]

In terms of Applicable Principles, Article 60 states:

60. The Commission shall draw inspiration from international law on human and peoples' rights, particularly from the provisions of various African instruments on Human and Peoples' Rights, the Charter of the United Nations, the Charter of the Organization of African Unity, the Universal Declaration of Human Rights, other instruments adopted by the United Nations and by African countries in the field of Human and Peoples' Rights,

---

31 Ibid., at Article 48.
32 Ibid., at Article 49.
33 Ibid., at Article 50.
34 Ibid., at Article 52.

as well as from the provisions of various instruments adopted within the Specialized Agencies of the United Nations of which the Parties to the present Charter are members.[35]

Finally, Article 61 holds:

> 61. The Commission shall also take into consideration, as subsidiary measures to determine the principles of law, other general or special international conventions, laying down rules expressly recognized by Member States of the Organization of African Unity, African practices consistent with international norms on Human and Peoples' Rights, customs generally accepted as law, general principles of law recognized by African States as well as legal precedents and doctrine.[36]

Protocol to the African Charter on Human and Peoples' Rights on the Establishment of an African Court on Human and Peoples' Rights The Preamble of the Protocol to the African Charter on Human and Peoples' Rights on the Establishment of an African Court on Human and Peoples' Rights 2003 states:

> The Member States of the Organization of African Unity hereinafter referred to as the OAU, States Parties to the African Charter on Human and Peoples' Rights,
>
> Considering that the Charter of the Organization of African Unity recognizes that freedom, equality, justice, peace and dignity are essential objectives for the achievement of the legitimate aspirations of the African Peoples;
>
> Noting that the African Charter on Human and Peoples' Rights reaffirms adherence to the principles of Human and Peoples' Rights, freedoms and duties contained in the declarations, conventions and other instruments adopted by the Organization of African Unity, and other international organizations;
>
> Recognizing that the two-fold objective of the African Commission on Human and Peoples' Rights is to ensure on the one hand promotion and on the other protection of Human and Peoples' Rights, freedom and duties;
>
> Recognizing further, the efforts of the African Charter on Human and Peoples' Rights in the promotion and protection of Human and Peoples' Rights since its inception in 1987;
>
> Firmly convinced that the attainment of the objectives of the African Charter on Human and Peoples' Rights requires the establishment of an African Court on

---

35   Ibid., at Article 60.
36   Ibid., at Article 61.

Human and Peoples' Rights to complement and reinforce the functions of the African Commission on Human and Peoples' Rights.[37]

Important for equal rights and appreciation for maternity issues, an African Court of Human and Peoples' Rights, is established under Article 1:

> 1. There shall be established within the Organization of African Unity an African Court of Human and Peoples' Rights hereinafter referred to as 'the Court', the organization, jurisdiction and functioning of which shall be governed by the present Protocol.[38]

The relationship between the Court and the Commission is enunciated under Article 2:

> 2. The Court shall, bearing in mind the provisions of this Protocol, complement the protective mandate of the African Commission on Human and Peoples' Rights hereinafter referred to as 'the Commission', conferred upon it by the African Charter on Human and Peoples' Rights, hereinafter referred to as 'the Charter'.[39]

The Jurisdiction of the Court is established under Article 3:

> 3. The jurisdiction of the Court shall extend to all cases and disputes submitted to it concerning the interpretation and application of the Charter, this Protocol and any other relevant Human Rights instrument ratified by the States concerned. In the event of a dispute as to whether the Court has jurisdiction, the Court shall decide.[40]

The Court may issue advisory opinions as outlined under Article 4:

> 4. At the request of a Member State of the OAU, the OAU, any of its organs, or any African organization recognized by the OAU, the Court may provide an opinion on any legal matter relating to the Charter or any other relevant human rights instruments, provided that the subject matter of the opinion is not related to a matter being examined by the Commission. The Court shall give reasons for its advisory opinions provided that every judge shall be entitled to deliver a separate of dissenting decision.[41]

---

37 Protocol to the African Charter on Human and Peoples' Rights on the Establishment of an African Court on Human and Peoples' Rights, at the Preamble.

38 Ibid., at Article 1.

39 Ibid., at Article 2.

40 Ibid., at Article 3.

41 Ibid., at Article 4.

Access to the Court is established under Article 5:

> 5. The following are entitled to submit cases to the Court:
>   The Commission
>   The State Party, which had lodged a complaint to the Commission
>   The State Party against which the complaint has been lodged at the Commission
>   The State Party whose citizen is a victim of human rights violation
>   African intergovernmental organizations
>   When a State Party has an interest in a case, it may submit a request to the Court to be permitted to join.
>   The Court may entitle relevant non-governmental organizations (NGOs) with observer status before the Commission, and individuals to institute cases directly before it ....[42]

The issue of admissibility of cases is examined in Article 6:

> 6. The Court, when deciding on the admissibility of a case instituted under Article 5 ... of this Protocol, may request the opinion of the Commission which shall give it as soon as possible.
>   The Court shall rule on the admissibility of cases taking into account the provisions of Article 56 of the Charter.
>   The Court may consider cases or transfer them to the Commission.[43]

Article 7 establishes the Sources of Law:

> 7. The Court shall apply the provision of the Charter and any other relevant human rights instruments ratified by the States concerned.[44]

Importantly, the independence of the Court is underlined in Article 17:

> 17. The independence of the judges shall be fully ensured in accordance with international law.
>   No judge may hear any case in which the same judge has previously taken part as agent, counsel or advocate for one of the parties or as a member of a national or international court or a commission of enquiry or in any other capacity. Any doubt on this point shall be settled by decision of the Court.[45]

Evidence is stressed under Article 26:

---

42   Ibid., at Article 5.
43   Ibid., at Article 6.
44   Ibid., at Article 7.
45   Ibid., at Article 17.

26. The Court shall hear submissions by all parties and if deemed necessary, hold an enquiry. The States concerned shall assist by providing relevant facilities for the efficient handling of the case.

   The Court may receive written and oral evidence including expert testimony and shall make its decision on the basis of such evidence.[46]

Findings of the Court are provided for under Article 27:

27. If the Court finds that there has been violation of a human or peoples' rights, it shall make appropriate orders to remedy the violation, including the payment of fair compensation or reparation.

   In cases of extreme gravity and urgency, and when necessary to avoid irreparable harm to persons, the Court shall adopt such provisional measures as it deems necessary.[47]

The Judgment of Court is underlined under Article 28:

28. The Court shall render its judgment within ninety (90) days of having completed its deliberations.

   The judgment of the Court decided by majority shall be final and not subject to appeal.

   Without prejudice to sub-Article 2 …, the Court may review its decision in the light of new evidence under conditions to be set out in the Rules of Procedure.

   The Court may interpret its own decision.

   The judgment of the Court shall be read in open court, due notice having been given to the parties.

   Reasons shall be given for the judgment of the Court.

   If the judgment of the court does not represent, in whole or in part, the unanimous decision of the judges, any judge shall be entitled to deliver a separate or dissenting opinion.[48]

Finally, Article 30 provides for the execution of judgment:

30. The States Parties to the present Protocol undertake to comply with the judgment in any case to which they are parties within the time stipulated by the Court and to guarantee its execution.[49]

46　Ibid., at Article 26.
47　Ibid., at Article 27.
48　Ibid., at Article 28.
49　Ibid., at Article 30.

Protocol on Rights of Women in Africa   Important for women, in the Preamble to the Protocol on Rights of Women in Africa 2003, the State Parties to the Protocol on the Rights of Women in Africa undertake the agreement:

> CONSIDERING that Article 66 of the African Charter on Human and Peoples' Rights provides for special protocols or agreements, if necessary, to supplement the provisions of the African Charter, and that the OAU Assembly of Heads of State and Government meeting in its Thirty-first Ordinary Session in Addis Ababa, Ethiopia, in June 1995, endorsed by resolution AHG/Res.240 (XXXI) the recommendation of the African Commission on Human and Peoples' Rights to elaborate a Protocol on the Rights of Women in Africa;

> CONSIDERING that Article 2 of the African Charter on Human and Peoples' Rights enshrines the principle of non-discrimination on the grounds of race, ethnic group, color, sex, language, religion, political or any other opinion, national and social origin, fortune, birth or other status;

> FURTHER CONSIDERING that Article 18 of the African Charter on Human and Peoples' Rights calls on all Member States to eliminate every discrimination against women and to ensure the protection of the rights of women as stipulated in international declarations and conventions;

> NOTING that Articles 60 and 61 of the African Charter on Human and Peoples' Rights recognize regional and international human rights instruments and African practices consistent with international norms on human and peoples' rights as being important reference points for the application and interpretation of the African Charter;

> RECALLING that women's rights have been recognized and guaranteed in all international human rights instruments, notably the Universal Declaration of Human Rights, the International Covenant on Civil and Political Rights, the International Covenant on Economic, Social and Cultural Rights, the Convention on the Elimination of All Forms of Discrimination Against Women and all other international conventions and covenants relating to the rights of women as being inalienable, interdependent and indivisible human rights;

> NOTING that women's rights and women's essential role in development have been reaffirmed in the United Nations Plans of Action on the Environment and Development in 1992, on Human Rights in 1993, on Population and Development in 1994 and on Social Development in 1995;

> FURTHER NOTING that the Plans of Action adopted in Dakar and in Beijing call on all Member States of the United Nations, which have made a solemn commitment to implement them, to take concrete steps to give greater attention

to the human rights of women in order to eliminate all forms of discrimination and of gender-based violence against women;

BEARING IN MIND related Resolutions, Declarations, Recommendations, Decisions and other Conventions aimed at eliminating all forms of discrimination and at promoting equality between men and women;

CONCERNED that despite the ratification of the African Charter on Human and Peoples' Rights and other international human rights instruments by the majority of Member States, and their solemn commitment to eliminate all forms of discrimination and harmful practices against women, women in Africa still continue to be victims of discrimination and harmful practices;

FIRMLY CONVINCED that any practice that hinders or endangers the normal growth and affects the physical, emotional and psychological development of women and girls should be condemned and eliminated, and DETERMINED to ensure that the rights of women are protected in order to enable them to enjoy fully all their human rights.[50]

Under Article 1, 'discrimination against women' is defined as any distinction, exclusion or restriction based on sex, or any differential treatment whose objective or effects compromise or destroy the recognition, enjoyment or the exercise by women, regardless of their marital status, of human rights and fundamental freedoms in all spheres of life.[51] Further, 'harmful practices (HPs)' is defined as all behavior, attitudes and practices which negatively affect the fundamental rights of women and girls, such as their right to life, health and bodily integrity.[52]

Importantly, Article 2(1) is paramount in the fight for the elimination of discrimination against women in general and women in particular who suffer double discrimination:

> 2. 1. State Parties shall combat all forms of discrimination against women through appropriate legislative measures. In this regard they shall:
>   i. include in their national constitutions and other legislative instruments the principle of equality between men and women and ensure its effective application;
>   ii. enact and effectively implement appropriate national legislative measures to prohibit all forms of harmful practices which endanger the health and general well-being of women and girls;
>   iii. integrate a gender perspective in their policy decisions, legislation, development plans, activities and all other spheres of life;

---

50   Protocol on the Rights of Women in Africa, at the Preamble.
51   Ibid., at Article 1.
52   Ibid., at Article 1.

iv. take positive action in those areas where discrimination against women in law and in fact continues to exist.[53]

Further, Article 2(2) holds:

2. 2. State Parties shall modify the social and cultural patterns of conduct of men and women through specific actions, such as:
   i. public education, with a view to achieving the elimination of harmful cultural and traditional practices and all other practices which are based on the idea of the inferiority or the superiority of either of the sexes, or on stereotyped roles for men and women;
   ii. support local, national, regional and continental initiatives directed at eradicating all forms of discrimination against women.[54]

It is recognized in Article 3 that women contribute to the preservation of those African values that are based on the principles of equality, dignity, justice and democracy, and in this regard, the State Parties shall ensure that women enjoy rights and dignity inherent in all human beings, and adopt appropriate measures to prohibit any exploitation and degradation of women.[55]

Article 4 establishes that women shall be entitled to respect of their lives and the integrity of their person.[56] Additionally, Article 5 holds that State Parties shall take appropriate measures to prohibit all forms of violence against women whether physical, mental, verbal or sexual, domestic and family, whether they take place in the private sphere or in society and public life.[57] Further, Article 6 establishes that State Parties shall condemn all harmful practices which affect the fundamental human rights of women and girls and which are contrary to recognized international standards, and undertake to take all the necessary measures to create public awareness regarding harmful practices through information, formal and informal education, communication campaigns and outreach programs targeting all stakeholders; and to rehabilitate victims of harmful practices by providing them with social support services such as health services to meet their health care needs, emotional and psychological counseling, and skills training aimed at making them self-supporting in order to facilitate their re-integration into their families, communities and in other sectors of the society.[58]

Importantly, on the issue of marriage, Article 7 guarantees that State Parties shall ensure that men and women enjoy equal rights and are regarded as equal partners in marriage. They shall enact appropriate national legislative measures to

53   Ibid., at Article 2(1).
54   Ibid., at Article 2(2).
55   Ibid., at Article 3.
56   Ibid., at Article 4.
57   Ibid., at Article 5.
58   Ibid., at Article 6.

ensure that during her marriage, the woman shall have the right to acquire her own property and to administer and manage it freely; and in cases of joint ownership of property the husband and wife shall have the same rights.[59]

The right to education and training for the advancement of women is outlined in Article 12, which establishes that State Parties shall take all appropriate measures to eliminate all forms of discrimination against women and girls in the sphere of education and training; and eliminate all references in textbooks and syllabuses to the stereotypes which perpetuate such discrimination. Further, State Parties shall take specific positive action to increase literacy among women; promote education and training for women and girls at all levels and in all disciplines; and promote the retention of girls in schools and other training institutions.[60]

In looking at the important concern of economic and social welfare rights, Article 13 is critical for equal rights in employment, protecting in particular the economic value of the work of women in the home, the guarantee of adequate pre- and post-natal maternity leave and the importance of equal parental responsibility, under sections viii, ix and xii respectively:

> 13. State Parties shall guarantee women equal opportunities to work. In this respect, they shall:
>   i. promote equality in access to employment;
>   ii. promote the right to equal remuneration for jobs of equal value for men and women;
>   iii. ensure transparency in employment and dismissal relating to women in order to address issues of sexual harassment in the workplace;
>   iv. allow women freedom to choose their occupation, and protect them from exploitation by their employers;
>   v. create conditions to promote and support the occupations and economic activities dominated by women, in particular, within the informal sector;
>   vi. encourage the establishment of a system of protection and social insurance for women working in the informal sector;
>   vii. introduce a minimum age of work and prohibit children below that age from working, and prohibit the exploitation of children, especially the girl-child;
>   viii. take the necessary measures to recognize the economic value of the work of women in the home;
>   ix. guarantee adequate pre and post-natal maternity leave;
>   x. ensure equality in taxation for men and women;
>   xi. recognize the right of salaried women to the same allowances and entitlements as those granted to salaried men for their spouses and children;

---

59   Ibid., at Article 7.
60   Ibid., at Article 12.

xii. recognize motherhood and the upbringing of children as a social function for which the State, the private sector and both parents must take responsibility.[61]

Finally, Article 19 guarantees that women shall have the right to fully enjoy their right to sustainable development, and that State Parties shall take all appropriate measures to ensure that in the implementation of trade and economic policies and programs such as globalization, the negative effects on women are minimized.[62]

South Africa

The Role of Women in South Africa

South Africa has a total population of 48,687,000 people.[63] In terms of the economically active population, 5,481,903 men and 3,631,944 women were employed, compared with 2,039,917 men and 2,631,730 women who were unemployed. According to staff profiles of all companies, women account for only 12% of executive directors and senior management, 26% of junior middle management, 29% of professionals, 27% of technicians and associate professionals, 54% of clerical and administrative workers, 51% of service and sales workers, 56% of skilled agricultural and fishery workers, 5% of craft and related trades, 17% of operators and assemblers, and 20% of laborers and related workers. Further, women represent only 22% of total permanent employees and 40% of temporary and casual workers. In terms of education level, there were 3,557,303 men and 4,108,495 women who were listed as having no schooling, and 657,674 men and 655,965 women who were listed at the other end of the spectrum in terms of having completed higher education, with most men at 4,372,582 men and women at 5,197,104 falling within the category of having some high school.[64]

Legislation

Interim Constitution and Schedule 4   Important for appreciation for maternity issues, the Preamble of the interim Constitution of the Republic of South Africa, 1993 (Act No. 200) states:

In humble submission to Almighty God,

We, the people of South Africa declare that

---

61   Ibid., at Article 13.
62   Ibid., at Article 19.
63   South African Census.
64   Ibid.

WHEREAS there is a need to create a new order in which all South Africans will be entitled to a common South African citizenship in a sovereign and democratic constitutional state in which there is equality between men and women and people of all races so that all citizens shall be able to enjoy and exercise their fundamental rights and freedoms;

AND WHEREAS in order to secure the achievement of this goal, elected representatives of all the people of South Africa should be mandated to adopt a new Constitution in accordance with a solemn pact recorded as Constitutional Principles;

AND WHEREAS it is necessary for such purposes that provision should be made for the promotion of national unity and the restructuring and continued governance of South Africa while an elected Constitutional Assembly draws up a final Constitution;

NOW THEREFORE the following provisions are adopted as the Constitution of the Republic of South Africa.[65]

The Constitutional Principles for the Republic of South Africa are contained in Schedule 4 of the Interim Constitution, and important for equal rights, Principle I guarantees equality:

I.   The Constitution of South Africa shall provide for the establishment of one sovereign state, a common South African citizenship and a democratic system of government committed to achieving equality between men and women and people of all races.[66]

In addition, Principle II also guarantees fundamental rights, freedoms and civil liberties:

II. Everyone shall enjoy all universally accepted fundamental rights, freedoms and civil liberties, which shall be provided for and protected by entrenched and justiciable provisions in the Constitution ....[67]

Important for equal rights and maternity issues, the prohibition against discrimination and the promotion of equality are contained within Principle III, which includes 'all other forms of discrimination':

---

65   Interim Constitution of South Africa, at the Preamble.
66   Ibid., at Schedule 4, Principle I.
67   Ibid., at Principle II.

III. The Constitution shall prohibit ... gender and all other forms of discrimination and shall promote ... gender equality ....[68]

Further, the fundamental guarantee of equality of all before the law is contained in Principle V, which includes all disadvantaged by discrimination:

V. The legal system shall ensure the equality of all before the law and an equitable legal process. Equality before the law includes laws, programs or activities that have as their object the amelioration of the conditions of the disadvantaged, including those disadvantaged on the grounds ... gender.[69]

The Supremacy clause is contained in Principle IV, which states that the Constitution shall be the supreme law of the land; it shall be binding on all organs of state at all levels of government.[70] In addition, the separation of powers for objectivity and accountability is contained in Principle VI, which establishes that there shall be a separation of powers between the legislature, executive and judiciary, with appropriate checks and balances to ensure accountability, responsiveness and openness.[71] Finally, the important role of the judiciary is outlined in Principle VII:

VII. The judiciary shall be appropriately qualified, independent and impartial and shall have the power and jurisdiction to safeguard and enforce the Constitution and all fundamental rights.[72]

Under Fundamental Rights contained in Chapter 3, Section 8 deals with equality:

8. 1. Every person shall have the right to equality before the law and to equal protection of the law.
   2. No person shall be unfairly discriminated against, directly or indirectly, and, without derogating from the generality of this provision, on one or more of the following grounds in particular: ... gender, sex ....
   3. a. This section shall not preclude measures designed to achieve the adequate protection and advancement of persons or groups or categories of persons disadvantaged by unfair discrimination, in order to enable their full and equal enjoyment of all rights and freedoms.
   4. *Prima facie* proof of discrimination on any of the grounds specified in subsection (2) shall be presumed to be sufficient proof of unfair

---

68 Ibid., at Principle III.
69 Ibid., at Principle V.
70 Ibid., at Principle IV.
71 Ibid., at Principle VI.
72 Ibid., at Principle VII.

discrimination as contemplated in that subsection, until the contrary is established.[73]

Constitution of South Africa   The Constitution of the Republic of South Africa was first adopted by the Constitutional Assembly on 8 May 1996 (Act 108 of 1996), and was signed into law on 10 December 1996. As an integration of ideas from ordinary citizens, civil society and political parties represented in and outside of the Constitutional Assembly, the Constitution of South Africa represents the collective wisdom of the South African people and has been arrived at by general agreement. The objective in this process was to ensure that the final Constitution be legitimate, credible and accepted by all South Africans.

The Preamble of the Constitution of the Republic of South Africa reads:

> We, the people of South Africa,
> Recognize the injustices of our past;
> Honour those who suffered for justice and freedom in our land;
> Respect those who have worked to build and develop our country; and
> Believe that South Africa belongs to all who live in it, united in our diversity.
> We therefore, through our freely elected representatives, adopt this Constitution as the supreme law of the Republic so as to
> Heal the divisions of the past and establish a society based on democratic values, social justice and fundamental human rights;
> Lay the foundations for a democratic and open society in which government is based on the will of the people and every citizen is equally protected by law;
> Improve the quality of life of all citizens and free the potential of each person; and
> Build a united and democratic South Africa able to take its rightful place as a sovereign state in the family of nations.
> May God protect our people.
> Nkosi Sikelel' iAfrika. Morena boloka setjhaba sa heso.
> God seën Suid-Afrika. God bless South Africa.
> Mudzimu fhatutshedza Afurika. Hosi katekisa Afrika.[74]

The Founding Provisions of the Republic of South Africa are found in Chapter 1, with Section 1 of the Constitution stressing equality and the advancement of human rights:

> 1. The Republic of South Africa is one, sovereign, democratic state founded on the following values:
>   a. Human dignity, the achievement of equality and the advancement of human rights and freedoms.

---

73   Ibid., at Section 8.
74   Constitution of South Africa, at the Preamble.

     b.   Non-racialism and non-sexism.

     c.   Supremacy of the constitution and the rule of law.[75]

The Supremacy Clause is found in Section 2:

    2.   This Constitution is the supreme law of the Republic; law or conduct inconsistent with it is invalid, and the obligations imposed by it must be fulfilled.[76]

Important for equal rights, the right to equality is espoused in Section 3:

    3. 2.   All citizens are
         a.   equally entitled to the rights, privileges and benefits of citizenship; and
         b.   equally subject to the duties and responsibilities of citizenship.[77]

The Bill of Rights for South Africa is contained in Chapter 2. Section 7 states:

    7. 1.   This Bill of Rights is a cornerstone of democracy in South Africa. It enshrines the rights of all people in our country and affirms the democratic values of human dignity, equality and freedom.
        2.   The state must respect, protect, promote and fulfil the rights in the Bill of Rights.
        3.   The rights in the Bill of Rights are subject to the limitations contained or referred to in Section 36, or elsewhere in the Bill.[78]

Further, the limitation of rights is strictly contained in Section 36:

    36. 1.   The rights in the Bill of Rights may be limited only in terms of law of general application to the extent that the limitation is reasonable and justifiable in an open and democratic society based on human dignity, equality and freedom, taking into account all relevant factors, including
         a.   the nature of the right;
         b.   the importance of the purpose of the limitation;
         c.   the nature and extent of the limitation;
         d.   the relation between the limitation and its purpose; and
         e.   less restrictive means to achieve the purpose.

---

75   Ibid., at Section 1.
76   Ibid., at Section 2.
77   Ibid., at Section 3.
78   Ibid., at Section 7.

2. Except as provided in subsection (1) or in any other provision of the Constitution, no law may limit any right entrenched in the Bill of Rights.[79]

Application and jurisdiction of the Bill of Rights are outlined in Section 8:

8. 1. The Bill of Rights applies to all law, and binds the legislature, the executive, the judiciary and all organs of state.
    2. A provision of the Bill of Rights binds a natural or a juristic person if, and to the extent that, it is applicable, taking into account the nature of the right and the nature of any duty imposed by the right.
    3. When applying a provision of the Bill of Rights to a natural or juristic person in terms of subsection (2), a court:
        a. in order to give effect to a right in the Bill, must apply, or if necessary develop, the common law to the extent that legislation does not give effect to that right; and
        b. may develop rules of the common law to limit the right, provided that the limitation is in accordance with Section 36(1).
    4. A juristic person is entitled to the rights in the Bill of Rights to the extent required by the nature of the rights and the nature of that juristic person.[80]

In terms of equality for all regardless of maternity discrimination, Section 9 goes on to outline and guarantee the important concept of equal protection, including maternity discrimination in Section 9(3), as related to pregnancy specifically:

9. 1. Everyone is equal before the law and has the right to equal protection and benefit of the law.
    2. Equality includes the full and equal enjoyment of all rights and freedoms. To promote the achievement of equality, legislative and other measures designed to protect or advance persons, or categories of persons, disadvantaged by unfair discrimination may be taken.
    3. The state may not unfairly discriminate directly or indirectly against anyone on one or more grounds, including…gender, sex, pregnancy….
    4. No person may unfairly discriminate directly or indirectly against anyone on one or more grounds in terms of subsection (3). National legislation must be enacted to prevent or prohibit unfair discrimination.
    5. Discrimination on one or more of the grounds listed in subsection (3) is unfair unless it is established that the discrimination is fair.[81]

---

79 Ibid., at Section 36(1).
80 Ibid., at Section 8.
81 Ibid., at Section 9.

On human dignity, Section 10 states that everyone has inherent dignity and the right to have their dignity respected and protected.[82]

Further, Section 16 provides for freedom of expression, which does not extend to hate speech:

16. 1. Everyone has the right to freedom of expression ....
    2. The right in subsection (1) does not extend to
       b. incitement of imminent violence; or
       c. advocacy of hatred that is based on...gender, and that constitutes incitement to cause harm.[83]

In the interpretation of the Bill of Rights, Section 39 stresses the importance of human dignity and equality:

39. 1. When interpreting the Bill of Rights, a court, tribunal or forum:
       a. must promote the values that underlie an open and democratic society based on human dignity, equality and freedom;
       b. must consider international law; and
       c. may consider foreign law.
    2. When interpreting any legislation, and when developing the common law or customary law, every court, tribunal or forum must promote the spirit, purport and objects of the Bill of Rights.
    3. The Bill of Rights does not deny the existence of any other rights or freedoms that are recognized or conferred by common law, customary law or legislation, to the extent that they are consistent with the Bill.[84]

In safeguarding the right to employment under the principle of freedom of trade, occupation and profession, important for equal rights, Section 22 states that every citizen has the right to choose their trade, occupation or profession freely, and the practice of a trade, occupation or profession may be regulated by law.[85] In terms of labor relations, Section 23 establishes that everyone has the right to fair labor practices, and every worker has the right to form and join a trade union; to participate in the activities and programs of a trade union; and to strike.[86] Further, in looking at the important right to education as a tool for tolerance, Section 29 states that everyone has the right to a basic education, including adult basic education; and to further education, which the state, through reasonable measures, must make progressively available and accessible.[87]

---

82 Ibid., at Section 10.
83 Ibid., at Section 16.
84 Ibid., at Section 39.
85 Ibid., at Section 22.
86 Ibid., at Section 23.
87 Ibid., at Section 29.

In guaranteeing the right to administrative action, Section 33 states that everyone has the right to administrative action that is lawful, reasonable and procedurally fair.[88] Importantly, the right to access to the courts is outlined in Section 34, which holds that everyone has the right to have any dispute that can be resolved by the application of law decided in a fair public hearing before a court or, where appropriate, another independent and impartial tribunal or forum.[89] In order to guarantee rights enumerated under the Constitution, Section 38 ensures the enforcement of such rights, by holding that anyone listed has the right to approach a competent court, alleging that a right in the Bill of Rights has been infringed or threatened, and the court may grant appropriate relief, including a declaration of rights. The persons who may approach a court are anyone acting in their own interest; anyone acting on behalf of another person who cannot act in their own name; anyone acting as a member of, or in the interest of, a group or class of persons; anyone acting in the public interest; and an association acting in the interest of its members.[90]

The importance of the Constitutional Court is outlined in Section 167:

> 167. 3. The Constitutional Court
>   a. is the highest court in all constitutional matters;
>   b. may decide only constitutional matters, and issues connected with decisions on constitutional matters; and
>   c. makes the final decision whether a matter is a constitutional matter or whether an issue is connected with a decision on a constitutional matter.[91]

Further, the powers of the courts in constitutional matters are outlined in Section 172(1):

> 172. 1. When deciding a constitutional matter within its power, a court
>   a. must declare that any law or conduct that is inconsistent with the Constitution is invalid to the extent of its inconsistency; and
>   b. may make any order that is just and equitable, including i. an order limiting the retrospective effect of the declaration of invalidity; and ii. an order suspending the declaration of invalidity for any period and on any conditions, to allow the competent authority to correct the defect.[92]

Under the establishment and governing principles, Section 181 lists several important institutions mandated to strengthen constitutional democracy, namely

---

88   Ibid., at Section 33.
89   Ibid., at Section 34.
90   Ibid., at Section 38.
91   Ibid., at Section 167.
92   Ibid., at Section 172.

the Public Protector; the Human Rights Commission; the Commission for the Promotion and Protection of the Rights of Cultural, Religious and Linguistic Communities; the Auditor-General; and the Electoral Commission.[93] The functions of the Human Rights Commission are listed under Section 184, which states that it must promote respect for human rights and a culture of human rights; promote the protection, development and attainment of human rights; and monitor and assess the observance of human rights in the Republic. Finally, the Human Rights Commission has the powers, as regulated by national legislation, necessary to perform its functions, including the power to investigate and to report on the observance of human rights; to take steps to secure appropriate redress where human rights have been violated; and to carry out research; and to educate.[94]

Employment Equity Act   Important for appreciation for maternity issues, the Preamble of the Employment Equity Act 1998, an Act to provide for employment equity and to provide for matters incidental thereto, states:

Recognizing

> that as a result of apartheid and other discriminatory laws and practices, there are disparities in employment, occupation and income within the national labor market; and that those disparities create such pronounced disadvantages for certain categories of people that they cannot be redressed simply by repealing discriminatory laws,

Therefore, in order to

> promote the constitutional right of equality and the exercise of true democracy; eliminate unfair discrimination in employment; ensure the implementation of employment equity to redress the effects of discrimination; achieve a diverse workforce broadly representative of our people; promote economic development and efficiency in the workforce; and give effect to the obligations of the Republic as a member of the International Labour Organization.[95]

According to Section 3, the Act must be interpreted in compliance with the Constitution so as to give effect to its purpose; taking into account any relevant code of good practice issued in terms of this Act or any other employment law; and in compliance with the international law obligations of the Republic, in particular those contained in the Discrimination (Employment and Occupation) Convention (No. 111) 1958.[96] Important for equal rights and maternity issues, the purpose of the Act is defined

---

93   Ibid., at Section 181.
94   Ibid., at Section 184.
95   Employment Equity Act, South Africa, at the Preamble.
96   Ibid., at Section 3.

in Section 2 as to achieve equity in the workplace by promoting equal opportunity and fair treatment in employment through the elimination of unfair discrimination; and implementing affirmative action measures to redress the disadvantages in employment experienced by designated groups, in order to ensure their equitable representation in all occupational categories and levels in the workforce.[97]

Crucially, the elimination and the prohibition of unfair discrimination for people regardless of pregnancy and family responsibility specifically are called for in Sections 5 and 6(1) respectively:

> 5. Every employer must take steps to promote equal opportunity in the workplace by eliminating unfair discrimination in any employment policy or practice.[98]
>
> 6. 1. No person may unfairly discriminate, directly or indirectly, against an employee, in any employment policy or practice, on one or more grounds, including ... gender, sex, pregnancy ... family responsibility ....[99]

Article 6(2) allows for affirmative action programs and bona fide occupational qualifications:

> 6. 2. It is not unfair discrimination to:
>   a. take affirmative action measures consistent with the purpose of this Act; or
>   b. distinguish, exclude or prefer any person on the basis of an inherent requirement of a job.[100]

Further, Section 15 goes on to outline affirmative action measures which are permitted:

> 15. 1. Affirmative action measures are measures designed to ensure that suitably qualified people from designated groups have equal employment opportunities and are equitably represented in all occupational categories and levels in the workforce of a designated employer.
>   2. Affirmative action measures implemented by a designated employer must include:
>   a. measures to identify and eliminate employment barriers, including unfair discrimination, which adversely affect people from designated groups;

---

97 Ibid., at Section 2.
98 Ibid., at Section 5.
99 Ibid., at Section 6(1).
100 Ibid., at Section 6(2).

    b. measures designed to further diversity in the workplace based on equal dignity and respect of all people;

    c. making reasonable accommodation for people from designated groups in order to ensure that they enjoy equal opportunities and are equitably represented in the workforce of a designated employer;

    d. subject to subsection (3), measures to:

        i. i. ensure the equitable representation of suitably qualified people from designated groups in all occupational categories and levels in the workforce; and

        ii. ii. retain and develop people from designated groups and to implement appropriate training measures, including measures in terms of an Act of Parliament providing for skills development.

3. The measures referred to in subsection (2)(d) include preferential treatment and numerical goals, but exclude quotas.[101]

According to the burden of proof outlined in Section 11, whenever unfair discrimination is alleged in terms of this Act, the employer against whom the allegation is made must establish that it is fair.[102] Further, to combat maternity discrimination in the workplace, Section 20 outlines the requirement of an employment equity plan:

20. 1. A designated employer must prepare and implement an employment equity plan which will achieve reasonable progress towards employment equity in that employer's workforce.

    2. An employment equity plan prepared in terms of subsection (1) must state:

      a. the objectives to be achieved for each year of the plan;

      b. the affirmative action measures to be implemented as required by subsection 15(2);

      c. where underrepresentation of people from designated groups has been identified by the analysis, the numerical goals to achieve the equitable representation of suitably qualified people from designated groups within each occupational category and level in the workforce, the timetable within which this is to be achieved, and the strategies intended to achieve those goals;

      d. the timetable for each year of the plan for the achievement of goals and objectives other than numerical goals;

      e. the duration of the plan, which may not be shorter than one year or longer than five years;

---

101 Ibid., at Section 15.
102 Ibid., at Section 11.

f. the procedures that will be used to monitor and evaluate the implementation of the plan and whether reasonable progress is being made towards implementing employment equity;

g. the internal procedures to resolve any dispute about the interpretation or implementation of the plan;

h. the persons in the workforce, including senior managers, responsible for monitoring and implementing the plan; and

i. any other prescribed matter.[103]

The functions of the Commission for Employment Equity are enumerated in Section 30:

30. 1. The Commission advises the Minister on:
  a. codes of good practice issued by the Minister;
  b. regulations made by the Minister; and
  c. policy and any other matter concerning this Act.

2. In addition to the functions in subsection (1) the Commission may:
  a. make awards recognizing achievements of employers in furthering the purpose of this Act;
  b. research and report to the Minister on any matter relating to the application of this Act, including appropriate and well-researched norms and benchmarks for the setting of numerical goals in various sectors; and
  c. perform any other prescribed function.[104]

Under Section 35, a labor inspector has the authority to enter, question and inspect as provided,[105] and under Section 36, he must request and obtain a written undertaking from a designated employer to comply within a specified period, if the inspector has reasonable grounds to believe that the employer has failed to consult with employees; conduct an analysis; prepare and implement an employment equity plan; submit and publish its annual report; prepare a successive employment equity plan; assign responsibility to a senior manager; inform its employees; or keep records.[106] Under Section 37, a labor inspector may issue a compliance order to a designated employer if that employer has failed to act,[107] and finally, under Section 40, a designated employer may appeal to the Labor Court against a compliance order of the Director-General within 21 days after receiving that order.[108]

---

103 Ibid., at Section 20.
104 Ibid., at Section 30.
105 Ibid., at Section 35.
106 Ibid., at Section 36.
107 Ibid., at Section 37.
108 Ibid., at Section 40.

In terms of a Code of Good Practice, the process of developing a plan has three sequential phases: planning, development, and implementation and monitoring, according to the Employment Equity Act. The planning phase of the process should include assignment of responsibility and accountability to senior managers; a communication, awareness and training program; consultation with relevant stakeholders; an analysis of existing employment policies, procedures, and practices; an analysis of the existing workforce profile; an analysis of relevant demographic information; and the development of meaningful benchmark comparisons. The development phase should include objectives set; corrective measures formulated; time frames established; the plan drawn up; resources identified and allocated for the implementation of the plan; and the plan communicated. The implementation and monitoring phase should include implementation; monitoring and evaluating progress; reviewing the plan; and reporting on progress.

In order to identify any barriers that may be responsible for the underrepresentation or underutilization of employees from designated groups, including senior workers, a review of all employment policies, practices and procedures specifically, as well as the working environment in general, should be undertaken of employment policy or practices, such as recruitment, selection, pre-employment testing and induction that could be biased, inappropriate or unaffirming; practices related to succession and experience planning, and related promotions and transfers to establish whether designated groups are excluded or adversely impacted; utilization and job assignments to establish whether designated groups are able meaningfully to participate and contribute; current training and development methodologies and strategies; remuneration structures and practices such as equal remuneration for work of equal value; employee benefits related to retirement, risk and medical aid to establish whether designated groups have equal access; disciplinary practices which may have a disproportionately adverse effect on designated groups that may not be justified; the number and nature of dismissals, voluntary terminations and retrenchments of employees from designated groups that may indicate internal or external equity-related factors contributing to such terminations; and corporate culture which may be characterized by exclusionary social and other practices. All practices should be assessed in terms of cross-group fairness, and the review should take into account more subtle or indirect forms of discrimination and stereotyping, which could result in certain groups of people not being employed in particular jobs, or which could preclude people from being promoted.

Finally, affirmative action measures should be developed in terms of appointing members from designated groups for transparent and unbiased recruitment strategies; increasing the pool of available candidates; training, promoting and retaining people from designated groups; ensuring that members of designated groups are appointed in such positions that they are able meaningfully to participate in corporate decision-making processes; and transforming the corporate culture of the past in a way that affirms diversity in the workplace and harnesses the potential of all employees.

Promotion of Equality and Prevention of Unfair Discrimination Act   Important
for appreciation for maternity issues, the Preamble of the Promotion of Equality
and Prevention of Unfair Discrimination Act 2000 states:

> The consolidation of democracy in our country requires the eradication of social
> and economic inequalities, especially those that are systematic in nature, which
> were generated in our history by colonialism, apartheid and patriarchy, and
> which brought pain and suffering to the great majority of our people ...;
>
> The Constitution provides for the enactment of national legislation to prevent or
> prohibit unfair discrimination and to promote the achievement of equality;
>
> This implies the advancement, special legal and other measures, of historically
> disadvantaged individuals, communities and social groups who were dispossessed
> of their land and resources, deprived of their human dignity and who continue
> to endure the consequences;
>
> This Act endeavours to facilitate the transition to a democratic society, united
> in its diversity, marked by human relations that are caring and compassionate,
> and guided by the principles of equality, fairness, equity, social progress, justice
> human dignity and freedom.[109]

'Prohibited grounds' are defined under Section 1, which includes pregnancy
specifically:

> a.   ... gender, sex, pregnancy ....; or
> b.   any other ground where discrimination based on that other ground:
>   i.   causes or perpetuates systemic disadvantage:
>   ii. undermines human dignity; or
>   iii. adversely affects the equal enjoyment of a person's rights and freedoms
>   in a serious manner that is comparable to discrimination on a ground in
>   paragraph (a).[110]

The objects of the Act are enumerated in Section 2:

> 2.   The objects of this Act are:
>   a.   to enact legislation required by section 9 of the Constitution;
>   b.   to give effect to the letter and spirit of the Constitution, in particular:
>   i.   the equal enjoyment of all rights and freedoms by every person;
>   ii. the promotion of equality;

---

109   Promotion of Equality and Prevention of Unfair Discrimination Act, South
Africa, at the Preamble.

110   Ibid., at Chapter 1, Section 1.

iii. the values of...non-sexism contained in section 1 of the Constitution;

iv. the prevention of unfair discrimination and protection of human dignity as contemplated in sections 9 and 10 of the Constitution;

v. the prohibition of advocacy of hatred, based on ... gender ..., that constitutes incitement to cause harm as contemplated in section 16(2)(c) of the Constitution and section 12 of this Act;

c. to provide for measures to facilitate the eradication of unfair discrimination, hate speech and harassment, particularly on the grounds of ... gender;

d. to provide for procedures for the determination of circumstances under which discrimination is unfair;

e. to provide for measures to educate the public and raise public awareness on the importance of promoting equality and overcoming unfair discrimination, hate speech and harassment;

f. to provide remedies for victims of unfair discrimination, hate speech and harassment and persons whose right to equality has been infringed;

g. to set out measures to advance persons disadvantaged by unfair discrimination;

h. to facilitate further compliance with international law obligations including treaty obligations in terms of, amongst others, the Convention on the Elimination of All Forms of Racial Discrimination and the Convention on the Elimination of All Forms of Discrimination against Women.[111]

Further, the guiding principles are contained in Section 4:

4. 1. In the adjudication of any proceedings which are instituted in terms of or under this Act, the following principles should apply:

a. The expeditious and informal processing of cases, which facilitate participation by the parties to the proceedings;

b. access to justice to all persons in relevant judicial and other dispute resolution forums;

c. the use of rules of procedure ... and criteria to facilitate participation;

d. the use of corrective or restorative measures in conjunction with measures of a deterrent nature;

e. the development of special skills and capacity for persons applying this Act in order to ensure effective implementation and administration thereof.

2. In the application of this Act the following should be recognised and taken into account:

---

111 Ibid., at Section 2.

    a.   The existence of systemic discrimination and inequalities, particularly in respect of…gender…in all spheres of life as a result of past and present unfair discrimination, brought about by colonialism, the apartheid system and patriarchy; and

    b.   the need to take measures at all levels to eliminate such discrimination and inequalities.[112]

It is understood that by virtue of Section 5, the Act binds the State and all persons,[113] and by virtue of Section 6, neither the State nor any person may unfairly discriminate against any person.[114] In terms of the burden of proof in maternity discrimination cases, Section 13 stipulates:

13. 1. If the complainant makes out a prima facie case of discrimination:

    a.   the respondent must prove, in the facts before the court, that the discrimination did not take place as alleged; or

    b.   the respondent must prove that the conduct is not based on one or more of the prohibited grounds.

   2. If the discrimination did take place:

    a.   on a ground in paragraph (a) of the definition of 'prohibited grounds' … then it is unfair, unless the respondent proves that the discrimination is fair;

    b.   on a ground in paragraph (b) of the definition of 'prohibited grounds', then it is unfair

       i.   if one or more of the conditions set out in paragraph (b) of the definition of 'prohibited grounds' is established; and

      ii. unless the respondent proves that the discrimination is fair.[115]

Further, Section 14 establishes the determination of fairness or unfairness:

14. 1. It is not unfair discrimination to take measures designed to protect or advance persons or categories of persons disadvantaged by unfair discrimination or the members of such groups or categories of persons.

   2. In determining whether the respondent has proved that the discrimination is fair, the following must be taken into account:

    a.   The context;

    b.   the factors referred to in subsection (3);

    c.   whether the discrimination reasonably and justifiably differentiates between persons according to objectively determinable criteria, intrinsic to the activity concerned.

---

112   Ibid., at Section 4.
113   Ibid., at Section 5.
114   Ibid., at Section 6.
115   Ibid., at Section 13.

3. The factors referred to in subsection (2)(b) include the following:
    a. Whether the discrimination impairs or is likely to impair human dignity;
    b. the impact or likely impact of the discrimination on the complainant;
    c. the position of the complainant in society and whether he or she suffers from patterns of disadvantage or belongs to a group that suffers from patterns of disadvantage;
    d. the nature and extent of the discrimination;
    e. whether the discrimination is systematic in nature;
    f. whether the discrimination has a legitimate purpose;
    g. whether and to what extent the discrimination achieves its purpose;
    h. whether there are less restrictive and less disadvantageous means to achieve the purpose;
    i. whether and to what extent the respondent has taken such steps as being reasonable in the circumstances to:
        i.   address the disadvantage which arises from or is related to one or more of the prohibited grounds; or
        ii. accommodate diversity.[116]

Importantly, under Section 25, the State has a duty to promote equality and, as such, the State must, where necessary with the assistance of the relevant constitutional institutions, develop awareness of fundamental rights in order to promote a climate of understanding, mutual respect and equality; take measures to develop and implement programs in order to promote equality; and where necessary or appropriate develop action plans to address any unfair discrimination, hate speech or harassment. It must also enact further legislation that seeks to promote equality and to establish a legislative framework in line with the objectives of the Act; develop codes of practice as contemplated in the Act in order to promote equality; develop guidelines, including codes in respect of reasonable accommodation; provide assistance, advice and training on issues of equality; develop appropriate internal mechanisms to deal with complaints of unfair discrimination, hate speech or harassment; and conduct information campaigns to popularize the Act.[117] Finally, Section 28 provides for special measures to promote equality:

28. 1. If it is proved in the prosecution of any offence that unfair discrimination on the grounds of … gender … played a part in the commission of the offence, this must be regarded as an aggravating circumstance for purposes of sentence.
    2. The South African Human Rights Commission must, in its report referred to in section 15 of the Human Rights Commission Act, 1994 (Act No. 54 of 1994), include an assessment on the extent to which

---

116   Ibid., at Section 14.
117   Ibid., at Section 25.

unfair discrimination on the grounds of ... gender ... persists in the Republic, the effects thereof and recommendations on how best to address the problems.

3. a. The State, institutions performing public functions and all persons have a duty and responsibility, in particular to:

    i.   eliminate discrimination on the grounds of ... gender ...;
    ii. promote equality in respect of ... gender ....

    b. In carrying out the duties and responsibilities referred to in paragraph (a), the State, institutions performing public functions and, where appropriate and relevant, juristic and non-juristic entities, must:

    i.   audit laws, policies and practices with a view to eliminating all discriminatory aspects thereof;
    ii. enact appropriate laws, develop progressive policies and initiate codes of practice in order to eliminate discrimination on the grounds of ... gender ...;
    iii. adopt viable action plans for the promotion and achievement of equality in respect of ... gender ...; and
    iv. give priority to the elimination of unfair discrimination and the promotion of equality in respect of ... gender ....[118]

Basic Conditions of Employment Act   The purpose of the Basic Conditions of Employment Act (No. 75 of 1997) is to give effect to the right to fair labor practices referred to in section 23(1) of the Constitution by establishing and making provision for the regulation of basic conditions of employment; and thereby to comply with the obligations of the Republic as a member state of the International Labour Organization; and to provide for matters connected therewith. Section 1 defines what is considered an employee: any person, excluding an independent contractor, who works for another person or for the State and who receives, or is entitled to receive, any remuneration; and any other person who in any manner assists in carrying on or conducting the business of an employer.[119] Section 2 outlines the purpose of the Act:

2. The purpose of this Act is to advance economic development and social justice by fulfilling the primary objects of this Act which are

    a. to give effect to and regulate the right to fair labour practices conferred by section 23(1) of the Constitution
    i.   by establishing and enforcing basic conditions of employment; and
    ii. by regulating the variation of basic conditions of employment;

    b. to give effect to obligations incurred by the Republic as a member state of the International Labour Organization.[120]

---

118   Ibid., at Section 28.
119   Basic Conditions of Employment Act, South Africa, at Section 1.
120   Ibid., at Section 2.

Section 3 deals with the application of the Act:

> 3. 1. This Act applies to all employees and employers except
>   a. members of the National Defence Force, the National Intelligence Agency, the South African Secret Service and the South African National Academy of Intelligence; and
>   b. unpaid volunteers working for an organisation serving a charitable purpose.
>   2. This Act applies to persons undergoing vocational training except to the extent that any term or condition of their employment is regulated by the provisions of any other law.[121]

Independent contractors are not covered by the Act. Further, atypical working patterns benefit from Section 84, in the calculation of periods of service for the purposes of the Act, in that it allows separate periods of employment with the same employer to be added together provided that the breaks in employment are less than 12 months.[122]

Section 7 deals with the regulation of working time:

> 7. Every employer must regulate the working time of each employee
>   a. in accordance with the provisions of any Act governing occupational health and safety;
>   b. with due regard to the health and safety of employees;
>   c. with due regard to the Code of Good Practice on the Regulation of Working Time issued under section 87(1)(a); and
>   d. with due regard to the family responsibilities of employees.[123]

Further, also relevant to family responsibilities, Section 10 notes that employers cannot require employees to work overtime except with agreement, including a collective agreement, and that it cannot be more than three hours a day or ten hours a week,[124] and night work can only be required with agreement under Section 17.[125] In terms of daily and weekly rest periods, Section 15 notes:

> 15. 1. An employer must allow an employee
>   a. a daily rest period of at least twelve consecutive hours between ending and recommencing work; and

---

121 Ibid., at Section 3.
122 Ibid., at Section 84.
123 Ibid., at Section 7.
124 Ibid., at Section 10.
125 Ibid., at Section 17.

b. a weekly rest period of at least 36 consecutive hours which, unless otherwise agreed, must include Sunday.[126]

Importantly for the protection of employees before and after the birth of a child, Section 26 stipulates:

26. 1. No employer may require or permit a pregnant employee or an employee who is nursing her child to perform work that is hazardous to her health or the health of her child.

2. During an employee's pregnancy, and for a period of six months after the birth of her child, her employer must offer her suitable, alternative employment on terms and conditions that are no less favourable than her ordinary terms and conditions of employment, if

a. the employee is required to perform night work, as defined in section 17(1) or her work poses a danger to her health or safety or that of her child; and

b. it is practicable for the employer to do so.[127]

Crucially, in terms of maternity leave, Section 25 stipulates:

25. 1. An employee is entitled to at least four consecutive months' maternity leave.

2. An employee may commence maternity leave

a. at any time from four weeks before the expected date of birth, unless otherwise agreed; or

b. on a date from which a medical practitioner or a midwife certifies that it is necessary for the employee's health or that of her unborn child.

3. No employee may work for six weeks after the birth of her child, unless a medical practitioner or midwife certifies that she is fit to do so.

4. An employee who has a miscarriage during the third trimester of pregnancy or bears a stillborn child is entitled to maternity leave for six weeks after the miscarriage or stillbirth, whether or not the employee had commenced maternity leave at the time of the miscarriage or stillbirth.

5. An employee must notify an employer in writing, unless the employee is unable to do so, of the date on which the employee intends to

a. commence maternity leave; and

b. return to work after maternity leave.

6. Notification in terms of subsection (5) must be given

a. at least four weeks before the employee intends to commence maternity leave;

---

126 Ibid., at Section 15.
127 Ibid., at Section 26.

    b. if it is not reasonably practicable to do so, as soon as is reasonably practicable.[128]

Further, in terms of family responsibility leave, Section 27 requires:

27. 1. This section applies to an employee
    a. who has been in employment with an employer for longer than four months; and
    b. who works for at least four days a week for that employer.

    2. An employer must grant an employee, during each annual leave cycle, at the request of the employee, three days' paid leave, which the employee is entitled to take
    a. when the employee's child is born;
    b. when the employee's child is sick; or
    c. in the event of the death of
      i. the employee's spouse or life partner; or
      ii. the employee's parent, adoptive parent, grandparent, child, adopted child, grandchild or sibling.

    3. Subject to subsection (5), an employer must pay an employee for a day's family responsibility leave
    a. the wage the employee would ordinarily have received for work on that day; and
    b. on the employee's usual pay day.

    4. An employee may take family responsibility leave in respect of the whole or a part of a day.

    5. Before paying an employee for leave in terms of this section, an employer may require reasonable proof of an event contemplated in subsection (2) for which the leave was required.

    6. An employee's unused entitlement to leave in terms of this section lapses at the end of the annual leave cycle in which it accrues.

    7. A collective agreement may vary the number of days and the circumstances under which leave is to be granted in terms of this section.[129]

Labor market concentration in farm and domestic work are issues for women, and according to Section 37(1)(c), farm and domestic workers are entitled to four weeks' termination notice, the same as employees who have been employed for more than a year.[130] Since lack of education can be an important issue for women workers, illiterate employees can give notice orally and any employee who receives a notice is entitled to have it explained orally. Finally, a proposal that pregnant South African schoolgirls be allowed maternity leave has sparked heated

---

128   Ibid., at Section 25.

129   Ibid., at Section 27.

130   Ibid., at Section 37.

debate in the country amid fears that this could encourage teen pregnancies. South Africa is under pressure to deal with the high number of teenagers who drop out of school and fail to continue their education once they become mothers. It is one of only a few countries in sub-Saharan Africa that allows pregnant girls to return to school after they give birth. It is estimated that around 72,000 girls countrywide between the ages of 13 and 19 years stop attending school as a result of pregnancy each year. There has since also been talk of special classes for pregnant girls where nurses could give lessons on baby care and other issues for mothers. Young girls in schools should not be treated differently from any other pregnant women in South Africa, since working mothers are entitled to four months' maternity leave.

Overall, the Basic Conditions of Employment Act confers a right to four consecutive months' unpaid maternity leave, which means that an employer is not obliged to pay its employee any remuneration whilst the employee is on maternity leave.[131] The principle is that payment during maternity leave is covered by the Unemployment Insurance Act, if the employee qualifies as a 'contributor'. The new Unemployment Insurance Act 2002, which came into effect on 1 April 2002, has done away with the distinction between low- and high-income earners so that all employees, regardless of their income, are entitled to become 'contributors', subject to some exceptions, and are entitled to maternity benefits from the Unemployment Insurance Fund. Notwithstanding that there is no legal obligation on them to do so, certain employers pay employees who are on maternity leave either partial or full remuneration either in terms of a contractual arrangement between them or in terms of a customary practice. If there has been a practice of paying maternity benefits, the employer would be obliged to grant benefits in accordance with the practice because a practice can over a period become a term and condition of employment.

Since an employee is entitled to four months' unpaid maternity leave, it is important to determine which payments constitute 'remuneration' and which payments constitute 'benefits'; this is because only remuneration is unpaid during maternity leave. In a number of recent judgments, 'remuneration' has been held to include an employee's basic salary and allowances paid to an employee for the purposes of enabling an employee to work, such as travelling and entertainment allowances, and to exclude benefits such as an employer's contribution to retirement and medical aid funds. However, where an employer is able to show that its contributions to the medical aid fund do form part of the employee's remuneration, the employer will be under no obligation to pay such contributions during the course of maternity leave. If the employer has contractually agreed to contribute a specified percentage to the employee's medical aid membership, then there is a greater inference of a separate obligation to pay such contributions during maternity leave.

If an employee qualifies for maternity benefits in terms of the new Unemployment Insurance Act, she will be entitled to receive such benefits from the Fund. Any

---

131   Sack, Shelley, Deloitte & Touche, 2002.

additional benefits from the employer's side would have to be determined with reference to the employee's contract of employment, a company policy dealing with this issue or an established practice. In the absence of a provision stipulating that such contributions form part of the employee's remuneration, the contributions to such funds would constitute a 'benefit', a separate obligation to pay such contributions during maternity leave, and the employer would be obliged to continue to pay the employee's medical aid and retirement fund contributions during maternity leave. Should the employer wish to introduce a policy that excludes the payment of medical aid and retirement fund contributions during maternity leave then it is recommended that the employer: record an agreement that any contributions by the employer to the medical aid and retirement funds constitute 'remuneration' as defined in the legislation; record that employees will not be remunerated during the course of maternity leave, including contributions to the medical aid fund and retirement fund; and the employee will be responsible for the payment of medical aid contributions in total during the course of maternity leave.[132]

Unemployment Insurance Act Maternity benefits are dealt with under the Unemployment Insurance Act (No. 63 of 2001). Section 24 guarantees the right to maternity benefits:

24. 1. … a contributor who is pregnant is entitled to the maternity benefits contemplated in this Part for any period of pregnancy or delivery and the period thereafter, if application is made in accordance with prescribed requirements and the provisions of this Part.
    3. When taking into account any maternity leave paid to the contributor in terms of any other law or any collective agreement or contract of employment, the maternity benefit may not be more than the remuneration the contributor would have received if the contributor had not been on maternity leave.
    4. For purposes of this section the maximum period of maternity leave is 17, 32 weeks.
    5. A contributor who has a miscarriage during the third trimester or bears a still-born child is entitled to a maximum maternity benefit of six weeks after the miscarriage or stillbirth.[133]

Finally, Section 25 covers the application for maternity benefits:

25. 1. An application for maternity benefits must be made in the prescribed form at an employment office at least eight weeks before childbirth.
    2. The Commissioner may on good cause shown

---

132 Ibid.
133 Unemployment Insurance Act, South Africa, at Section 24.

      a.   accept an application after the period of eight weeks referred to in
         subsection (1);

      b.   extend the period of submission of the application up to a period of
         six months after the date of childbirth.

3. The claims officer must investigate the application and, if necessary, request further information.

4. If the application complies with the provisions of this Chapter, the claims officer must
   a. approve the application;
   b. determine
      i. the amount of the benefits for purposes of section 13(3);
      ii. the benefits the applicant is entitled to in terms of section 13(4); and
   c. stipulate how the benefits are to be paid.

5. If the application does not comply with the provisions of this Chapter, the claims officer must advise the applicant in writing that the application is defective and of the reasons why it is defective.[134]

Overall, the way to combat discrimination is neither to deny its existence or its systemic roots, nor to trivialize its impact, and those who deny it must be challenged because it is such denial that potentially entrenches inherited inequalities. We need to strengthen and in some cases revolutionize the democratic institutions and their capacity to deal with the barriers that perpetuate social exclusion and discrimination on the grounds of maternity. In order to change entrenched discriminatory perceptions and prejudices, educational programs that popularize a rights-based approach to addressing discrimination should be developed for civil society as a whole. It is necessary to address discrimination and inequality in its many institutional and social forms. This includes changing the skewed distribution of resources through the equitable distribution of State funds, a program of economic empowerment, including senior economic empowerment, affirmative action, land reform and social development. It requires the transformation, in terms of composition, culture and focus, of institutions such as the judiciary, public service, private sector and academia. Essential to this are programs to promote tolerance in all institutions of social development. It is clear that much needs to be done to ensure that all people enjoy their constitutional rights.

Conclusion

African States should share experiences on best practices in order to complement each other so as to ensure effective maternity mainstreaming in legislation and court cases; continue to ensure that equal rights issues are integrated in all development

---

134   Ibid., at Section 25.

programs and plans; develop common indicators for monitoring equal rights issues at local, regional, national and international levels; and encourage and support the initiation and coordination of periodical conference/seminars on equal rights and development. Indeed, a renewal of commitment to maternity equality is overdue in Africa, where there is a great disparity in the level of human rights protection available to its inhabitants. Almost all African countries have constitutions or civil codes that prohibit discrimination. However, the level of protection varies from nation to nation, and entrenched attitudes and practices, as well as limited resources, limit the practical effect, in the pursuit of *Pregnant Pause.*

Chapter 6

Pregnant Pause in Canada, Mexico and the United States

Introduction

In the quest for appreciation for maternity issues in *Pregnant Pause*, this chapter will examine efforts against maternity discrimination in North America. It will review discrimination legislation in Canada, namely: the Canadian Constitution, the Canadian Bill of Rights, the Canadian Human Rights Act and the Canada Employment Equity Act; then minimally in Mexico, namely: the Constitución Política de los Estados Unidos Mexicanos, Ley Federal de Trabajo and the Ley del Seguro Social; and finally in the United States, namely: the Declaration of Independence, the Federalist Papers, the American Constitution, the Equal Pay Act, the Civil Rights Act and the Pregnancy Discrimination Act, and the Family and Medical Leave Act. Although neighbors, Canada and the United States have had separate histories and thus have undergone very different paths, with some rights having more of an impact in one country than the other.

Canada

The Role of Women in Canada

The British model of government, which has influenced greatly the Canadian structure, sees the legislature making the laws and the judiciary applying them, with parliamentary supremacy not founded on democratic ideals, but rather on a narrow power struggle.[1] Canada is a relatively young nation, founded officially by Confederation in 1867. While present Canada endorses multiculturalism, it is a country founded on the tale of 'two solitudes', English and French or Anglophone and Francophone, which lies at the heart of many a legal debate. While Canada is an officially bilingual country composed of 10 provinces and three territories, it is important to note that the province of Quebec now remains by contrast officially unilingually Francophone.

---

1   Mandel, Michael, *The Charter of Rights and the Legalization of Politics in Canada*, Wall & Thompson, Toronto, 1989, p.4.

Canada has a total population of 33,311,389 people.[2] Importantly, women have experienced growth in the labor force over the years; however, women are still considerably less likely to be in the workforce than men, as 5,844,800 women are employed, while 514,700 are unemployed.[3] Labor force participation rates are at 72.5% for men and 57.4% for women.[4] Men account for 6,613,000 of full-time jobs, compared to 4,384,000 for women, and 783,000 of part-time jobs, compared to 1,725,000 for women. The unemployment rate was 7.3% for women and 7.8% for men.[5] Part-time work continues to be more significant for women than for men. Women are more likely to work part-time, accounting for 69% of all part-time employment. Some women work part-time because of family responsibilities, with young women more likely than older women to be in part-time positions.[6] Women have less tenure in employment than men, with an average ratio of 81 months compared to 108 months at the same job. Older women have greater job tenure than younger women, but still less tenure than men. This is due in part to the tradition of many women interrupting their work in order to raise a family.

Unemployed women are more likely than men to be new job market entrants who have never worked, and are twice as likely as men to be re-entrants who have not worked in the past five years. Women are also more likely to have left their job for personal responsibilities, in keeping with tradition. However, women are unemployed for shorter periods, and are less likely to experience extended periods of unemployment, with older women more likely than younger women to be unemployed for longer periods.

Women have made gains in some professional occupations. In management and professional positions, women number 2,258,000, compared to 2,190,000 men, having made tremendous gains, due in part to changes in occupational definitions. However, women still occupy positions of less power and influence, predominating in the clerical sector, numbering 1,578,000 compared with 392,000 men. Women are also underrepresented among self-employed workers, with women accounting for roughly 10% of such workers, in comparison with roughly 20% for male workers. However, there has been an increase in the last decade in the number of women running their own businesses.

The increased workforce participation of women is due in part to the higher levels of educational attainment. The university enrolment of women declines the higher the level of education. Women earned 72,884 bachelor and first professional degrees, compared to 53,276 for men, while women earned only 1,059 doctorates, compared to 2,588 for men. The gap will narrow in the future, since women form the majority of students attending university. Women with high levels of education are more likely than other women to be employed in the labor force

---

2   Canadian Census.
3   Statistics Canada, *Women in the Labour Force*, p.8.
4   Minister of Industry, *Canada Yearbook*.
5   United Nations, *The World's Women: Trends and Statistics*.
6   Statistics Canada, *Women in the Labour Force*, p.14.

and are less likely to work part-time or be unemployed. As well, female graduates have a higher income than other women. Young women are better educated than their male counterparts, with the reverse true for the older population. Women with high levels of educational attainment are less likely than other women to work part-time. However, women are more likely than their male counterparts to work part-time regardless of educational qualifications, with female university graduates over three times more likely than male graduates to have part-time employment. Women who have graduated from a post-secondary institution have lower unemployment rates than other women. However, women with a university degree have a higher unemployment rate than similarly qualified men. As well, at all levels of educational attainment, women are less likely than men to be employed.

Rapid growth has occurred in labor force participation rates for those women with children in the last decade. However, women with pre-school children are less likely than those with school-aged children to be employed. In general, women are less likely than men to be in the labor force, and women with children are more likely than other women to be employed part-time. Further, female lone parents are less likely to be employed than women in two-parent families with children. Women continue to be responsible for most of the unpaid domestic work even when employed, devoting two hours more per day than men. Domestic work activities account for most of the total unpaid work time of employed women. Employed women are nearly three times more likely than men to be absent from work because of personal family responsibilities. Importantly, most female homemakers spend more time on unpaid household activities than the employed do at their jobs, but these women are not included in national labor market surveys.[7]

The past 30 years have seen the growth of dual-earner families. The number of dual-earner families has gone from 33% to 60% in recent years. The traditional family of a bread-winning husband and a stay-at-home wife has been radically changed, in less than a generation, into one where both spouses work outside the home. As well, a recent trend has been the emergence of women as primary earners and sole earners within families.[8] An interesting aspect of women working outside the home has been the growing proportion of working couples in which the wife earns more than the husband. Over the last 30 years, the proportion of women as the primary wage earner has risen from 11% to 25%. As well, changes have occurred in single-earner families, which has seen the proportion of families with the wife as the earning spouse grow over the years from 2% to 20%.

Despite all the progress, women cannot match men's earning power. Women's earnings overall continue to be significantly below those of men in all occupations and in all educational groups. Primary earner wives were more likely to be employed in managerial professional occupations, 48% compared to 35% for primary earner husbands; however, at the same time, these women earned one-third less than their

---

7   Ibid.

8   Crompton, Susan, and Geran, Leslie, *Women as Main Wage-Earners*, Perspectives.

male counterparts. Outside of the managerial professional occupations, almost 80% of female primary earners worked in clerical, sales or service jobs; 60% of male primary earners worked in blue-collar occupations. One factor for the differential is the work pattern. Women primary earners were considerably less likely to have worked full-time than their male counterparts, 86% to 96% respectively. Another phenomenon has been the steady increase in families in which the wife was the only spouse earner. This can be traced to the general ageing of the population. Sole-earner wives and their husbands are generally older, with 43% of such wives and 60% of such husbands aged 55 and over. In contrast, in families in which the sole wage earner is the husband, 47% of these men are between the ages of 25 and 44. The generation gap suggests that the growth of female sole-earner families is mainly due to the fact that husbands retire and the younger wives continue to work. Overall, wives are the primary wage earners in one-quarter of dual-earner families and the sole earner in one-fifth of families. At the same time, however, women's salaries still lag behind men's in similar situations.[9]

The importance of women wage earners has grown throughout the years. Women's advancements in the labor force have contributed to another recent trend of female entrepreneurs.[10] The representation of women among the self-employed has jumped to account for one in three entrepreneurs, up from one in four previously. Women account for 40% in the rise of self-employment. Two-thirds of women entrepreneurs work full-time. While both the full-time and part-time self-employment rates have doubled among women, the rate for male entrepreneurs has fallen 90%. In addition, women account for 22% of all employers. Due to retirement, there is a particularly high rate of entrepreneurship for both sexes, with 34% of women and 55% of men aged 65 and over self-employed. In looking at the different sectors and among self-employed women, 37% work in the service industry, 21% in sales, 17% in the retail trade, 13% in business, and 11% in health and social services. In contrast, among self-employed men, 21% work in sales, 17% in the construction trade, and 13% in managerial and administrative occupations. Interestingly, average annual earnings for entrepreneur women are lower than for men, and several factors account for this: part-time work is more prevalent among women entrepreneurs; women entrepreneurs are concentrated in industries with lower earnings; the number of female employers is considerably lower than that of men; and the proportion of self-employed women with a university degree is lower than that of men.[11]

Women have made considerable progress in the labor force. However, much still needs to be done to improve the lives of women, who often have to work twice as hard.

---

9   Ibid., at p.29.
10   Cohen, Gary L., *Women Entrepreneurs*, Perspectives.
11   Ibid.

Legislation

Canadian Constitution   The Canadian Constitution, which includes the Canadian Charter of Rights and Freedoms, was proclaimed into force and entrenched on 17 April 1982.[12] It is made up of three separate documents: the British North America Act and its various amendments, the Constitution Act and its amending formula, and the Canadian Charter of Rights and Freedoms, encompassing Articles 1 to 34 inclusively. In terms of the Charter of Rights and Freedoms, its purpose is to protect and safeguard the rights and freedoms enumerated, and to contain governmental action within reasonable limits. The supremacy of the Constitution is contained in Section 52(1) of the Constitution Act:

> 52. 1. The Constitution of Canada is the supreme law of Canada and any law that is inconsistent with the provisions of the Constitution is, to the extent of the inconsistency, of no force or effect.[13]

Section 32 provides for its application to the Parliament and government of Canada, as well as to the legislature and government of each province.[14]

In terms of civil rights, important for protection against discrimination, which should include maternity discrimination, Section 15, which came into effect on 17 April 1985 after a three-year implemented delay, guarantees equality of rights and also deals with affirmative action programs to help reverse the discrimination process:

> 15. 1. Every individual is equal before and under the law and has the right to the equal protection and equal benefit of the law without discrimination and, in particular, without discrimination based on ... sex ....
>
> 2. Subsection (1) does not preclude any law, program or activity that has as its object the amelioration of conditions of disadvantaged individuals or groups including those that are disadvantaged because of ... sex ....[15]

Further, the Charter implements equality through Section 28, which cannot be overridden by legislation or act of Parliament:

> 28. Notwithstanding anything in this Charter, the rights and freedoms referred to in it are guaranteed equally to male and female persons.[16]

---

12 Canadian Constitution, Canada.

13 Canadian Constitution, the Canadian Charter of Rights and Freedoms, Canada, at Section 52(1).

14 Canadian Constitution, Canada, at Section 32.

15 Canadian Constitution, the Canadian Charter of Rights and Freedoms, Canada, at Section 15.

16 Ibid., at Section 28.

In terms of provisions in denial of rights, the infamous 'notwithstanding' clause is Section 33, allowing the Canadian provinces to opt out of the Constitution for successive and infinite five-year periods:

> 33. Parliament or the legislature of a province may expressly declare in an Act of Parliament or of the legislature ... that the Act or a provision thereof shall operate notwithstanding a provision included in ... Section ... 15 of this Charter.[17]

The Canadian Constitution extends power to judges to review legislative action on the basis of congruence with protected values in the Charter, and treats the judicial branch of government as a partner with the legislative and executive branches, in determining the rights of citizens. However, Section 33, the overriding clause, will ensure that legislatures rather than judges have the final say on important matters of public policy, so that laws offensive to certain provisions of the Charter may be upheld.

Further, importantly, Section 1 of the Charter is also an overriding clause:

> 1. The Canadian Charter of Rights and Freedoms set out is subject only to such reasonable limits prescribed by law as can be demonstrably justified in a free and democratic society.[18]

Thus, fundamental freedoms, as well as legal and equality rights, can be subjected to this notwithstanding clause. Remarkably, the right against maternity discrimination is not absolute, since the Canadian Charter of Rights and Freedoms may be used to strengthen inequalities, by weighing in on the side of power, and undermine popular movements.

In terms of the burden of proof, Section 1 of the Charter has two functions: first, it guarantees the rights and freedoms set out in the provisions which follow it; and second, it states explicitly the exclusive justificatory criteria, outside of Section 33 of the Charter, against which limitations on those rights and freedoms may be measured. The onus of proving that a limitation on any Charter right is reasonable and demonstrably justified in a free and democratic society rests upon the party seeking to uphold the limitation. Limits on constitutionally guaranteed rights are clearly exceptions to the general guarantee. The presumption is that Charter rights are guaranteed unless the party invoking Section 1 can bring itself within the exceptional criteria justifying their being limited. The standard of proof under Section 1 is a preponderance of probabilities. Proof beyond a reasonable doubt would be unduly onerous on the party seeking to limit the right, because concepts such as 'reasonableness', 'justifiability' and 'free and democratic society' are not amenable to such a standard. Nevertheless, the preponderance of probability test must be applied rigorously.

---

17   Ibid., at Section 33.
18   Ibid., at Section 1.

The Supreme Court of Canada uses the purposive approach to interpret the Charter, whereby the underlying purpose of the legislative provision and the nature of the interest are identified. A two-step procedure is utilized to see whether the limit of the Charter contained in Section 1 can uphold an infringement of a right. Two questions are asked: (1) has the right been violated?; and (2) can the violation be justified under Section 1? The burden of proof is such that the onus of establishing a *prima facie* infringement of the Charter is on the person alleging it, while the onus of justifying a reasonable limit on the protected right is on the party invoking Section 1. Two criteria must be satisfied in order to come within Section 1 of the Charter: (1) the objective of the limiting measure must be sufficiently important, and the concerns must be pressing and substantial to justify overriding a constitutionally protected right; and (2) the means must be reasonable and demonstrably justified according to a proportionality test, which balances the interests of society against those of individuals. There are three components to the test: (1) the measure must be carefully designed to achieve the stated objective, and must not be arbitrary, unfair or irrational; (2) the measure should impair the right as little as possible; and (3) proportionality must exist between the effect of the limiting measure and its objectives (*Regina v. Oakes*, [1986] 1 SCR 103).[19]

Canadian Bill of Rights   In addition to the Canadian Constitution, there is the Canadian Bill of Rights, enacted on 10 August 1960. In terms of fundamental freedoms, human rights are guaranteed in Section 1, which mentions equality before the law and the protection of the law:

1. It is hereby recognized and declared that in Canada there have existed and shall continue to exist without discrimination by reason of ... sex, the following human rights and fundamental freedoms, namely,
    a. the right of the individual to life, liberty, security of the person and enjoyment of property and the right not to be deprived thereof except by due process of law;
    b. the right of the individual to equality before the law and the protection of the law.[20]

Canadian Human Rights Act (CHRA)   The Canadian Human Rights Act (CHRA) was implemented and came into force on 1 March 1978, and prohibits discrimination in all federal and federally regulated organizations. The provinces and territories have similar laws forbidding discrimination in their areas of jurisdiction. Complaints are handled by the Canadian Human Rights Commission and a number of provincial commissions. The CHRA has been very influential for those seeking relief from human rights abuses and discrimination through a channel other than the traditional court system, namely the Canadian Human Rights Tribunal

---

19   *Regina* v. *Oakes*, [1986] 1 SCR 103.
20   Canadian Bill of Rights, Canada, at Section 1.

(CHRT). It implements a complaint process through a commission, which assumes that systemic discrimination does not exist but for a few cases. This differs from a proactive approach, which places an obligation on the employer to determine if systemic wage discrimination exists and to remedy it within a time frame. The Canadian Human Rights Commission (CHRC) administers the CHRA, in trying to ensure the principles of equal opportunity and non-discrimination within the federal jurisdiction that is the federal public service and federally regulated employers. The CHRA features a 'duty of accommodation' which requires employers to address the needs of people who are protected under the CHRA, and creates a smaller permanent human rights tribunal, which will improve the ability to hear and make decisions about cases effectively and efficiently. Importantly, the purpose of the CHRA is outlined in Section 2, which specifically mentions family status:

> 2. The purpose of this Act is to extend the laws in Canada to give effect, within the purview of matters coming within the legislative authority of Parliament, to the principle that all individuals should have an opportunity equal with other individuals to make for themselves the lives that they are able and wish to have and to have their needs accommodated, consistent with their duties and obligations as members of society, without being hindered in or prevented from doing so by discriminatory practices based on ... sex, ... family status ....[21]

Further, important for maternity discrimination cases, Section 3(1), which mentions family status, states:

> 3. 1. For all purposes of this Act, ... sex, ... family status ... are prohibited grounds of discrimination.[22]

Sections 7 and 10 go on to enumerate what is considered to be discriminatory:

> 7. It is a discriminatory practice, directly or indirectly:
>   a. to refuse to employ or continue to employ any individual, or
>   b. in the course of employment, to differentiate adversely in relation to an employee, on a prohibited ground of discrimination. [1976~77, c.33, s.7.3][23]
>
> 10. It is a discriminatory practice for an employer, employee organization or organization of employers:
>   a. to establish or pursue a policy or practice, or

---

21 Canadian Human Rights Act, Canada, at Section 2.
22 Ibid., at Section 3(1).
23 Ibid., at Section 7.

b. to enter into an agreement affecting recruitment, referral, hiring, promotion, training, apprenticeship, transfer or any other matter relating to employment or prospective employment, that deprives or tends to deprive an individual or class of individuals of any employment opportunities on a prohibited ground of discrimination. [1976~77, c.33, s.10; 1980~81~82~83, c.143, s.5][24]

Further, under Section 11, it is discriminatory directly or indirectly to refuse to employ or, in the course of employment, to differentiate adversely against an employee in recruitment, referral, hiring, promotion, training or transfer policies:

11. 2. In assessing the value of work performed by employees employed in the same establishment, the criterion to be applied is the composite of the skill, effort and responsibility required in the performance of the work and the conditions under which the work is performed.[25]

However, Section 15(1) allows for a *bona fide* occupational exception:

15. 1. It is not a discriminatory practice if
    a. any refusal, exclusion, expulsion, suspension, limitation, specification or preference in relation to any employment is established by an employer to be based on a *bona fide* occupational requirement.[26]

Further, special programs are allowed under Section 16, which mentions family status:

16. It is not a discriminatory practice for a person to adopt or carry out a special program, plan or arrangement designed to prevent disadvantages that are likely to be suffered by, or to eliminate or reduce disadvantages that are suffered by, any group of individuals when those disadvantages would be or are based on or related to the ... sex, ... family status ... of members of that group, by improving opportunities respecting goods, services, facilities, accommodation or employment in relation to that group.[27]

The CHRA looks at comparable worth, applying the same wages where respective work is shown to be equal in value through a combination of skill, effort, responsibility and working conditions, and thereby makes comparisons between dissimilar jobs. It is a discriminatory practice to establish different wages, so that if people do work of equal value in the same establishment then they must be

---

24   Ibid., at Section 10.
25   Ibid., at Section 11.
26   Ibid., at Section 15(1).
27   Canadian Human Rights Act, Canada, at Section 16.

paid equally. Discriminatory practices for wage inequities include segregated employment, exclusion of those categorically from the existing evaluation system, undervaluation of certain positions, fewer promotion opportunities, senior rules disadvantaging some groups, and discriminatory transfers, promotion and layoffs.[28] Discrimination includes practices or attitudes, whether by design or impact, which have the effect of limiting the individual's right to the opportunities generally available because of attributes such as maternity characteristics rather than actual characteristics. There are, however, some reasonable factors to permit a pay difference, such as periodic pay increases for length of service or working in remote locations. The CHRC only has jurisdiction over the federal public service and federally regulated employers in the quest for equal pay for work of equal value, and one drawback to the federal law is that it is limited to comparisons within the same establishment.

In terms of the onus of proof with respect to a complaint under the Act, the evidentiary burden in discrimination cases involving the refusal of employment appears clear and constant through all Canadian jurisdictions: a complainant must first establish a *prima facie* case of discrimination, and once that is done the burden shifts to the respondent to provide a reasonable explanation for the otherwise discriminatory behavior. Thereafter, assuming the employer has provided an explanation, the complainant has the eventual burden of showing that the explanation provided was merely 'pretext' and that the true motivation behind the employer's actions was in fact discriminatory (*Basi v. Canadian National Railway* (1984), 9 CHRR 4. D/5029, 5037 (CHR Tribunal)).[29]

Thus, in an employment complaint, the Commission usually establishes a *prima facie* case by proving that: (1) the complainant was qualified for the particular employment; (2) the complainant was not hired; and (3) someone no better qualified but lacking the distinguishing feature which is the gravamen of the human rights complaint subsequently obtained the position. If these elements are proved, there is an evidentiary onus on the respondent to provide an explanation of events equally consistent with the conclusion that discrimination on the basis prohibited by the Code is not the correct explanation of what occurred (*Shakes v. Rex Pak Ltd.* (1982), 3 CHRR D/1001, 1002).[30] Should the respondent provide evidence of a non-discriminatory reason for refusing to employ the complainant, then the complainant and the Commission can still establish that the reason advanced for non-employment is in fact a pretext, and that discrimination on an unlawful ground was one of the operative reasons for the respondent's actions (*Blake v. Ministry of Correctional Services and Mimico Correctional Institute* (1984), 5 CHRR D/2417 (Ontario)).[31]

---

28   Labor Canada, *Equal Pay for Work of Equal Value*, Ottawa, 1986, p.21.

29   *Basi v. Canadian National Railway* (1984), 9 CHRR 4. D/5029, 5037 (CHR Tribunal).

30   *Shakes v. Rex Pak Ltd.* (1982), 3 CHRR D/1001, 1002.

31   *Blake v. Ministry of Correctional Services and Mimico Correctional Institute* (1984), 5 CHRR D/2417 (Ontario).

The ultimate onus of proof to establish the complaint on a balance of probabilities lies with the complainant and the Commission. Discrimination can be established by direct evidence or by circumstantial evidence, which is evidence that is consistent with the fact that is sought to be proven and inconsistent with any other rational conclusion, since it is not necessary to find that the respondent intended to discriminate against the complainant, it is sufficient to establish the complaint if it is found, on the balance of probabilities, that the respondent in fact discriminated against the complainant on one of the grounds alleged in their complaint (*Ontario Human Rights Commission v. Simpsons-Sears Ltd.*, [1985] SCR 536, 547).[32]

There are three essential steps in developing a special program: to identify as problems, areas within the organization in which the labor force is unrepresentative; to determine how the problems relate to organization policies, practices and procedures, both formal and informal; and to formulate solutions that aim to remove existing barriers and to provide for equitable representation. The criteria that indicate the need for a special program are: observable absence of members of certain groups in particular job categories or in the organization as a whole; existence of particularly high unemployment rates among certain groups; internal complaints and grievances from employees; external complaints by individuals or groups; inability of the organization to recruit or retain employees in terms of high turnover; and complaints filed with the CHRC alleging discriminatory practices. The primary objective of a special program is to increase the overall representation of the organization's labor force in some specific way. In setting objectives specific to the organization, the following factors must be considered: objectives should be quantitative, namely targets or goals; objectives should aim to correct underutilization or overconcentration where they occur in an organization; objectives must be specific as to target group and should also specify job category and geographical area; and objectives must be attainable within specific and reasonable timeframes. A special program is intended to be a temporary measure that should not outlive the identified problem of disadvantage, although the achievement of objectives will result in permanent organizational changes; objectives should realistically reflect the ability of the organization to respond to change; objectives must take into consideration the continuing rights of individuals, especially employees, not belonging to designated target groups; and objectives should be framed with care to be sensitive to the feelings and expectations of staff, including members of the target groups.

Canada Employment Equity Act   Important for female workers, the purpose of the Canada Employment Equity Act, assented to 15 December 1995, as outlined in Section 2, is to achieve equality in the workplace so that no person shall be denied employment opportunities or benefits for reasons unrelated to ability and, in the fulfillment of that goal, to correct the conditions of disadvantage in employment

---

32   *Ontario Human Rights Commission v. Simpsons-Sears Ltd.*, [1985] SCR 536, 547.

experienced by members of certain groups, and by giving effect to the principle that employment equity means more than treating persons in the same way but also requires special measures and the accommodation of differences.[33] It covers the federal government, including the public service and crown corporations, as well as federally regulated private sector employers with 100 or more employees, and addresses four designated groups: persons with disabilities, women, Aboriginal peoples and visible minorities. The Canadian Human Rights Commission (CHRC) is responsible for enforcing the obligations of employers to implement employment equity. Section 5 establishes a duty of employers:

> 5. Every employer shall implement employment equity by
>   a. identifying and eliminating employment barriers against persons in designated groups that result from the employer's employment systems, policies and practices that are not authorized by law; and
>   b. instituting such positive policies and practices and making such reasonable accommodations as will ensure that persons in designated groups achieve a degree of representation in each occupational group in the employer's workforce that reflects their representation in
>   i. the Canadian workforce, or
>   ii. those segments of the Canadian workforce that are identifiable by qualification, eligibility or geography and from which the employer may reasonably be expected to draw employees.[34]

Further, Section 6 states that the obligation to implement employment equity does not require an employer to take a particular measure to implement employment equity where the taking of that measure would cause undue hardship to the employer; to hire or promote unqualified persons; with respect to the public sector, to hire or promote persons without basing the hiring or promotion on selection according to merit in cases where the Public Service Employment Act requires that hiring or promotion be based on selection according to merit; or to create new positions in its workforce.[35]

Section 10 provides for the implementation of an employment equity plan:

> 10. 1. The employer shall prepare an employment equity plan that
>   a. specifies the positive policies and practices that are to be instituted by the employer in the short term for the hiring, training, promotion and retention of persons in designated groups and for the making of reasonable accommodations for those persons, to correct the underrepresentation of those persons identified by the analysis ...;

---

33 Canada Employment Equity Act, Canada, at Section 2.
34 Ibid., at Section 5.
35 Ibid., at Section 6.

b. specifies the measures to be taken by the employer in the short term for the elimination of any employment barriers identified by the review ...;

c. establishes a timetable for the implementation of the matters referred to in paragraphs (a) and (b);

d. where underrepresentation has been identified by the analysis, establishes short term numerical goals for the hiring and promotion of persons in designated groups in order to increase their representation in each occupational group in the workforce in which underrepresentation has been identified and sets out measures to be taken in each year to meet those goals;

e. sets out the employer's longer term goals for increasing the representation of persons in designated groups in the employer's workforce and the employer's strategy for achieving those goals; and

f. provides for any other matter that may be prescribed.[36]

Finally, under Section 29, a Tribunal may, in the same manner and to the same extent as a superior court of record, summon and enforce the attendance of witnesses and compel them to give oral and written evidence on oath and to produce such documents and things as the Tribunal considers necessary for a full review; administer oaths; and receive and accept such evidence and other information, whether on oath or by affidavit or otherwise, as the Tribunal sees fit, whether or not that evidence or information would be admissible in a court of law.[37]

Citizenship offers a sense of belonging in one's country and gives each individual the right to participate in society and in its economic and political systems. It confers the protection of the State within Canada and abroad, while requiring individuals to obey this country's laws. In terms of a more complete set of rights, popular conceptions of citizenship incorporate an increasingly complete set of rights. From 'civil rights' such as freedom of speech, thought and faith, citizenship came to include 'political rights' as expressed by the right to hold office or to vote. Most recently, twentieth-century citizenship is understood to comprise not only these but also 'social and economic rights'. These are the level of well-being and security that are required to exist in a society. They represent a commitment that there will be no internal 'borders' and that all those who call a particular country home can participate fully in the life of the community. In terms of the legislative review process, the Government needs to establish an ongoing strategy and process to review laws, regulations, policies, practices and rules to remove barriers to full participation and ensure the equality of all people. Canada's labor market is evolving; new types of jobs are appearing in the workplace as others disappear. Governments are trying to respond to these changes and are working to ensure that all Canadians can participate in the new economy.

36　Ibid., at Section 10.
37　Ibid., at Article 29.

The legal workplace duty to accommodate requires the elimination of employment standards, rules, practices or other requirements that discriminate on prohibited grounds.[38] The Supreme Court of Canada case *Meiorin: British Columbia (Public Service Employee Relations Commission) (BCPSERC) v. The British Columbia Government and Service Employees Union (BCGSEU)* [1999], 35 C.H.R.R. D/257 (S.C.C.)[39] (gender discrimination at the workplace), established that accommodation is to be the norm, in line with affirmative action and employment equity work. It requires employers to design workplace standards that do not discriminate, and developed the three-step *Meiorin* Test to determine if the employer has established a standard that is a *bona fide* occupational requirement; the employer must: (1) Demonstrate the standard was adopted for a purpose rationally connected to the performance of the job; (2) Honestly believe the standard is necessary to fulfill the legitimate, work-related purpose; and (3) Show the standard is reasonably necessary to the accomplishment of the legitimate, work-related purpose, so that it is impossible to accommodate workers without undue hardship to the employer. To deal with step 3, the following questions are asked: Have alternatives been considered?; If so, why were these alternatives not adopted?; Must all workers meet a single standard, or could different standards be adopted?; Does the standard treat some more harshly than others?; If so, was the standard designed to minimize this differential treatment?; What steps were taken to find accommodations?; Is there evidence of undue hardship if accommodation were to be provided?; Have all parties who are required to accommodate played their roles? The Court did say accommodation would be the norm 'in so far as is reasonably possible', and accommodation is not required if it causes undue hardship.[40] To be considered undue hardship, financial costs must be so great as to alter the essential nature of the enterprise or affect its viability, and may include: financial cost, health and safety, impact on the collective agreement, interference with other workers' rights, employee morale, the size of the operation and the adaptability of the workforce and facilities.[41]

In terms of inclusion, the principle of inclusiveness implied in Canadian citizenship gives the Government a base for its approach to today's requirements. While the federal government aims for and expects that its laws will not discriminate in their intent or effect, the reality is that, while many laws do not actively discriminate against Canadians from minority groups, their effects are discriminatory. In terms of an inclusive labor market, a vision of inclusion is one in which programs and services are designed in consultation with people from various

---

38   Hatfield, Robert, Duty to Accommodate, *Just Labour*, vol. 5 (Winter 2005).

39   *Meiorin: British Columbia (Public Service Employee Relations Commission) (BCPSERC) v. The British Columbia Government and Service Employees Union (BCGSEU)* [1999], 35 C.H.R.R. D/257 (S.C.C.).

40   Ibid.

41   *Central Alberta Dairy Pool v. Alberta (Human Rights Commission)* [1990] 2 S.C.R. 489.

groups, in which employers hire individuals on the basis of their skills and abilities, and accommodating different ways to get work done happens as a matter of course in the workplace. Inclusiveness should be a matter of 'business as usual'. A secure income is fundamental to the ability to enjoy the rights of citizenship, since without a secure income an individual cannot satisfy the most basic living needs.[42]

As used in human rights laws, discrimination means making a distinction between certain individuals or groups based on a prohibited ground of discrimination. The Canadian Human Rights Act and provincial human rights codes forbid discrimination in employment, with exceptions in some cases regarding mandatory retirement and *bona fide* occupational requirements.[43] The province of Quebec prohibits discrimination in the private and public sectors, amending the Quebec Charter of Rights and Freedoms, which is both a charter of rights and a human rights act, to prohibit discrimination based on pregnancy in Section 10 entitled Right to Equal Recognition and Exercise of Rights and Freedoms:

> 10. Every person has a right to full and equal recognition and exercise of his human rights and freedoms, without distinction, exclusion or preference based on ... sex, pregnancy ....
> Discrimination exists where such a distinction, exclusion or preference has the effect of nullifying or impairing such right.
> 1. No one may harass a person on the basis of any ground mentioned in section 10.[44]

In terms of maternity leave, maternity benefits for working mothers and parents remain the responsibility of the federal government. Female employees are entitled to a standard 17 weeks' unpaid, job-protected maternity leave. In addition, both male and female employees are granted up to 37 weeks' unpaid, job-protected parental leave, 35 weeks for women if being combined with maternity leave for a total of 52 weeks. Unlike in the U.S., however, employees in Canada pay into an Employee Insurance Fund from their paychecks. Depending on how much they have paid in, how long they have been working, and how much they earn, employees who take maternity leave, parental leave, sick leave, or are laid off will receive money from this fund and will therefore earn a percentage of their wage throughout their entire leave from work.

Canada's Employment Insurance (EI) gives paid maternity leave for 15 weeks.[45] To receive maternity benefits, the woman is required to have worked for 600 hours in the last 52 weeks or since the last claim. If the baby is hospitalized, then the 17-week limit can be extended for every week the child is in the hospital up to 52 weeks following the week of the child's birth. In terms of parental benefits, these

---

42   Ibid.
43   Human Resources and Social Development Canada.
44   Quebec Charter of Rights and Freedoms, at Section 10.
45   Human Resources Development Canada, Labour Program.

are payable either to the biological or adoptive parents while they are caring for a newborn or an adopted child, up to a maximum of 35 weeks. To receive parental benefits, one is required to have worked for 600 hours in the last 52 weeks or since the last claim. Despite the fact that maternity leave is intended for female employees, fathers are allowed to take maternity leave in grave circumstances; in the event the birth mother dies or is totally disabled, an employee who is the father of the child shall be entitled to both maternity and parental leave without pay.

In Canadian Labor Legislation, the employment standards legislation of all Canadian jurisdictions provides for a minimum period of unpaid maternity leave for eligible pregnant employees, which is 18 weeks in Alberta, British Columbia, Quebec and Saskatchewan, and 17 weeks in all other jurisdictions. This leave can usually be supplemented by adding a period of parental leave, and in some jurisdictions, it is also possible to obtain an extended maternity leave. While some collective agreements merely adhere to minimum labor standards, many others provide a longer period of leave. In terms of extended maternity leave, an additional period of maternity leave may sometimes be granted, in case of medical complications following childbirth, or if the actual date of birth is later than expected. Extensions to maternity leave are provided in the labor standards legislation of most Canadian provinces and territories. Seven jurisdictions guarantee at least six weeks of postnatal leave. Although unconditional in Alberta and British Columbia, the minimum period of leave in Ontario and Newfoundland legislation applies only to employees who are not taking parental leave. In Prince Edward Island and Saskatchewan, only employees giving birth later than the expected date of delivery are eligible. As regards the Yukon, the six-week minimum period pertains solely to employees with pregnancy-related health problems. In Nova Scotia, there is a provision for a minimum of one week of leave after childbirth. Five jurisdictions – Alberta, Manitoba, the Northwest Territories, Nunavut, Quebec – provide for an extension of maternity leave if the actual date of delivery occurs after the estimated date of delivery, with the extension the equivalent to the period of time between the two dates. In the Northwest Territories and Nunavut, it is limited to a maximum of six weeks. In Quebec, the extension is only available to employees who have less than two weeks of regular maternity leave remaining after delivery. In Alberta, Quebec, British Columbia and Saskatchewan, it is possible to extend a maternity leave by up to six weeks if the medical condition of the mother or child prevents the employee from returning to work. Since leave can also be extended by using vacation credits, it may be necessary for some employees to rely on their sick leave credits to extend their maternity leave, considering the health risks associated with a pregnancy, and the potential complications following childbirth.

Maternity benefits (EI) are payable to the natural mother in the period surrounding the birth of a child, and may start from eight weeks before the expected date of birth to the week of actual delivery. Fifteen weeks of maternity benefits are allowed after a two-week waiting period and can be collected within 17 weeks of the actual week of confinement or week of expected confinement, whichever is later. However, the 17-week limit can be extended and payments delayed for every week a baby is confined to the hospital, for up to 52 weeks following the week of the child's birth. It may also be possible to receive sickness benefits in addition to the maximum weeks of maternity benefits should an employee be unable to work because of complications due to pregnancy or childbirth or by reason of an unrelated illness. Benefits usually cover 55% of a claimant's weekly insurable earnings, to a maximum of $413 per week. To be eligible, an employee must have worked a minimum number of hours in the previous 52 weeks or since the start of her last claim. There is also the possibility of retaining some work attachment while receiving benefits, thereby allowing parents to earn the greater of $50 or 25% of their weekly benefits, without penalty. Supplemental insurance benefits for employees on a maternity or parental leave provided by employers do not affect EI benefits, as long as the combined income of the benefit and supplement do not exceed 100% of an employee's normal weekly salary.

In terms of legislative provisions regarding the reinstatement of employees following a maternity leave, every Canadian jurisdiction requires employers to reinstate employees who have taken a maternity leave to their former position or to a comparable one with equivalent wages and benefits. In the latter case, federal jurisdiction employers must in addition offer a position in the same location. Employees covered by Quebec's *Act Respecting Labour Standards* must be reinstated in the same position at the end of their maternity leave or of a parental leave not exceeding 12 weeks; they may be reassigned to a comparable position after a parental leave of greater than 12 weeks' duration. In British Columbia, Nunavut, the Northwest Territories, the Yukon, Ontario, Prince Edward Island and Quebec, employees are to receive any wage rate or benefit increases to which they would have been entitled had they remained at work during the leave period. Moreover, eight jurisdictions, Alberta, British Columbia, the Northwest Territories, Nunavut, Nova Scotia, Ontario, the Yukon, provide that if an employer suspends or discontinues operations during an employee's maternity leave, the employee is to be reinstated upon resumption of operations. In Alberta, this requirement only extends for 12 months after the end of the leave. In Nova Scotia, Ontario and the Yukon, reinstatement is to proceed in accordance with the existing seniority system or practice. Although Quebec's legislation does not specifically mention a suspension of operations, it stipulates that an employee who would have been laid off had she not been on maternity leave shall keep, with respect to rehiring, the same rights as the employees who were laid off. Employees under federal jurisdiction must be notified as soon as possible if a reorganization affects their wages and benefits during their maternity or parental leave. Historically, the right to return to their job has been one of the key concerns of employees taking a leave of absence related to the birth or adoption of a child. Where an employee's position has disappeared, an employee may be assigned a comparable position, as some of the examples above indicate.[46]

---

46   Ibid.

Mexico

Legislation

Constitución Política de los Estados Unidos Mexicanos   The equality of all persons before the law is guaranteed by the *Constitución Política de los Estados Unidos Mexicanos*, the Political Constitution of the United Mexican States.[47] Article 1 establishes that all individuals shall enjoy the guarantees set down by the Constitution, which may not be restricted or suspended, except in those cases and conditions established therein.[48] Article 4 goes on to state that men and women are equal under the Law.[49] In terms of equality in employment, Article 123(7) establishes that equal work performed in the same post with the same hours worked and conditions of efficiency shall also be remunerated with the same salary.[50]

Ley Federal de Trabajo   The entitlement to equal opportunities is set down in Article 3 and Article 164 of the *Ley Federal de Trabajo* (LFT), the Federal Labor Law.[51] Article 1 provides that no discrimination may be established between workers.[52] Article 1 states that no discrimination may be established between workers on the basis of race, gender, age, religion, political opinion or social rank.[53] Article 2 states that women shall have the same rights and obligations as men.[54] In terms of equality in employment, Article 133(1) states that it is prohibited for an employer to refuse to contract an individual because of their age or gender.[55] Article 86 establishes that equal work performed in the same post with the same hours worked and conditions of efficiency shall also be remunerated with the same salary.[56]

As regards maternity leave, Article 170 establishes the obligation of employers to provide female workers with six weeks leave before and six weeks after childbirth at full salaries.[57] This period may be extended as necessary, and in the event of a worker being unable to work as the result of pregnancy or childbirth, she is entitled to 50% of her salary for a period of up to 60 days in addition to the 12 weeks at full pay. Further, during the period of lactation, women are entitled to two extra half-hour rest periods in order to feed their infants. Importantly, as long as more than a year has not elapsed from the date of childbirth, women are entitled

---

47   *Constitución Política de los Estados Unidos Mexicanos*, Mexico.
48   Ibid., at Article 1.
49   Ibid., at Article 4.
50   Ibid., at Article 123(7).
51   *Ley Federal de Trabajo*, Mexico, at Articles 3 and 164.
52   Ibid., at Article 1.
53   Ibid., at Article 1.
54   Ibid., at Article 2.
55   Ibid., at Article 133(1).
56   Ibid., at Article 86.
57   Ibid., at Article 170.

to return to the position they formerly occupied, and are entitled to have pre- and post-natal periods included in their seniority.

In terms of work risk indemnification financed by a premium paid by the employer, Article 166 establishes that pregnant or lactating women may not be assigned to unhealthy or dangerous work, industrial night work, in commercial or service establishments after 10 p.m. or for overtime, as a means of protecting the health of women.[58]

Although there is no unemployment insurance *per se*, Articles 50 and 52 of the LFT establish an obligation on the part of employers to pay compensation to unfairly dismissed workers, and they would also have the option to be reinstated to the same job.[59] If the worker is discharged without justification and his employment is for a specified period, the worker is entitled to receive a severance payment equal to the wages received for half of the time of work with the same employer. For those workers with more than one year of service, the severance payment is equal to six months' wages for the first year of service plus 20 days' wages for each additional year of service. For workers with labor contracts of unspecified duration, the severance payment is equal to three months' wages, and they would also have the right to receive wages for the period between the day of dismissal and the day the severance compensation is paid. If a worker asks to be reinstated and the employer refuses, he has the right to receive 20 days' wages for each year of service in addition to the above.

Ley del Seguro Social Article 109 of the *Ley del Seguro Social* (LSS), the Social Security Law, states that in the event of a female insurance worker losing her job and having made at least eight continuous weekly contributions to the *Instituto Mexicano del Seguro Social* (IMSS), Mexican Institute of Social Security, she shall be entitled to receive all necessary medical, maternity, surgical, pharmaceutical and hospital assistance for eight weeks following dismissal.[60] Likewise, female workers involved in strikes are entitled to medical benefits for the duration of the strike, a requirement that applies equally to male workers.

In terms of retirement income and health benefits, the social security system covers a broad range of social insurance, including retirement and dismissal due to old age, work risks, illness and maternity, disability and life, and nursery facilities for children, as well as other social benefits. The system is financed by premiums paid by employers and employees, and by contributions from the federal government. Premiums paid by the employer are equal to 8.5% of insurable earnings plus 13.9% of the minimum wage in the *Distrito Federal* for illness insurance plus a variable portion for work risks insurance. Employees' premiums are equal to 2% of their insurable earnings. In the case of workers receiving the minimum

---

58   Ibid., at Article 166.

59   Ibid., at Articles 50 and 52.

60   *Ley del Seguro Social*, Mexico, Article 109.

wage, according to Article 36, employers are obliged to pay the entire premium.[61] Contributions to the retirement insurance scheme are administered by means of individual accounts handled by private companies known as *Administradores de Fondos para el Retiro de los Trabajadores* (AFORES), Worker Retirement Fund Administrators. The IMSS offers nursery facilities for children aged 43 days to four years of insured female workers, as provided by Article 206,[62] and the premium is entirely covered by the employer, as stated in Article 212.[63] Any female worker losing her job is entitled to make use of the nursery service for a further four weeks, according to Article 207.[64] As of July 1997, contributions for the retirement insurance scheme are administered by means of individual accounts handled by private companies known as *Administradores de Fondos para el Retiro de los Trabajadores* (AFORES), Worker Retirement Fund Administrators.

United States of America

The Role of Women in America

The American model sees judicial activism and the judicial power as fundamentally legislative in character, with royal power displaced and overthrown, but class power remaining, with the upper class combining the popular republican form of government. As of December 2009, the United States has a total population of 308,116,474 people.[65] Concerning the employment status of the population 16 years and older in the civilian labor force, 74,517,000 are men, of these 3,281,000 are unemployed, and 65,937,000 are women, of these 2,835,000 are unemployed.[66] In terms of unemployment, reasons given for the unemployment of both sexes were: lost their job; left their job; re-entered the workforce; or remained non-entrants. The rates for women and men were higher for re-entrants and non-entrants.[67] Additionally, men and women continue to occupy different professions. In terms of the major occupational groups, managerial and professional has 20,297,000 men and 20,196,000 women; technical, sales and administrative support 14,174,000 men and 25,367,000 women; service occupations 7,459,000 men and 11,212,000 women; precision production, craft and repair 12,975,000 men and 1,410,000 women; operators, fabricators and laborers 13,816,000 men and 4,187,000 women; and farming, forestry and fishing 2,515,000 men and 729,000 women.[68] Further, at

---

61   Ibid., at Article 36.
62   Ibid., at Article 206.
63   Ibid., at Article 212.
64   Ibid., at Article 207.
65   United States Census Bureau.
66   United States Census Bureau, Women in the United States.
67   United States Census Bureau, Statistical Abstract.
68   United States Census Bureau, Women in the United States.

the top of the career ladder, in the managerial and professional category, there are 10,877,000 men (15.3%) and 8,888,000 women (14.1%) in the decision-making executive, administrator and managerial areas. However, 9,420,000 men (13.2%) and 11,309,000 women (17.9%) are in the support service professional specialty area.[69] In looking more closely at the legal profession, women still account for only 29% of attorneys and judges, up from 15.8% a decade earlier.[70]

In terms of earnings of full-time year-round workers aged 15 years and older, most men (12,631,000 or 22.0%) are found in the $35,000 to $49,999 range, while most women (9,410,000 or 23.3%) are less well off in the $25,000 to $34,999 range. The highest level, $75,000 and over, held 13% of the male figures and only 3.7% of the female figures.[71] Women still earn roughly 75% of what men earn, with the wage gap persisting.[72] Of the total money income of families by type, most of the married couples (33.6%) are in the $75,000 and more range, while male householders (19.3%) are lower in the $50,000 to $74,999 range, and female householders (15.2%) even lower in the $25,000 to $34,999 range.[73]

In terms of educational attainment of the population 25 years and older, of the 83,611,000 total male population and 91,620,000 total female population, 13,215,000 males and 14,638,000 females have less than a high school diploma, and 70,395,000 males and 76,982,000 females are high school graduates or more. In other terms, 60,359,000 males and 70,025,000 females have less than a university bachelor's degree, and 23,251,000 males and 21,595,000 females have a university bachelor's degree or more. On opposite scales, there are 5,918,000 men and 6,261,000 women who have less than ninth grade education, and 8,342,000 men and 6,664,000 women who hold an advanced university degree.[74] Education has had an important impact on the lives of both sexes, but especially women. Female labor force participation rates are at 47.2% for those with less than high school, 68.9% for high school graduates, 77.3% for those with some university and 82.5% for university graduates, while male labor force participation rates are at 72% for those with less than high school, 86.9% for high school graduates, 90.1% for those with some university and 93.8% for university graduates.[75]

In the United States, the return on education for women is particularly high for those with a third-level qualification. Looking at earnings data for full-time women classified by educational attainment, women without a high school diploma earned only 40% as much as women with a college degree, and women with just some college education or an associate degree made just 67% of the earnings of their counterparts with a four-year degree. However, regardless of

---

69   Ibid.
70   United States Census Bureau, Statistical Abstract.
71   United States Census Bureau, Women in the United States.
72   United States Census Bureau, Statistical Abstract.
73   United States Census Bureau, Women in the United States.
74   Ibid.
75   United States Census Bureau, Statistical Abstract.

education level, female full-time workers earned less than men, with the gap being relatively similar for all of the education groups. In looking at temporary contract and part-time workers, and in particular weekly hours worked by men and women full-time in the United States, men were more than twice as likely as women to work 49 or more hours in a week, and women were three times as likely as men to work 35 to 39 hours per week. The possible reasons for the difference in work hours could be attributed to women being more likely to be engaged in family caretaking responsibilities, or to men being more likely to work in occupations and industries where overtime or extended hours are required or frequently available. In looking at discrimination, while the unadjusted gender pay gap in the United States is around 73%, the gap narrowed to 81% after adjusting for human capital differences and to 88% when adjusting for other variables such as occupation and industry. So while the gap in pay was reduced significantly after accounting for other variables, a substantial proportion remained due to discrimination.[76] Women continue to make significant strides in the labor force. However, women still lag behind men overall, making it more difficult for women to advance in their career and in life.

Legislation

Declaration of Independence   The concepts of equality and good government, found in the American judicial system, were equally important principles to the Founding Fathers of the United States. The Declaration of Independence, the bedrock of the United States jurisprudence system, was enshrined on 4 July 1776. It fundamentally states:

> We hold these truths to be self-evident, that all men are created equal; that they are endowed by their Creator with certain unalienable rights; that among these are life, liberty and the pursuit of happiness. That, to secure these rights, governments are instituted among men, deriving their just powers from the consent of the governed; that whenever any form of government becomes destructive of these ends, it is the right of the people to alter or to abolish it, and to institute a new government, laying its foundation on such principles, and organize its powers in such form, as to them shall seem most likely to effect their safety and happiness.[77]

Federalist Papers   Influential thinkers, such as Jefferson, Madison and Jay, believed in a national government and a Bill of Rights, which they outlined in the Federalist Papers 1787–88. Government is seen as essential to the security of liberty, with every citizen ceding some rights for the protection thereof. The

---

76   Department of Justice, Equality & Law Reform, *Developing Sectoral Strategies to Address Gender Pay Gaps.*

77   Declaration of Independence, United States.

diversities in the faculties of men are recognized as where property rights originate. The objective of government is to secure the public good and private rights against the danger of factions, with the most common source of faction being the unequal distribution of property. The purpose of the Union is the common defense of the members, so that the means are proportionate to the ends. Government must act before the public and must be derived from the body of society. The Constitution is founded on the assent and ratification of the people, and every man who values liberty must cherish the attachment to the Union and preserve it.

Among the three branches of government, the Judicial branch is considered the least dangerous to the political rights of the Constitution. The Executive branch dispenses the honors and holds the sword, the Legislative branch controls the purse and prescribes the rules to regulate duties and rights, and the Judiciary has no influence over the sword or the purse, needing the aid of the Executive for the efficacy of judgments. Oppression can proceed from the Courts, but liberty will not be endangered if the branches are separate. The Constitution is the fundamental law of the land. 'We, the people of the United States, to secure the blessings of liberty to ourselves and our prosperity, do ordain and establish this Constitution for the United States of America.' As a recognition of popular rights, the judgments of many unite into one, with the voluntary consent of a whole people.[78] The Federalist Papers give us an important insight into the making of the Constitution, showing us early on the concept of equality of man and the formation of one government out of many people. The importance of the Judiciary must not be overlooked, as it is a major contributor of policy through its judgments, often itself influencing the sword, the Executive, and the purse, the Legislative. American constitutionalism is the product of the revolutionary movement in political thought of Hobbes, the parent of the modern American political process.[79] The chief purpose of political institutions is the management of social conflict. According to Hobbes, the only source of public authority is the private need of independently situated political actors, with a prior right to act based on self-defined standards of conscience and interest. If used wisely, the Constitution can serve to remedy injustices, including maternity discrimination.

United States Constitution   In terms of civil rights, the Fifth and Fourteenth Amendments of the Constitution, ratified in 15 December 1791 and 9 July 1868 respectively, are of paramount importance in the fight for human rights, including maternity rights. With the due process clause of the Fifth Amendment including an equal protection component, the Fifth and Fourteenth Amendments provide due process of law and equal protection to citizens from federal and state actions respectively. Thus, they prohibit government from invidious discrimination:

---

78 Federalist Papers, United States.
79 Coleman, Frank, *Hobbes and America*, University of Toronto, Toronto, 1977, p.3.

Amendment V

No person shall ... be deprived of life, liberty, or property, without due process of law ....[80]

Amendment XIV

1. No state shall make or enforce any law which shall abridge the privileges or immunities of citizens of the United States; nor shall any state deprive any person of life, liberty, or property, without due process of law; nor deny to any person within its jurisdiction the equal protection of the laws.[81]

The 39th Article of the Magna Carta of 1215 is a foundation for the Fifth and Fourteenth Amendments of the American Constitution regarding due process and the rights of life, liberty and property. The Magna Carta states:

No free man shall be taken or imprisoned or dispossessed, or outlawed or banished, or in any way destroyed, nor will we go upon him nor send upon him, except by the legal judgement of his peers or by the law of the land.[82]

In addition, the Nineteenth Amendment, ratified 18 August 1920, was an initial step in granting equality for women:

Amendment XIX

The right of citizens of the United States to vote shall not be denied or abridged by the United States or by any State on account of sex.

Congress shall have power to enforce this article by appropriate legislation.[83]

The American Founding Fathers designed the United States Constitution to be a set of broad guidelines established by free and intelligent men for the government of free and intelligent people for successive generations. It has survived for over 200 years due to the common sense of the American people, the prudence of their representatives, and the calculated wisdom of its judicial interpreters, the Supreme Court of the United States.[84] Chief Justice Marshall said of the Constitution: 'It was intended to endure for ages to come and consequentially to be adapted to the various crises of human affairs' (*McCullough v. Maryland*, 4 Wheaton 415 (1819)).[85] It was a common opinion that each branch of government in matters pertaining to itself be the final judge of its own powers. However, it was the

---

80   Ibid., at Amendment V.

81   Ibid., at Amendment XIV.

82   Magna Carta, Great Britain.

83   Ibid., at Amendment XIX.

84   North, Arthur, *The Supreme Court, Judicial Process and Judicial Politics*, Appleton Century Crofts, New York, 1964, p.2.

85   *McCullough v. Maryland*, 4 Wheaton 415 (1819).

function of the judiciary, and especially the Supreme Court, to construe in the last resort the meaning of the Constitution, with its opinion final and binding. Justice Hughes stated: 'We are under a Constitution but the Constitution is what the judges say it is.' The United States Constitution, through Article 6(2) known as the Supremacy Clause, is the supreme law of the land:

> 6. 2. This Constitution, and the Laws of the United States which shall be made in Pursuance thereof; and all Treaties made, or which shall be made, under the Authority of the United States, shall be the supreme Law of the Land; and the Judges in every State shall be bound thereby, any Thing in the Constitution or Laws of any State to the Contrary notwithstanding.[86]

The seminal case of *Marbury v. Madison*, 1 Cranch 137 (1803), brought forth the important principles that: (1) the Constitution is the supreme law of the land; (2) the powers granted to various branches of government are limited; and (3) the sole and essential function of the Court is to determine which law should prevail in conflict of laws.[87]

In a dynamic society, the creativity of judges is important for the development of the law and the adaptability of the Constitution to the needs of modern society, according to the Realist Theory. Courts are the best means for recognizing social change, in order to focus social attitudes on unachieved goals and assist in their attainment through a decision-making process of judgments and thus policy-making, according to the Free Legal Decision Sociological Jurisprudence Theory.[88] History has a record of the past and provides the Court with a reservoir of social wisdom and political insight. It points out the evils against which the great constitutional clauses were designed as remedies. The adjudicative process depends on a delicate symbiotic relationship, whereby the Court must know us better than we know ourselves, acting as a voice of the spirit to remind us of our better selves.[89] It provides a stimulus and quickens moral education. However, the roots of the Supreme Court's decisions must be already in the nation. The aspirations voiced by the Court must be those the community is willing not only to avow but in the end to live by. For the power of the great constitutional decisions rests upon the accuracy of the Court's perceptions of this kind of common will and upon its ability ultimately to command a consensus. The rule of law, the capacity to command free assent, is the substitute for power.[90] Law is the fabric of a free

---

86   United States Constitution, United States, at Article 6(2).

87   *Marbury v. Madison*, 1 Cranch 137 (1803).

88   North, Arthur, *The Supreme Court, Judicial Process and Judicial Politics*, Appleton Century Crofts, New York, 1964, p.8.

89   Cox Archibald, *The Role of the Supreme Court in American Government*, Oxford University Press, New York, 1976, p.117.

90   Cox, Archibald, Civil Rights, *The Constitution and the Court*, Harvard University Press, Cambridge, 1967, p.21.

society, organized with a minimum of force and a maximum of reason, in an ideal sense of right and justice. Thus, a neutral government, with its various branches, serves only as a participant in the inhumanities of its citizens.

In terms of the burden of proof in discrimination cases, the United States Supreme Court examines the cause of action to see whether a plaintiff is a member of a class, which as a matter of law can invoke the power of the court, and thus, the equal protection clause and the due process clause of the Constitutional Amendments confer a constitutional right to be free from discrimination (*Davis v. Passman*, 442 US 228 (1979)).[91] Importantly, over the years, in examining court challenges, the United States Supreme Court has developed three different levels of review and accompanying burden of proof, depending upon the type of action brought in a legal proceeding. The Court will first examine the legislative purpose of the governmental action alleged to be contrary to the constitutional amendments, and the plaintiff's burden to prove his case will then come into play. The three levels of review are: (1) the minimum rationality level applied to see the rational basis for the means to the ends so that a law will survive as long as it does not serve an important government objective or is not substantially related to the achievement of the objective; (2) the heightened scrutiny level where the defendant government must show that the restriction has a substantial relationship to an important government interest, applied in quasi-suspect classifications, such as gender discrimination cases; and (3) most importantly, the strict scrutiny level where the defendant government must show a compelling interest for the restriction, a hard burden to meet, applied in suspect classifications affecting fundamental rights, such as racial discrimination cases. Thus, the concept of the burden of proof is an important element in court cases. In the fight for equal rights without regard to maternity, some would say one's maternity characteristics should be considered suspect and thus be subject to the highest level of review of strict scrutiny.

In addition, although the American Constitution is the paramount tool for redressing wrongs, the judicial system in the United States has seen the use of two acts, the Equal Pay Act and the Civil Rights Act, as alternatives to the Constitution, with the latter having been the most successful in guarding against discrimination.

Equal Pay Act Important for women, the Equal Pay Act 1963 establishes that it is unlawful for an employer to pay unequal wages for equal work based on a discriminatory distinction.[92] An exception is made where there is a system of (1) seniority; (2) merit; (3) earnings based on quantity or quality of production; or (4) something other than gender. Section 16 of the Equal Pay Act states:

> 16. No employer having employees ... shall discriminate, within any establishment ... between employees on the basis of sex by paying wages to employees in

---

91   *Davis v. Passman*, 442 US 228 (1979).
92   Equal Pay Act, United States.

such establishment at a rate less than the rate at which he pays wages to employees of the opposite sex in such establishment for equal work on jobs the performance of which requires equal skill, effort and responsibility, and which are performed under similar working conditions except where such payment is made pursuant to 1) a seniority system, 2) a merit system, 3) a system which measures earnings by quantity or quality of product or 4) a differential based on any other factor other than sex.[93]

The Equal Pay Act only includes jobs that are very much alike or closely related, considered virtually or substantially identical (*Brennan v. City Stores*, 479 F.2d. 235 (1973)).[94] Jobs though not identical can be considered equal for Equal Pay Act standards if there is only an insubstantial difference in skill, effort and responsibility (*Murphy v. Miller Brewer Co.*, 307 F.Supp. 829 (1969)).[95] For the Equal Pay Act, there is discrimination when there is a different wage rate for equal work, that is, work which requires equal skill, effort and responsibility under similar working conditions (*Corning Glass v. Brennan*, 417 US 188 (1974)).[96] Equal protection is violated only by intentional discrimination, and a different impact standing alone is not enough. Further, there is no legal duty to undo the effects of previous discrimination (*American Nurses' Association v. State of Illinois*, 783 F.2d. 716 (1986)).[97] In terms of the burden of proof, the plaintiff has the burden of establishing that equal pay for equal work was not received, and then the defendant, in rebutting a *prima facie* case, must show the different wages were based on seniority, merit, a quantitative or qualitative system, or reasons other than sex (*Spaulding v. University of Washington*, 740 F.2d. 686 (1984)).[98] The court, however, is concerned with the actual job performance and content, not job description, titles or classifications, and the scrutiny is done on a case-by-case basis so that if skill is irrelevant to job requirements, it is not considered. Therefore, a non-job-related pretext can act as a shield for invidious discrimination.

Civil Rights Act and Pregnancy Discrimination Act   Important for discrimination cases, including maternity discrimination, Title VII, the Civil Rights Act 1964, incorporating some of the provisions of the earlier Equal Pay Act with the Bennett Act Amendment, was implemented to safeguard important civil liberties, and serves to strengthen legislation, thereby helping the courts rule against discrimination. Importantly, Section 703(a) guards against discrimination in employment:

---

93   Ibid., at Section 16.
94   *Brennan v. City Stores*, 479 F.2d. 235 (1973).
95   *Murphy v. Miller Brewer Co.*, 307 F.Supp. 829 (1969).
96   *Corning Glass Works v. Brennan*, 417 US 188 (1974).
97   *American Nurses' Association v. State of Illinois*, 783 F.2d. 716 (1986).
98   *Spaulding v. University of Washington*, 740 F.2d. 686 (1984).

703. a. It shall be an unlawful employment practice for an employer, (1) to fail or refuse to hire or to discharge any individual, or otherwise to discriminate against any individual with respect to his compensation, terms, conditions, or privilege of employment, because of such individual's ... sex ... or (2) to limit, segregate, or classify his employees or applicants for employment in any way which would deprive or tend to deprive any individual of employment opportunities or otherwise adversely affect his status as an employee, because of such individual's ... sex .....[99]

Training programs are covered under Section 703(d):

703. d. It shall be an unlawful employment practice for any employer, labor organization, or joint labor management committee controlling apprenticeship or other training or retraining, including on the job training programs to discriminate against any individual because of his ... sex ... in admission to, or employment in, any program established to provide apprenticeship or other training.[100]

A *bona fide* occupational qualification exception is outlined in Section 703(e):

703. e. Notwithstanding any other provision of this subchapter, (1) it shall not be an unlawful employment practice for an employer to hire and employ employees, for an employment agency to classify, or refer for employment any individual, for a labor organization to classify its membership or to classify or refer for employment any individual, or for an employer, labor organization, or joint labor management committee controlling apprenticeship or other training or retraining programs to admit or employ any individual in any such program, on the basis of his ... sex ... in those certain instances where ... sex ... is a bona fide occupational qualification reasonably necessary to the normal operation of that particular business or enterprise.[101]

Section 703(h) covers unequal pay:

703. h. Notwithstanding any other provision of this title, it shall be a lawful employment practice for an employer to apply different standards of compensation, or different terms, conditions, or privileges of employment pursuant to a bona fide seniority or merit system, or a system which measures earnings by quantity or quality of production or to employees who work different locations, provided that such are not

---

99   Civil Rights Act, United States, at Section 703(a).
100   Ibid., at Section 703(d).
101   Ibid., at Section 703(e).

the result of an intention to discriminate because of ... sex .... It shall not be an unlawful employment practice under this title for any employer to differentiate upon the basis of sex in determining the amount of wages or compensation paid to employees of such employer if such differentiation is authorized by the provisions of Section 6(d) of the Fair Standards Act.[102]

Section 703(j) guards against preferential treatment:

703. j. Nothing contained in this subchapter shall be interpreted to require any employer, employment agency, labor organization, or joint labor management committee subject to this subchapter to grant preferential treatment to any individual or to any group because of the ... sex ... of such individual or group on account of an imbalance which may exist with respect to the total number or percentage of persons of any ... sex ... employed by any employer, referred or classified for employment by any employment agency or labor organization, admitted to membership or classified by any labor organization, or admitted to, or employed in, any apprenticeship or other training program, in comparison with the total number or percentage of persons of such ... sex ... in any community, State, section, or other area, or in the available work force in any community, State, section, or other area.[103]

The establishment of a discriminatory employment practice based on disparate impact is noted in Section 703(k):

703. k. 1. A. An unlawful employment practice based on disparate impact is established under this title only if
  i. a complaining party demonstrates that a respondent uses a particular employment practice that causes a disparate impact on the basis of ... sex ... and the respondent fails to demonstrate that the challenged practice is job related for the position in question and consistent with business necessity.[104]

Further, the duty of a complainant party in a discrimination case is outlined in Section 703(m):

703. m. Except as otherwise provided in this title, an unlawful employment practice is established when the complaining party demonstrates that

---

102   Ibid., at Section 703(h).
103   Ibid., at Section 703(j).
104   Ibid., at Section 703(k).

... sex ... was a motivating factor for any employment practice, even though other factors also motivated the practice.[105]

Section 706(g) provides for adjudicative relief:

706. g. If the court finds that the respondent has intentionally engaged in or is intentionally engaging in an unlawful employment practice charged in the complaint, the court may enjoin the respondent from engaging in such unlawful employment practice, and order such affirmative action as may be appropriate, which may include, but is not limited to, reinstatement or hiring of employees, with or without back pay ..., or any other equitable relief as the court deems appropriate .... No order of the court shall require the admission or reinstatement of an individual as a member of a union, or the hiring, reinstatement, or promotion of an individual as an employee, or the payment to him of any back pay, if such individual was refused admission, suspended, or expelled, or was refused employment or advancement or was suspended or discharged for any reason other than discrimination on account of ... sex ... or in violation of section 704(a).[106]

Finally, opposition to a discriminatory practice is protected under Section 704(a):

704. a. It shall be an unlawful employment practice for an employer to discriminate against any of his employees or applicants for employment, for an employment agency, or joint labor management committee controlling apprenticeship or other training or retraining, including on the job training programs, to discriminate against any individual, or for a labor organization to discriminate against any member thereof or applicant for membership, because he has opposed any practice made an unlawful employment practice by this subchapter, or because he has made a charge, testified, assisted, or participated in any manner in an investigation, proceeding, or hearing under this subchapter.[107]

The Pregnancy Discrimination Act 1978 amended the Civil Rights Act by requiring that employers treat pregnant workers the same as other employees with temporary medical disabilities in all conditions of employment, such as pay and fringe benefits, including paid sick days, health insurance coverage, and temporary disability insurance. It also forbids employers from discriminating against pregnant women or forcing them to take pregnancy leave. The law does not require employers to provide paid leave, but if they provide it for some medical conditions, they

---

105   Ibid., at Section 703(m).
106   Ibid., at Section 706(g).
107   Ibid., at Section 704(a).

must include pregnancy. Discrimination on the basis of pregnancy, childbirth, or related medical conditions constitutes unlawful sex discrimination under Title VII, which covers employers with 15 or more employees, including state and local governments. Women who are pregnant or affected by pregnancy-related conditions must be treated in the same manner as other applicants or employees with similar abilities or limitations. Section 701(k) states:

> 701. k. The terms 'because of sex' or 'on the basis of sex' include, but are not limited to, because of or on the basis of pregnancy, childbirth, or related medical conditions; and women affected by pregnancy, childbirth, or related medical conditions shall be treated the same for all employment-related purposes, including receipt of benefits under fringe benefit programs, as other persons not so affected but similar in their ability or inability to work, and nothing in section 2000e-2(h) of this title [section 703(h)] shall be interpreted to permit otherwise. This subsection shall not require an employer to pay for health insurance benefits for abortion, except where the life of the mother would be endangered if the fetus were carried to term, or except where medical complications have arisen from an abortion: Provided, That nothing herein shall preclude an employer from providing abortion benefits or otherwise affect bargaining agreements in regard to abortion.[108]

In general, the Civil Rights Act eliminates artificial, arbitrary and unnecessary barriers to employment in the form of invidious discrimination, unless there is a demonstrably reasonable measure of job performance (*Griggs v. Duke Power Co.*, 401 US 424 (1971)).[109] Title VII prohibits discrimination allowing for compensation, thus recognizing equal pay as a legal right (*American Federation of State, County and Municipal Employees v. Washington*, 770 F.2d. 1401 (1985)).[110] In terms of the burden of proof, the plaintiff has the burden to show he belongs to a group, has applied for a job, was qualified for the job that the employer tried to fill but was rejected, and the employer continued to seek applicants (*McDonnell Douglas Corp. v. Green*, 411 U.S. 792 (1973)),[111] and then the defendant, in rebutting a *prima facie* case, is required to show the absence of a discriminatory motive for his actions. However, this was later revised by the court, so that the defendant is not required to show the absence, but must merely articulate a legitimate non-discriminatory reason for the employee's rejection (*Board of Trustees of Keene State College v. Sweeney*, 439 US 24 (1978)).[112]

---

108   Civil Right Act, at Section 701(k) (Pregnancy Discrimination Act).

109   *Griggs v. Duke Power Co.*, 401 US 424 (1971).

110   *American Federation of State, County and Municipal Employees v. Washington*, 770 F.2d. 1401 (1985).

111   *McDonnell Douglas Corp. v. Green*, 411 US 792 (1973).

112   *Board of Trustees of Keene State College v. Sweeney*, 439 US 24 (1978).

The Civil Rights Act is often used to fight discrimination in compensation, with a differentiation made between disparate treatment and disparate impact. Disparate treatment is concerned with direct or circumstantial discriminatory motives, which lack well-defined criteria (*Spaulding v. University of Washington*, 740 F.2d. 686 (1984)),[113] and involves intent or motive as an essential element of liability concerning the effects of a chosen policy, with awareness alone of adverse consequences on a group being insufficient (*American Federation of State, County and Municipal Employees v. Washington*, 770 F.2d. 1401 (1985)).[114] In a disparate treatment approach, the plaintiff is required to show by a preponderance of the evidence the overt motive, and then the defendant, in rebutting a *prima facie* case, must prove that it was non-discriminatory either by the four exceptions, by necessity or by a *bona fide* occupational qualification. On the other hand, disparate impact is more than an inference of discriminatory impact of outwardly neutral employment practices and adversity (*Spaulding v. University of Washington*, 740 F.2d. 686 (1984)),[115] and does not need a profession of intent by the employer to discriminate, only a clearly delineated employment practice (*American Federation of State, County and Municipal Employees v. Washington*, 770 F.2d. 1401 (1985)).[116] In a disparate impact approach, the plaintiff need only show the disproportionate impact, and then the defendant, in rebutting a *prima facie* case, must show that it was non-discriminatory.

Family and Medical Leave Act   The Family and Medical Leave Act 1993 (FMLA) provides eligible workers with unpaid time off to meet family responsibilities, such as caring for a new baby or an adopted child, or for looking after a sick child, spouse, or parent. The FMLA applies to employees who work 20 or more weeks in a year and have worked at least 12 months for their current employer and who work for a firm employing at least 50 workers. The federal policy ensures that eligible employees receive up to 12 weeks of unpaid leave annually, leave may be taken all at once or intermittently, and for part or all of a day; continued health insurance benefits, if ordinarily provided by the employer; and a guarantee of return to the same, or an equivalent, job. However, the FMLA only requires unpaid leave. The purpose of the Act is outlined in Section 825.101:

> 825. 101. a.FMLA is intended to allow employees to balance their work and family life by taking reasonable unpaid leave for medical reasons, for the birth ... of a child .... The Act is intended to balance the demands of the workplace with the needs of families, to promote

---

113   *Spaulding v. University of Washington*, 740 F.2d. 686 (1984).

114   *American Federation of State, County and Municipal Employees v. Washington*, 770 F.2d. 1401 (1985).

115   *Spaulding v. University of Washington*, 740 F.2d. 686 (1984).

116   *American Federation of State, County and Municipal Employees v. Washington*, 770 F.2d. 1401 (1985).

the stability and economic security of families, and to promote national interests in preserving family integrity. It was intended that the Act accomplish these purposes in a manner that accommodates the legitimate interests of employers, and in a manner consistent with the Equal Protection Clause of the Fourteenth Amendment in minimizing the potential for employment discrimination on the basis of sex, while promoting equal employment opportunity for men and women.

b. The FMLA was predicated on two fundamental concerns, the needs of the American workforce, and the development of high-performance organizations .... (W)orkers need reassurance that they will not be asked to choose between continuing their employment, and meeting their personal and family obligations or tending to vital needs at home.

c. The FMLA is both intended and expected to benefit employers as well as their employees. A direct correlation exists between stability in the family and productivity in the workplace. FMLA will encourage the development of high-performance organizations. When workers can count on durable links to their workplace they are able to make their own full commitments to their jobs. The record of hearings on family and medical leave indicate the powerful productive advantages of stable workplace relationships, and the comparatively small costs of guaranteeing that those relationships will not be dissolved while workers attend to pressing family health obligations or their own serious illness.[117]

The employers covered are outlined in Section 825.104:

825. 104. a. An employer covered by FMLA is any person engaged in commerce or in any industry or activity affecting commerce, who employs 50 or more employees for each working day during each of 20 or more calendar workweeks in the current or preceding calendar year .... Public agencies are covered employers without regard to the number of employees employed. Public as well as private elementary and secondary schools are also covered employers without regard to the number of employees employed.[118]

The employees covered are outlined in Section 825.110:

825. 110. a. An 'eligible employee' is an employee of a covered employer who:
  1. Has been employed by the employer for at least 12 months, and

---

117   Family and Medical Leave Act, United States, at Section 825.101.
118   Ibid., at Section 825.104.

2. Has been employed for at least 1,250 hours of service during the 12-month period immediately preceding the commencement of the leave, and
3. Is employed at a worksite where 50 or more employees are employed by the employer within 75 miles of that worksite.

b. The 12 months an employee must have been employed by the employer need not be consecutive months, provided

1. Subject to the exceptions provided in paragraph (b)(2) of this section, employment periods prior to a break in service of seven years or more need not be counted in determining whether the employee has been employed by the employer for at least 12 months.[119]

Section 825.120 deals specifically with the leave for pregnancy or birth:

825. 120. a. General rules. Eligible employees are entitled to FMLA leave for pregnancy or birth of a child as follows:

1. Both the mother and father are entitled to FMLA leave for the birth of their child.
2. Both the mother and father are entitled to FMLA leave to be with the healthy newborn child (i.e., bonding time) during the 12-month period beginning on the date of birth. An employee's entitlement to FMLA leave for a birth expires at the end of the 12-month period beginning on the date of the birth. If state law allows, or the employer permits, bonding leave to be taken beyond this period, such leave will not qualify as FMLA leave …. Under this section, both the mother and father are entitled to FMLA leave even if the newborn does not have a serious health condition.
3. A husband and wife who are eligible for FMLA leave and are employed by the same covered employer may be limited to a combined total of 12 weeks of leave during any 12-month period if the leave is taken for birth of the employee's son or daughter or to care for the child after birth, for placement of a son or daughter with the employee for adoption or foster care or to care for the child after placement, or to care for the employee's parent with a serious health condition. This limitation on the total weeks of leave applies to leave taken for the reasons specified as long as a husband and wife are employed by the 'same employer'….
4. The mother is entitled to FMLA leave for incapacity due to pregnancy, for prenatal care, or for her own serious health condition following the birth of the child. Circumstances may

---

119   Ibid., at Section 825.110.

require that FMLA leave begin before the actual date of birth of a child. An expectant mother may take FMLA leave before the birth of the child for prenatal care or if her condition makes her unable to work. The mother is entitled to leave for incapacity due to pregnancy even though she does not receive treatment from a health care provider during the absence, and even if the absence does not last for more than three consecutive calendar days....

5. The husband is entitled to FMLA leave if needed to care for his pregnant spouse who is incapacitated or if needed to care for her during her prenatal care, or if needed to care for the spouse following the birth of a child if the spouse has a serious health condition.

6. Both the mother and father are entitled to FMLA leave if needed to care for a child with a serious health condition .... Thus, a husband and wife may each take 12 weeks of FMLA leave if needed to care for their newborn child with a serious health condition, even if both are employed by the same employer, provided they have not exhausted their entitlements during the applicable 12-month FMLA leave period.

b. Intermittent and reduced schedule leave. An eligible employee may use intermittent or reduced schedule leave after the birth to be with a healthy newborn child only if the employer agrees....[120]

The amount of leave is determined according to Section 825.200:

825. 200. a. Except in the case of leave to care for a covered service member with a serious injury or illness, an eligible employee's FMLA leave entitlement is limited to a total of 12 workweeks of leave during any 12-month period for any one, or more, of the following reasons:

1. The birth of the employee's son or daughter, and to care for the newborn child;

b. An employer is permitted to choose any one of the following methods for determining the '12-month period' in which the 12 weeks of leave entitlement described in paragraph (a) of this section occurs:

1. The calendar year;

2. Any fixed 12-month 'leave year', such as a fiscal year, a year required by State law, or a year starting on an employee's 'anniversary' date;

3. The 12-month period measured forward from the date any employee's first FMLA leave under paragraph (a) begins; or,

---

120   Ibid., at Section 825.120.

> 4. A 'rolling' 12-month period measured backward from the date an employee uses any FMLA leave as described in paragraph (a).
>
> c. Under methods in paragraphs (b)(1) and (b)(2) of this section an employee would be entitled to up to 12 weeks of FMLA leave at any time in the fixed 12-month period selected. An employee could, therefore, take 12 weeks of leave at the end of the year and 12 weeks at the beginning of the following year. Under the method in paragraph (b)(3) of this section, an employee would be entitled to 12 weeks of leave during the year beginning on the first date FMLA leave is taken; the next 12-month period would begin the first time FMLA leave is taken after completion of any previous 12-month period. Under the method in paragraph (b)(4) of this section, the 'rolling' 12-month period, each time an employee takes FMLA leave the remaining leave entitlement would be any balance of the 12 weeks which has not been used during the immediately preceding 12 months.[121]

The entitlement to reinstatement is covered under Section 825.214:

> 825. 214. General rule. On return from FMLA leave, an employee is entitled to be returned to the same position the employee held when leave commenced, or to an equivalent position with equivalent benefits, pay, and other terms and conditions of employment. An employee is entitled to such reinstatement even if the employee has been replaced or his or her position has been restructured to accommodate the employee's absence.[122]

Further, protection for employees who request leave is provided for under Section 825.220, which includes the definition of interference:

> 825. 220. a. The FMLA prohibits interference with an employee's rights under the law, and with legal proceedings or inquiries relating to an employee's rights. More specifically, the law contains the following employee protections:
>
> 1. An employer is prohibited from interfering with, restraining or denying the exercise of (or attempts to exercise) any rights provided by the Act.
> 2. An employer is prohibited from discharging or in any other way discriminating against any person (whether or not an employee)

---

121   Ibid., at Section 825.200.
122   Ibid., at Section 825.214.

for opposing or complaining about any unlawful practice under the Act.

3. All persons (whether or not employers) are prohibited from discharging or in any other way discriminating against any person (whether or not an employee) because that person has
   i. Filed any charge, or has instituted (or caused to be instituted) any proceeding under or related to this Act;
   ii. Given, or is about to give, any information in connection with an inquiry or proceeding relating to a right under this Act;
   iii. Testified, or is about to testify, in any inquiry or proceeding relating to a right under this Act.

b. Any violations of the Act or of these regulations constitute interfering with, restraining, or denying the exercise of rights provided by the Act. An employer may be liable for compensation and benefits lost by reason of the violation, for other actual monetary losses sustained as a direct result of the violation, and for appropriate equitable or other relief, including employment, reinstatement, promotion, or any other relief tailored to the harm suffered. 'Interfering with' the exercise of an employee's rights would include, for example, not only refusing to authorize FMLA leave, but discouraging an employee from using such leave. It would also include manipulation by a covered employer to avoid responsibilities under FMLA, for example:

   1. Transferring employees from one worksite to another for the purpose of reducing worksites, or to keep worksites, below the 50-employee threshold for employee eligibility under the Act;
   2. Changing the essential functions of the job in order to preclude the taking of leave;
   3. Reducing hours available to work in order to avoid employee eligibility.

c. The Act's prohibition against 'interference' prohibits an employer from discriminating or retaliating against an employee or prospective employee for having exercised or attempted to exercise FMLA rights. For example, if an employee on leave without pay would otherwise be entitled to full benefits (other than health benefits), the same benefits would be required to be provided to an employee on unpaid FMLA leave. By the same token, employers cannot use the taking of FMLA leave as a negative factor in employment actions, such as hiring, promotions or disciplinary actions; nor can FMLA leave be counted under 'no fault' attendance policies. See Sec. 825.215.

d. Employees cannot waive, nor may employers induce employees to waive, their prospective rights under FMLA...

e. Individuals, and not merely employees, are protected from retaliation for opposing (e.g., filing a complaint about) any practice which is unlawful under the Act. They are similarly protected if they oppose any practice which they reasonably believe to be a violation of the Act or regulations.[123]

Section 825.400 deals with enforcement of the rights under the FMLA:

825. 400. a. The employee has the choice of:
    1. Filing, or having another person file on his or her behalf, a complaint with the Secretary of Labor, or
    2. Filing a private lawsuit....
b. If the employee files a private lawsuit, it must be filed within two years after the last action which the employee contends was in violation of the Act, or three years if the violation was willful.
c. If an employer has violated one or more provisions of FMLA, and if justified by the facts of a particular case, an employee may receive one or more of the following: Wages, employment benefits, or other compensation denied or lost to such employee by reason of the violation; or, where no such tangible loss has occurred, such as when FMLA leave was unlawfully denied, any actual monetary loss sustained by the employee as a direct result of the violation, such as the cost of providing care, up to a sum equal to 26 weeks of wages for the employee in a case involving leave to care for a covered service member or 12 weeks of wages for the employee in a case involving leave for any other FMLA qualifying reason. In addition, the employee may be entitled to interest on such sum, calculated at the prevailing rate. An amount equaling the preceding sums may also be awarded as liquidated damages unless such amount is reduced by the court because the violation was in good faith and the employer had reasonable grounds for believing the employer had not violated the Act. When appropriate, the employee may also obtain appropriate equitable relief, such as employment, reinstatement and promotion. When the employer is found in violation, the employee may recover a reasonable attorney's fee, reasonable expert witness fees, and other costs of the action from the employer in addition to any judgment awarded by the court.[124]

Finally, filing a complaint with the Federal Government, Section 825.401 states:

---

123   Ibid., at Section 825.220.
124   Ibid., at Section 825.400.

825. 401. a. A complaint may be filed in person, by mail or by telephone, with the Wage and Hour Division, Employment Standards Administration, U.S. Department of Labor. A complaint may be filed at any local office of the Wage and Hour Division....

b. (b) A complaint filed with the Secretary of Labor should be filed within a reasonable time of when the employee discovers that his or her FMLA rights have been violated. In no event may a complaint be filed more than two years after the action which is alleged to be a violation of FMLA occurred, or three years in the case of a willful violation.

c. (c) No particular form of complaint is required, except that a complaint must be reduced to writing and should include a full statement of the acts and/or omissions, with pertinent dates, which are believed to constitute the violation.[125]

The concept of the burden of proof is an important element in court cases, especially those impacting gender. The court must choose among three levels of scrutiny in evaluating a case: rational basis, the lowest level, where the plaintiff must show that there is no rational basis for the State restriction, which is a hard burden to meet; heightened scrutiny, the intermediary level, where the defendant government must show that the restriction has a substantial relationship to an important government interest, which is used in gender cases; and strict scrutiny, the highest level, where the defendant government must show a compelling interest for the restriction, a hard burden to meet which is used in such suspect cases as race. Women have been discriminated against for centuries, often being put on a pedestal or being treated as inferior citizens. Because of the unresponsive rendering of rights through the rational basis test the burden of proof, the lowest level, the heightened scrutiny test was developed to better protect women. However, today more than ever, there is a greater push to better recognize gender discrimination and elevate it to the strict scrutiny test, the highest level of review. Just over a century ago, the Court distinguished between the sexes. In a demand by a woman to practice as an attorney, the Court, in *Bradwell v. State*, 16 Wall. 130 (1873), enunciated the role of women in society, in distinguishing between womanhood and personhood:

That God designed the sexes to occupy different spheres of action, and that it belonged to men to make, apply, and execute the laws, was regarded as an almost axiomatic truth .... In view of these facts, we are certainly warranted in saying that when the legislature gave to this court the power of granting licenses to practice law, it was with not the slightest expectation that this privilege would be extended to women.[126]

125 Ibid., at Section 825.401.
126 *Bradwell v. State*, 16 Wall. 130 (1873).

In denying her claim, Mr. Justice Bradley stated:

> The civil law, as well as nature herself, has always recognized a wide difference
> in the respective spheres and destinies of man and woman. Man is, or should be,
> woman's protector and defender. The natural and proper timidity and delicacy
> which belongs to the female sex evidently unfits it for many of the occupations
> of civil life .... The harmony, not to say the identity, of interests and views which
> belong, or should belong, to the family institution is repugnant to the idea of a
> woman adopting a distinct and independent career from that of her husband.[127]

The Court went on to state:

> The paramount destiny and mission of woman are to fulfill the noble and benign
> offices of wife and mother. This is the law of the Creator. And the rules of civil
> society must be adapted to the general constitution of things, and cannot be
> based upon exceptional cases.[128]

Hence, certain virtues were seen as prerogatives within the domain of a particular
gender, and this way of thinking persisted for a long time with the help of the
courts. The Court continued to hold that the 'Fourteenth Amendment did not
tear history up by the roots; the fact that women may have achieved the virtues
that men have long claimed as their prerogatives and now indulge in vices that
men have long practiced, does not preclude the States from drawing a sharp line
between the sexes, since the Constitution does not require legislatures to reflect
sociological insight, or shifting social standards' (*Goesaert v. Cleary*, 335 U.S.
464, 466 (1948)).[129]

In using the rationality test, the least protective, the Court continued to see
certain virtues as the prerogatives of the domain of men, even though it was
recognized by the legal system that there had been many changes in the social
position of women. In a case involving the denial of a woman's opportunity to
serve the judicial system as a juror, the Court found that 'despite the enlightened
emancipation of women from the restrictions and protections of bygone years, and
their entry into many parts of community life formerly considered to be reserved
to men, woman is still regarded as the center of home and family life' (*Hoyt v.
Florida*, 368 U.S. 57, 62 (1961)).[130] The lowest standard of scrutiny, the rationality
test, finds that the State has a legitimate interest in regulating an activity within
its jurisdiction. Under the rationality test, a Statute should be reviewed keeping in
mind that: (1) The equal-protection clause of the 14th Amendment does not take
from the state the power to classify in the adoption of police laws, but admits of

---

127   Ibid.
128   Ibid.
129   *Goesaert v. Cleary*, 335 U.S. 464, 466 (1948).
130   *Hoyt v. Florida*, 368 U.S. 57, 62 (1961).

the exercise of a wide scope of discretion in that regard, and avoids what is done only when it is without any reasonable basis, and therefore is purely arbitrary; (2) A classification having some reasonable basis does not offend against that clause merely because it is not made with mathematical nicety, or because in practice it results in some inequality; (3) When the classification in such a law is called in question, if any state of facts reasonably can be conceived that would sustain it, the existence of that state of facts at the time the law was enacted must be assumed; and (4) One who assails the classification in such a law must carry the burden of showing that it does not rest upon any reasonable basis, but is essentially arbitrary (*Lindsley v. Natural Carbonic Gas Co.*, 220 U.S. 61, 78 (1911)).[131] Thus, the Court pronounced that the governmental classification will not offend the Constitution's equal protection clause 'simply because it is not made with material nicety' (*Dandridge v. William*, 397 U.S. 471, 485 (1970)).[132] 'To be able to find fault with a law is not to demonstrate its invalidity. It may seem unjust and oppressive, yet be free from judicial interference .... The problems of government are practical ones and may justify, if they do not require, rough accommodations, – illogical, it may be, and unscientific .... What is best is not always discernible; the wisdom of any choice may be disputed or condemned. Mere errors of government are not subject to our judicial review. It is only its palpably arbitrary exercises which can be declared void under the 14th Amendment' (*Metropolis Theatre Co. v. City of Chicago*, 228 U.S. 61, 69 (1913)).[133] 'A statutory discrimination will not be set aside if any state of facts reasonably may be conceived to justify it,' but it will fail if the unequal distinction 'rests on grounds wholly irrelevant to the achievement of the State's objective' (*McGowan v. Maryland*, 366 U.S. 420, 425 (1961)).[134] As such, this lowest standard was not adequate to meet the needs of women, and hence, gender discrimination persisted.

A different outlook of women was taken in the 1970s. Gender discrimination was not as readily upheld by the Court, unless it met the higher intermediate level, the heightened scrutiny test, which required the justification for limiting a right be substantially related to an important government objective. The first case in which the heightened scrutiny test was used was *Reed v. Reed*, 404 U.S. 71 (1971), in which a restriction based on gender was struck down.[135] Where a statutory scheme 'provides that different treatment be accorded ... on the basis of ... sex; it thus establishes a classification subject to scrutiny under the Equal Protection Clause. In applying that clause, this Court has consistently recognized that the Fourteenth Amendment does not deny to States the power to treat different classes of persons in different ways. The Equal Protection Clause of that amendment does, however, deny to States the power to legislate that different treatment be accorded to persons

---

131   *Lindsley v. Natural Carbonic Gas Co.*, 220 U.S. 61, 78 (1911).
132   *Dandridge v. William*, 397 U.S. 471, 485 (1970).
133   *Metropolis Theatre Co. v. City of Chicago*, 228 U.S. 61, 69 (1913).
134   *McGowan v. Maryland*, 366 U.S. 420, 425 (1961).
135   *Reed v. Reed*, 404 U.S. 71 (1971).

placed by a statute into different classes on the basis of criteria wholly unrelated to the objective of that statute' (*Reed v. Reed*, 404 U.S. 71, 76 (1971)).[136] A classification 'must be reasonable, not arbitrary, and must rest upon some ground of difference having a fair and substantial relation to the object of the legislation, so that all persons similarly circumstanced shall be treated alike' (*F.S. Royster Guano Co. v. Com of Virginia*, 253 U.S. 412, 415 (1920)).[137] A mandatory preference solely on the basis of gender through an arbitrary legislative choice was forbidden. The Court stated that the classification must be reasonable not arbitrary, and must rest upon a ground which is fair and substantially related to the objective of the legislation.

Even though the Court purported to apply 'any rational basis', the lowest standard, the language used in the judgment in *Reed* resulted in a more stringent standard for gender cases. It was an important case, which hinted at a special type of scrutiny, higher than the mere rational basis test. Further decisions drained the previous reasoning of *Bradwell*, *Goesart* and *Hoyt*. In contravention of *Hoyt*, the court in *Taylor v. Louisiana*, 419 U.S. 522 (1975), dismissed the antiquated notion that society cannot spare any women from the home.[138] 'The thought is that the factors which tend to influence the action of women are the same as those which influence the action of men – personality, background, economic status – and not sex .... The truth is that the two sexes are not fungible; a community made up exclusively of one is different from a community composed of both; the subtle interplay of influence one on the other is among the imponderables .... Yet a flavor, a distinct quality is lost if either sex is excluded' (*Ballard v. United States*, 329 U.S. 187, 194 (1946)).[139] Further, contrary to the principles enunciated in *Bradwell*, the classification effectuated by the challenged statute denies the equal protection of the laws, as guaranteed by the Fourteenth Amendment. Notwithstanding the 'old notions' cited by the state court that it is the man's primary responsibility to provide a home, that it is salutary for him to have education and training before he assumes that responsibility, and that females tend to mature and marry earlier than males, there is nothing rational in the statutory distinction between males and females, ... thus imposing criteria wholly unrelated to the objective of that statute' (*Stanton v. Stanton*, 421 U.S. 7, 17 (1975)).[140]

The seminal far-reaching case of *Craig v. Boren*, 429 U.S. 190 (1976) was the first Supreme Court decision to officially recognize the heightened scrutiny test for gender.[141] It noted that *Reed* emphasized that statutory classifications which distinguish between males and females are subject to scrutiny under the Equal Protection Clause. Therefore, to withstand constitutional challenge, 'classifications by gender must serve important governmental objectives and must

---

136   *Reed v. Reed*, 404 U.S. 71, 76 (1971).
137   *F.S. Royster Guano Co. v. Com of Virginia*, 253 U.S. 412, 415 (1920).
138   *Taylor v. Louisiana*, 419 U.S. 522 (1975).
139   *Ballard v. United States*, 329 U.S. 187, 194 (1946).
140   *Stanton v. Stanton*, 421 U.S. 7, 17 (1975).
141   *Craig v. Boren*, 429 U.S. 190 (1976).

be substantially related to achievement of those objectives' (*Craig v. Boren*, 429 U.S. 190, 197 (1976)).[142] *Craig* further noted that *Reed* 'provided the underpinning for decisions that have invalidated statutes employing gender as an inaccurate proxy for other, more germane bases of classification. Hence, "archaic and overbroad" generalizations could not justify use of a gender line in determining eligibility for certain governmental entitlements. Similarly, increasingly outdated misconceptions concerning the role of females in the home rather than in the "marketplace and world of ideas" were rejected as loose-fitting characterizations incapable of supporting state statutory schemes that were premised upon their accuracy. In light of the weak congruence between gender and the characteristic or trait that gender purported to represent, it was necessary that the legislatures choose either to realign their substantive laws in a gender-neutral fashion, or to adopt procedures for identifying those instances where the sex-centered generalization actually comported with fact' (*Craig v. Boren*, 429 U.S. 190, 199 (1976)).[143]

It is important to understand that the intermediate level of scrutiny, used for gender discrimination cases, is a lower burden than the one used for fundamental rights or suspect classifications, which requires an overwhelming and compelling state interest to contravene a right. This higher burden, the strict scrutiny test, is used for racial and national origin classifications only. In *Craig*, the distinction on the basis of sex was found not to be invidious, in this case being against males who were not considered to be a discreet and insular minority, therefore an inoffensive legislative purpose. The minority opinion still rejected the notion of a higher standard beyond the rational basis test, holding that a more active review was reserved for discriminated members of discrete insular minorities, and women were not included in this. While invalidating a discriminatory statute, the Court, in a unanimous decision, further stressed that the party wishing to uphold a classification on the basis of gender must show 'an exceedingly persuasive justification' for it (*Kirchberg v. Feenstra*, 450 U.S. 455 (1981)).[144]

In the fight against gender discrimination, the court has sometimes moved beyond the concept of equality for women. The Supreme Court has recognized the concept of 'benign' discrimination, when one is being treated differently as a means for compensation for past and present injustices. The problem occurs when one is compensated and the other is denied compensation, and they were not parties to the original injustice. One of the first modern cases to deal with benign discrimination found that a state law is not arbitrary although it 'discriminate[s] in favor of a certain class ... if the discrimination is founded upon a reasonable distinction, or difference in state policy', one of cushioning the financial impact of spousal loss upon the sex for which that loss imposes a disproportionately heavy burden (*Kahn v. Shevin*, 416 U.S. 351, 355 (1974)).[145] The Court made a distinction

---

142 *Craig v. Boren*, 429 U.S. 190, 197 (1976).
143 *Craig v. Boren*, 429 U.S. 190, 199 (1976).
144 *Kirchberg v. Feenstra*, 450 U.S. 455 (1981).
145 *Kahn v. Shevin*, 416 U.S. 351, 355 (1974).

between gender and race, but allowed benign discrimination. To remedy past discrimination, the Court permitted the favoring of women by rejecting gender equality, finding that men had more of an opportunity in the past and emphasizing the prior treatment in society toward the sexes (*Schlesinger v. Ballard*, 419 U.S. 498 (1975)).[146] In the case of *Orr v. Orr*, 440 U.S. 268 (1979),[147] Justice Brennan had cautioned against classifications on the basis of sex, in that 'legislative classifications which distribute benefits and burdens on the basis of gender carry the inherent risk of reinforcing stereotypes about the "proper place" of women and their need for special protection. Thus, even statutes purportedly designed to compensate for and ameliorate the effects of past discrimination must be carefully tailored. Where ... the State's compensatory and ameliorative purposes are as well served by a gender-neutral classification as one that gender classifies and therefore carries with it the baggage of sexual stereotypes, the State cannot be permitted to classify on the basis of sex. And this is doubly so where the choice made by the State appears to redound – if only indirectly – to the benefit of those without need for special solicitude' (*Orr v. Orr*, 440 U.S. 268, 283 (1979)).[148]

Importantly, equal rights advocates and women's groups have rallied to argue for the adoption of the highest standard of review, that of strict scrutiny to gender discrimination cases. It requires a precisely tailored objective to a compelling government interest, with no less drastic means available. It is used where there has been 'a history of purposeful unequal treatment ... and a position of political powerlessness' (*San Antonio Independent School Division v. Rodriguez*, 411 U.S. 1, 16 (1973)).[149] The closest that the United States Supreme Court has come to the strict scrutiny test for gender differentiations was in the important case of *Frontiero v. Richardson*, 411 U.S. 677 (1973). Judges Brennan, Douglas, White and Marshall decided that gender 'frequently bears no relation to ability to perform or contribute to society', so that statutory distinctions based on gender have invidious effects.[150] Under 'traditional' equal protection analysis, a legislative classification must be sustained unless it is 'patently arbitrary' and bears no rational relationship to a legitimate governmental interest. Therefore, the departure from 'traditional' rational-basis analysis with respect to sex-based classifications is clearly justified:

> There can be no doubt that our Nation has had a long and unfortunate history of sex discrimination. Traditionally, such discrimination was rationalized by an attitude of 'romantic paternalism' which, in practical effect, put women, not on a pedestal, but in a cage .... As a result of notions such as these, our statute books gradually became laden with gross, stereotyped distinctions between the sexes

---

146   *Schlesinger v. Ballard*, 419 U.S. 498 (1975).
147   *Orr v. Orr*, 440 U.S. 268 (1979).
148   *Orr v. Orr*, 440 U.S. 268, 283 (1979).
149   *San Antonio Independent School Division v. Rodriguez*, 411 U.S. 1, 16 (1973).
150   *Frontiero v. Richardson*, 411 U.S. 677 (1973).

and, indeed, throughout much of the 19th century the position of women in our society was, in many respects, comparable to that of blacks under the pre-Civil War slave codes. Neither slaves nor women could hold office, serve on juries, or bring suit in their own names, and married women traditionally were denied the legal capacity to hold or convey property or to serve as legal guardians of their own children. And although blacks were guaranteed the right to vote in 1870, women were denied even that right – which is itself 'preservative of other basic civil and political rights' until adoption of the Nineteenth Amendment half a century later. It is true, of course, that the position of women in America has improved markedly in recent decades.[151]

Judges Brennan, Douglas, White and Marshall found that gender should be a suspect classification like race and national origin:

> Nevertheless, it can hardly be doubted that, in part because of the high visibility of the sex characteristic, women still face pervasive, although at times more subtle, discrimination in our educational institutions, in the job market and, perhaps most conspicuously, in the political arena. Moreover, since sex, like race and national origin, is an immutable characteristic determined solely by the accident of birth, the imposition of special disabilities upon the members of a particular sex because of their sex would seem to violate 'the basic concept of our system that legal burdens should bear some relationship to individual responsibility...'.[152]

Justice Brennan postulated the suspect nature of gender comparing it to race. Gender is to be considered as immutable, like race is, since one cannot change one's gender, and gender like race has historically been suspect to invidious discrimination, relegating an entire class to an inferior legal status without regard to actual individual capabilities. Members of both groups carry an obvious badge by sight, causing *de jure* discrimination not simply *de facto* discrimination:

> And what differentiates sex from such nonsuspect statuses as intelligence or physical disability, and aligns it with the recognized suspect criteria, is that the sex characteristic frequently bears no relation to ability to perform or contribute to society. As a result, statutory distinctions between the sexes often have the effect of invidiously relegating the entire class of females to inferior legal status without regard to the actual capabilities of its individual members .... Congress itself has concluded that classifications based upon sex are inherently invidious, and this conclusion of a coequal branch of Government is not without significance to the question presently under consideration.[153]

---

151   *Frontiero v. Richardson*, 411 U.S. 677, 686 (1973).
152   *Frontiero v. Richardson*, 411 U.S. 677, 687 (1973).
153   *Frontiero v. Richardson*, 411 U.S. 677, 688 (1973).

Any statutory scheme which draws a sharp line between the sexes, solely for the purpose of achieving administrative convenience, necessarily commands 'dissimilar treatment for men and women who are ... similarly situated', and therefore involves the 'very kind of arbitrary legislative choice forbidden by the Constitution'. Therefore, 'With these considerations in mind, we can only conclude that classifications based upon sex, like classifications based upon race, alienage, or national origin, are inherently suspect, and must therefore be subjected to strict judicial scrutiny.'[154]

In terms of family leave, starting a family on the right track is what a government should do toward creating a productive, satisfied workforce, and happier, better-balanced families. Maternity leave, often called parental or family leave, is the time a mother or father takes off from work for the birth of a child. In March 2009, President Barack Obama created the White House Council on Women and Girls, which is tasked with ensuring that all government agencies include the welfare of females when formulating policy; one of its priorities will be to evaluate and develop 'policies that establish a balance between work and family'. In looking at maternity leave discrimination, mothers and children benefit from paid maternity leave: Women with any combination of paid vacation or sick time tend to take more time off after childbirth, resulting in positive health effects for both women and children; women workers who have some form of paid leave take on average 10.5 weeks off after childbirth, while women without any paid leave take 6.6 weeks; the majority of new mothers report one or more physical side effects five weeks after childbirth, and those who had a Cesarean section had significantly more health impacts; and newborns have decreased access to follow-up care, lower rates of immunization, and decreased breastfeeding by four and one-half weeks on average as a result of early returns to work.[155] In the United States, only 8% of workers have paid family leave to care for newborns and other family members. Managerial and professional workers and those in larger establishments have a distinct advantage over service and blue-collar workers and those employed in smaller firms. Full-time workers are nearly twice as likely as part-timers to have paid family leave. Workers in the Pacific Northwest and New England are also more likely to have paid family leave.[156] Among countries with comparable per capita income, those in the G7, the United States provides the fewest mandated maternity leave benefits in both length of leave and amount of paid time off.[157]

In terms of factors related to employment and maternity leave, in the 1970s, the common expectation that women would leave work upon becoming pregnant began to change, and there was an increase in the proportion of families with a

---

154   *Frontiero v. Richardson*, 411 U.S. 677 (1973).

155   Institute for Women's Policy Research, *Maternity Leave in the United States, Paid Parental Leave Is Still Not Standard, Even Among the Best U.S. Employers*.

156   Ibid.

157   Gould, Elise, *Economic Snapshot for May 6, 2009, No paid leave for new U.S. moms*.

second income.[158] A little over half of all American women with a child under 1 year of age are in the labor force. A child's birth often requires changes in a mother's work schedule. In terms of age and educational attainment of first-time mothers, young women giving birth in their late teens and early twenties are just beginning to start families at ages when other women are completing high school and entering college. Women who have delayed childbearing until their late twenties and thirties are more likely to have completed their schooling and accumulated more years of work experience than their younger counterparts. Education and experience can influence income levels and job security, which may in turn influence their decisions about working during pregnancy and how soon to return to work after their first birth. Age at first birth and the educational attainment of new mothers have changed over time. The average age at first birth increased from 21.4 years in 1970 to 24.9 years in 2000. The percentage of first births that were to women aged 30 and over increased between 1970 and 2000, from 4% to 24%. At the same time, the percentage of first births that were to women under 20 years of age dropped from 36% to 23%. In terms of employment history before the first birth, mothers who had their first child between 2001 and 2003, 74% had worked for at least a six-month period in their lives, an increase since the early 1960s, when it was 60% of new mothers. Age is related to whether women have worked before having their first child. For women 30 years and older, 9 out of 10 women who had a first birth in 2001–2003 had worked for at least six consecutive months, compared with 55% of women under 22 years of age. The proportion of first time mothers working full-time during pregnancy was 40% in 1961–1965, increased to over 50% by the late 1970s, and stayed above 50% through 2003. The proportion of first-time mothers working part-time during pregnancy in 1961–1965 was 5%, 11% in 1981–1985 and between 9% and 12% since then.

In terms of women who worked during pregnancy, first-time mothers under age 22 had lower rates of employment during pregnancy than older first-time mothers; 30% of new mothers under age 18 worked while pregnant, compared with 85% of mothers 30 and older. Women who had their first child before their first marriage rather than within or after their first marriage, were less likely to have worked during pregnancy, 53%, 75%, and 84%, respectively. Women who have their first child prior to marriage are generally younger, more likely to be a minority race or Hispanic, and to have lower levels of education. In contrast, women who have their first birth during or after their first marriage are more likely to be older and already in the labor force at the time they become pregnant.

In terms of the duration of work during pregnancy, among all first-time mothers who worked while pregnant, 87% worked into their last trimester, less than three months before their child's birth, while 64% worked into their last month of pregnancy. Older mothers were more likely than younger mothers to work closer to the end of their pregnancies. Eighty-nine per cent of mothers 22 and older worked

---

158   Johnson, Tallese D., *Maternity Leave and Employment Patterns, 2007*, U.S. Census Bureau, Washington, D.C.

into the last three months of their pregnancy, compared with 82% of mothers less than 22 years of age. During the 1980s, a larger proportion of college educated women began to work into the last trimester of their pregnancy than women with less than a high school education; by 2001–2003, 91% of college graduates who worked during their pregnancy were employed into their last trimester, compared with 82% of women who had not graduated from high school. Some women may be motivated to maintain ties to the labor force because of career goals or because their jobs offer attractive leave benefits and do not penalize them for choosing to become mothers. They may also feel they have too much invested in their careers in terms of education, training, and wages to leave the labor force. For 2000–2002, older first-time mothers were more likely to work in the first few months after giving birth than younger first-time mothers. Twenty-eight per cent of mothers 30 or older were working within three months, compared with 15% of mothers less than 18 years old.

In terms of how late into pregnancy first-time mothers have worked since 1961, for the 1961–1965 first-birth cohort, 13% of those who worked during pregnancy reported they stopped working during their first trimester, six or more months before the birth, while 35% worked one month or less before their child's birth. By 1986–1990, the percentage of women who left work in their first trimester had declined to 5%, while the proportion working one month or less before their child's birth more than doubled to 76%. During 1991–1995, 7% of women left work in their first trimester, compared with 4% by the 2001–2003 birth cohort, while the proportion working one month or less before their child's birth increased from 73% in 1991–1995 to 80% in 2001–2003.

In terms of maternity leave arrangements, both paid and unpaid leave were more likely to be used after the child's birth, 43% and 34%, respectively, than during pregnancy, 22% and 16%, respectively. Of women who plan to return to work after having their child, many may work as long as possible into their pregnancy in order to have more leave available to use once their child is born.

In terms of educational attainment, this has increased among all mothers since 1970. In 2000, 25% of mothers had completed 16 or more years of school, compared with 9% in 1970. Among mothers aged 30 to 34, the proportion completing 16 or more years of school increased from 15% to 43%. During this time, an increasing proportion of women 25 to 34 years old continued their education beyond high school. The proportion who had completed four or more years of college approximately doubled from 12% in 1970 to 23% by 1990. By 2006, the proportion with a bachelor's degree or more education had reached 33%. For new mothers in 2001–2003, those with a bachelor's degree or higher were more likely to have worked during pregnancy, 82%, than women with less education, 30% to 75% of women in other educational categories. Educational attainment and age at first birth are related to the likelihood of working during pregnancy. At every level of educational attainment, women 25 or older at the time of their first birth had higher rates of working during pregnancy than younger first-time mothers. Women who became mothers later in life were more likely to have worked at some time prior to their first birth, probably because they had more years of potential working life before their first birth than mothers who had their first birth at younger ages. This finding may reflect a decision to postpone pregnancy in order to gain more work experience, regardless of their level of education. Further, women with a high school degree, some college, or a bachelor's degree or more were more likely to work in the first three months after their child's birth, 30% or more, than women with less than a high school degree, 14%. Women with less than a high school degree were most likely not to work at all in the year after their first child's birth, 62%. Among all mothers, 14% of mothers with less than a high school education were working within three months of their child's birth, compared with 32% of mothers with a bachelor's degree or more. Women who worked later into their pregnancy were more likely to return to work sooner than those who left work earlier in their pregnancy; 45% of women who stopped working one month or less prior to their child's birth were back at work within three months of their birth, but in comparison, 17% of women who left six or more months before their child's birth went back to work within three months.

Overall, since the 1960s, women have experienced gains in education beyond the high school years and have continued to delay childbearing to older ages. Today, women are staying longer at work, returning more rapidly after having their first child and choosing to incorporate work life with childbearing and childrearing.[159]

Conclusion

Legislation has indeed made an impact on discrimination. However, legislation can only help to change attitudes if it operates in conjunction with other policies to promote equal rights and educate employers and workers about their obligations and rights; experience has shown that changing hearts and minds on discrimination is far from easy, and that it is only through doing so that equal respect and treatment of all people will become possible.[160] The keys to the future for equal rights and tolerance of maternity issues in North America are the implementation and development of the law, the deepening in understanding of specific legal issues relating to human rights in the courts, and the raising of the level of awareness of legal rights and obligations, in the pursuit of *Pregnant Pause*. Martin Luther King Jr., in his struggle for civil rights, stated:

> I have a dream that one day every valley shall be exalted, every hill and mountain shall be made plain, and the crooked places shall be made straight and the glory of the Lord will be revealed and all flesh shall see it together. This is our hope ....
> And when we allow freedom to ring, when we let it ring from every village and

---

159   Ibid.

160   Hornstein, Zmira, *Outlawing age discrimination: Foreign lessons, UK choices*, The Policy Press.

hamlet, from every state and city, we will be able to join hands and to sing in the words of the old Negro spiritual, 'Free at last, free at last; thank God Almighty, we are free at last.'[161]

---

161   King Jr., Martin Luther, March on Washington, 1963.

Chapter 7

Pregnant Pause in the North American Free Trade Agreement

Introduction

In the quest for appreciation for maternity issues in employment and trade in *Pregnant Pause*, this chapter will examine efforts against maternity discrimination in the area of the North American Free Trade Agreement (NAFTA), which at the time was the largest economic and legal undertaking ever attempted, having an important impact on the labor force generally and on particular classes of workers specifically. It will look at NAFTA from its inception, examining first its benefits and then its drawbacks. It will also look at the North American Agreement on Labor Cooperation (NAALC) and the Free Trade Area of the Americas (FTAA), as well as legislation of the Americas, namely the American Declaration of the Rights and Duties of Man, the American Convention on Human Rights, the Statute of the Inter-American Court on Human Rights, and the Inter-American Democratic Charter.

Toward the North American Free Trade Agreement (NAFTA)

There were several developments in the relationship between the United States and British North America, what was to become Canada. The War of 1812 brought an end to the fear of American annexation of Canada, with a new view of commercial and economic rivalry between the two countries. The Canadian national sentiment favored trade with the United States through transportation via the railways and the waterways.[1] The Elgin-Marcy Reciprocity Treaty 1854 was the first major trade pact between the United States and Canada. Reciprocity was an attempt to create, in North America, a single market area covering several distinct political jurisdictions, where specified types of products were freely exchanged for a partial and limited economic union between British North America and the United States.[2] The American Civil War influenced the economic development of British North America, with new markets in the United States opening for Canadian exports. However, the Treaty was abrogated by the United States on 17 March 1866, due

---

1   Hamelin, Jean, *Histoire du Québec*, Edisem, St. Hyacinthe, 1976, p.371.

2   Easterbrook, W.T. and Aitken, Hugh, *Canadian Economic History*, Macmillan, Toronto, 1976, p.362.

to several antagonizing factors for the United States, namely British support for the Confederacy during the Civil War, new Canadian tariffs, the disastrous effects on timber- and grain-growing regions of the United States, the resentment by farming and lumber interests to Canadian competition, the jealousy by shipping and forwarding interests in Buffalo and Philadelphia of the St Lawrence Route and of the Grand Trunk Railway system with the Victoria Bridge completion in Montreal in 1860 furthering competition, and the manufacturing interests blaming Canadian tariffs for the decline of certain exports.[3] While Canada's policy in economic relations was to favor east–west relations, the natural tendencies were the opposite, north–south.

The 1911 Free Trade Agreement allowed Canada to build up its own manufacturing protection tariff.[4] With the exception of Britain, Canada was the chief trading partner of the United States.[5] American President Taft negotiated for full-scale reciprocity for better trade relations between the United States and Canada, since common interests called for special arrangements, and Canadians and Americans were reminded that there were 3,000 miles of joint border between the two countries. Most American tariffs on manufacturing goods were reduced, while most Canadian manufacturing tariffs remained. Canadian Prime Minister Laurier was the first continentalist Prime Minister to appreciate that Canada shares North America with the United States, which shapes the national destiny; however, subsequent Canadian Prime Minister Borden opposed the trade legislation and did not put the reciprocity agreement to a vote, with the United States rescinding its vote eight years later.

The General Agreement on Tariffs and Trade (GATT) 1947 had as its purpose to promote global trade between members through a reduction in tariffs. Canada wished for trade on a liberalized basis, the first Article of GATT, and same treatment. GATT provided for an impressive reduction of tariffs, with some even impeding economic efficiency, production, competition and growth. It permitted the United States and Canada to enter into free trade, with an agreement to remove customs duties and other restrictions on substantially all bilateral trade.[6] Over the last years of GATT and the advent of the World Trade Organization (WTO), Canadian exports multiplied 10 times, the national wealth more than tripled and

---

3   Fry, Earl, 'Trends in Canada-U.S. Free Trade Discussions', in A.R. Riggs and Tom Welk, *Canadian-American Free Trade: Historical, Political and Economic Dimensions*, The Institute for Research in Public Policy, Montreal, 1987, p.28.

4   d'Aquino, Thomas, 'Truck and Trade with the Yankees, The Case for a Canada-U.S. Comprehensive Trade Agreement', in A.R. Riggs and Tom Velk, *Canadian-American Free Trade: Historical, Political and Economic Dimensions*, The Institute for Research on Public Policy, Montreal, 1987, p.74.

5   Velk, Tom, and Riggs, A.R., 'The Ongoing Debate Over Free Trade', in A.R. Riggs and Tom Velk, *Canadian-American Free Trade: (The Sequel) Historical, Political and Economic Dimensions*, The Institute for Research on Public Policy, Montreal, 1988, p.93.

6   General Agreement on Tariffs and Trade, at Article 24.

the number of jobs doubled.[7] War-time demands required greater cooperation on a continental basis, with Canada and Mexico being prime sources of raw materials for American factories. Private negotiations on free trade once again took place in 1947 between American President Truman and Canadian Prime Minister King, with the latter approving the agreement at first but later vetoing it because of fear that the Canadian public would label it continentalist and anti-British.[8]

There is a regional aspect to the overall economic evolution of the North American continent. Canada's industrial development has been North American, with its development based on its natural resources, and its expansion characterized by large-scale monopolistic industries. Over time, Canada's dealings with Britain and the United States changed. Canada once had an autonomous relationship with Britain, producing an un-American sentiment. Britain used to be the major investor in Canada. However, over the years, the United States has replaced it. Canada went from dependence on Britain to dependence on the United States, thus producing a foreign-controlled economy. In addition, the nature of foreign investment had changed, since the British invested indirectly through obligations and finance, while the Americans invested directly, usually as proprietors funding production. The Canadian policy, interestingly, was to increase tariffs and oblige U.S. companies wishing to do business to build factories in Canada. Therefore, the United States penetrated the Canadian economy by installing branch plants for American-made products. Today, Canada sends more than three-quarters of all its exports to the United States, accounting for 25% of its annual gross national product.[9] The policy process resulted in the overwhelming trade dependence of Canada on the United States over the years, with Canada's trade pattern from the outset based on the importing of manufactured goods in return for the exporting of staples to more advanced industrialized economies as the engine of growth of the Canadian economy.[10] The commercial rather than industrial bias of the Canadian capitalist class, along with dependent branch plant industrialization, flowed from the unequal alliance with American foreign ownership and capital; Canada was within the tight embrace of the American empire, and occupied whatever room was left open by U.S. capital, becoming the exemplary client State.[11]

---

7   Laun, Louis, 'U.S.-Canada Free Trade Negotiations: Historical Opportunities', in A.R. Riggs and Tom Velk, *Canadian-American Free Trade: Historical, Political and Economic Dimensions*, The Institute for Research in Public Policy, Montreal, 1987, p.205.

8   Fry, Earl, 'Trends in Canada-U.S. Free Trade Discussions', in A.R. Riggs and Tom Velk, *Canadian-American Free Trade: Historical, Political and Economic Dimensions*, The Institute for Research in Public Policy, Montreal, 1987, p.9.

9   Ibid., at p.27.

10   Watkins, Mel, 'The Political Economy of Growth', in Wallace Clement and Glen Williams, *The New Canadian Political Economy*, McGill-Queen's University Press, Kingston, 1989, p.17.

11   Laun, Louis, 'U.S.-Canada Free Trade Negotiations: Historical Opportunities', in A.R. Riggs and Tom Velk, *Canadian-American Free Trade: Historical, Political and Economic Dimensions*, The Institute for Research in Public Policy, Montreal, 1987, p.205.

The service industry has subtle impediments, with discrimination being a barrier because of immigration labor laws, which are most evident today with illegal immigration at an all-time high. National treatment calls for no regulatory distinction between foreign and domestic firms, which is good if there are similar industries for reciprocity and market access.[12] These laws restrict one country's firms from transferring staff to the other country. Trade in services encompasses a large number of areas, having different characteristics of trade and efforts for international rule-making.

The 1989 Canada United States Free Trade Agreement (FTA) had as its goal to remove all or most remaining barriers to cross-border trade in goods and services, and to create an enlarged body of agreed rules to govern trade. President Ronald Reagan called the document, signed on 2 January 1988, the most important bilateral trade negotiation ever undertaken by the United States. It was horizontal, not sectoral, for market access, and called for mutual restraint on unilateral commercial policies. The United States absorbs 80% of Canada's exports, in a southward flow,[13] has an economy 10 times bigger than Canada's, affording the latter greater access to opportunities. This Free Trade Agreement was the biggest trade agreement ever reached between two countries, in excess of $200 billion in trade of goods and services.[14]

North American Free Trade Agreement (NAFTA)

In 1991, Canada, the United States and Mexico began negotiations for the North American Free Trade Agreement (NAFTA). The free trade agenda shifted from a sectoral approach to a comprehensive accord among the three countries because of a difficulty in matching sectors and in accommodating regional concerns. The 1989 Canada United States Free Trade Agreement laid the foundation for NAFTA, which secured Canada's economic relationship with the United States. Prior to NAFTA coming into effect on 1 January 1994, trade between the United States and Canada had never been larger and was growing faster than the rest of the economy. In addition, the flow of trade and investment among the United States, Canada and Mexico was $500 billion per year. Mexico has a rapidly growing market of over 85

---

12   Neufeld, E.P., 'Financial and Economic Dimensions of Free Trade', in A.R. Riggs and Tom Velk, *Canadian-American Free Trade: Historical, Political and Economic Dimensions*, The Institute for Research on Public Policy, Montreal, 1987, p.152.

13   d'Aquino, Thomas, 'Truck and Trade with the Yankees, The Case for a Canada-U.S. Comprehensive Trade Agreement', in A.R. Riggs and Tom Velk, *Canadian-American Free Trade: Historical, Political and Economic Dimensions*, The Institute for Research on Public Policy, Montreal, 1987, p.74.

14   Velk, Tom, and Riggs, A.R., 'The Ongoing Debate Over Free Trade', in A.R. Riggs and Tom Velk, *Canadian-American Free Trade: (The Sequel) Historical, Political and Economic Dimensions*, The Institute for Research on Public Policy, Montreal, 1988, p.3.

million people, which historically was hard to penetrate because of strict Mexican barriers to trade. Before NAFTA, Mexico was restrictive on foreign investment. However, with NAFTA, Mexican tariffs are phased out over time. Mexico's border is aligned with the United States and its coastline faces Europe and Asia. It has a key global strategic advantage with its unique geographic position, and is considered the gateway to Latin America, being ranked twelfth in area among the world's nations.[15] The regulatory environment must ensure the rules of the game are clear and uniformly applied, subject to monitoring.

NAFTA was the biggest trade agreement ever signed at the time, covering 360 million consumers and far-reaching to remove all tariffs and liberalize non-tariff barriers to trade. It regulates trade in services, liberalizes investment, promotes specialization and implements a mechanism for a binding resolution to disputes, which is unprecedented in free trade. The objectives of NAFTA are the removal of tariff and non-tariff barriers for goods and services, the neutralization of government policies, practices and procedures, and a consistency with the GATT agreement to cover all trade.[16] The long-term goals of free trade are the improvement of real income wages and production, an increase in the number of jobs, a reduction of protectionism, a decrease in competitive pressures from developing and newly industrialized countries, and the mitigation of pressures due to global imbalances.[17]

NAFTA provided that tariffs would be removed within 10 years in the traditional sectors, accounting for half of the trade, and removed either immediately, in five years or exceptionally in 20 years for the remainder, moving toward a harmonized system of tariff nomenclature. It has quantitative restrictions, which build on GATT, and has a sectoral perspective as to agriculture, foods, automotives and energy. There are new elements to the agreement, which include the restriction of investment, the freedom in the future to regulate in conformity with the basic principles of non-discrimination, and the principles of national treatment, right of establishment and right of commercial presence. NAFTA sets out strict rules of origin to qualify for preferential duties, requiring that products originate in North America.

The NAFTA Secretariat, comprising the Canadian, American and Mexican Sections, is an organization established by the Free Trade Commission, pursuant to the North American Free Trade Agreement. It is responsible for the administration of the dispute settlement provisions of the Agreement, and its mandate includes the

---

15   Mexican Investment Board, *Mexico Your Partner for Growth, Regulatory Reform and Competition Policy, Setting the Incentives for an Efficient Economy*, Mexico, 1994, p.1.

16   Laun, Louis, 'U.S.-Canada Free Trade Negotiations: Historical Opportunities', in A.R. Riggs and Tom Velk, *Canadian-American Free Trade: Historical, Political and Economic Dimensions*, The Institute for Research in Public Policy, Montreal, 1987, p.208.

17   Harris, Richard, 'Some Observations on the Canada-U.S. Free Trade Deal', in A.R. Riggs and Tom Velk, *Canadian-American Free Trade: (The Sequel) Historical, Political and Economic Dimensions*, The Institute for Research on Public Policy, Montreal 1988, p.52.

provision of assistance to the Commission, and support for various non-dispute-related committees and working groups. Each national Section maintains a court-like registry relating to panel, committee and tribunal proceedings. A similar administrative body, the Binational Secretariat, existed under the Canada United States Free Trade Agreement (FTA). The Parties have established permanent national Section offices, which are 'mirror-images' of one another, and are located in Ottawa, Washington and Mexico City respectively.

Importantly, the principle dispute settlement mechanisms of NAFTA are found in Chapters 11, 14, 19 and 20 of the Agreement. NAFTA establishes a mechanism for the settlement of disputes that assures both equal treatment among Parties in accordance with the principle of international reciprocity and due process before an impartial tribunal. Alternatively, the investor may choose the remedies available in the host country's domestic courts. An important feature of the arbitral provisions is the enforceability in domestic courts of final awards by arbitration tribunals. NAFTA provides for a trade commission in charge of political management, which includes a dispute settlement mechanism in the form of a panel, with an important role of the Commission to consider matters relating to the Agreement which are under dispute. When general disputes concerning NAFTA are not resolved through consultation within a specified period of time, the matter may be referred at the request of either Party to a non-binding panel. Various third-party provisions are necessarily included, as a third party that considers it has a substantial interest in a disputed matter is entitled to join consultations or a proceeding as a complaining Party on written notice, but it does not join as a complainant, upon written notice, it is entitled to attend hearings, make written and oral submissions and receive written submissions of the disputing Parties. There is also a provision for an advisory committee to be established to provide recommendations to the Commission on the use of arbitration and other procedures for the resolution of international private commercial disputes, and if nothing results from the notification of a consultation action, then a panel review ensues with recommendations that are binding if both sides agree. The dispute settlement is also binding when one side believes that a surge of imports is damaging to it, thereby receiving compensation while the other side is snapped back to a most-favored nation tariff. This procedure was in effect for the first 10 years of the agreement, providing steps for negotiation, legislation specificity and panel review. The settlement mechanism calls for compulsory consultation on changes of law and an evaluation procedure by a panel, with the right to retaliate or withdraw if the panel so favors. NAFTA also provides, for the first time, a system of settling private investment disputes in that those between an investor from a NAFTA country and another NAFTA government can be settled at the investor's option by binding international arbitration, with all investors treated equally. The dispute settlement provisions call for the rapid and fair settlement of disputes, including the use of impartial panels, and there are three basic steps to the process: first, consultation among the three countries for a satisfactory settlement; second, if the first round fails, the NAFTA trade commission, comprising cabinet-level representatives, will examine the case for interpretation of trade rules; and third, if the second round fails, in order to promote an impartial decision, the issue will be reviewed by a specially selected panel, which is composed of five members chosen from a trilaterally agreed roster, with two panelists from the complaining party selected by the defending party, two from the defending party nominated by the complainant and the panel's chair allowed to be a representative from the third NAFTA country or another neutral country chosen by mutual agreement or drawn by lot.

In terms of employment, cross-border trade in services was first included in the Canada United States Free Trade Agreement, and NAFTA has extended these codes of binding rules and principles with procedures to encourage the recognition of licenses and certificates through mutually acceptable professional standards and criteria, such as education, experience and professional development. It opens up temporary entry across the border for over 60 professions. Further, there is a provision as to access for temporary personnel in the service and manufacturing sectors, as well as business recognition of professional and sales services in the spirit of freedom of movement. This latter aspect, however, has not yet been extended to blue-collar workers. As such, Canada's service industry is the fastest growing sector of the economy, accounting for the employment of roughly 10 million Canadians and two-thirds of the workforce, as well as providing 90% of all new jobs in Canada in the last several years. Canada's export of services around the world totals an average of $24 billion per year, with business and professional services accounting for 20% of these exports. Virtually all services are covered by NAFTA, with key sectors being: accounting, architecture, land transport, publishing, consulting, commercial education, environmental services, enhanced telecommunications, advertising, broadcasting, construction, tourism, engineering, health care, management and legal services. Each country has also excluded certain sensitive sectors from coverage, such that Mexico will not liberalize services of public notaries, which are specifically reserved to Mexicans by the Mexican Constitution, and Canada has retained its cultural exclusion, which affects the entertainment and publishing industries. NAFTA does not remove or weaken licensing and certification requirements but, consistent with the principle of non-discrimination, licensing of professionals, such as lawyers, doctors and accountants, are based on objective criteria aimed at ensuring competence, not nationality, so that NAFTA does not permit American, Mexican or Canadian professionals to practice in the other member countries, unless they have undergone the same licensing and certification procedures as a national professional. Overall, NAFTA obliges one country's service providers to treat the other country's no less favorably than their own for domestic and cross-border sales, distribution and the right of establishment of facilities, providing for mutually acceptable professional licensing standards. However, the equal employment provision in the Member States must go further to protect against any form of discrimination, including maternity discrimination.

The Preamble of the North American Free Trade Agreement states:

The Government of Canada, the Government of the United Mexican States and the Government of the United States of America, resolved to:

STRENGTHEN the special bonds of friendship and cooperation among their nations;

CONTRIBUTE to the harmonious development and expansion of world trade and provide a catalyst to broader international cooperation;

CREATE an expanded and secure market for the goods and services produced in their territories;

REDUCE distortions to trade;

ESTABLISH clear and mutually advantageous rules governing their trade;

ENSURE a predictable commercial framework for business planning and investment;

BUILD on their respective rights and obligations under the *General Agreement on Tariffs and Trade* and other multilateral and bilateral instruments of cooperation;

ENHANCE the competitiveness of their firms in global markets;

FOSTER creativity and innovation, and promote trade in goods and services that are the subject of intellectual property rights;

CREATE new employment opportunities and improve working conditions and living standards in their respective territories;

UNDERTAKE each of the preceding in a manner consistent with environmental protection and conservation;

PRESERVE their flexibility to safeguard the public welfare;

PROMOTE sustainable development;

STRENGTHEN the development and enforcement of environmental laws and regulations; and

PROTECT, enhance and enforce basic workers' rights.[18]

---

18   North American Free Trade Agreement, at the Preamble.

Under the agreement, in terms of service providers, Article 1201 applies to measures adopted or maintained by a Party relating to cross-border trade in services by service providers of another Party, including measures respecting the production, distribution, marketing, sale and delivery of a service; the purchase or use of, or payment for, a service; the access to and use of distribution and transportation systems in connection with the provision of a service; the presence in its territory of a service provider of another Party; and the provision of a bond or other form of financial security as a condition for the provision of a service.[19] Articles 1202 and 1203 provide that each Party shall accord to service providers of another Party treatment no less favorable than that it accords, in like circumstances, to service providers of any other Party or of a non-Party.[20] Further, Article 1208 maintains that each Party shall set out in its Schedule to Annex VI its commitments to liberalize quantitative restrictions, licensing requirements, performance requirements or other non-discriminatory measures.[21] Professional services are defined in Article 1213 as services, the provision of which requires specialized post-secondary education, or equivalent training or experience, and for which the right to practice is granted or restricted by a Party, but does not include services provided by tradespersons or vessel and aircraft crew members.[22]

Important to all workers, including female workers, Article 1210 provides for licensing and certification requirements:

> 1210. 1. With a view to ensuring that any measure adopted or maintained by a Party relating to the licensing or certification of nationals of another Party does not constitute an unnecessary barrier to trade, each Party shall endeavor to ensure that any such measure:
>   a. is based on objective and transparent criteria, such as competence and the ability to provide a service;
>   b. is not more burdensome than necessary to ensure the quality of a service; and
>   c. does not constitute a disguised restriction on the cross-border provision of a service.
>
> 2. … a Party shall not be required to extend to a service provider of another Party the benefits of recognition of education, experience, licenses or certifications obtained in another country, whether such recognition was accorded unilaterally or by arrangement or agreement with that other country. The Party according such recognition shall afford any interested Party an adequate opportunity to demonstrate that education, experience, licenses or certifications obtained in that other Party's

---

19   Ibid., at Article 1201.
20   Ibid., at Article 1202, 1203.
21   Ibid., at Article 1208.
22   Ibid., at Article 1213.

territory should also be recognized or to negotiate and enter into an agreement or arrangement of comparable effect.

3. ... a Party shall eliminate any citizenship or permanent residency requirement for the licensing and certification of professional service providers in its territory ....[23]

Further, licensing and certification standards for professionals are provided for in Annex 1210.A.2.:

Annex 1210.A.2. The Parties shall encourage the relevant bodies in their respective territories to develop mutually acceptable standards and criteria for licensing and certification of professional service providers and to provide recommendations on mutual recognition to the Commission.[24]

Additionally, Annex 1210.A.3. provides for standards and criteria to be developed:

Annex 1210.A.3. The standards and criteria referred to in paragraph 2 may be developed with regard to the following matters:
a. education: accreditation of schools or academic programs;
b. examinations: qualifying examinations for licensing, including alternative methods of assessment such as oral examinations and interviews;
c. experience: length and nature of experience required for licensing;
d. conduct and ethics: standards of professional conduct and the nature of disciplinary action for non-conformity with those standards;
e. professional development and re-certification: continuing education and ongoing requirements to maintain professional certification;
f. scope of practice: extent of, or limitations on, permissible activities;
g. local knowledge: requirements for knowledge of such matters as local laws, regulations, language, geography or climate; and
h. consumer protection: alternatives to residency requirements, including bonding, professional liability insurance and client restitution funds, to provide for the protection of consumers.[25]

Finally, Annex 1210.B.1. provides that each Party shall, in implementing its obligations and commitments regarding foreign legal consultants as set out in its relevant Schedules and subject to any reservations therein, ensure that a national

---

23 Ibid., at Article 1210.
24 Ibid., at Annex 1210.A.2.
25 Ibid., at Annex 1210.A.3.

of another Party is permitted to practice or advise on the law of any country in which that national is authorized to practice as a lawyer.[26]

In terms of the temporary entry for people to conduct business, Chapter 16 and specifically Article 1601 specify:

> 1601. This Chapter reflects the preferential trading relationship between the Parties, the desirability of facilitating temporary entry on a reciprocal basis and of establishing transparent criteria and procedures for temporary entry, and the need to ensure border security and to protect the domestic labor force and permanent employment in their respective territories.[27]

Article 1602 outlines the general obligations:

> 1602. 1. Each Party shall apply its measures relating to the provisions of this Chapter in accordance with Article 1601 and, in particular, shall apply expeditiously those measures so as to avoid unduly impairing or delaying trade in goods or services or conduct of investment activities under this Agreement.
> 2. The Parties shall endeavor to develop and adopt common criteria, definitions and interpretations for the implementation of this Chapter.[28]

Additional requirements are noted in Annex 1603, in order to gain entry for different classes of individuals in employment situations. Section A provides for business visitors:

> Annex 1603.A.1. Each Party shall grant temporary entry to a business person seeking to engage in a business activity set out in Appendix 1603.A.1, without requiring that person to obtain an employment authorization, provided that the business person otherwise complies with existing immigration measures applicable to temporary entry, on presentation of:
> a. proof of citizenship of a Party;
> b. documentation demonstrating that the business person will be so engaged and describing the purpose of entry; and
> c. evidence demonstrating that the proposed business activity is international in scope and that the business person is not seeking to enter the local labor market.
> 2. Each Party shall provide that a business person may satisfy the requirements of paragraph 1(c) by demonstrating that:

---

26 Ibid., at Annex 1210.B.1.
27 Ibid., at Article 1601.
28 Ibid., at Article 1602.

a. the primary source of remuneration for the proposed business activity is outside the territory of the Party granting temporary entry; and

b. the business person's principal place of business and the actual place of accrual of profits, at least predominantly, remain outside such territory.

A Party shall normally accept an oral declaration as to the principal place of business and the actual place of accrual of profits. Where the Party requires further proof, it shall normally consider a letter from the employer attesting to these matters as sufficient proof.

3. Each Party shall grant temporary entry to a business person seeking to engage in a business activity other than those set out in Appendix 1603.A.1, without requiring that person to obtain an employment authorization, on a basis no less favorable than that provided under the existing provisions of the measures set out in Appendix 1603.A.3, provided that the business person otherwise complies with existing immigration measures applicable to temporary entry.

4. No Party may:

a. as a condition for temporary entry under paragraph 1 or 3, require prior approval procedures, petitions, labor certification tests or other procedures of similar effect; or

b. impose or maintain any numerical restriction relating to temporary entry under paragraph 1 or 3.

5. Notwithstanding paragraph 4, a Party may require a business person seeking temporary entry under this Section to obtain a visa or its equivalent prior to entry. Before imposing a visa requirement, the Party shall consult with a Party whose business persons would be affected with a view to avoiding the imposition of the requirement. With respect to an existing visa requirement, a Party shall consult, on request, with a Party whose business persons are subject to the requirement with a view to its removal.[29]

Section B provides for traders and investors:

Annex 1603.B.1. Each Party shall grant temporary entry and provide confirming documentation to a business person seeking to:

a. carry on substantial trade in goods or services principally between the territory of the Party of which the business person is a citizen and the territory of the Party into which entry is sought, or

b. establish, develop, administer or provide advice or key technical services to the operation of an investment to which the business person or the business person's enterprise has committed, or is in the process of committing, a substantial amount of capital, in a

---

29 Ibid., at Annex 1603.A.

capacity that is supervisory, executive or involves essential skills, provided that the business person otherwise complies with existing immigration measures applicable to temporary entry.

2. No Party may:
    a. as a condition for temporary entry under paragraph 1, require labor certification tests or other procedures of similar effect; or
    b. impose or maintain any numerical restriction relating to temporary entry under paragraph 1.
3. Notwithstanding paragraph 2, a Party may require a business person seeking temporary entry under this Section to obtain a visa or its equivalent prior to entry.[30]

Section C provides for intra-company transferees:

Annex 1603.C.1. Each Party shall grant temporary entry and provide confirming documentation to a business person employed by an enterprise who seeks to render services to that enterprise or a subsidiary or affiliate thereof, in a capacity that is managerial, executive or involves specialized knowledge, provided that the business person otherwise complies with existing immigration measures applicable to temporary entry. A Party may require the business person to have been employed continuously by the enterprise for one year within the three-year period immediately preceding the date of the application for admission.

2. No Party may:
    a. as a condition for temporary entry under paragraph 1, require labor certification tests or other procedures of similar effect; or
    b. impose or maintain any numerical restriction relating to temporary entry under paragraph 1.
3. Notwithstanding paragraph 2, a Party may require a business person seeking temporary entry under this Section to obtain a visa or its equivalent prior to entry. Before imposing a visa requirement, the Party shall consult with a Party whose business persons would be affected with a view to avoiding the imposition of the requirement. With respect to an existing visa requirement, a Party shall consult, on request, with a Party whose business persons are subject to the requirement with a view to its removal.[31]

Section D provides for professionals:

Annex 1603.D.1. Each Party shall grant temporary entry and provide confirming documentation to a business person seeking to engage in a business

---

30 Ibid., at Annex 1603.B.
31 Ibid., at Annex 1603.C.

activity at a professional level in a profession set out in Appendix 1603. D.1, if the business person otherwise complies with existing immigration measures applicable to temporary entry, on presentation of:

a. proof of citizenship of a Party; and

b. documentation demonstrating that the business person will be so engaged and describing the purpose of entry.

2. No Party may:

a. as a condition for temporary entry under paragraph 1, require prior approval procedures, petitions, labor certification tests or other procedures of similar effect; or

b. impose or maintain any numerical restriction relating to temporary entry under paragraph 1.

3. Notwithstanding paragraph 2, a Party may require a business person seeking temporary entry under this Section to obtain a visa or its equivalent prior to entry. Before imposing a visa requirement, the Party shall consult with a Party whose business persons would be affected with a view to avoiding the imposition of the requirement. With respect to an existing visa requirement, a Party shall consult, on request, with a Party whose business persons are subject to the requirement with a view to its removal.

4. Notwithstanding paragraphs 1 and 2, a Party may establish an annual numerical limit, which shall be set out in Appendix 1603.D.4, regarding temporary entry of business persons of another Party seeking to engage in business activities at a professional level in a profession set out in Appendix 1603.D.1, if the Parties concerned have not agreed otherwise prior to the date of entry into force of this Agreement for those Parties. In establishing such a limit, the Party shall consult with the other Party concerned.

5. A Party establishing a numerical limit pursuant to paragraph 4, unless the Parties concerned agree otherwise:

a. shall, for each year after the first year after the date of entry into force of this Agreement, consider increasing the numerical limit set out in Appendix 1603.D.4 by an amount to be established in consultation with the other Party concerned, taking into account the demand for temporary entry under this Section;

b. shall not apply its procedures established pursuant to paragraph 1 to the temporary entry of a business person subject to the numerical limit, but may require the business person to comply with its other procedures applicable to the temporary entry of professionals; and

c. may, in consultation with the other Party concerned, grant temporary entry under paragraph 1 to a business person who practices in a profession where accreditation, licensing, and certification requirements are mutually recognized by those Parties.

6. Nothing in paragraph 4 or 5 shall be construed to limit the ability of a business person to seek temporary entry under a Party's applicable immigration measures relating to the entry of professionals other than those adopted or maintained pursuant to paragraph 1.[32]

Finally, Appendix 1603.D.1 outlines the different professions provided for under NAFTA, along with the minimum educational requirements and alternative credentials.[33]

There are a number of institutions that are part of NAFTA. Article 2001 provides for the Free Trade Commission:

2001. 1. The Parties hereby establish the Free Trade Commission, comprising cabinet-level representatives of the Parties or their designees.
2. The Commission shall:
    a. supervise the implementation of this Agreement;
    b. oversee its further elaboration;
    c. resolve disputes that may arise regarding its interpretation or application;
    d. supervise the work of all committees and working groups established under this Agreement ...; and
    e. consider any other matter that may affect the operation of this Agreement.
3. The Commission may:
    a. establish, and delegate responsibilities to, ad hoc or standing committees, working groups or expert groups;
    b. seek the advice of nongovernmental persons or groups; and
    c. take such other action in the exercise of its functions as the Parties may agree.[34]

Further, Article 2002 provides for the Secretariat:

2002. 1. The Commission shall establish and oversee a Secretariat comprising national Sections.
2. Each Party shall:
    a. establish a permanent office of its Section;
    b. be responsible for
        i.   the operation and costs of its Section, and
        ii. the remuneration and payment of expenses of panelists and members of committees and scientific review boards established under this Agreement, as set out in Annex 2002.2;

---

32 Ibid., at Annex 1603.D.
33 Ibid., at Appendix 1603.D.1.
34 Ibid., at Article 2001.

    c. designate an individual to serve as Secretary for its Section, who shall be responsible for its administration and management; and

    d. notify the Commission of the location of its Section's office.

3. The Secretariat shall:

    a. provide assistance to the Commission;

    b. provide administrative assistance to

       i. panels and committees established under Chapter Nineteen (Review and Dispute Settlement in Antidumping and Countervailing Duty Matters), in accordance with the procedures established pursuant to Article 1908, and

       ii. panels established under this Chapter, in accordance with procedures established pursuant to Article 2012; and

    c. as the Commission may direct

       i. support the work of other committees and groups established under this Agreement, and

       ii. otherwise facilitate the operation of this Agreement.[35]

Importantly, in terms of a dispute settlement, cooperation is stressed under Article 2003:

> 2003. The Parties shall at all times endeavor to agree on the interpretation and application of this Agreement, and shall make every attempt through cooperation and consultations to arrive at a mutually satisfactory resolution of any matter that might affect its operation.[36]

Recourse to dispute settlement procedures is enunciated under Articles 1606 and 2004:

> 1606. 1. A Party may not initiate proceedings under Article 2007 (Commission – Good Offices, Conciliation and Mediation) regarding a refusal to grant temporary entry under this Chapter or a particular case arising under Article 1602(1) unless:
>
>   a. the matter involves a pattern of practice; and
>
>   b. the business person has exhausted the available administrative remedies regarding the particular matter.
>
>   2. The remedies referred to in paragraph (1) (b) shall be deemed to be exhausted if a final determination in the matter has not been issued by the competent authority within one year of the institution of an administrative proceeding, and the failure to issue a determination is not attributable to delay caused by the business person.[37]

---

35 Ibid., at Article 2002.

36 Ibid., at Article 2003.

37 Ibid., at Article 1606.

2004. Except for the matters covered in Chapter Nineteen (Review and Dispute Settlement in Antidumping and Countervailing Duty Matters) and as otherwise provided in this Agreement, the dispute settlement provisions of this Chapter shall apply with respect to the avoidance or settlement of all disputes between the Parties regarding the interpretation or application of this Agreement or wherever a Party considers that an actual or proposed measure of another Party is or would be inconsistent with the obligations of this Agreement or cause nullification or impairment in the sense of Annex 2004.[38]

Further, in terms of panel proceedings, a request for an arbitral panel is contained in Article 2008:

2008. 1. If the Commission has convened pursuant to Article 2007(4), and the matter has not been resolved within:
   a. 30 days thereafter,
   b. 30 days after the Commission has convened in respect of the matter most recently referred to it, where proceedings have been consolidated pursuant to Article 2007(6), or
   c. such other period as the consulting Parties may agree,
   any consulting Party may request in writing the establishment of an arbitral panel. The requesting Party shall deliver the request to the other Parties and to its Section of the Secretariat.
2. On delivery of the request, the Commission shall establish an arbitral panel.
3. A third Party that considers it has a substantial interest in the matter shall be entitled to join as a complaining Party on delivery of written notice of its intention to participate to the disputing Parties and its Section of the Secretariat. The notice shall be delivered at the earliest possible time, and in any event no later than seven days after the date of delivery of a request by a Party for the establishment of a panel.
4. If a third Party does not join as a complaining Party in accordance with paragraph 3, it normally shall refrain thereafter from initiating or continuing:
   a. a dispute settlement procedure under this Agreement, or
   b. a dispute settlement proceeding in the GATT on grounds that are substantially equivalent to those available to that Party under this Agreement,
   regarding the same matter in the absence of a significant change in economic or commercial circumstances.

---

38   Ibid., at Article 2004.

5. Unless otherwise agreed by the disputing Parties, the panel shall be established and perform its functions in a manner consistent with the provisions of this Chapter.[39]

The rules of procedure are outlined in Article 2012:

2012. 1. The Commission shall establish by January 1, 1994, Model Rules of Procedure, in accordance with the following principles:
   a. the procedures shall assure a right to at least one hearing before the panel as well as the opportunity to provide initial and rebuttal written submissions; and
   b. the panel's hearings, deliberations and initial report, and all written submissions to and communications with the panel shall be confidential.
2. Unless the disputing Parties otherwise agree, the panel shall conduct its proceedings in accordance with the Model Rules of Procedure.
3. Unless the disputing Parties otherwise agree within 20 days from the date of the delivery of the request for the establishment of the panel, the terms of reference shall be:

'To examine, in the light of the relevant provisions of the Agreement, the matter referred to the Commission (as set out in the request for a Commission meeting) and to make findings, determinations and recommendations as provided in Article 2016(2)'.[40]

Third party participation is permitted under Article 2013:

2013. A Party that is not a disputing Party, on delivery of a written notice to the disputing Parties and to its Section of the Secretariat, shall be entitled to attend all hearings, to make written and oral submissions to the panel and to receive written submissions of the disputing Parties.

The panel's final report is contained in Article 2017:

2017. 1. The panel shall present to the disputing Parties a final report, including any separate opinions on matters not unanimously agreed, within 30 days of presentation of the initial report, unless the disputing Parties otherwise agree.[41]

Implementation of the final report is stressed under Article 2018:

---

39   Ibid., at Article 2008.
40   Ibid., at Article 2012.
41   Ibid., at Article 2017.

2018. 1. On receipt of the final report of a panel, the disputing Parties shall agree on the resolution of the dispute, which normally shall conform with the determinations and recommendations of the panel, and shall notify their Sections of the Secretariat of any agreed resolution of any dispute.[42]

Importantly, non-implementation and the suspension of benefits are provided for under Article 2019:

2019. 1. If in its final report a panel has determined that a measure is inconsistent with the obligations of this Agreement or causes nullification or impairment in the sense of Annex 2004 and the Party complained against has not reached agreement with any complaining Party on a mutually satisfactory resolution pursuant to Article 2018(1) within 30 days of receiving the final report, such complaining Party may suspend the application to the Party complained against of benefits of equivalent effect until such time as they have reached agreement on a resolution of the dispute.

2. In considering what benefits to suspend pursuant to paragraph 1:

a. a complaining Party should first seek to suspend benefits in the same sector or sectors as that affected by the measure or other matter that the panel has found to be inconsistent with the obligations of this Agreement or to have caused nullification or impairment in the sense of Annex 2004; and

b. a complaining Party that considers it is not practicable or effective to suspend benefits in the same sector or sectors may suspend benefits in other sectors.[43]

In terms of domestic proceedings and a private commercial dispute settlement, Article 2020 provides for referrals of matters from judicial or administrative proceedings:

2020. 1. If an issue of interpretation or application of this Agreement arises in any domestic judicial or administrative proceeding of a Party that any Party considers would merit its intervention, or if a court or administrative body solicits the views of a Party, that Party shall notify the other Parties and its Section of the Secretariat. The Commission shall endeavor to agree on an appropriate response as expeditiously as possible.

2. The Party in whose territory the court or administrative body is located shall submit any agreed interpretation of the Commission to the court or administrative body in accordance with the rules of that forum.

---

42   Ibid., at Article 2018.
43   Ibid., at Article 2019.

3. If the Commission is unable to agree, any Party may submit its own views to the court or administrative body in accordance with the rules of that forum.[44]

Further, private rights are guaranteed under Article 2021:

2021. No Party may provide for a right of action under its domestic law against any other Party on the ground that a measure of another Party is inconsistent with this Agreement.[45]

Finally, Article 2022 provides for alternative dispute resolution:

2022. 1. Each Party shall, to the maximum extent possible, encourage and facilitate the use of arbitration and other means of alternative dispute resolution for the settlement of international commercial disputes between private parties in the free trade area.

2. To this end, each Party shall provide appropriate procedures to ensure observance of agreements to arbitrate and for the recognition and enforcement of arbitral awards in such disputes.[46]

North American Agreement on Labor Cooperation (NAALC)

The North American Agreement on Labor Cooperation (NAALC) 1993, a side agreement to NAFTA, promotes the enforcement of national labor laws and transparency in their administration, important for equal rights of workers, including female workers. Through NAALC, the NAFTA partners seek to improve working conditions and living standards in all three countries, and commit themselves to promoting principles that protect, enhance and enforce basic workers' rights. To accomplish these goals, the NAALC creates mechanisms for cooperative activities and intergovernmental consultations, as well as for independent evaluations and dispute settlement related to the enforcement of labor laws. Public submissions made under the NAALC have led to public hearings, ministerial consultations and action plans to address concerns raised. In addition, the NAFTA partners have established cooperative programs and technical exchanges on a number of issues such as industrial relations, health and safety, child labor, gender equity and migrant worker issues. The agreement reflects the shared recognition of the United States, Mexico, and Canada that their mutual prosperity depends on the promotion of fair and open competition based on innovation and rising levels of productivity and quality with due regard for the importance of labor laws and principles. The

---

44 Ibid., at Article 2020.
45 Ibid., at Article 2021.
46 Ibid., at Article 2022.

Agreement increases cooperation and promotes greater understanding among the Parties in a broad range of labor areas; establishes the obligation of each Party to ensure the enforcement of its domestic labor laws; provides mechanisms to permit problem-solving consultations; enables the Parties to initiate evaluations of patterns of practice by independent committees of experts; and allows for dispute settlement procedures.

The general obligation of each Party is to ensure the effective enforcement of its own labor law. Specific obligations refer to publication of labor laws and related regulations and procedures, and to promotion of awareness of and compliance with them. Other obligations include government enforcement actions for promoting compliance and effective enforcement of its labor law, covering such matters as: appointing and training of inspectors, monitoring compliance and examining suspected violations; carrying out inspections, mandatory reporting and record keeping; encouraging worker-management committees; providing mediation, conciliation, or arbitration services; and initiating in a timely manner enforcement actions seeking appropriate remedies. Each Party is committed to ensuring access by persons with a legally recognized interest to administrative, judicial and related tribunals, including recourse to procedures by which labor rights can be enforced in a binding fashion. The Agreement also provides that such tribunals and proceedings before them would be fair and comply with due process.

A trinational Labor Commission is created to facilitate the achievement of the objectives of the Agreement and to deal with labor issues in a cooperative and consultative manner that duly respects the three nations' sovereignty. The Labor Commission consists of a Ministerial Council, an International Coordinating Secretariat (ICS), and three National Administrative Offices (NAOs). The Ministerial Council consists of the labor Ministers from the three signatory countries, who supervise the implementation of the Agreement, including directing the work of the ICS, and promote cooperative activities. An ICS, under the direction of the Ministerial Council, carries out the day-to-day work of the Commission, and is responsible for assisting the Council in its work, for gathering and periodically publishing information on labor matters in Canada, the United States and Mexico, for planning and coordinating cooperative activities, and for supporting any working groups or evaluation committees established by the Ministerial Council. The NAOs, established by each Party, serve as a point of contact for and facilitate the provision of information to other Parties on domestic law and practice, receive public communications, conduct preliminary reviews and promote the exchange of information relevant to the Agreement.

As to resolution of disputes, if the Council cannot resolve a dispute involving a Party's alleged persistent pattern of failure to effectively enforce labor laws with respect to health and safety, child labor and minimum wage, relating to a situation involving mutually recognized labor laws and the production of goods or services traded between the Parties, any Party may request an arbitral panel, which will be established on a two-thirds vote of the council, and panelists will normally be chosen from a previously agreed roster of experts, including experts on labor matters. With the approval of the disputing Parties, a panel may seek information and technical advice from any person or body that it deems appropriate, and the report of the panel will be made publicly available five days after it is transmitted to the Parties. If a panel makes a finding that a Party has engaged in a persistent pattern of failure to effectively enforce its labor laws, the Parties may, within 60 days, agree on a mutually satisfactory action plan to remedy the non-enforcement. If there is no agreed action plan, then between 60 and 120 days after the final panel report, the panel may be reconvened to evaluate an action plan proposed by the Party complained against or to set out an action plan in its stead. Further, the panel would also make a determination on the imposition of monetary enforcement assessments on the alleged offending Party. The panel may be reconvened at any time to determine if an action plan is being fully implemented, and if not, the panel is to impose a monetary enforcement assessment on the alleged offending Party. In the event that a Party complained against fails to pay a monetary enforcement assessment or continues in its failure to enforce its labor law and minimum wage, the Party is liable for ongoing enforcement actions. In the case of Canada, the Commission, on the request of a complaining Party, collects the monetary enforcement assessment and enforces an action plan in summary proceedings before a Canadian court of competent jurisdiction. In the case of Mexico and the United States, the complaining Party or Parties may suspend NAFTA benefits based on the amount of the assessment. Sadly, an important element of any labor agreement is missing: specific protection for maternity leave rights and safeguards against maternity discrimination.

The Preamble to the North American Agreement on Labor Cooperation (NAALC) states that the Government of the United States of America, the Government of Canada and the Government of the United Mexican States undertake the agreement:

> RECALLING their resolve in the North American Free Trade Agreement (NAFTA) to:
>
> create an expanded and secure market for the goods and services produced in their territories,
>
> enhance the competitiveness of their firms in global markets,
>
> create new employment opportunities and improve working conditions and living standards in their respective territories, and
>
> protect, enhance and enforce basic workers' rights;
>
> AFFIRMING their continuing respect for each Party's constitution and law;

DESIRING to build on their respective international commitments and to strengthen their cooperation on labor matters;

RECOGNIZING that their mutual prosperity depends on the promotion of competition based on innovation and rising levels of productivity and quality;

SEEKING to complement the economic opportunities created by the NAFTA with the human resource development, labor-management cooperation and continuous learning that characterize high-productivity economies;

ACKNOWLEDGING that protecting basic workers' rights will encourage firms to adopt high-productivity competitive strategies;

RESOLVED to promote, in accordance with their respective laws, high-skill, high-productivity economic development in North America by:
investing in continuous human resource development, including for entry into the workforce and during periods of unemployment;
promoting employment security and career opportunities for all workers through referral and other employment services;
strengthening labor-management cooperation to promote greater dialogue between worker organizations and employers and to foster creativity and productivity in the workplace;
promoting higher living standards as productivity increases;
encouraging consultation and dialogue between labor, business and government both in each country and in North America;
fostering investment with due regard for the importance of labor laws and principles;
encouraging employers and employees in each country to comply with labor laws and to work together in maintaining a progressive, fair, safe and healthy working environment;

BUILDING on existing institutions and mechanisms in Canada, Mexico and the United States to achieve the preceding economic and social goals; and

CONVINCED of the benefits to be gained from further cooperation between them on labor matters.[47]

The objectives of the agreement are outlined in Article 1:

1. a. improve working conditions and living standards in each Party's territory;
   b. promote, to the maximum extent possible, the labor principles set out in Annex 1;

---

47 North American Agreement on Labor Cooperation (NAALC), at the Preamble.

    c. encourage cooperation to promote innovation and rising levels of productivity and quality;

    d. encourage publication and exchange of information, data development and coordination, and joint studies to enhance mutually beneficial understanding of the laws and institutions governing labor in each Party's territory;

    e. pursue cooperative labor-related activities on the basis of mutual benefit;

    f. promote compliance with, and effective enforcement by each Party of, its labor law; and

    g. foster transparency in the administration of labor law.[48]

As such, the Preamble to NAALC reaffirms relevant provisions of the Preamble to NAFTA and adds further shared goals related to labor matters while not specifically mentioning maternity rights. Importantly, each Party is committed, in accordance with its domestic laws, to promote equal pay and to eliminate employment discrimination, important for equal rights in employment. Further, each is committed to the following labor principles: the freedom of association, the right to bargain collectively, the right to strike, prohibition of forced labor, restrictions on labor by children and young people, minimum employment standards, prevention of occupational accidents and diseases, compensation in cases of work accidents or occupational diseases, and protection of migrant workers. The Agreement sets forth the following general objectives: improving working conditions and living standards, promoting compliance with and effective enforcement of labor laws, promoting the Agreement's principles through cooperation and coordination, and promoting the publication and exchange of information to enhance the mutual understanding of the Parties' laws, institutions and legal systems.

Specifically, in terms of Obligations of the Parties and the Levels of Protection, Article 2 holds:

    2. Affirming full respect for each Party's constitution, and recognizing the right of each Party to establish its own domestic labor standards, and to adopt or modify accordingly its labor laws and regulations, each Party shall ensure that its labor laws and regulations provide for high labor standards, consistent with high quality and productivity workplaces, and shall continue to strive to improve those standards in that light.[49]

Importantly, government enforcement action is established under Article 3, which states that each Party shall promote compliance with and effectively enforce its labor law through appropriate government action, such as:

---

48   Ibid., at Article 1.
49   Ibid., at Article 2.

3. a. appointing and training inspectors;
   b. monitoring compliance and investigating suspected violations, including through on-site inspections;
   c. seeking assurances of voluntary compliance;
   d. requiring record keeping and reporting;
   e. encouraging the establishment of worker-management committees to address labor regulation of the workplace;
   f. providing or encouraging mediation, conciliation and arbitration services; or
   g. initiating, in a timely manner, proceedings to seek appropriate sanctions or remedies for violations of its labor law.[50]

Critical for discrimination cases, the agreement safeguards private action in Article 4:

4. 1. Each Party shall ensure that persons with a legally recognized interest under its law in a particular matter have appropriate access to administrative, quasijudicial, judicial or labor tribunals for the enforcement of the Party's labor law.
   2. Each Party's law shall ensure that such persons may have recourse to, as appropriate, procedures by which rights arising under:
      a. its labor law, including in respect of occupational safety and health, employment standards, industrial relations and migrant workers, and
      b. collective agreements,
      can be enforced.[51]

Further, under procedural guarantees, Article 5 establishes:

5. 1. Each Party shall ensure that its administrative, quasijudicial, judicial and labor tribunal proceedings for the enforcement of its labor law are fair, equitable and transparent and, to this end, each Party shall provide that:
      a. such proceedings comply with due process of law;
      b. any hearings in such proceedings are open to the public, except where the administration of justice otherwise requires;
      c. the parties to such proceedings are entitled to support or defend their respective positions and to present information or evidence; and
      d. such proceedings are not unnecessarily complicated and do not entail unreasonable charges or time limits or unwarranted delays.
   2. Each Party shall provide that final decisions on the merits of the case in such proceedings are:

---

50   Ibid., at Article 3.
51   Ibid., at Article 4.

a. in writing and preferably state the reasons on which the decisions are based;
b. made available without undue delay to the parties to the proceedings and, consistent with its law, to the public; and
c. based on information or evidence in respect of which the parties were offered the opportunity to be heard.

3. Each Party shall provide, as appropriate, that parties to such proceedings have the right, in accordance with its law, to seek review and, where warranted, correction of final decisions issued in such proceedings.

4. Each Party shall ensure that tribunals that conduct or review such proceedings are impartial and independent and do not have any substantial interest in the outcome of the matter.

5. Each Party shall provide that the parties to administrative, quasijudicial, judicial or labor tribunal proceedings may seek remedies to ensure the enforcement of their labor rights. Such remedies may include, as appropriate, orders, compliance agreements, fines, penalties, imprisonment, injunctions or emergency workplace closures.

6. Each Party may, as appropriate, adopt or maintain labor defense offices to represent or advise workers or their organizations.

7. Nothing in this Article shall be construed to require a Party to establish, or to prevent a Party from establishing, a judicial system for the enforcement of its labor law distinct from its system for the enforcement of laws in general.

8. For greater certainty, decisions by each Party's administrative, quasijudicial, judicial or labor tribunals, or pending decisions, as well as related proceedings shall not be subject to revision or reopened under the provisions of this Agreement.[52]

In terms of cooperation for appreciation for maternity issues in the workplace, Article 11 underlines the importance of labor practices and cooperative activities for equality:

11. 1. The Council shall promote cooperative activities between the Parties, as appropriate, regarding:
a. occupational safety and health;
b. child labor;
c. migrant workers of the Parties;
d. human resource development;
e. labor statistics;
f. work benefits;
g. social programs for workers and their families;

---

52   Ibid., at Article 5.

      h. programs, methodologies and experiences regarding productivity improvement;

      i. labor-management relations and collective bargaining procedures;

      j. employment standards and their implementation;

      k. compensation for work-related injury or illness;

      l. legislation relating to the formation and operation of unions, collective bargaining and the resolution of labor disputes, and its implementation;

      m. the equality of women and men in the workplace;

      n. forms of cooperation among workers, management and government;

      o. the provision of technical assistance, at the request of a Party, for the development of its labor standards; and

      p. such other matters as the Parties may agree.

2. In carrying out the activities referred to in paragraph 1, the Parties may, commensurate with the availability of resources in each Party, cooperate through:

      a. seminars, training sessions, working groups and conferences;

      b. joint research projects, including sectoral studies;

      c. technical assistance; and

      d. such other means as the Parties may agree.

3. The Parties shall carry out the cooperative activities referred to in paragraph 1 with due regard for the economic, social, cultural and legislative differences between them.[53]

Importantly, Article 49 defines labor law, which should include maternity in Article 49.1(g) under 'other grounds':

49. 1. For purposes of this Agreement:
'labor law' means laws and regulations, or provisions thereof, that are directly related to:

      a. freedom of association and protection of the right to organize;

      b. the right to bargain collectively;

      c. the right to strike;

      d. prohibition of forced labor;

      e. labor protections for children and young persons;

      f. minimum employment standards, such as minimum wages and overtime pay, covering wage earners, including those not covered by collective agreements;

      g. elimination of employment discrimination on the basis of grounds such as race, religion, age, sex, or other grounds as determined by each Party's domestic laws;

---

53   Ibid., at Article 11.

    h.   equal pay for men and women;

    i.   prevention of occupational injuries and illnesses;

    j.   compensation in cases of occupational injuries and illnesses;

    k.   protection of migrant workers.[54]

Further, in Article 7 of Annex 1, labor principles are outlined, which stress the elimination of employment discrimination, and should include maternity under 'other grounds':

> Annex 1. The following are guiding principles that the Parties are committed to promote, subject to each Party's domestic law, but do not establish common minimum standards for their domestic law. They indicate broad areas of concern where the Parties have developed, each in its own way, laws, regulations, procedures and practices that protect the rights and interests of their respective workforces.
>
> 7.   Elimination of employment discrimination on such grounds as race, religion, age, sex or other grounds, subject to certain reasonable exceptions, such as, where applicable, *bona fide* occupational requirements or qualifications and established practices or rules governing retirement ages, and special measures of protection or assistance for particular groups designed to take into account the effects of discrimination.[55]

NAFTA, according to its critics, is not free, since Canada has paid a high price to gain greater access to the American and Mexican markets. Canadian consumers have seen prices rise along with the advent of the Goods and Services Tax, and thousands of jobs have been lost, with unemployment hovering around the 9% level.[56] The structural adjustment costs, such as a rise in unemployment, tend to be underestimated by free trade advocates. Further, the agreement is also not about trade, and is more about the creation of a new continental model of development for the regulation of capitalism.[57] It serves more as a corporate bill of rights entrenching deregulation and market orientation in an international treaty, while at the same time eroding the national economic, as well as social and political institutions. Neo-conservatives in Canada and the Unites States wanted a deregulated continental model of development to increase capital mobility in order to restore profitability. Unfortunately, corporate managers have worked in a continent-wide drive to bring down wages and welfare state spending, by playing communities off against one another, doing away with crucial social programs.

---

54   Ibid., at Article 49.

55   Ibid., at Annex 1, Article 7.

56   Merrett, Christopher, *Free Trade, Neither Free Nor About Trade*, Black Rose Books, New York, 1996, p.270.

57   Ibid., at p.95.

The hidden goal is to harmonize and integrate Canadian standards and institutions with the United States and, as a result, Canada's economy, political system and labor practices have been significantly altered due to closer ties with the United States economy. Canada has been forced to acquiesce to the continental model of development by continental market forces and American geopolitical pressures. Free trade is designed to restructure society to suit corporate needs, causing a threat to communities by capital-enhanced geographic mobility, which is not universally beneficial.

Many have benefited, but in the eyes of the critics, many more have been hurt. Sovereignty has been compromised and the three most important industries for Canada – wood exports, agriculture and automobile manufacturing – have been hurt. 'The burden of Free Trade driven restructuring was shared unequally on a national, regional, class and gender basis.'[58] The critics argue that the new capital labor accord relies on domination instead of negotiation. Canadian workers are suffering from a 'whiplash process', being forced concessions on wage benefits and work rules, and failure to acquiesce has resulted in relocation out of Canada. Mergers, temporary and part-time workers, and cheap labor increase competitiveness at a cost, free-trade-generated jobs not materializing as promised by the advocates. The Continental Model has led to polarization and segmentation of the Canadian labor force, and the discourse of universality has ended, so that there is more social inequality across Canada. The Welfare State is viewed as an impediment to profit in the eyes of business, which has chipped away at it, giving way to a 'policy of stealth'; and with deregulation, budget cuts and privatization, importance is given to corporate profit at the expense of social equality.

'Continental free trade has helped to create a neo-conservative utopia where issues such as social justice and regional equality have become relics' of a bygone era.[59] While opponents of free trade are said to suffer from 'emporiophobia', a fear of free trade, the effects of free trade are something to fear, since hemispheric free trade is now a possibility. It was argued that there would be a 'sucking sound' of jobs going south of the border, ultimately to Mexico.[60] However, no tripartite treaty will disturb the overwhelming dominance that accrues to the United States, because of its geographic position, between Canada and Mexico. A borderland is a region jointly shared by two nations that houses people with common social characteristics in spite of the political boundaries between them, and thus the United States has a strong influence on the other two countries bordering it. The outflow of investment and the hemorrhaging of profits and service payments out of Canada is intrinsically intertwined with NAFTA.[61] According to the critics, the human and economic debris will be with us for as long as we can see into the

---

58   Ibid., at p.271.

59   Ibid., at p.279.

60   McPhail, Brenda, *NAFTA Now*, University Press of America, Lanham, 1985, p.44.

61   Hurtig, Mel, *The Betrayal of Canada*, Stoddart Publishing, Toronto, 1991, p.303.

future. The single most important impact of NAFTA is the decline in the overall standard of living of Canadians, which has coincided with the agreements. We must be careful to reform democracy and political institutions so citizens and not just corporate business benefit from change. There is presently more foreign ownership and control in Canada, with fewer and poorer jobs. More imports of goods and services should be sourced in Canada, but there is a failure to develop new competitive products while at the same time having less diversification of exports.

Northrop Frye pointed out long ago about Canada, 'Why go to the trouble of annexing a country that is so easy to exploit without taking any responsibility for it?'[62] Economic penetration has proven simpler than military force. NAFTA, according to its critics, is a neo-conservative Americanization of Canada.[63] The pre-agreement years saw trade on a multilateral level, without abandoning national control of the foreign market. However, the agreement itself is seen as a straightjacket, because it is difficult to introduce new measures to strengthen or expand national control of firms and industries. It can be argued that it is a dangerous and indefensible gamble for Canada to commit to a binding dispute settlement mechanism with a trading partner, the United States, which has such a disproportionate power. NAFTA has set up a trading bloc designed to fit Canada and Mexico into the American model of development, keeping Europe and Japan out. Mexico is an attractive site for low-wage production of standardized industrial goods, and with this come Canadian and American job losses, with production shifts to Mexico and a downward pressure on wages. Workers have been displaced from industries and are vulnerable to competition from low-wage countries, with the loss especially to low-income jobs. While the job crisis existed before free trade and was not confined to Canada, NAFTA does nothing for basic labor.

There is a conflict between the profitability of individual corporations and the pressures of global capabilities against human needs for high employment levels, decent pay, healthy working conditions and job security. To serve the corporate profit, what has occurred is a decrease in full-time employment and an increase in part-time and temporary employment at the expense of benefits, as well as an increase in unemployment and in welfare levels. As such, this has been 'the longest and deepest unemployment crisis since the Great Depression', with inappropriate monetary policy playing a major role.[64]

There is a gap in the free trade effect between the top corporate executive and the average shop-floor worker. Free trade encourages self-reinforcing cycles of destructive competition, exerting great pressure on the Continent. It has eliminated

---

62   Ibid., at p.89.

63   Watkins, Mel, 'The Political Economy of Growth', in Wallace Clement and Glen Williams, *The New Canadian Political Economy*, McGill-Queen's University Press, Kingston, 1989, p.3.

64   Campbell, Bruce, *Free Trade, Destroyer of Jobs*, Canadian Centre for Policy Alternatives, Ottawa, 1993, p.2.

jobs, depressed incomes and standards. The effects of investment diversion and export harassment far outweigh the positive effects of tariff reductions. There is a one-sided advantage for a corporate elite that is globally competitive, increasing profits, surviving and growing unfettered by government controls, and securing the highest rate of return for the interests of financial capital. Decent jobs and decent living standards have become unimportant. However, employment needs of society must be paramount and, therefore, corporate interests must yield to broader public interests. NAFTA is tilted in the wrong direction. Multilateral trading arrangements with the European Community and Japan would be alternatives to NAFTA and its shortfalls. Canada's social programs are a contrast to those of the United States. Americanization is balkanizing Canada. Regional equality is promised, but individuals, families, communities and regions are being abandoned. Canada was founded on the national principle of building strong communities and regions to serve the needs of residents, not to deplete these areas in order to supply land and factories for economic interests. With lay-offs and closures, there is a bitter legacy of unemployment, poverty and inequality, with society becoming distinctly harsher. Those who are able to thrive are doing very well, but the societal gap is growing so that there is a chasm between rich and poor, young and old, black and white, men and women, non-disabled and disabled, with a disappearing middle class. There is a severe strain on the societal fabric, with a sacrificing of the needs of many for the demands of few.

Among those who were opposed to NAFTA, well-known Canadian Mitchell Sharp stated it best:

> From the very beginnings of our country, we have sought to preserve a separate identity, to live in harmony with our next door neighbour but as an independent country. By entering into this ... preferential agreement, we would be deciding no longer to resist the continental pull. On the contrary, we would be accelerating the process of the Americanisation of Canada.[65]

Many believe that free trade challenges the fundamentals of Canada's nationhood, with its powers limited by interdependence and domination from foreign multinationals. The benefits of free trade do not fall equally. Free trade serves to undermine full employment,[66] but the first essential ingredient for free trade should be a commitment to full employment. Sufficient independence for blueprint choices and for flexible alternatives for long-term planning is needed, looking away from integration.

By operating under the deceptive banner of 'free' trade, multinational corporations are working hard to expand their control over the international

---

65   Axworthy, Lloyd, 'Free Trade, The Costs for Canada', in A.R. Riggs and Tom Velk, *Canadian-American Free Trade: (The Sequel) Historical, Political and Economic Dimensions*, The Institute for Research on Public Policy, Montreal, 1988, p.38.

66   Ibid., at p.39.

economy, and to dismantle vital health, safety and environmental protections, which in recent decades have been won by citizens' movements across the globe. According to consumer advocate Ralph Nader, this serves to devalue jobs, depress wage levels, make workplaces less safe, destroy family farms and undermine consumer protections.[67] Because of NAFTA, large global companies have capitalized on poverty in the Third World, including China and India, by lowering safety and wages in employment. As such, workers, consumers and communities will continue to lose, while short-term profits soar and big business wins, in a threat to move south. Thus the centralization of commercial power is unsound, as the allocation of power to lower levels of government bodies tends to increase citizen power. There is a need for community-oriented production in smaller-scale operations, along with more flexibility and adaptability to local needs for sustainable production methods and democratic controls. There is a race 'to the bottom', pitting State against State, for the lowest wage levels, lowest environmental policies and lowest consumer safety standards.[68]

NAFTA has forced Canada to harmonize its social and economic policies to conform to the United States at the expense of its citizens. Free trade calls for privatization and deregulation, but policy intervention is needed to reduce unemployment and raise wage rates. There has been a shift away from service-type jobs, with pressure to decrease wages and provide fewer benefits for the sake of the almighty American dollar. There has been major job loss by sourcing services outside Canada but also outside the United States.[69] It is important to negotiate over the right of establishment and the right to national treatment. Manufacturing is vulnerable to trade liberalization, which will lead to an increase in unemployment and adverse working conditions, and the United States has an advantage over Canada, because of cheap material, capital intensiveness and technological advancement. As well, in the food industry, Canada is again at a disadvantage due to its size and climate. So too in the electrical field where the United States is again favored, because of a rationalization of production for specializations. Overall, there is a 'going south' policy, since Canadian firms want to locate elsewhere, while still having access to the Canadian market, but at the same time, by phasing out import restrictions, the domestic sector is not protected. American legislation for North American realignment, it is argued, will curtail equal rights legislation, since equal pay is too costly for the industry. Free trade erodes the domestic service economy and should be a means only, not an end.[70]

---

67   Nader, Ralph, *The Case Against Free Trade*, Earth Island Press, San Francisco, 1993, p.1.

68   Ibid., at p.6.

69   Griffin Cohen, Marjorie, *Free Trade and the Future of Women's Work, Manufacturing and Service Industries*, Garamond Press, Toronto, 1987, p.16.

70   Ibid., at p.49.

American Declaration of the Rights and Duties of Man

Important for equal rights, including appreciation for maternity issues, the Preamble of the American Declaration of the Rights and Duties of Man 1948 states:

All men are born free and equal, in dignity and in rights, and, being endowed by nature with reason and conscience, they should conduct themselves as brothers one to another.

The fulfilment of duty by each individual is a prerequisite to the rights of all. Rights and duties are interrelated in every social and political activity of man. While rights exalt individual liberty, duties express the dignity of that liberty.

Duties of a juridical nature presuppose others of a moral nature which support them in principle and constitute their basis.

In as much as spiritual development is the supreme end of human existence and the highest expression thereof, it is the duty of man to serve that end with all his strength and resources.

Since culture is the highest social and historical expression of that spiritual development, it is the duty of man to preserve, practice and foster culture by every means within his power.

And, since moral conduct constitutes the noblest flowering of culture, it is the duty of every man always to hold it in high respect.

WHEREAS:

The American peoples have acknowledged the dignity of the individual, and their national constitutions recognize that juridical and political institutions, which regulate life in human society, have as their principal aim the protection of the essential rights of man and the creation of circumstances that will permit him to achieve spiritual and material progress and attain happiness;

The American States have on repeated occasions recognized that the essential rights of man are not derived from the fact that he is a national of a certain state, but are based upon attributes of his human personality;

The international protection of the rights of man should be the principal guide of an evolving American law;

The affirmation of essential human rights by the American States together with the guarantees given by the internal regimes of the states establish the initial system of protection considered by the American States as being suited to the present social and juridical conditions, not without a recognition on their part that they should increasingly strengthen that system in the international field as conditions become more favourable.[71]

In terms of equal rights and equality, Article II guarantees the right to equality before the law, which should include maternity under 'any other factor':

> II. All persons are equal before the law and have the rights and duties established in this Declaration, without distinction as to race, sex, language, creed or any other factor.[72]

Further, important for advancement, the right to education is guaranteed under Article XII:

> XII. Every person has the right to an education, which should be based on the principles of liberty, morality and human solidarity.
>
> Likewise every person has the right to an education that will prepare him to attain a decent life, to raise his standard of living, and to be a useful member of society. The right to an education includes the right to equality of opportunity in every case, in accordance with natural talents, merit and the desire to utilize the resources that the state or the community is in a position to provide. Every person has the right to receive, free, at least a primary education.[73]

In addition, important in the fight against maternity discrimination in employment, the right to work and to fair remuneration are contained in Article XIV:

> XIV. Every person has the right to work, under proper conditions, and to follow his vocation freely, in so far as existing conditions of employment permit. Every person who works has the right to receive such remuneration as will, in proportion to his capacity and skill, assure him a standard of living suitable for himself and for his family.[74]

The scope of the rights of man is outlined in Article XXVIII:

> XXVIII. The rights of man are limited by the rights of others, by the security of all, and by the just demands of the general welfare and the advancement of democracy.[75]

---

71 American Declaration of the Rights and Duties of Man, at the Preamble.
72 Ibid., at Article II.
73 Ibid., at Article XII.
74 Ibid., at Article XIV.
75 Ibid., at Article XXVIII.

In terms of duties, the duty to obey the law is contained in Article XXXIII:

> XXXIII. It is the duty of every person to obey the law and other legitimate commands of the authorities of his country and those of the country in which he may be.[76]

Further, the duty to work is contained in Article XXXVII:

> XXXVII. It is the duty of every person to work, as far as his capacity and possibilities permit, in order to obtain the means of livelihood or to benefit his community.[77]

American Convention on Human Rights

The Preamble of the American Convention on Human Rights 1978, which entered into force on 18 July 1978, states:

> The American states signatory to the present Convention,
>
> *Reaffirming* their intention to consolidate in this hemisphere, within the framework of democratic institutions, a system of personal liberty and social justice based on respect for the essential rights of man;
>
> *Recognizing* that the essential rights of man are not derived from one's being a national of a certain state, but are based upon attributes of the human personality, and that they therefore justify international protection in the form of a convention reinforcing or complementing the protection provided by the domestic law of the American states;
>
> *Considering* that these principles have been set forth in the Charter of the Organization of American States, in the American Declaration of the Rights and Duties of Man, and in the Universal Declaration of Human Rights, and that they have been reaffirmed and refined in other international instruments, worldwide as well as regional in scope;
>
> *Reiterating* that, in accordance with the Universal Declaration of Human Rights, the ideal of free men enjoying freedom from fear and want can be achieved only if conditions are created whereby everyone may enjoy his economic, social, and cultural rights, as well as his civil and political rights.[78]

---

76   Ibid., at Article XXXIII.
77   Ibid., at Article XXXVII.
78   American Convention on Human Rights, at the Preamble.

Important for equal rights, Article 1 stresses the obligation to respect rights, which should include maternity under 'any other social condition':

> 1. 1. The States Parties to this Convention undertake to respect the rights and freedoms recognized herein and to ensure to all persons subject to their jurisdiction the free and full exercise of those rights and freedoms, without any discrimination for reasons of race, color, sex, language, religion, political or other opinion, national or social origin, economic status, birth, or any other social condition.
>   2. For the purposes of this Convention, 'person' means every human being.[79]

Important for maternity discrimination cases, the right to equal protection is guaranteed under Article 24:

> 24. All persons are equal before the law. Consequently, they are entitled, without discrimination, to equal protection of the law.[80]

Further, freedom of movement and residence, critical for employment opportunities, is guaranteed under Article 22:

> 22. 1. Every person lawfully in the territory of a State Party has the right to move about in it, and to reside in it subject to the provisions of the law.
>   2. Every person has the right to leave any country freely, including his own.
>   3. The exercise of the foregoing rights may be restricted only pursuant to a law to the extent necessary in a democratic society to prevent crime or to protect national security, public safety, public order, public morals, public health, or the rights or freedoms of others.
>   4. The exercise of the rights recognized in paragraph 1 may also be restricted by law in designated zones for reasons of public interest.
>   5. No one can be expelled from the territory of the state of which he is a national or be deprived of the right to enter it.
>   6. An alien lawfully in the territory of a State Party to this Convention may be expelled from it only pursuant to a decision reached in accordance with law.
>   7. Every person has the right to seek and be granted asylum in a foreign territory, in accordance with the legislation of the state and international conventions, in the event he is being pursued for political offenses or related common crimes.
>   8. In no case may an alien be deported or returned to a country, regardless of whether or not it is his country of origin, if in that country his right

---

79 Ibid., at Article 1.
80 Ibid., at Article 24.

to life or personal freedom is in danger of being violated because of his race, nationality, religion, social status, or political opinions.
9. The collective expulsion of aliens is prohibited.[81]

In terms of civil and political rights, the right to Juridical Personality is contained in Article 3:

3. Every person has the right to recognition as a person before the law.[82]

Further, domestic legal effects are outlined in Article 2:

2. Where the exercise of any of the rights or freedoms referred to in Article 1 is not already ensured by legislative or other provisions, the States Parties undertake to adopt, in accordance with their constitutional processes and the provisions of this Convention, such legislative or other measures as may be necessary to give effect to those rights or freedoms.[83]

Crucially, the right to judicial protection is guaranteed under Article 25:

25. 1. Everyone has the right to simple and prompt recourse, or any other effective recourse, to a competent court or tribunal for protection against acts that violate his fundamental rights recognized by the constitution or laws of the state concerned or by this Convention, even though such violation may have been committed by persons acting in the course of their official duties.
2. The States Parties undertake:
   a. to ensure that any person claiming such remedy shall have his rights determined by the competent authority provided for by the legal system of the state;
   b. to develop the possibilities of judicial remedy; and
   c. to ensure that the competent authorities shall enforce such remedies when granted.[84]

In addition, Article 28 contains a federal clause:

28. 1. Where a State Party is constituted as a federal state, the national government of such State Party shall implement all the provisions of

---

81 Ibid., at Article 22.
82 Ibid., at Article 3.
83 Ibid., at Article 2.
84 Ibid., at Article 25.

the Convention over whose subject matter it exercises legislative and judicial jurisdiction.[85]

As well, in terms of economic, social and cultural rights, Article 26 provides for progressive development:

26. The States Parties undertake to adopt measures, both internally and through international cooperation, especially those of an economic and technical nature, with a view to achieving progressively, by legislation or other appropriate means, the full realization of the rights implicit in the economic, social, educational, scientific, and cultural standards set forth in the Charter of the Organization of American States ....[86]

There are a number of competent organs involved as outlined in Article 33:

33. The following organs shall have competence with respect to matters relating to the fulfillment of the commitments made by the States Parties to this Convention:
   a. the Inter-American Commission on Human Rights, referred to as 'The Commission'; and
   b. the Inter-American Court of Human Rights, referred to as 'The Court'.[87]

In terms of the Inter-American Commission on Human Rights, Article 35 outlines the organization:

35. The Commission shall represent all the member countries of the Organization of American States.[88]

The functions of the Inter-American Commission on Human Rights are outlined in Article 41:

41. The main function of the Commission shall be to promote respect for and defense of human rights. In the exercise of its mandate, it shall have the following functions and powers:
   a. to develop an awareness of human rights among the peoples of America;
   b. to make recommendations to the governments of the member states, when it considers such action advisable, for the adoption of progressive

---

85   Ibid., at Article 28.
86   Ibid., at Article 26.
87   Ibid., at Article 33.
88   Ibid., at Article 35.

measures in favor of human rights within the framework of their domestic law and constitutional provisions as well as appropriate measures to further the observance of those rights;

c. to prepare such studies or reports as it considers advisable in the performance of its duties;

d. to request the governments of the member states to supply it with information on the measures adopted by them in matters of human rights;

e. to respond, through the General Secretariat of the Organization of American States, to inquiries made by the member states on matters related to human rights and, within the limits of its possibilities, to provide those states with the advisory services they request;

f. to take action on petitions and other communications pursuant to its authority under the provisions of Articles 44 through 51 of this Convention; and

g. to submit an annual report to the General Assembly of the Organization of American States.[89]

The competency to lodge petitions is outlined in Article 44:

44. Any person or group of persons, or any nongovernmental entity legally recognized in one or more member states of the Organization, may lodge petitions with the Commission containing denunciations or complaints of violation of this Convention by a State Party.[90]

Admissibility of petitions is outlined in Article 46:

46. 1. Admission by the Commission of a petition or communication … shall be subject to the following requirements:

a. that the remedies under domestic law have been pursued and exhausted in accordance with generally recognized principles of international law;

b. that the petition or communication is lodged within a period of six months from the date on which the party alleging violation of his rights was notified of the final judgment;

c. that the subject of the petition or communication is not pending in another international proceeding for settlement.

2. The provisions of paragraphs 1.a and 1.b of this article shall not be applicable when:

---

89   Ibid., at Article 41.
90   Ibid., at Article 44.

a. the domestic legislation of the state concerned does not afford due process of law for the protection of the right or rights that have allegedly been violated;

b. the party alleging violation of his rights has been denied access to the remedies under domestic law or has been prevented from exhausting them; or

c. there has been unwarranted delay in rendering a final judgment under the aforementioned remedies.[91]

The procedure is outlined in Article 48:

48. 1. When the Commission receives a petition or communication alleging violation of any of the rights protected by this Convention, it shall proceed as follows:

a. If it considers the petition or communication admissible, it shall request information from the government of the state indicated as being responsible for the alleged violations and shall furnish that government a transcript of the pertinent portions of the petition or communication. This information shall be submitted within a reasonable period to be determined by the Commission in accordance with the circumstances of each case.

b. After the information has been received, or after the period established has elapsed and the information has not been received, the Commission shall ascertain whether the grounds for the petition or communication still exist. If they do not, the Commission shall order the record to be closed.

c. The Commission may also declare the petition or communication inadmissible or out of order on the basis of information or evidence subsequently received.

d. If the record has not been closed, the Commission shall, with the knowledge of the parties, examine the matter set forth in the petition or communication in order to verify the facts. If necessary and advisable, the Commission shall carry out an investigation, for the effective conduct of which it shall request, and the states concerned shall furnish to it, all necessary facilities.

e. The Commission may request the states concerned to furnish any pertinent information and, if so requested, shall hear oral statements or receive written statements from the parties concerned.

f. The Commission shall place itself at the disposal of the parties concerned with a view to reaching a friendly settlement of the matter on the basis of respect for the human rights recognized in this Convention.

---

91   Ibid., at Article 46.

2. However, in serious and urgent cases, only the presentation of a petition or communication that fulfils all the formal requirements of admissibility shall be necessary in order for the Commission to conduct an investigation with the prior consent of the state in whose territory a violation has allegedly been committed.[92]

In terms of the Inter-American Court of Human Rights, the right of submission is outlined in Article 61:

61. 1. Only the States Parties and the Commission shall have the right to submit a case to the Court.[93]

The safeguarding of rights and the provision of measures are contained in Article 63:

63. 1. If the Court finds that there has been a violation of a right or freedom protected by this Convention, the Court shall rule that the injured party be ensured the enjoyment of his right or freedom that was violated. It shall also rule, if appropriate, that the consequences of the measure or situation that constituted the breach of such right or freedom be remedied and that fair compensation be paid to the injured party.

2. In cases of extreme gravity and urgency, and when necessary to avoid irreparable damage to persons, the Court shall adopt such provisional measures as it deems pertinent in matters it has under consideration. With respect to a case not yet submitted to the Court, it may act at the request of the Commission.[94]

In terms of procedure, Article 66 calls for reasons for judgments:

66. 1. Reasons shall be given for the judgment of the Court.[95]

Further, finality of judgment is contained in Article 67:

67. The judgment of the Court shall be final and not subject to appeal. In case of disagreement as to the meaning or scope of the judgment, the Court shall interpret it at the request of any of the parties, provided the request is made within ninety days from the date of notification of the judgment.[96]

---

92 Ibid., at Article 48.
93 Ibid., at Article 61.
94 Ibid., at Article 63.
95 Ibid., at Article 66.
96 Ibid., at Article 67.

Finally, compliance with the judgment is underlined in Article 68:

> 68. 1. The States Parties to the Convention undertake to comply with the judgment of the Court in any case to which they are parties.
>   2. That part of a judgment that stipulates compensatory damages may be executed in the country concerned in accordance with domestic procedure governing the execution of judgments against the state.[97]

Statute of the Inter-American Court on Human Rights

More specifically and carrying on from the American Convention on Human Rights, Article 1 of the Statute of the Inter-American Court on Human Rights 1980, which entered into force on 1 January 1980, outlines the nature of the legal organization:

> 1. The Inter-American Court of Human Rights is an autonomous judicial institution whose purpose is the application and interpretation of the American Convention on Human Rights. The Court exercises its functions in accordance with the provisions of the aforementioned Convention and the present Statute.[98]

The jurisdiction of the Court is contained in Article 2:

> 2. The Court shall exercise adjudicatory and advisory jurisdiction:
>   1. Its adjudicatory jurisdiction shall be governed by the provisions of Articles 61, 62 and 63 of the Convention, and
>   2. Its advisory jurisdiction shall be governed by the provisions of Article 64 of the Convention.[99]

The seat of the Court is contained in Article 3:

> 3. 1. The seat of the Court shall be San Jose, Costa Rica; however, the Court may convene in any member state of the Organization of American States (OAS) when a majority of the Court considers it desirable, and with the prior consent of the State concerned.[100]

Further, the composition of the Court is contained in Article 4:

---

97 Ibid., at Article 68.
98 Statute of the Inter-American Court on Human Rights, at Article 1.
99 Ibid., at Article 2.
100 Ibid., at Article 3.

4. 1. The Court shall consist of seven judges, nationals of the member states of the OAS, elected in an individual capacity from among jurists of the highest moral authority and of recognized competence in the field of human rights, who possess the qualifications required for the exercise of the highest judicial functions under the law of the State of which they are nationals or of the State that proposes them as candidates.
   2. No two judges may be nationals of the same State.[101]

The structure of the Court includes the Presidency as outlined in Article 12 and the Secretariat as outlined in Article 14:

12. 1. The Court shall elect from among its members a President and Vice-President who shall serve for a period of two years; they may be reelected.
    2. The President shall direct the work of the Court, represent it, regulate the disposition of matters brought before the Court, and preside over its sessions.[102]

14. 1. The Secretariat of the Court shall function under the immediate authority of the Secretary, in accordance with the administrative standards of the OAS General Secretariat, in all matters that are not incompatible with the independence of the Court.
    2. The Secretary shall be appointed by the Court. He shall be a full-time employee serving in a position of trust to the Court, shall have his office at the seat of the Court and shall attend any meetings that the Court holds away from its seat.
    3. There shall be an Assistant Secretary who shall assist the Secretary in his duties and shall replace him in his temporary absence.
    4. The Staff of the Secretariat shall be appointed by the Secretary General of the OAS, in consultation with the Secretary of the Court.[103]

In terms of the workings of the Court, Article 24 outlines the hearings, deliberations and decisions:

24. 1. The hearings shall be public, unless the Court, in exceptional circumstances, decides otherwise.
    2. The Court shall deliberate in private. Its deliberations shall remain secret, unless the Court decides otherwise.
    3. The decisions, judgments and opinions of the Court shall be delivered in public session, and the parties shall be given written notification thereof.

---

101   Ibid., at Article 4.
102   Ibid., at Article 12.
103   Ibid., at Article 14.

>In addition, the decisions, judgments and opinions shall be published, along with judges' individual votes and opinions and with such other data or background information that the Court may deem appropriate.[104]

Article 27 stresses the importance of relations with the host country, governments and organizations:

>27. 1. The relations of the Court with the host country shall be governed through a headquarters agreement. The seat of the Court shall be international in nature.
>
>2. The relations of the Court with governments, with the OAS and its organs, agencies and entities and with other international governmental organizations involved in promoting and defending human rights shall be governed through special agreements.[105]

Finally, Article 28 stresses the importance of the relations with the Inter-American Commission on Human Rights:

>28. The Inter-American Commission on Human Rights shall appear as a party before the Court in all cases within the adjudicatory jurisdiction of the Court, pursuant to Article 2(1) of the present Statute.[106]

Inter-American Democratic Charter

The Preamble of the Inter-American Democratic Charter 2001, which came into force on 11 September 2001, states:

>The General Assembly,
>
>CONSIDERING that the Charter of the Organization of American States recognizes that representative democracy is indispensable for the stability, peace, and development of the region, and that one of the purposes of the OAS is to promote and consolidate representative democracy, with due respect for the principle of nonintervention;
>
>RECALLING that the Heads of State and Government of the Americas, gathered at the Third Summit of the Americas, held from April 20 to 22, 2001 in Quebec City, adopted a democracy clause which establishes that any unconstitutional alteration or interruption of the democratic order in a state of the Hemisphere

---

104   Ibid., at Article 24.
105   Ibid., at Article 27.
106   Ibid., at Article 28.

constitutes an insurmountable obstacle to the participation of that state's government in the Summits of the Americas process;

REAFFIRMING that the participatory nature of democracy in our countries in different aspects of public life contributes to the consolidation of democratic values and to freedom and solidarity in the Hemisphere;

CONSIDERING that solidarity among and cooperation between American states require the political organization of those states based on the effective exercise of representative democracy, and that economic growth and social development based on justice and equity, and democracy are interdependent and mutually reinforcing;

BEARING IN MIND that the American Declaration on the Rights and Duties of Man and the American Convention on Human Rights contain the values and principles of liberty, equality, and social justice that are intrinsic to democracy;

REAFFIRMING that the promotion and protection of human rights is a basic prerequisite for the existence of a democratic society, and recognizing the importance of the continuous development and strengthening of the inter-American human rights system for the consolidation of democracy;

CONSIDERING that education is an effective way to promote citizens' awareness concerning their own countries and thereby achieve meaningful participation in the decision-making process, and reaffirming the importance of human resource development for a sound democratic system;

RECOGNIZING that the right of workers to associate themselves freely for the defense and promotion of their interests is fundamental to the fulfillment of democratic ideals.[107]

The anti-discrimination provision is contained in Article 9, which should include maternity:

The elimination of all forms of discrimination, especially gender, ethnic and race discrimination, as well as diverse forms of intolerance, the promotion and protection of human rights of indigenous peoples and migrants, and respect for ethnic, cultural and religious diversity in the Americas contribute to strengthening democracy and citizen participation.[108]

Workers' rights and labor standards are emphasized in Article 10:

---

107 Inter-American Democratic Charter, at the Preamble.
108 Ibid., at Article 9.

The promotion and strengthening of democracy requires the full and effective exercise of workers' rights and the application of core labor standards, as recognized in the International Labour Organization (ILO) Declaration on Fundamental Principles and Rights at Work ..., adopted in 1998, as well as other related fundamental ILO conventions. Democracy is strengthened by improving standards in the workplace and enhancing the quality of life for workers in the Hemisphere.[109]

The importance of claims and redress for grievances is outlined in Article 8:

Any person or group of persons who consider that their human rights have been violated may present claims or petitions to the inter-American system for the promotion and protection of human rights in accordance with its established procedures.

Member states reaffirm their intention to strengthen the inter-American system for the protection of human rights for the consolidation of democracy in the Hemisphere.[110]

Further, in terms of democracy and the inter-American system, Article 4 espouses the importance of transparency:

Transparency in government activities, probity, responsible public administration on the part of governments, respect for social rights, and freedom of expression and of the press are essential components of the exercise of democracy.

The constitutional subordination of all state institutions to the legally constituted civilian authority and respect for the rule of law on the part of all institutions and sectors of society are equally essential to democracy.[111]

Finally, in terms of human rights, Article 7 stresses the importance of democracy:

Democracy is indispensable for the effective exercise of fundamental freedoms and human rights in their universality, indivisibility and interdependence, embodied in the respective constitutions of states and in inter-American and international human rights instruments.[112]

Conclusion

By recognizing that we share a hemisphere, NAFTA sets an important precedent for north–south continental trade, and looks toward the future by allowing for

---

109   Ibid., at Article 10.
110   Ibid., at Article 8.
111   Ibid., at Article 4.
112   Ibid., at Article 7.

participation by other countries. Latin American countries have expressed an interest in becoming signatory members of the Free Trade Agreement. In addition, the Canadian Province of Quebec has already given thought to joining as a separate member in the event it becomes a separate nation, but wishes to maintain the current division of legislative powers, respect fully its unique social policy, language and culture, maintain a leeway to modernize and develop its economy, provide for transitional periods for businesses in less competitive sectors, adopt a dispute settlement mechanism, maintain its special status for agriculture and fisheries, and protect its right to decide on the Agreement in light of its interests. The Parties to the North American Free Trade Agreement (NAFTA) are cooperating to advance trade liberalization not only within North America with the NAFTA Superhighway, but also in the negotiations for the Free Trade Area of the Americas (FTAA), encompassing 34 countries. The FTAA would eliminate trade and investment barriers on virtually all goods and services traded by member countries, reduce prices for consumers and create new markets for producers throughout the hemisphere. However, more needs to be done to legislate for equal rights and tolerance specifically for maternity rights of workers. President John F. Kennedy stated with regard to the relationship between Canada and the United States: 'Geography has made us neighbors, history has made us friends, the economy has made us partners and necessity has made us allies.'[113] In this spirit, important in the fight against maternity discrimination, we need to work together to bring about full equality in the Americas, in the pursuit of *Pregnant Pause.*

---

113   President John F. Kennedy.

Chapter 8

Pregnant Pause in the United Kingdom and Ireland

Introduction

In the quest for appreciation for maternity issues in *Pregnant Pause*, this chapter will examine efforts against maternity discrimination in the United Kingdom and Ireland. It will review important legislation impacting equal rights, first in the United Kingdom, which encompasses England, Scotland, Wales and Northern Ireland, namely: the Sex Discrimination Act, the Equal Pay Act, the Equal Opportunities Commission (EOC) and the Code of Practice on Equal Pay, the Human Rights Act, and the Equality Act; and then in the Republic of Ireland, namely: the Constitution, the Employment Equality Act, the Equal Status Act, and the Maternity Protection Act and the Maternity Protection (Amendment) Act.

Great Britain

The Role of Women in Britain

There is a need for intervention in the area of public/private distinctions in the application of international human rights law. The State's accountability for violations committed by private actors has long been an important debate. Recent jurisprudence holds the states to a due diligence standard with regard to preventing and prosecuting crimes against women. This will be of critical relevance to Commonwealth governments and the Secretariat as part of their continuing priority work in the area of democracy, rule of law, and human rights. The increased participation of women at decision-making levels in conflict prevention, mediation and resolution is vital. Gender refers to the socially determined difference between women and men such as roles, attitudes, behaviors and values.[1] Gender identifies the biological differences between women and men. While sex is genetically determined, gender roles vary across cultures and over time, and are amenable to change. Gender is a relational term based on the fact that women and men have different life courses, and development policies affect them differently. Gender mainstreaming addresses these differences by making gender equality integral to

---

1   Commonwealth Office, Advancing the Commonwealth Agenda for Gender Equality into the New Millennium (2000–2005).

the process of policy making, planning and program delivery at all levels and in all sectors, focusing less on providing equal treatment for women and men, since equal treatment does not necessarily result in equal outcomes, and more on taking whatever steps are necessary to ensure equal outcomes. Gender mainstreaming is everyone's business and involves all social actors, including governments, civil society and the private sector.

The strategy to advance the Commonwealth agenda maintains a two-level approach, namely action related to policy priorities such as human rights, peace and political participation, and macroeconomics and social development; and action related to mechanisms for gender mainstreaming within both governments and the Secretariat. To achieve these goals, Commonwealth governments are committed to: (a) promote and protect women's human rights, promote women's awareness of their human rights, and also involve men in awareness raising through education about the human rights of women; (b) introduce and promote equal opportunities legislation, policies and practices in public and private sector employment, formal and non-formal education and ongoing vocational training; (c) introduce legal structures to provide effective and practical redress in cases of discrimination; (d) promote and increase women's participation in politics and decision-making by adopting measures to achieve the Commonwealth target of having women number no less than a third of decision-makers in the political, public and private sectors; (e) enhance the capacity of women for leadership in the public and private sectors, especially in areas with economic planning and budgeting; and (f) encourage the participation of women and women's organizations in the development of professional guidelines and codes of conduct or other appropriate self-regulatory mechanisms to promote balanced and non-stereotyped portrayals of women by the media.[2] Therefore, Commonwealth governments undertake to: (a) monitor and analyze the different impact of macroeconomic policy and economic reform programs on women and men, and develop strategies, mechanisms, and corrective measures to address gender imbalances in key areas, including national economic reforms and budgetary processes; (b) monitor and analyze the differential economic and social impact of current globalization trends to identify opportunities for and challenges to equal gender participation in micro- and small-scale enterprise, and in formal and informal economy, and develop strategies and policy frameworks, programs and corrective measures to address gender imbalances; (c) support vocational and information technology skills training to ensure equal access to emerging employment opportunities; and (d) integrate gender analysis in national planning and in the development and provision of social services and social safety nets.[3]

Gender mainstreaming is an essential element of good governance. It requires the implementation by sector of women-specific activities and projects. A number of obstacles continue to affect women's ability to participate fully and equally in

---

2   Commonwealth Secretariat, *Commonwealth Plan.*
3   Ibid.

decision-making in the political, public and private sectors. Traditional perceptions often limit the role of women to the household. Socioeconomic impediments affecting women in many countries include women's limited access to formal education, and the streaming of girls and women in traditional subject areas with the result that they are concentrated in low-waged, low-status occupational groups such as clerks, sales and personnel services. The political framework acts to inhibit the equal participation of women with the result of the lack of family-friendly policies, bias toward male candidates, and lack of funding, of training and of support in elections. More effort is required to address impediments to women's involvement in the political process such as family responsibilities, and to encourage women to transcend cultural barriers. Education systems have a role to play in providing encouragement for women's leadership and critical thinking skills. In the area of macroeconomic policy, efforts need to be made to address gender equality issues within structural adjustment and poverty alleviation programs, in particular the 'feminization of poverty', and economic empowerment, since limited progress has been achieved in integrating gender considerations in macroeconomic policies.

A gender management system is defined as 'a network of processes, mechanisms and structures to guide, monitor and evaluate' gender mainstreaming activities, and may be used in a sector or in an institution to address a particular issue. For effective gender mainstreaming, the following strategies need to be applied, namely: strengthening the political will at the local, national and global levels are essential for effective gender mainstreaming; changing policy, resource allocation and planning to make them gender-sensitive within organizations; collecting gender-disaggregated data to greatly benefit the process of gender mainstreaming as an excellent advocacy tool showing how policies impact differently on men and women; increasing the number of women and ultimately ensuring an equal amount of men and women in decision-making positions in the Government and all other sectors; providing all decision-makers with training and tools for gender awareness, analysis and planning; and successful mainstreaming for dynamic links to be forged between stakeholders, government, private sector, civil society, non-governmental organizations (NGOs), to ensure major advocacy efforts and a coordination of resources.

A vast amount of talent and human potential is wasted when women are denied full and equal citizenship. Organizations that represent women, non-governmental organizations (NGOs), trade unions and employers all have an important part to play in empowering women to reach their potential and claim their rights. There are still gross inequalities between the sexes. Millions of women still have to work harder than men to make a living, and many still shoulder the full responsibility for caring. They still have less control over income and assets, are subject to violence and intimidation, and often have no real say in important decisions that affect them. It is a situation that is not only unfair, but also lacks vision. It is in everyone's interests to realize the immense potential of women, since they have unique talents, skills, knowledge and insights. As technology continues to make

the world a smaller more interconnected place, women have what it takes to
flourish in this new economy.

The United Kingdom has a total population of 61,399,118 people.[4] In terms
of the gender pay gap in Great Britain, female employees who work full-time
earn 81% of the average gross hourly earnings of male full-time employees.[5]
The gender pay gap in hourly earnings is 19%. It is wider than this in weekly
earnings at 25%, because men work longer hours than women on average and are
more likely to receive overtime and other additional payments. Men receive £54
per week from additional payments on average, but women only £20 per week.
Women working part-time have lower average hourly earnings than women who
work full-time. There is a particularly large difference between the average hourly
earnings of women who work part-time and men who work full-time, resulting
in a gender pay gap of 41%. If full-time and part-time employees are combined,
the gender pay gap in hourly earnings is wider than for full-time employees, since
more women than men work part-time. The gender pay gap is narrower in Wales
for hourly, weekly and annual earnings than in England and Scotland. The main
reason for this is the low average male earnings in Wales; 18% of male full-time
employees in Wales earn less than £250 per week, compared with 12% in Britain
overall. The gap between the hourly earnings of women who work part-time and
men who work full-time is also wider in England at 42% than in Scotland at 37%
or Wales at 34%.

In terms of sectors and industries, average weekly earnings are higher for men
in the private sector than the public sector, but are higher for women in the public
sector. Consequently, the gender pay gap is much wider in the private sector at
29%, than in the public sector at 16%. Within the public sector, the gap is wider
in central government at 20%, than in public corporations at 16%, and local
government at 15%. A key explanation for the wider gender pay gap in the private
sector is likely to be the differing representation of women in the three highest
paid occupational groups. In the public sector, women comprise 53% of full-
time employees in these groups combined, and in the private sector, only 27%.
Among the nine major occupational groups, average hourly earnings of full-time
employees are highest for men working as managers and administrators, and for
women in professional occupations. Men have higher average hourly earnings
than women in all nine groups, but the extent of the gender pay gap varies, with
managers and administrators at 30%, sales occupations at 28%, and clerical and
secretarial occupations at 2%. Men make up the majority of employees in the
five highest paid occupations, but women predominate in four of the five lowest
paid. Women comprise around 27% of the 3.5 million self-employed.[6] The rate
of female self-employment has more than doubled over the last 20 years. Women

---

4   United Kingdom Census.

5   Equal Opportunities Commission, Women and Men in Britain, Pay and Income.

6   Department of Trade and Industry, Great Britain, *Key Facts about Women in the
Labour Market*.

start up one-third of new businesses and own 13% of all businesses. In looking at the role of women in senior management, of the 100 FTSE firms, only 7.2% of directorships are held by women. Women comprise just 24% of managers. In looking at women in the important sphere of the judiciary, only 5% of High Court judges are women.[7]

In terms of marital and parental status, women who are single have lower average hourly earnings than those who are either married/cohabiting or separated, divorced or widowed, and the pattern for men is the same.[8] However, the gender gap for all employees is widest in the married/cohabiting group at 27%, and the gap is wider than for full-time employees because a high proportion of married/cohabiting women work part-time, having lower earnings on average. The gender pay gap for all employees is higher for those with dependent children at 31%, than without at 18%. Among those with dependent children, the pay gap is at 22% for parents of 0 to 2 year olds, and 35% for parents of dependent children aged 11 or over.

In terms of qualification levels, average hourly earnings increase steadily for both women and men as qualifications rise. Among full-time employees, there are similar gender pay gaps for each qualification level, that is the gender pay gap for full-time employed graduates with a degree or equivalent is 19%, while the gap for those with no qualifications is at 18%. Women with a degree or equivalent qualification have double the average hourly earnings of those with no qualifications, and the pattern was the same for men.

Overall, unequal income is a major source of gender inequality which can result in women having reduced economic independence and a greater likelihood of poverty than men in old age. Income has seven component elements: earnings, self-employment income, occupational pensions and annuities, investment income, tax credits, benefit income and other income. Overall, the gender income gap is much wider than the gender pay gap. Women's average income is £191 per week and men's £368 per week. Women receive only 52% of men's income on average and the gender income gap is 48%. Income levels are highest for both women and men in England, lower in Scotland, and lowest in Wales. The gender income gap is widest in England at 49% and narrowest in Wales at 39%, and in Scotland, it is 46%.

In terms of the labor force in Great Britain, 67% of women and 79% of men aged 16 to 64 are in employment.[9] People aged 25 to 44 have the highest employment rates, that is, 73% for women and 88% for men. Only 9% of male employees work part-time, compared with 43% of female employees, and the largest group of male part-time employees is aged under 25. In terms of occupations, women form over 69% of administrative and secretarial, personal service, and sales and customer service occupations, while men make up over 69% of managers and senior officials, skilled trades, and process, plant and machine operatives. In looking at equal pay, female employees working full-time earn on average 18.8% less than the average

---

7   Government of the United Kingdom, *Equality in Practice*.

8   Equal Opportunities Commission, Women and Men in Britain, Pay and Income.

9   Equal Opportunities Commission, Facts About Women and Men in Great Britain.

hourly earnings of male full-time employees. Women's gross individual income, including income from employment, pensions, benefits and investments, is on average 51% less than men's gross individual income. In examining work–life balance, employment rates for women and men without dependent children are 67% and 74% respectively. In comparison, there is a wide gap between mothers and fathers with dependent children, where employment rates are 65% and 89% respectively. Women whose youngest child is aged under 5 have an employment rate of 53%, and those whose youngest child is 5 or over have an employment rate of 73%.

In terms of the labor force in Scotland, overall, 66% of women and 76% of men aged 16 to 64 are in employment.[10] People aged 25 to 44 have the highest employment rates, that is, 75% for women and 85% for men. Only 9% of male employees aged 16 and over work part-time, compared with 42% of female employees, and nearly half the male part-time employees are aged under 25. In terms of occupations, women form over 70% of administrative and secretarial, personal service, and sales and customer service occupations, while men make up over 80% in skilled trades, and process, plant and machine operatives. In looking at equal pay, female employees working full-time earn on average 18.6% less than the average hourly earnings of male full-time employees. Women's gross individual income, including income from employment, pensions, benefits and investments, is on average 46% less than men's gross individual income. In examining work–life balance, employment rates for women and men without dependent children are 65% and 70% respectively. In comparison, there is a wide gap between mothers and fathers with dependent children, where employment rates are 69% and 89% respectively. Over a quarter, that is 26% of women employees and 19% of men employees, have at least one type of flexible working arrangement.

In terms of the labor force in Wales, 59% of women and 74% of men aged 16–64 are in employment.[11] People aged 25 to 44 have the highest employment rates, that is, 72% for women and 85% for men. Only 9% of male employees aged 16 and over work part-time, compared with 46% of female employees. In terms of occupations, women form 69% or more of administrative and secretarial, personal service, and sales and customer service occupations, while men make up over 80% of skilled trades, and process, plant and machine operatives. In looking at equal pay, female employees working full-time earn on average 13.4% less than the average hourly earnings of male full-time employees. Women's gross individual income, including income from employment, pensions, benefits and investments, is on average 42% less than men's gross individual income. In examining work–life balance, employment rates for women and men without dependent children are 56% and 67% respectively. In comparison, there is a wide gap between mothers and fathers with dependent children, where employment rates are 64% and 87% respectively. Women whose youngest child is aged under 5 have the

---

10   Equal Opportunities Commission, Facts About Women and Men in Scotland.
11   Equal Opportunities Commission, *Facts About Women and Men in Wales*.

lowest employment rate of 49%, and those whose dependent children are 5 or over have an employment rate of 72%.

Legislation

At the outset, if a court determines that it is impossible to interpret an Act of Parliament in a way which is compatible with European convention rights, a formal declaration of incompatibility may be made, and it is then for the Government and Parliament to decide whether or not to amend it.

Sex Discrimination Act (SDA) Important for women, the Sex Discrimination Act 1975 (SDA) defines direct and indirect discrimination. Further, under the SDA, it is first up to the applicant to establish facts, which constitute a *prima facie* case of discrimination, as the burden of proof is initially on the employee to show on the balance of probabilities that her male comparator is doing the same or broadly similar work, or that her work has been rated as equivalent to his, or that her work is of equal value, and that his contract contains a more favorable term. The burden of proof then shifts from the applicant to the employer to show that there is a non-discriminatory reason for their actions, that is, the difference between the contracts is genuinely due to a material factor which is not the difference of gender. The material factor defense is the reason put forward by the employer to explain why the comparator, although doing equal work, is paid more than the applicant; to succeed in a defense, this factor must be significant and relevant; that is, it must be an important cause of the difference and apply to the jobs in question. The difference in pay must be genuinely due to the material factor which must not be tainted by gender discrimination. If the reason given for paying the comparator more is that he has certain skills which the applicant does not have, then the employer would have to demonstrate that these skills are necessary for the job, and genuinely applied during the performance of the job, and are not simply rewarded because past pay agreements recognized and rewarded skills which are no longer applicable; to succeed in a defense, the employer needs to show that the material factor accounts for the whole of the difference in pay.

Direct and indirect discrimination are defined in Section 1:

1. 1. In any circumstances relevant for the purposes of any provision of this Act ..., a person discriminates against a woman if:
    a. on the ground of her sex he treats her less favourably than he treats or would treat a man, or
    b. he applies to her a requirement or condition which he applies or would apply equally to a man but:
        i. which is such that the proportion of women who can comply with it is considerably smaller than the proportion of men who can comply with it, and

    ii. which he cannot show to be justifiable irrespective of the sex of the person to whom it is applied, and

b. iii. which is to her detriment because she cannot comply with it.[12]

In terms of sex discrimination against men, Section 2 holds that Section 1 is to be read as applying equally to the treatment of men, and for that purpose shall have effect with such modifications as are required.[13]

In looking at discrimination in the pre-employment stage, Section 6(1) states:

6. 1. It is unlawful for a person, in relation to employment by him at an establishment in Great Britain, to discriminate against a woman

    a. in the arrangements he makes for the purpose of determining who should be offered that employment, or

    b. in the terms on which he offers her that employment, or

    c. by refusing or deliberately omitting to offer her that employment.[14]

Further, in looking at discrimination in the employment stage, Section 6(2) states:

6. 2. It is unlawful for a person, in the case of a woman employed by him at an establishment in Great Britain, to discriminate against her:

    a. in the way he affords her access to opportunities for promotion, transfer or training, or to any other benefits, facilities or services, or by refusing or deliberately omitting to afford her access to them, or

    b. by dismissing her, or subjecting her to any other detriment.[15]

There is an exception to the rule where sex is a genuine occupational qualification, which is contained in Section 7:

7. 1. In relation to sex discrimination:

    a. section 6(1)(a) or (c) does not apply to any employment where being a man is a genuine occupational qualification for the job.

  2. Being a man is a genuine occupational qualification for a job only where:

    a. the essential nature of the job calls for a man for reasons of physiology (excluding physical strength or stamina) or, in dramatic performances or other entertainment, for reasons of authenticity, so that the essential nature of the job would be materially different if carried out by a woman; or

---

12 Sex Discrimination Act, UK, at Section 1.
13 Ibid., at Section 2.
14 Ibid., at Section 6(1).
15 Ibid., at Section 6(2).

b. the job needs to be held by a man to preserve decency or privacy ...; or

c. the nature or location of the establishment makes it impracticable for the holder of the job to live elsewhere than in premises provided by the employer ...;

d. the nature of the establishment, or of the part of it within which the work is done, requires it to be held by a man ...; or

e. the job needs to be held by a man because of restrictions imposed by the laws regulating the employment of women, or

f. the holder of the job provides individuals with personal services promoting their welfare or education, or similar personal services, and those services can most effectively be provided by a man, or

g. the job needs to be held by a man because it is likely to involve the performance of duties outside the United Kingdom in a country whose laws or customs are such that the duties could not, or could not effectively, be performed by a woman, or

h. the job is one of two to be held by a married couple.[16]

Section 48 allows for positive action by employers to overcome the effects of past discrimination, in terms of training and encouragement where few or no members of one sex have been doing particular work in the preceding 12 months.[17] The Equal Opportunity Employment Commission is recognized in Section 53:

53. 1. There shall be a body of Commissioners named the Equal Opportunities Commission ..., which shall have the following duties

a. to work toward the elimination of discrimination,

b. to promote equality of opportunity between men and women generally.[18]

The SDA prohibits sex discrimination against individuals in the areas of employment and education, in the provision of goods, facilities and services, and in the disposal or management of premises. The SDA prohibits direct and indirect sex discrimination. Direct sex discrimination is where a woman or man is treated less favorably than a person of the opposite sex in comparable circumstances is, or would be, because of their gender. The test is: was the treatment less favorable than the treatment which was or would be accorded to a person of the opposite sex?; and was the treatment less favorable because of the gender of the person involved? Indirect sex discrimination is where a condition or practice is applied to both sexes but it adversely affects a considerably larger proportion of one sex than the other, and it is not justifiable, irrespective of sex, to apply that condition

---

16 Ibid., at Section 7.
17 Ibid., at Section 48.
18 Ibid., at Section 53.

or practice. A recent amendment places the burden of proof with the employer, in line with the European Directives.

Employment-related claims are brought in the employment tribunal. Possible remedies for unlawful discrimination include a declaration that unlawful discrimination has occurred; compensation for financial loss, injury to feelings and injury to health with interest; in employment tribunals, a recommendation that the employer take action which will reduce the effect of discrimination on the complainant; and in a county court in England and Wales, or sheriff court in Scotland, an order that the discriminator stop the discrimination.

Gender segregation involves a form of labor market rigidity that prevents the allocation of the most appropriate worker to any given job slot, and is a failure of the market to allocate people to their most productive location. Gender discrimination in pay occurs primarily because women and men tend to do different jobs or to have different work patterns. As a result it is easy to undervalue the demands of work performed by one sex compared with the demands associated with jobs typically done by the other. Such differences can be reinforced by discriminatory recruitment, training, selection and promotion procedures which may restrict the range of work each sex performs. Gender segregation in employment is often historical, and consequently, it may be difficult to recognize the discriminatory effects of past pay and grading decisions based on traditional values ascribed to 'male' and 'female' work. Career progression and promotion in all sectors are mechanisms, which sustain and even widen the gender pay gap. Past discriminatory assumptions about the value of what has been regarded as men's or women's work may be reflected in current grading schemes. Men and women may be doing the same or very similar work but have different job titles and consequently be in separate grades, with the women's jobs being graded lower. They may also be doing different jobs, which are actually of equal value though the women are in lower grades. The grading scheme could fail to value the actual work done and result in discrimination.

Equal Pay Act (EPA), Equal Opportunities Commission (EOC) and the Code of Practice on Equal Pay   Important for equal rights in employment and in particular women, the Equal Pay Act 1970 (EPA) covers all contractual terms and not simply those relating to pay, with claims taken initially to an Industrial Tribunal. Genuine occupational qualification is recognized in Section 1(3):

> 1. 3. An equality clause shall not operate in relation to a variation between the woman's contract and the man's contract if the employer proves that the variation is genuinely due to a material factor which is not the difference of sex ... and that factor ... must be a material difference between the woman's case and the man's....[19]

---

19   Equal Pay Act, UK, at Section 1(3).

Section 2(1) guarantees the important right of tribunal recourse for redress:

> 2. 1. Any claim in respect of the contravention of a term modified or
> included by virtue of an equality clause, including a claim for arrears
> of remuneration or damages in respect of the contravention, may be
> presented by way of a complaint to an employment tribunal.[20]

In terms of maternity discrimination cases, the Code of Practice on Equal Pay is the main source of advice on implementing equal pay in the workplace and was issued by the Equal Opportunities Commission (EOC) in 1997. Employers must include an equality clause into individual contracts of employment. The EOC issued a Code of Practice for the purposes of the elimination of discrimination in employment; for guidance to employers, trade unions and employment agencies on measures that can be taken to achieve equality, and on what steps it is reasonably practicable for employers to take to ensure that their employees do not in the course of their employment act contrary to the law; and for the promotion of equality of opportunity in employment. The primary responsibility at law rests with each employer to ensure that there is no unlawful discrimination. The Code recommends the establishment and use of consistent criteria for selection, training, promotion, redundancy and dismissal that are made known to all employees, as part of good employment practices in eliminating disability discrimination. It is recommended that each individual should be assessed according to his personal capability to carry out a given job.

The EOC recommends that a pay systems review should involve the following stages. Stage 1: undertake a thorough analysis of the pay system to produce a breakdown of all employees, which covers job title, grade, whether part-time or full-time, with basic pay, performance ratings and all other elements of remuneration; stage 2: examine each element of the pay system against the data obtained in stage 1; stage 3: identify any elements of the pay system that the review indicates may be the source of any discrimination; stage 4: change any rules or practices, including those in collective agreements, which stages 1 to 3 have identified as likely to give rise to discrimination in pay, in consultation with employees, trade unions or staff representatives where appropriate. Stages 1 to 3 may reveal that practices and procedures in relation to recruitment, selection and access to training have contributed to discrimination in pay, and these should be addressed; stage 5: analyze the likely effects of any proposed changes in practice to the pay system before implementation, in order to identify and rectify any discrimination that could be caused; stage 6: give equal pay to current employees. Where the review shows that some employees are not receiving equal pay for equal work and the reasons cannot be shown to be free of bias, then a plan must be developed for dealing with this; stage 7: set up a system of regular monitoring to allow checks to be made to pay practices; and stage 8: draw up and publish an equal pay policy

---

20   Ibid., at Section 2(1).

with provision for assessing the new pay system or modification to a system in terms of discrimination.[21]

Human Rights Act (HRA)   The Human Rights Act (HRA), entitled An Act to give further effect to rights and freedoms guaranteed under the European Convention on Human Rights. Regarding the interpretation of legislation, Section 3 states:

3.   1.   So far as it is possible to do so, primary legislation and subordinate legislation must be read and given effect in a way which is compatible with the Convention rights.
     2.   This section
          a.   applies to primary legislation and subordinate legislation whenever enacted;
          b.   does not affect the validity, continuing operation or enforcement of any incompatible primary legislation; and
          c.   does not affect the validity, continuing operation or enforcement of any incompatible subordinate legislation if (disregarding any possibility of revocation) primary legislation prevents removal of the incompatibility.[22]

Further, the concept of declaration of incompatibility is covered under Section 4:

4.   1.   Subsection (2) applies in any proceedings in which a court determines whether a provision of primary legislation is compatible with a Convention right.
     2.   If the court is satisfied that the provision is incompatible with a Convention right, it may make a declaration of that incompatibility.
     3.   Subsection (4) applies in any proceedings in which a court determines whether a provision of subordinate legislation, made in the exercise of a power conferred by primary legislation, is compatible with a Convention right.
     4.   If the court is satisfied
          a.   that the provision is incompatible with a Convention right, and
          b.   that (disregarding any possibility of revocation) the primary legislation concerned prevents removal of the incompatibility,
          it may make a declaration of that incompatibility.[23]

Finally, in terms of Acts of Public Authorities, Section 6 states:

---

21   Equal Opportunities Commission, *Code of Practice on Equal Pay, UK*.
22   Human Rights Act, UK, at Section 3.
23   Ibid., at Section 4.

6. 1. It is unlawful for a public authority to act in a way which is incompatible with a Convention right.
   2. Subsection (1) does not apply to an act if
      a. as the result of one or more provisions of primary legislation, the authority could not have acted differently; or
      b. in the case of one or more provisions of, or made under, primary legislation which cannot be read or given effect in a way which is compatible with the Convention rights, the authority was acting so as to give effect to or enforce those provisions.
   3. In this section 'public authority' includes
      a. a court or tribunal, and
      b. any person certain of whose functions are functions of a public nature,

      but does not include either House of Parliament or a person exercising functions in connection with proceedings in Parliament.
   5. In relation to a particular act, a person is not a public authority by virtue only of subsection (3)(b) if the nature of the act is private.
   6. 'An act' includes a failure to act but does not include a failure to
      a. introduce in, or lay before, Parliament a proposal for legislation; or
      b. make any primary legislation or remedial order.[24]

Equality Act In terms of the Equality Act 2006, the general duty of the Commission is outlined in Section 3:

3. The Commission shall exercise its functions under this Part with a view to encouraging and supporting the development of a society in which
   a. people's ability to achieve their potential is not limited by prejudice or discrimination,
   b. there is respect for and protection of each individual's human rights,
   c. there is respect for the dignity and worth of each individual,
   d. each individual has an equal opportunity to participate in society, and
   e. there is mutual respect between groups based on understanding and valuing of diversity and on shared respect for equality and human rights.[25]

Equality and diversity are to be promoted under Section 8:

8. 1. The Commission shall, by exercising the powers conferred by this Part
      a. promote understanding of the importance of equality and diversity,
      b. encourage good practice in relation to equality and diversity,
      c. promote equality of opportunity,

---

24 Ibid., at Section 6.
25 Equality Act, UK, at Section 3.

 d. promote awareness and understanding of rights under the equality enactments,

 e. enforce the equality enactments,

 f. work towards the elimination of unlawful discrimination, and

 g. work towards the elimination of unlawful harassment.[26]

Importantly, human rights are to be promoted under Section 9:

9. 1. The Commission shall, by exercising the powers conferred by this Part

  a. promote understanding of the importance of human rights,

  b. encourage good practice in relation to human rights,

  c. promote awareness, understanding and protection of human rights, and

  d. encourage public authorities to comply with section 6 of the Human Rights Act (compliance with Convention rights).[27]

As to groups, Section 10 states:

10. 1. The Commission shall, by exercising the powers conferred by this Part

  a. promote understanding of the importance of good relations

   i. between members of different groups, and

   ii. between members of groups and others,

  b. encourage good practice in relation to relations

   i. between members of different groups, and

   ii. between members of groups and others,

  c. work towards the elimination of prejudice against, hatred of and hostility towards members of groups, and

  d. work towards enabling members of groups to participate in society.

 2. In this Part 'group' means a group or class of persons who share a common attribute in respect of any of the following matters

  c. gender.

 3. For the purposes of this Part a reference to a group (as defined in subsection (2)) includes a reference to a smaller group or smaller class, within a group, of persons who share a common attribute (in addition to the attribute by reference to which the group is defined) in respect of any of the matters specified in subsection (2)(a) to (g).[28]

Finally, in terms of monitoring of the law, Section 11 states:

---

26 Ibid., at Section 8.
27 Ibid., at Section 9.
28 Ibid., at Section 10.

11. 1. The Commission shall monitor the effectiveness of the equality and human rights enactments.

2. The Commission may
   a. advise central government about the effectiveness of any of the equality and human rights enactments;
   b. recommend to central government the amendment, repeal, consolidation (with or without amendments) or replication (with or without amendments) of any of the equality and human rights enactments;
   c. advise central or devolved government about the effect of an enactment (including an enactment in or under an Act of the Scottish Parliament);
   d. advise central or devolved government about the likely effect of a proposed change of law.[29]

Ireland

Legislation

Constitution of Ireland   The Constitution of Ireland (*Bunreacht Na hEireann*) was enacted by the People on 1 July 1937 and came into operation as from 29 December 1937. The Preamble of the Constitution of Ireland states:

> In the Name of the Most Holy Trinity, from Whom is all authority and to Whom, as our final end, all actions both of men and States must be referred,
>
> We, the people of Éire,
>
> Humbly acknowledging all our obligations to our Divine Lord, Jesus Christ, Who sustained our fathers through centuries of trial,
>
> Gratefully remembering their heroic and unremitting struggle to regain the rightful independence of our Nation,
>
> And seeking to promote the common good, with due observance of Prudence, Justice and Charity, so that the dignity and freedom of the individual may be assured, true social order attained, the unity of our country restored, and concord established with other nations,
>
> Do hereby adopt, enact, and give to ourselves this Constitution.[30]

---

29   Ibid., at Section 11.
30   Constitution of Ireland, Ireland, at the Preamble.

Fundamental freedoms are guaranteed as personal rights under Article 40:

> 40. 1. All citizens shall, as human persons, be held equal before the law.
>   This shall not be held to mean that the State shall not in its enactments
>   have due regard to differences of capacity, physical and moral, and of
>   social function.[31]

Employment Equality Act   In Ireland, the Employment Equality Act 1998 prohibits discrimination in employment and in other spheres of life on a number of grounds. The conception of equality in the EEA is based on individual merit, and moves towards the 'equality as rationality' end of the spectrum, addressing discrimination based on prejudice or stereotypes. The Act creates some positive duties to promote equality, despite the limits to positive action in favor of individuals. In addition, it established an Equality Authority with powers to develop codes of practice that have enhanced legal standing, and to promote equality through Equality Reviews and Action Plans. Positive measures are permitted under the Employment Equality Act, where the measures are 'intended to reduce or eliminate the effects of discrimination', and various provisions prevent challenges to measures targeted to disadvantaged groups, including seniors.

Important for equal rights, discrimination is outlined in Section 6, and in particular Sections 6(2)(c) as to family status:

> 6. 1. For the purposes of this Act, discrimination shall be taken to occur
>   where, on any of the grounds in *subsection (2)* (in this Act referred to as
>   'the discriminatory grounds'), one person is treated less favourably than
>   another is, has been or would be treated.
>   2. As between any 2 persons, the discriminatory grounds (and the
>   descriptions of those grounds for the purposes of this Act) are:
>   a. that one is a woman and the other is a man (in this Act referred to as
>   'the gender ground'),
>   c. that one has family status and the other does not (in this Act referred
>   to as 'the family status ground').[32]

In terms of comparators, Section 28, in particular Section 28(1)(b) dealing with family status, states:

> 28. 1. For the purpose of this Part, 'C' and 'D' represent 2 persons who differ
>   as follows:
>   b. in relation to the family status ground, C has family status and D
>   does not, or *vice versa*;

---

31 Ibid., at Article 40.
32 Ibid., at Section 6.

2. In the following provisions of this Part, any reference to C and D which does not apply to a specific discriminatory ground shall be treated as a reference to C and D in the context of each of the discriminatory grounds (other than the gender ground) considered separately.
3. Any reference in this Act to persons having the same relevant characteristic as C (or as D) shall be construed by reference to the discriminatory ground in relation to which the reference applies or, as the case may be, in relation to each of the discriminatory grounds (other than the gender ground) separately, so that
    b. in relation to the family status ground, the relevant characteristic is having the same, or the same lack of, family status as C (or, as the case may be, as D),
    and so on for each of the other discriminatory grounds.[33]

Indirect discrimination is prohibited under Article 22:

22. 1. Where a provision (whether in the nature of a requirement, practice or otherwise) which relates to any of the matters specified in ... section 8(1)...
    a. applies to both A and B,
    b. is such that the proportion of persons who are disadvantaged by the provisions is substantially higher in the case of those of the same sex as A than in the case of those of the same sex as B, and
    c. cannot be justified by objective factors unrelated to A's sex,
    then, for purposes of this Act, A's employer ... shall be regarded as discriminating against A on the gender ground contrary to section 8....[34]

Further, indirect discrimination is covered in Section 31:

31. 1. Where a provision (whether in the nature of a requirement, practice or otherwise) relating to employment:
    a. applies to all the employees or prospective employees of a particular employer who include C and D or, as the case may be, to a particular class of those employees or prospective employees which includes C and D,
    b. operates to the disadvantage of C, as compared with D, in relation to any of the matters specified in *paragraphs (a)* to *(e)* of *section 8(1)*,
    c. in practice can be complied with by a substantially smaller proportion of the employees or prospective employees having the same relevant characteristic as C when compared with the employees or prospective employees having the same relevant characteristic as D, and

---

33 Ibid., at Section 28.
34 Ibid., at Article 22.

    d. cannot be justified as being reasonable in all the circumstances of the case,

then ... for the purposes of this Act the employer shall be regarded as discriminating against C, contrary to *section 8*, on whichever of the discriminatory grounds gives rise to the relevant characteristics referred to in *paragraph (c)*.[35]

Discrimination by employers is outlined under Section 8:

8. 1. In relation to:
    a. access to employment,
    b. conditions of employment,
    c. training or experience for or in relation to employment,
    d. promotion or re-grading, or
    e. classification of posts,

    an employer shall not discriminate against an employee or prospective employee and a provider of agency work shall not discriminate against an agency worker.

  5. Without prejudice to the generality of *subsection (1)*, an employer shall be taken to discriminate against an employee or prospective employee in relation to access to employment if the employer discriminates against the employee or prospective employee:
    a. in any arrangements the employer makes for the purpose of deciding to whom employment should be offered, or
    b. by specifying, in respect of one person or class of persons, entry requirements for employment which are not specified in respect of other persons or classes of persons, where the circumstances in which both such persons or classes would be employed are not materially different.

  6. Without prejudice to the generality of *subsection (1)*, an employer shall be taken to discriminate against an employee or prospective employee in relation to conditions of employment if, on any of the discriminatory grounds, the employer does not offer or afford to that employee or prospective employee or to a class of persons of whom he or she is one:
    a. the same terms of employment (other than remuneration and pension rights),
    b. the same working conditions, and
    c. the same treatment in relation to overtime, shift work, short time, transfers, lay-offs, redundancies, dismissals and disciplinary measures,

---

35 Ibid., at Section 31.

as the employer offers or affords to another person or class of persons, where the circumstances in which both such persons or classes are or would be employed are not materially different.

7. Without prejudice to the generality of *subsection (1)*, an employer shall be taken to discriminate against an employee in relation to training or experience for, or in relation to, employment if, on any of the discriminatory grounds, the employer refuses to offer or afford to that employee the same opportunities or facilities for employment counselling, training (whether on or off the job) and work experience as the employer offers or affords to other employees, where the circumstances in which that employee and those other employees are employed are not materially different.

8. Without prejudice to the generality of *subsection (1)*, an employer shall be taken to discriminate against an employee in relation to promotion if, on any of the discriminatory grounds:
    a. the employer refuses or deliberately omits to offer or afford the employee access to opportunities for promotion in circumstances in which another eligible and qualified person is offered or afforded such access, or
    b. the employer does not in those circumstances offer or afford the employee access in the same way to those opportunities.[36]

As well, discrimination as to bodies is covered under Section 13:

13. A body which
    a. is an organisation of workers or of employers,
    b. is a professional or trade organisation, or
    c. controls entry to, or the carrying on of, a profession, vocation or occupation,
    shall not discriminate against a person in relation to membership of that body or any benefits, other than pension rights, provided by it or in relation to entry to, or the carrying on of, that profession, vocation or occupation.[37]

The exclusion of discrimination in certain employment is allowed by way of a *bona fide* occupational qualification as outlined in Article 25:

25. 1. Nothing in this Part of Part II applies to discrimination against A in respect of employment in a particular post if the discrimination results from preferring B on the ground that, by reference to one or more of subsections (2) to (4) the sex of B is or amounts to an occupational qualification for the post in question.

---

36   Ibid., at Section 8.
37   Ibid., at Section 13.

2. For the purposes of this section, the sex of B shall be taken to be an occupational qualification for a post where, on grounds of physiology (excluding physical strength or stamina) or on grounds of authenticity for the purpose of entertainment, the nature of the post

    a. requires a person of the same sex as B, and
    b. would be materially different if filled by a person of the same sex as A.

3. For the purposes of this section, the sex of B shall be taken to be an occupational qualification for a post where it is necessary that the post should be held by B because it is likely to involve the performance of duties outside the State in a place where the laws or customs are such that those duties could not reasonably be performed by a person who is of the same sex as A.

4. For the purposes of this section, the sex of B shall be taken to be an occupational qualification for a post

    a. where the duties of the post involve personal services and it is necessary to have persons of both sexes engaged in such duties, or
    b. where, because of the nature of the employment it is necessary to provide sleeping and sanitary accommodation for employees on a communal basis and it would be unreasonable to expect the provision of separate accommodation of that nature or impracticable for an employer so to provide.[38]

Further, the Employment Equality Act makes the principle of 'equal pay for like work' a term of every employment contract. Proving 'like work' means showing that the work of the person claiming equal pay, the claimant, is the same, similar or equal in value to the work of the appropriate comparator, the person with whom the claimant is comparing himself. The comparator must, among other things, be employed by the same or an associated employer, at the same time or during the previous or following three years. Section 7 states:

7. 1. Subject to *subsection (2)*, for the purposes of this Act, in relation to the work which one person is employed to do, another person shall be regarded as employed to do like work if:

    a. both perform the same work under the same or similar conditions, or each is interchangeable with the other in relation to the work,
    b. the work performed by one is of a similar nature to that performed by the other and any differences between the work performed or the conditions under which it is performed by each either are of small importance in relation to the work as a whole or occur with such irregularity as not to be significant to the work as a whole, or

---

38   Ibid., at Article 25.

     c.   the work performed by one is equal in value to the work performed by the other, having regard to such matters as skill, physical or mental requirements, responsibility and working conditions.
3. In any case where:
     a.   the remuneration received by one person ('the primary worker') is less than the remuneration received by another ('the comparator'), and
     b.   the work performed by the primary worker is greater in value than the work performed by the comparator, having regard to the matters mentioned in *subsection (1)(c)*,

     then, for the purposes of *subsection (1)(c)*, the work performed by the primary worker shall be regarded as equal in value to the work performed by the comparator.[39]

Equal remuneration is established under Article 19:

19. 1. It shall be a term of the contract under which A is employed that, subject to this Act, A shall at any time be entitled to the same rate of remuneration for the work which A is employed to do as B who, at that or any relevant time, is employed to do like work by the same or an associated employer.[40]

In addition, entitlement to equal remuneration is covered under Section 29:

29. 1. It shall be a term of the contract under which C is employed that, subject to this Act, C shall at any time be entitled to the same rate of remuneration for the work which C is employed to do as D who, at that or any other relevant time, is employed to do like work by the same or an associated employer.
    3. For the purposes of this Part, where D's employer is an associated employer of C's employer, C and D shall not be regarded as employed to do like work unless they both have the same or reasonably comparable terms and conditions of employment.
    4. Where a term of a contract of employment or a criterion applied to employees (including C and D):
     a.   applies to all employees of a particular employer or to a particular class of such employees (including C and D),
     b.   is such that the remuneration of those who fulfil the term or criterion is different from that of those who do not,
     c.   is such that the proportion of employees who can fulfil the term or criterion is substantially smaller in the case of the employees having

---

39   Ibid., at Section 7.
40   Ibid., at Article 19.

the same relevant characteristic as C when compared with the employees having the same relevant characteristic as D, and

d.   cannot be justified as being reasonable in all the circumstances of the case,

then, for the purposes of *subsection (1)*, C and D shall each be treated as fulfilling or, as the case may be, as not fulfilling the term or criterion, whichever results in the higher remuneration.

5.   Subject to *subsection (4)*, nothing in this Part shall prevent an employer from paying, on grounds other than the discriminatory grounds, different rates of remuneration to different employees.[41]

Further, a gender equality clause is guaranteed under Article 21:

21. 1.   If and so far as the terms of a contract of employment do not include (expressly or by reference to a collective agreement or otherwise) a gender equality clause, they shall be taken to include one.

2.   A gender equality clause is a provision relating to the terms of a contract of employment, other than a term relating to remuneration or pension rights, which has the effect that if

a.   A is employed in circumstances where the work done by A is not materially different from that done by B in the same employment, and

b.   at any time A's contract of employment would (but for the gender equality clause)

i.   contain a term which is or becomes less favourable to A than a term of a similar kind in B's contract of employment, or

ii.   not include a term corresponding to a term in B's contract of employment which benefits B,

then the terms of A's contract of employment shall be treated as modified so that the term in question is not less favourable to A or, as the case may be, so that they include a similar term benefiting A.

3.   A gender equality clause shall not operate in relation to a difference between A's contract of employment and B's contract of employment if the employer proves that the difference is genuinely based on grounds other than the gender ground.[42]

Important for equal rights, an equality clause is outlined under Section 30:

30. 1.   If and so far as the terms of a contract of employment do not include (expressly or by reference to a collective agreement or otherwise) a non-discriminatory equality clause, they shall be taken to include one.

---

41   Ibid., at Section 29.
42   Ibid., at Article 21.

2. A non-discriminatory equality clause is a provision relating to the terms of a contract of employment, other than a term relating to remuneration or pension rights, which has the effect that if:

    a. C is employed in circumstances where the work done by C is not materially different from that done by D in the same employment, and

    b. at any time C's contract of employment would (but for the non-discriminatory equality clause):

        i. contain a term which is or becomes less favourable to C than a term of a similar kind in D's contract of employment, or

        ii. not include a term corresponding to a term in D's contract of employment which benefits D,

    then the terms of C's contract of employment shall be treated as modified so that the term in question is not less favourable to C or, as the case may be, so that they include a similar term benefiting C.

3. A non-discriminatory equality clause shall not operate in relation to a difference between C's contract of employment and D's contract of employment if the employer proves that the difference is genuinely based on grounds which are not among those specified in *paragraphs (a) to (h)* of *section 28(1)*.[43]

Harassment in the workplace is covered under Section 32:

32. 1. If, at a place where C is employed (in this section referred to as 'the workplace'), or otherwise in the course of C's employment, another individual ('E') harasses C by reference to the relevant characteristic of C and:

    a. C and E are both employed at that place or by the same employer,

    b. E is C's employer, or

    c. E is a client, customer or other business contact of C's employer and the circumstances of the harassment are such that C's employer ought reasonably to have taken steps to prevent it,

    then, for the purposes of this Act, the harassment constitutes discrimination by C's employer, in relation to C's conditions of employment, on whichever discriminatory ground is relevant to persons having the same relevant characteristic as C.

6. If, as a result of any act or conduct of E another person ('F') who is C's employer would, apart from this subsection, be regarded … as discriminating against C, it shall be a defence for F to prove that F took such steps as are reasonably practicable:

    a. … to prevent C being treated differently in the workplace or otherwise in the course of C's employment and, if and so far as any such treatment has occurred, to reverse the effects of it, and

---

43 Ibid., at Section 30.

b.   ... to prevent E from harassing C (or any class of persons of whom C is one).[44]

Importantly, positive action is established under Article 24 in that the provisions of this Act are without prejudice to measures to promote equal opportunity for men and women, in particular by removing existing inequalities which affect women's opportunities in the areas of access to employment, vocational training and promotion, and working conditions.[45] Further, positive action for workers is permitted as contained in Section 33, and in particular Section 33(1)(*a*):

33. 1.   Nothing in this Part or *Part II* shall prevent the taking of such measures ... in order to facilitate the integration into employment, either generally or in particular areas or a particular workplace.
    3.   Nothing in this Part or *Part II* shall render unlawful the provision, by or on behalf of the State, of training or work experience for a disadvantaged group of persons if the Minister certifies that, in the absence of the provision in question, it is unlikely that that disadvantaged group would receive similar training or work experience.[46]

In addition, an exception exists as to family matters in Section 26:

26. 1.   Nothing in this Act shall make it unlawful for an employer to arrange for or provide treatment which confers benefits on women in connection with pregnancy and maternity (including breastfeeding) or adoption.
    2.   This Act does not apply to discrimination on the gender ground in employment which consists of the performance of services of a personal nature, such as the care of an elderly or incapacitated person in that person's home, where the sex of the employee constitutes a determining factor.[47]

The Equality Authority has important legal powers, not to decide on disputes but to work generally for the elimination of discrimination and the promotion of equal opportunities. It can develop Codes of Practice, carry out equality reviews in particular employment, draw up Equality Action Plans, and serve Substantive Notices. The Authority has broad powers to ensure the development of a proactive equality-conscious approach to equal opportunities in the workplace. The functions of the Equality Authority are outlined under Section 39:

39. The Authority shall have, in addition to the functions assigned to it by any other provision of this Act or of any other Act, the following general functions:

---

44   Ibid., at Section 32.
45   Ibid., at Article 24.
46   Ibid., at Section 33.
47   Ibid., at Section 26.

    a. to work towards the elimination of discrimination in relation to employment;

    b. to promote equality of opportunity in relation to the matters to which this Act applies.[48]

The forum for seeking redress is covered under Section 77:

77. 1. A person who claims:

    a. to have been discriminated against by another in contravention of this Act,

    b. not to be receiving remuneration in accordance with an equal remuneration term,

    c. not to be receiving a benefit under an equality clause, or

    d. to have been penalised in circumstances amounting to victimisation,

may, subject to *subsections (2)* to *(8)*, seek redress by referring the case to the Director.

2. If a person claims to have been dismissed:

    a. in circumstances amounting to discrimination by another in contravention of this Act, or

    b. in circumstances amounting to victimisation,

then, subject to *subsection (3)*, a claim for redress for the dismissal may be brought to the Labour Court and shall not be brought to the Director.

3. If the grounds for such a claim as is referred to in *subsection (1)* or *(2)* arise:

    a. under *Part III*, or

    b. in any other circumstances (including circumstances amounting to victimisation) to which the Equal Pay Directive or the Equal Treatment Directive is relevant,

then ... the person making the claim may seek redress by referring the case to the Circuit Court, instead of referring it to the Director under *subsection (1)* or, as the case may be, to the Labour Court under *subsection (2)*.[49]

Crucially, enforcement of determinations, decisions and mediated settlements is outlined under Section 91:

91. 1. If an employer or any other person who is bound by the terms of:

    a. a final determination of the Labour Court under this Part, or

    b. a final decision of the Director under this Part,

---

48   Ibid., at Section 39.
49   Ibid., at Section 77.

fails to comply with the terms of the determination or decision then, on an application under this section, the Circuit Court shall make, subject to *section 93*, an order directing the person affected (that is to say, the employer or other person concerned) to carry out the determination or decision in accordance with its terms.

2. If an employer or the person who is a party to a settlement ... fails to give effect, in whole or in part, to the terms of the settlement, then, on an application under this section, the Circuit Court may make an order directing the person affected (that is to say, the employer or the person who is a party to the settlement) to carry out those terms or, as the case may be, the part of those terms to which the application relates; but the Circuit Court shall not, by virtue of this subsection, direct any person to pay any sum or do any other thing which (had the matter been dealt with otherwise than by mediation) could not have been provided for by way of redress ....

4. An application under this section may be made:
   a. by the complainant, or
   b. in a case where the Authority is not the complainant, then, by the Authority with the consent of the complainant if the Authority considers that the determination, decision or settlement is unlikely to be implemented without its intervention.

5. On an application under this section, the Circuit Court shall exercise its functions under *subsection (1)* or *(2)* on being satisfied:
   a. of the existence and terms of the determination, decision or settlement, and
   b. of the failure by the person affected to comply with those terms.[50]

Equal Status Act   Important for equal rights, the Equal Status Act 2000 protects against discrimination, which is outlined in Section 3, and in particular Sections 3(2)(c) as to family status:

3. 1. For the purposes of this Act, discrimination shall be taken to occur where:
   a. on any of the grounds specified in *subsection (2)* (in this Act referred to as 'the discriminatory grounds') which exists at present or previously existed but no longer exists or may exist in the future, or which is imputed to the person concerned, a person is treated less favourably than another person is, has been or would be treated,
   b. i. a person who is associated with another person is treated, by virtue of that association, less favourably than a person who is not so associated is, has been or would be treated, and

---

50   Ibid., at Section 91.

> ii. similar treatment of that person on any of the discriminatory grounds would, by virtue of *paragraph (a)*, constitute discrimination,
>
> or
>
> c. i. a person is in a category of persons who share a common characteristic by reason of which discrimination may, by virtue of *paragraph (a)*, occur in respect of those persons,
>
>   ii. the person is obliged by the provider of a service ... to comply with a condition (whether in the nature of a requirement, practice or otherwise) but is unable to do so,
>
>   iii. substantially more people outside the category than within it are able to comply with the condition, and
>
>   iv. the obligation to comply with the condition cannot be justified as being reasonable in all the circumstances of the case.
>
> 2. As between any two persons, the discriminatory grounds (and the descriptions of those grounds for the purposes of this Act) are:
>
>   a. that one is male and the other is female (the 'gender ground'),
>
>   c. that one has family status and the other does not or that one has a different family status from the other (the 'family status ground'),
>
>   j. that one:
>
>   i. has in good faith applied for any determination or redress provided for in *Part II or III*,
>
>   iv. has opposed by lawful means an act which is unlawful under this Act, or
>
>   v. has given notice of an intention to take any of the actions specified in *subparagraphs (i)* to *(iv)*, and the other has not (the 'victimisation ground').[51]

Further, clubs are given special treatment under Section 9, which specifically mentions family status under Section 9(1)(a)(i):

> 9. 1. ... a club shall not be considered to be a discriminating club by reason only that
>
>   a. if its principal purpose is to cater only for the needs of
>
>   i. persons of a particular gender, ... family status....[52]

Certain measures are not prohibited under Section 14:

> 14. Nothing in this Act shall be construed as prohibiting:
>
>   a. the taking of any action that is required by or under:
>
>   i. any enactment or order of a court,

---

51 Equal Status Act, at Section 3.
52 Ibid., at Section 9.

　　　ii.　any act done or measure adopted by the European Union, by the European Communities or institutions thereof or by bodies competent under the Treaties establishing the European Communities, or

　　　iii.　any convention or other instrument imposing an international obligation on the State, or

　b.　preferential treatment or the taking of positive measures which are *bona fide* intended to:

　　　i.　promote equality of opportunity for persons who are, in relation to other persons, disadvantaged or who have been or are likely to be unable to avail themselves of the same opportunities as those other persons, or

　　　ii.　cater for the special needs of persons, or a category of persons, who, because of their circumstances, may require facilities, arrangements, services or assistance not required by persons who do not have those special needs.[53]

Importantly, redress in respect of prohibited grounds is covered under Section 21:

21. 1.　A person who claims that prohibited conduct has been directed against him or her may, subject to this section, seek redress by referring the case to the Director.

　2.　Before seeking redress under this section the complainant:

　a.　shall, within 2 months after the prohibited conducted is alleged to have occurred, or, where more than one incident of prohibited conduct is alleged to have occurred, within 2 months after the last such occurrence, notify the respondent in writing of:

　　　i.　the nature of the allegation,

　　　ii.　the complainant's intention, if not satisfied with the respondent's response to the allegation, to seek redress by referring the case to the Director, and

　b.　may in that notification, with a view to assisting the complainant in deciding whether to refer the case to the Director, question the respondent in writing so as to obtain material information and the respondent may, if the respondent so wishes, reply to any such questions.[54]

Finally, mediation is provided for under Section 24:

24. 1.　Subject to *subsection (2)*, if at any time after a case has been referred to the Director under section 21 it appears to the Director that the case is

---

53　Ibid., at Section 14.
54　Ibid., at Section 21.

one which could be resolved by mediation, the Director shall refer the case for mediation to an equality mediation officer.

2. If the complainant or the respondent objects to a case being dealt with by way of mediation, the Director shall not exercise his or her powers under this section....

3. Mediation shall be conducted in private.

5. If, after a case has been referred to an equality mediation officer, it appears to the equality mediation officer that the case cannot be resolved by mediation, the officer shall issue a notice to that effect to the complainant and the respondent.[55]

Maternity Protection Act and Maternity Protection (Amendment) Act The Maternity Protection Act 1994 is entitled an Act to implement Council Directive 92/85/EEC of 19 October 1992 on the introduction of measures to encourage improvements in the safety and health at work of pregnant workers and workers who have recently given birth or are breastfeeding, to re-enact with amendments the provisions of the Maternity Protection of Employees Acts, 1981 and 1991, to entitle a male employee to leave in certain cases where the mother of his child dies, to extend as a consequence of the above-mentioned provisions the protection against unfair dismissals conferred by the Unfair Dismissals Act, 1977, and to provide for related matters. Ireland has a population of 4,459,547 people.[56] In Ireland, if one becomes pregnant while in employment, one is entitled to take maternity leave. The Maternity Protection (Amendment) Act 2004 is entitled an Act to amend and extend the Maternity Protection Act 1994, to amend the Redundancy Payments Act 1967 and the Unfair Dismissals Act 1977, to revoke in part and enact in respect of certain proceedings the European Communities (Burden of Proof in Gender Discrimination Cases) Regulations 2001 which gave effect to Council Directive 97/80/EC of 15 December 1997 on the burden of proof in cases of discrimination based on sex and to provide for related matters. The entitlement to a basic period of maternity leave from employment extends to all female employees in Ireland, including casual workers, regardless of how long one has been working for the organization or the number of hours worked per week. One is generally entitled to 26 weeks' maternity leave together with 16 weeks' additional unpaid maternity leave. One may qualify for Maternity Benefits, which is a Department of Social and Family Affairs payment, if one has sufficient PRSI (Pay Related Social Insurance) contributions. However, an employee's contract could provide for additional rights to payment during the leave period, so that the employee could receive full pay less the amount of Maternity Benefit payable. Time spent on maternity leave is treated as though one has been in employment, and this time can be used to accumulate annual leave and public holiday entitlement.

---

55 Ibid., at Section 24.
56 Ireland Census.

In looking at the Maternity Protection Act 1994, in terms of entitlement to maternity leave, Section 8 states:

> 8. 1. Subject to this Part, a pregnant employee shall be entitled to leave, to be known (and referred to in this Act) as 'maternity leave', from her employment for a period (in this Part referred to as 'the minimum period of maternity leave') of not less than 14 consecutive weeks.
>   2. The Minister may by order, made with the consent of the Minister for Social Welfare and the consent of the Minister for Finance, amend *subsection (1)* so as to extend the period mentioned in that subsection.[57]

Section 2 of the 2004 Act amends Section 8:

> 2. The Principal Act is amended by the substitution of the following section for Section 8:
>   8. 1. Subject to this Part, a pregnant employee shall be entitled to leave, to be known (and referred to in this Act) as 'maternity leave', from her employment for a period (in this Part referred to as 'the minimum period of maternity leave') of not less than
>   a. 18 consecutive weeks, or
>   b. 18 weeks part of which is postponed in accordance with section 14B, as may be appropriate.[58]

Employer notification is required under Section 9:

> 9. 1. Entitlement to the minimum period of maternity leave shall be subject to a pregnant employee
>   a. having, as soon as reasonably practicable but not later than four weeks before the commencement of maternity leave, notified in writing her employer (or caused her employer to be so notified) of her intention to take maternity leave; and
>   b. having, at the time of the notification, given to her employer or produced for her employer's inspection a medical or other appropriate certificate confirming the pregnancy and specifying the expected week of confinement.
>   2. A notification under this section may be revoked by a further notification in writing by the employee concerned to her employer.[59]

Importantly, Section 10 guarantees an allocation of a minimum period of maternity leave:

---

57 Maternity Protection Act, at Section 8.
58 Maternity Protection (Amendment) Act, at Section 2.
59 Maternity Protection Act, at Section 9.

10. 1.   Subject to *subsection (2)* and *sections 11* to *13*, the minimum period of maternity leave shall commence on such day as the employee selects, being not later than four weeks before the end of the expected week of confinement, and shall end on such day as she selects, being not earlier than four weeks after the end of the expected week of confinement.

    2.   Where an employee is employed under a contract for a fixed term and that term expires before the day which, apart from this subsection, would be the last day of her maternity leave, then

        a.   notwithstanding any other provision in this Part, the last day of her maternity leave shall be the day on which the term expires; and

        b.   nothing in this Part shall affect the termination of the employee's contract of employment on that day.[60]

Section 3 of the 2004 Act amends Section 10:

    3.   Section 10(1) of the Principal Act is amended by the substitution of 'not later than two weeks before the end of the expected week of confinement' for 'not later than four weeks before the end of the expected week of confinement'.[61]

Further, Section 11 deals with the variation in allocation of the minimum period of maternity leave:

11. 1.   Where it is certified by a registered medical practitioner or otherwise to the satisfaction of the Minister and the Minister for Social Welfare that, for an employee specified in the certificate, the minimum period of maternity leave should for a medical reason so specified commence on a date so specified, and the certificate is produced for inspection by the employer concerned within such period as may be prescribed by regulations made by the Minister under this section, the minimum period of maternity leave for that employee shall commence on the date so specified.

    2.   Where a certificate under this section is issued and the requirement in *subsection (1)* relating to the production of the certificate for the employer's inspection is complied with, the employee specified in the certificate.

        a.   shall be taken to have informed her employer of her pregnancy (if she had not previously done so); and

        b.   shall be deemed to have complied also with *section 9 (1) (a)*.[62]

---

60   Ibid., at Section 10.
61   Maternity Protection (Amendment) Act, at Section 3.
62   Maternity Protection Act, at Section 11.

Finally, Section 12 deals with the possible extension of maternity leave:

12. 1. Where the date of confinement of a pregnant employee occurs in a week after the expected week of confinement, the minimum period of maternity leave shall be extended by such number of consecutive weeks (subject to a maximum of four consecutive weeks) after the week in which the date of confinement occurs as ensures compliance with *section 10*.

2. Where the minimum period of maternity leave is proposed to be extended under this section, the employee concerned shall

   a. as soon as practicable after the proposal for such extension, notify in writing her employer (or cause her employer to be so notified) of the proposed extension; and

   b. as soon as practicable after the date of confinement, confirm in writing to her employer the notification under *paragraph (a)* and specify the duration of the extension.[63]

With regard to commencement of maternity leave, early confinement, Section 13 states:

13. 1. Where, in relation to a pregnant employee, the date of confinement occurs in a week that is four weeks or more before the expected week of confinement, the employee shall, where the circumstances so require, be deemed to have complied with *section 9 (1) (a)* if the notification required by that section is given in the period of 14 days commencing on the date of confinement.

2. Notwithstanding *section 10 (1)*, but subject to regulations under section 11, the minimum period of maternity leave for an employee referred to in *subsection (1)* shall be a period of not less than 14 consecutive weeks commencing on whichever of the following is the earlier

   a. the first day of maternity leave taken in accordance with *section 10*; and

   b. the date of confinement.[64]

Section 4 of the 2004 Act amends Section 13:

4. Section 13 of the Principal Act is amended by the substitution of the following subsection for subsection (2):

2. Notwithstanding section 10(1), but subject to regulations under section 11, the minimum period of maternity leave for an employee referred to in subsection (1) shall be a period of not less than

   a. 18 consecutive weeks, or

---

63   Ibid., at Section 12.
64   Ibid., at Section 13.

      b. 18 weeks part of which is postponed in accordance with section 14B, as may be appropriate, commencing on whichever of the following is the earlier
  - i. the first day of maternity leave taken in accordance with section 10, or
  - ii. the date of confinement.[65]

Section 14 deals with the possible entitlement to additional maternity leave:

14. 1. An employee who has taken maternity leave shall, if she so wishes, be entitled in accordance with this section to further leave, to be known (and referred to in this Act) as 'additional maternity leave', for a maximum period of four consecutive weeks commencing immediately after the end of her maternity leave.
  2. An employee shall be entitled to additional maternity leave, whether or not the minimum period of maternity leave has been extended under *section 12*.
  3. Entitlement to additional maternity leave shall be subject to an employee having notified in writing her employer (or caused her employer to be so notified) … of her intention to take such leave.[66]

Section 5 of the 2004 Act amends Section 14:

5. Section 14 of the Principal Act is amended
  a. by the substitution of the following subsection for subsection (1):
    1. An employee who has taken maternity leave shall, if she so wishes, be entitled in accordance with this section to further leave from her employment, to be known (and referred to in this Act) as 'additional maternity leave', for a maximum period of
      a. 8 consecutive weeks commencing immediately after the end of her maternity leave, or
      b. 8 weeks, all or part of which is postponed in accordance with section 14B, commencing either in accordance with that section or immediately after the end of her maternity leave, as may be appropriate.[67]

In addition, Section 7 of the 2004 Act states:

7. The Principal Act is amended by the insertion of the following section after section 14A (inserted by *section 6* of this Act):

---

65 Maternity Protection (Amendment) Act, at Section 4.
66 Maternity Protection Act, at Section 14.
67 Maternity Protection (Amendment) Act, at Section 5.

14B. 1. Subject to subsection (2), an employee who is on maternity leave or is additional maternity leave in entitled to, or is on, additional maternity leave may, if the child in connection with whose birth she is on, or is entitled to, that leave (in this section referred to as 'the child') is hospitalised, request in writing (or cause a written request to be submitted to) her employer to postpone

    a.   part of the maternity leave,

    b.   part of the maternity leave and the additional maternity leave, or

    c.   the additional maternity leave or part of it, as may be appropriate,

    in accordance with this section.

  2. An employee may make a request under paragraph (*a*) or (*b*) of subsection (1) to postpone part of her maternity leave with effect from a date she selects only if the period of maternity leave taken by her on that date is not less than 14 weeks and not less than 4 of those weeks are after the end of the week of confinement.

Further, Section 15 deals with the right to time off from work for ante-natal or post-natal care:

15. 1. For the purpose of receiving ante-natal or post-natal care or both, an employee shall be entitled to time off from her work, without loss of pay, in accordance with regulations made under this section by the Minister.

  2. Without prejudice to the generality of *subsection (1)*, regulations under this section may make provision in relation to all or any of the following matters

    a.   the amount of time off to which an employee shall be entitled under this section;

    b.   the terms or conditions relating to such time off;

    c.   the notice to be given in advance by an employee so entitled to her, employer (including any circumstances in which such notice need not be given);

    d.   the evidence to be furnished by an employee so entitled to her employer of any appropriate medical or related appointment.[68]

Section 9 of the 2004 Act states:

9. The Principal Act is amended by the insertion of the following section after section 15A (inserted by *section 8* of this Act):

15B. 1. An employee who is breastfeeding shall be entitled, without loss of pay, at the work option of her employer to either

---

68   Maternity Protection Act, at Section 15.

    a. time off from her work for the purpose of breastfeeding in the workplace in accordance with regulations made under this section by the Minister where facilities for breastfeeding are provided in the workplace by her employer, or

    b. a reduction of her working hours in accordance with regulations made under this section by the Minister for the purpose of breastfeeding otherwise than in the workplace.

2. An employer shall not be required to provide facilities for breastfeeding in the workplace if the provision of such facilities would give rise to a cost, other than a nominal cost, to the employer.[69]

Interestingly, fathers are only entitled to maternity leave if the mother dies within 24 weeks of the birth. In these circumstances, the father may be entitled to a period of leave, the extent of which depends on the actual date of the mother's death. Where a father qualifies for leave under these circumstances, he also has an optional right to the additional maternity leave. In the case of the death of the mother, Section 16 provides some guarantees:

16. 1. If a woman (in this section referred to as 'the mother') who has been delivered of a living child dies at any time before the expiry of the fourteenth week following the week of her confinement, the father of the child (if he is employed under a contract of employment) shall he entitled in accordance with this section to leave from his employment for a period ending as follows

    a. if the mother dies before the expiry of the tenth week following the week of her confinement, the period ends at the end of that tenth week; and

    b. if the mother dies at any time after the expiry of that tenth week, the period ends at the end of the fourteenth week following the week of her confinement.

2. Entitlement to leave under *subsection (1)* shall be subject to the father

    a. notifying his employer in writing (or causing his employer to be so notified) not later than the day on which his leave begins of the death of the mother, of his intention to take leave under *subsection (1)* and of the length of the leave to which he believes he is so entitled; and

    b. if requested by his employer, causing his employer to be supplied, as soon as is reasonably practicable, with a copy of the death certificate made in respect of the mother and of the birth certificate in respect of the child.

3. The period of leave under *subsection (1)* shall commence within 7 days of the mother's death; and in this section

---

69   Maternity Protection (Amendment) Act, at Section 9.

    a. a period of such leave which ends as mentioned in *paragraph (a) of subsection (1)* is referred to as '*subsection (1) (a)* leave'; and

    b. a period of such leave which ends as mentioned in *paragraph (b)* of that subsection is referred to as '*subsection (1) (b)* leave'.

4. A father who has taken *subsection (1) (a)* leave shall, if he so wishes, be entitled to further leave for a maximum period of four consecutive weeks commencing immediately after the end of his *subsection (1) (a)* leave.

5. Entitlement to further leave under *subsection (4)* shall be subject to the father having notified in writing his employer (or caused his employer to be so notified) in accordance with *subsection (6)* of his intention to take such leave.[70]

Section 10 of the 2004 Act amends Section 10:

10. Section 16 of the Principal Act is amended

    a. by the substitution of the following subsection for subsection (1):

        1. If a woman who has been delivered of a living child (in this section referred to as 'the mother') dies at any time before the expiry of the twenty-fourth week following the week of her confinement, the father of the child (if he is employed under a contract of employment) shall be entitled in accordance with this section to leave from his employment for a period ending as follows

            a. if the mother dies before the expiry of the sixteenth week following the week of her confinement, the period ends, subject to section 16B, at the end of that sixteenth week, and

            b. if the mother dies at any time after the expiry of that sixteenth week, the period ends, subject to sections 16A and 16B, at the end of the twenty-fourth week following the week of her confinement,

        4. A father who has taken subsection (1)(a) leave shall, if he so wishes, be entitled to further leave from his employment for a maximum period of

            a. 8 consecutive weeks commencing immediately after the end of his subsection (1)(a) leave, or

            b. 8 weeks, all or part of which is postponed in accordance with section 16B, commencing either in accordance with that section or immediately after the end of his subsection (1)(a) leave, as may be appropriate.[71]

---

70   Maternity Protection Act, at Section 16.

71   Maternity Protection (Amendment) Act, at Section 10.

In terms of those employees defined in Section 17, pregnant employees, employees who have recently given birth and employees who are breastfeeding,[72] Section 18 provides for leave for health and safety reasons:

18. 1. If, by regulations under the 1989 Act implementing the 1992 Directive, an employer is required to move an employee to whom this Part applies to other work (whether as a result of a risk assessment or because the employee cannot be required to perform night work), but
     a. it is not technically or objectively feasible for the employer to move the employee as required by the regulations, or
     b. such a move cannot reasonably be required on duly substantiated grounds, or
     c. the other work to which the employer proposes to move the employee is not suitable for her,
     the employee shall be granted leave from her employment under this section.
   3. For the purposes of *subsection (1) (c)*, other work is suitable for an employee if it is
     a. of a kind which is suitable in relation to the employee concerned, as an employee to whom this Part applies; and
     b. appropriate for the employee to do in all the circumstances.
   4. For the first 21 days of leave granted to an employee by an employer under this section in any relevant period, the employee shall be entitled to receive from the employer remuneration of an amount determined in accordance with regulations.[73]

Section 22 deals with the preservation or suspension of certain rights while on protective leave:

22. 1. During a period of absence from work by an employee while on
     a. maternity leave,
     b. *subsection (1) (a)* leave, as defined in *section 16 (3)*, or
     c. leave granted under *section 18*,
     and during a period of natal care absence, the employee shall be deemed to have been in the employment of the employer and, accordingly, while so absent the employee shall, subject to *subsection (6)* and *section 24*, be treated as if she had not been so absent; and such absence shall not affect any right (other than, except in the case of natal care absence, the employee's right to remuneration during such absence), whether conferred by statute, contract or otherwise, and related to the employee's employment.

---

72 Maternity Protection Act, at Section 17.
73 Ibid., at Section 18.

2. In respect of a period of absence from work by an employee while on
    a. additional maternity leave,
    b. *subsection (1) (b)* leave, as defined in *section 16 (3)*, or
    c. further leave under *section 16 (4)*,
    the period of employment before such absence shall be regarded as
    continuous with the employee's employment following such absence in
    respect of any right (other than the right to remuneration during such
    absence) whether conferred by statute, contract or otherwise, and related
    to the employee's employment.[74]

Importantly, a general right to return to work on expiry of protective leave is
guaranteed in Section 26:

26. 1. Subject to this Part, on the expiry of a period during which an employee
        was absent from work while on protective leave, the employee shall be
        entitled to return to work
        a. with the employer with whom she was working immediately before
            the start of that period or, where during the employee's absence from
            work there was a change of ownership of the undertaking in which
            she was employed immediately before her absence, with the owner
            (in this Act referred to as 'the successor') of the undertaking at the
            expiry of the period of absence,
        b. in the job which the employee held immediately before the start of
            that period, and
        c. under the contract of employment under which the employee was
            employed immediately before the start of that period, or, where a
            change of ownership such as is referred to in *paragraph (a)* has
            occurred, under a contract of employment with the successor which
            is identical to the contract under which the employee was employed
            immediately before the start of that period, and (in either case) under
            terms or conditions not less favourable than those that would have been
            applicable to the employee if she had not been so absent from work.
    3. In this section 'job', in relation to an employee, means the nature of the
        work which she is employed to do in accordance with her contract of
        employment and the capacity and place in which she is so employed.[75]

Section 18 of the 2004 Act amends Section 26:

18. Section 26 of the Principal Act is amended
    a. in subsection (1)(*a*), by the substitution of with the employer with whom
        she or he was working immediately before the start of that period or,

---

74 Ibid., at Section 22.
75 Ibid., at Section 26.

where during the employee's absence from work there was a change of ownership of the undertaking in which she or he was employed immediately before her or his absence for with the employer with whom she was working immediately before the start of that period or, where during the employee's absence from work there was a change of ownership of the undertaking in which she was employed immediately before her absence,

    b. in subsection (1)(*c*), by the substitution of and (in either case) under terms or conditions

        i. not less favourable than those that would have been applicable to the employee, and

       ii. that incorporate any improvement to the terms or conditions of employment to which the employee would have been entitled, if she or he had not been so absent from work for and (in either case) under terms or conditions not less favourable than those that would have been applicable to the employee if she had not been so absent from work.[76]

Further, Section 27 deals with the right to suitable alternative work in certain circumstances on return to work:

27. 1. Where an employee is entitled to return to work in accordance with *section 26* but it is not reasonably practicable for the employer or the successor to permit the employee to return to work in accordance with that section, the employee shall, subject to this Part, be entitled to be offered by the employer, the successor or an associated employer suitable alternative work under a new contract of employment.

    2. Work under a new contract of employment constitutes suitable alternative work for the purposes of this Act if

        a. the work required to be done under the contract is of a kind which is suitable in relation to the employee concerned and appropriate for the employee to do in the circumstances; and

        b. the terms or conditions of the contract relating to the place where the work under it is required to be done, the capacity in which the employee concerned is to be employed and any other terms or conditions of employment are not substantially less favourable to the employee than those of her contract of employment immediately before the start of the period of absence from work while on protective leave.[77]

Section 19 of the 2004 Act amends Section 27:

---

76 Maternity Protection (Amendment) Act, at Section 18.
77 Maternity Protection Act, at Section 27.

19. Section 27(2) of the Principal Act is amended by the substitution of the following paragraph for paragraph (*b*):

  b. the terms or conditions of the contract

    i. relating to the place where the work under it is required to be done, the capacity in which the employee concerned is to be employed and any other terms or conditions of employment are not less favourable to the employee than those of her or his contract of employment immediately before the start of the period of absence from work while on protective leave, and

    ii. incorporate any improvement to the terms or conditions of employment to which the employee would have been entitled if she or he had not been so absent from work during that period.

The procedure for the referral of disputes to the rights commissioner is outlined under Section 31:

31. 1. The referral of a dispute shall be initiated by the employee or the relevant employer giving a notice in writing, containing such particulars (if any) as may be prescribed, to a rights commissioner

    a. within the period of six months from the date on which the employer is informed of the initial circumstances relevant to the dispute, that is to say, that the employee is pregnant, has recently given birth or is breastfeeding or, in the case of an employee who is the father of a child, that the child's mother has died; or

    b. if the rights commissioner is satisfied that exceptional circumstances prevented the giving of the notice within the period specified in *paragraph (a)*, within such period, not exceeding 12 months from the date so specified, as the rights commissioner considers reasonable.[78]

Redress is guaranteed in Section 32:

32. 1. On the hearing of a dispute a rights commissioner or the Tribunal shall

    a. in the case of a rights commissioner, make a decision in relation to the dispute, or

    b. in the case of the Tribunal, make a determination in relation to the dispute,

    and may give to the parties concerned such directions as the rights commissioner or the Tribunal, as the case may be, considers necessary or expedient for the resolution of the dispute.

  2. If a decision or determination under *subsection (1)* is in favour of the employee then, without prejudice to the power to give directions

---

78   Ibid., at Section 31.

under that subsection, the rights commissioner or Tribunal may order such redress for the employee as the rights commissioner or Tribunal considers appropriate, either or both of the following

a. the grant of leave for such period as may be so specified;
b. an award of compensation in favour of the employee to be paid by the relevant employer.

3. Compensation under *subsection (2) (b)* shall be of such amount as the rights commissioner or Tribunal deems just and equitable having regard to all the circumstances of the case but shall not exceed 20 weeks' remuneration in respect of the employee's employment calculated in such manner as may be prescribed.[79]

An appeal from the decision of the rights commissioner is provided for under Section 33:

33. 1. A party concerned may appeal to the Tribunal from a decision of a rights commissioner in relation to a dispute and the Tribunal shall hear the parties and any evidence relevant to the appeal tendered by them and shall make a determination in relation to the appeal.[80]

Section 22 of the 2004 Act amends Section 33:

22. The Principal Act is amended by the insertion of the following section after section 33:

33A. 1. In this section 'discrimination' means

a. a failure, which gives rise to a dispute, to comply with a provision of Parts II to IV, or
b. an unfair dismissal (within the meaning of the 1977 Act) of an employee resulting wholly or mainly from
   i.   the employee's pregnancy, attendance at ante-natal classes, giving birth or breastfeeding or any matters connected therewith, or
   ii. the exercise or proposed exercise by the employee of the right under this Act to any form of protective leave or natal care absence, within the meaning of Part IV, or to time off from work to attend ante-natal classes in accordance with section 15A (inserted by *section 8* of the *Maternity Protection (Amendment) Act 2004*), or to time off from work or a reduction of working hours for breastfeeding in accordance with section 15B (inserted by *section 9* of the *Maternity Protection (Amendment) Act 2004*).

---

79   Ibid., at Section 32.
80   Ibid., at Section 33.

Further, an appeal to High Court on point of law is provided for under Section 34:

34. 1. The Tribunal may refer a question of law arising in proceedings before it under this Part to the High Court for determination by it.
    2. A party to proceedings before the Tribunal under this Part may appeal to the High Court from a determination of the Tribunal on a point of law.[81]

Finally, enforcement of decisions and determinations is protected under Section 37:

37. 1. A decision of a rights commissioner or a determination of the Tribunal in proceedings under this Part may provide that the decision or determination shall be carried out before a specified date.
    2. Where a decision of a rights commissioner or a determination of the Tribunal does not provide as mentioned in *subsection (1)*, the decision or determination shall be deemed, for the purposes of this section, to provide that it shall be carried out within four weeks from the date on which it is communicated to the parties.
    3. If a party fails to carry out the terms of a decision of a rights commissioner or of a determination of the Tribunal in relation to a dispute within the period appropriate under *subsection (1)* or *subsection (2)*, the Circuit Court shall, on application to it in that behalf by
        a. the other party, or
        b. the Minister, if of the opinion that it is appropriate to make the application having regard to all the circumstances,
        without hearing the party in default or any evidence (other than in relation to the failure), make an order directing that party to carry out the decision or determination in accordance with its terms.[82]

Conclusion

Due to the overall legislation, employer behavior has changed in countries with anti-discrimination laws in that explicit discrimination, especially in recruitment, has reduced. Discriminating against workers on the basis of their maternity rights is unfair to individuals and harmful to the economy. The principle is that redressing this inequality is a shared responsibility by all aspects of government stakeholders in maternity analysis, planning and training. The State's accountability for violations committed by private actors has long been an important debate. This will be of

---

81   Ibid., at Section 34.
82   Ibid., at Section 37.

critical relevance to Commonwealth governments and the Secretariat as part of their continuing priority work in the area of democracy, rule of law, and human rights. The increased participation of all, especially women at decision-making levels in conflict prevention, mediation and resolution is vital, in the pursuit of *Pregnant Pause.*

Chapter 9

Pregnant Pause in the European Union

Introduction

In the quest for appreciation for maternity issues in *Pregnant Pause*, this chapter will examine efforts against maternity discrimination in the European Union (EU). As well as examining the European Court of Justice, it will review the European Union treaties from their inception, as well as other important legislation, namely: the Treaty of Paris, the Treaty of Rome, the Maastricht Treaty, the Treaty of Amsterdam, the Treaty Establishing a Constitution for Europe and the Charter of Fundamental Rights of the European Union, the Treaty of Lisbon, the European Convention for the Protection of Human Rights and Fundamental Freedoms (ECHR), and the European Social Charter. Finally, important European Council legislation affecting equal rights will be analyzed: Council Recommendation 84/635/EEC on the promotion of positive action for women; Council Decision 2000/750/EC Establishing a Community Action Program to Combat Discrimination (2001 to 2006); Council Directive 97/80/EC on the burden of proof in cases of discrimination based on sex; Council Directive 2000/78/EC Establishing a General Framework for Equal Treatment in Employment and Occupation; Council Directive 96/34/EC Establishing a General Framework Agreement on Parental Leave; Council Directive 86/613/EEC on the application of the principle of equal treatment between men and women engaged in an activity, including agriculture, in a self-employed capacity, and on the protection of self-employed women during pregnancy and motherhood; and Council Directive 92/85/EEC on the introduction of measures to encourage improvements in the safety and health at work of pregnant workers and workers who have recently given birth or are breastfeeding.

The Role of Women in Europe

In the labor force, women account for roughly 40% of the workforce, up significantly from 10 years ago. The employment rate is at 52.6% for women and at 71.6% for men. In terms of part-time employment as a percentage of all employment, 33.5% of women and only 6.2% of men work part-time. Therefore, part-time employment continues to be more important for women. In terms of employment sectors, men and women continue to pursue careers in different occupations and to occupy different positions. In terms of unemployment, the rate of unemployment for women remains higher, with women at 10.9% and men at 7.9%.[1] Men account for 4.3% and women for 6.3% of unemployment in the higher education level, 6.5% and 9.3% respectively in the upper secondary and post-secondary education level, and 10% and 13.8% respectively in the pre-primary, primary and lower secondary level. In terms of long-term unemployment defined as 12 months or longer, women account for 47.3% and men for 44.7%. Further, women account for 34% and men for 53.4% of those considered not in the labor market. Women feel threatened because of their lack of qualifications, their position in non-secure jobs, and the difficulty in professional re-entry.

Women continue to earn less than their male counterparts. A wide pay gap persists between women and men in all European Union Member States, and in addition to the gap arising from a variety of factors, there is an unexplained difference in wages, which is presumed to be due to discrimination. The earnings of women as a percentage of men's vary from a low of 61.2% for the United Kingdom to a high of 82.4% in Sweden.[2] In the EU as a whole, women doing the same work as men are paid only 76% of the gross hourly wage men earn, and the employment rate for women is 51.2%, compared to 70.8% for men, with 83% of part-time workers being women. Gender differences in salaries persist and even have increased in some countries, despite the economic activity of women and egalitarian legislation.[3] The significant trends show that pay differentials between men and women are narrow for young people, grow with time, and peak at the middle and at the end of careers.[4]

As for sectors and occupations, the gap between the wages of men in supervisory and managerial positions and those in subordinate positions is much greater than for women. Men gain more from promotion than do women. It is likely that men when promoted are promoted to higher levels than are women so that gender differences in career progression are likely to exacerbate the gender pay gap. Significant differences in earnings between men and women remain within sectors. In sectors with a relatively high share of female employment, earnings for both men and women are below the national average, and female-dominated sectors are low-paid sectors. The most important factors contributing to the gender pay gap in the EU are earnings differences between men and women with children; a high concentration of women in low-paying sectors and occupations; and lower earnings for women in female-dominated sectors and occupations that cannot be explained by productivity differences between sectors and occupations.[5]

----

1   Eurostat, *Yearbook, Statistical Guide to Europe*, Brussels.

2   Ibid.

3   Commission of the European Communities, *The Position of Women on the Labour Market*, p.52.

4   Ibid.

5   Department of Justice, Equality & Law Reform, *Developing Sectoral Strategies to Address Gender Pay Gaps*.

Although women who spend a long time with an individual employer appear to gain a greater financial return as a consequence than do men, especially during the initial years of their working careers, the relationship between the overall length of the working career and the financial rewards for staying in the labor market is more favorable for men than for women, as periods out of the labor market do adversely affect earnings. In looking at family status and caring, men who are married with children tend to have higher wages than single men without children. However, women do not benefit from a similar pay premium, and in fact married women with children have lower average wages than those of single women without children, with the number of children a woman has often impacting on her earnings.[6]

In terms of education, recent trends have brought about an increase in the level of education for women, but the types of fields chosen do not lend themselves to profitable job prospects. However, education is proven to help overcome some discrimination but not all. In the EU, men obtain a higher return on educational attainment levels and specific skills than women in all Member States. Further, Europe has experienced an increased divorce rate, a falling birth rate, a longer life expectancy and a positive net balance of migration. Marriage and children are no longer the sole limits to women. Due to the various characteristics of the different States, the birth of children has had a different effect on women's level of participation in the workforce, namely no influence (Denmark), a minimal impact (France), part-time work (Germany, United Kingdom), and a drop with the birth of the first child (Netherlands, Ireland).[7] Interestingly, less than half of all women in the EU have children, and over a quarter of women are heads of households.[8]

Overall, there are a number of important trends impacting women in Europe. The majority of women between the ages of 25 and 49 now work, despite having young children.[9] This is a major difference from the once strict family imperatives, showing that women have made a bid for more autonomy in their lives and their careers. Now, 80% of women are employees and no longer work in family firms. Further, of those employed part-time, roughly 80% of these are women.[10] Interestingly, in the entrepreneur area, of those who are self-employed, 22.1% are women. This integration into the labor force allows women to encounter a different universe from the family unit. In the industries which have expanded to adjust for the employment of women, an increasing proportion of these jobs have been part-time, lending themselves to the realities of many women who combine work and family. The share of women in employment has increased everywhere in the European Union, even in countries where part-time work is relatively unimportant. However, women

---

6   Ibid.

7   Commission of the European Communities, *The Position of Women on the Labour Market*, p.52.

8   Commission of the European Communities, *Equal Opportunities for Women in the Community*, Brussels.

9   Eurostat, *Statistics in Focus*, Brussels.

10   Commission of the European Communities, *Europe*, Brussels.

find themselves most often in small non-unionized businesses, and are thus more vulnerable to wage inequity. As well, they predominate in the tertiary service sector, which accounts for 54% of male employment and 79% of female employment.[11]

In recent years, the promotion of gender equality between men and women, particularly in the areas of economic and social life, has come to the forefront of the public policy agenda in the EU.[12] As more and more women enter the labor market in all countries across the European Union, ensuring that men and women receive equal treatment in the workplace becomes all the more important. The position of women relative to men in the labor market has improved greatly over the last few decades and this has included a narrowing of the gender pay gap. Employment equality legislation has played an important part. As well, economic and social factors have had an effect, as there are now an increasing number of women entering what were traditionally viewed as male-dominated occupations and an increasing proportion of women entering senior management positions. In addition, there has been an increase in the participation of women in third-level education, which has thus increased the overall average level of education of the female workforce. However, in terms of the gender pay gap in the EU, women on average earn less than men in all EU Member States, as women's earnings as a percentage of men's stands at around 83%.

It is important that equality for women be achieved in securing access to jobs, which are commensurate with skill levels. Women are still lagging behind due to horizontal segregation, with a concentration in feminine jobs, and vertical segregation, with difficulty acceding to higher positions in the occupational hierarchy. The system has failed to reward women's skills, and even provides guises for discrimination. The demographic changes on the horizon will bring about a further need for qualified workers, including women. However, women remain underutilized and are still considered as reserve labor. This attitude is a barrier to progressive legislation. In addition, women and men face even more challenges as they choose whether to step out of the labor force in order to raise their children or they stay in the labor force and hire outside assistance for their children; thus maternity and paternity leave are important concerns in combining parental responsibilities with career aspirations. Although European laws have gone a long way to improving the plight of women in the EU, in reality, women have yet to enjoy the equality they are entitled to in theory.

Legislation

Initially, many centuries ago, Europe was united within the Roman Empire. Throughout its history, the European continent has naturally been restless, fragile,

---

11   Ibid.

12   Department of Justice, Equality & Law Reform, *Developing Sectoral Strategies to Address Gender Pay Gaps.*

contradictory, competitive and pluralistic, divided by ethnicity, language and religion. National ambitions and self-interest have been the predominant political forces throughout the twentieth century. However, with the two World Wars and the threat of the Cold War, European integration by peaceful methods was seriously reconsidered as an alternative to the independent and aggressive nation state. With democratic governments reinstated in liberated Europe in the post-war era, the restructuring of the region began. A Congress of Europe was held in The Hague in 1948, bringing together leading figures from France, Britain, the Netherlands, Belgium, Germany, Italy and elsewhere. Britain's Prime Minister Churchill referred to the idea of a setting up of 'a kind of United States of Europe', which made a powerful impact.[13] Political integration is the peaceful creation of a larger political unit out of several separate ones, which voluntarily give up some powers to a central authority and renounce the use of force toward the other units.[14] In Europe, a political structure at a supranational level exists. Only continental-wide superpowers can think of solving their major problems at the national level, but for smaller powers like Europe, it requires wider alliance decisions. It is a multi-tiered approach to government and decision-making that is working.

Treaty of Paris

The advocates of integration sought to escape from national rivalries. Thus came the flagship of European integration, the European Communities. The first of these was the Coal and Steel Community, also known as the Treaty of Paris signed on 18 April 1951, which entered into force on 23 July 1952 and expired on 23 July 2002.[15] It removed the coal and steel industries from full national control to a supranational stewardship. The High Authority, which it created, was presided over by Jean Monnet and comprised delegates from the Member States, making decisions in consultation with the Assembly. The Treaty of Paris was regarded only as a starting point, with the success foreseen in this sector expected to spread to others. The Preamble of the Treaty of Paris wrote of safeguarding world peace, establishing an economic community, and substituting essential interests for age-old rivalries and conflicts.[16] Monnet, the most influential of the founding fathers of the European Economic Community, insisted on cooperation across national frontiers in a sector by sector approach at the Messina Conference held in 1955, with the foreign ministers of the six countries involved to meet at. They resolved that the moment had come to go a step further towards the construction of Europe

---

13   Nicoll, William and Salmon, Trevor, *Understanding the New European Community*, Prentice Hall, Exeter, 1994, p.11.

14   Daltrop, Anne, *Political Realities, Politics and the European Community*, Longman, London, 1982, p.2.

15   Treaty of Paris.

16   Nicoll, William and Salmon, Trevor, *Understanding the New European Community*, Prentice Hall, Exeter, 1994, at p.13.

by setting up a customs union with no internal tariff barriers, only a common external tariff.

Treaty of Rome

The Treaty of Rome was signed by France, Italy, West Germany, Luxembourg, the Netherlands and Belgium on 25 March 1957, and entered into force on 1 January 1958, creating the European Economic Community (EEC). The European Community was set up by the Treaty of Rome to maintain peace in Europe and to foster prosperity through cooperation. With the Treaty of Rome, the European Economic Community States transferred to the Community the power to conclude treaties with international organizations and with non-member countries.[17] Lord Denning, a leading constitutional expert, stated 'the Treaty of Rome is like an incoming tide. It flows into the estuaries and up the rivers. It cannot be held back.'[18] The Member States agreed to work together for an integrated multinational economy for the free movement of labor and capital in the Community, while having joint institutions and common policies toward underdeveloped regions of the Community and toward those outside the Community. The Treaty gave the community institutions power to take the necessary steps to adjust national legal rules through harmonization procedures. This was required in order to remove national legal arrangements inhibiting the free movement of products, people and resources. The larger market allowed for a more rational use of resources and provided for higher productivity. By 1 July 1968, all internal tariffs had been abolished among the Member States for a Community-wide production and distribution of products and services,[19] and with the abolition of tariffs encouraging mutual trade, intra-Community trade in manufactured products was about 50% higher than previously. The long-term implications of the Treaty of Rome were a system of majority voting among the representatives of the national governments in the Council, a supranational bureaucracy over which national governments would have little control, a directly elected European Parliament and a commitment by the Member States to work for a closer union.

In accordance with Article 3 of the Treaty of Rome, the activities of the Community include:

> 3. a. the elimination as between Member States, of customs duties and quantitative restrictions on the import and export of goods, and of all other measures having equivalent effect;
>   b. a common commercial policy;

---

17   Ibid., at p.20.
18   Ibid., at p.99.
19   Daltrop, Anne (1982), Political Realities, Politics and the European Community, Longman, London, 1982, p.18.

    c.   an internal market characterised by the abolition, as between Member States, of obstacles to the free movement of goods, persons, services and capital;

    d.   measures concerning the entry and movement of persons in the internal market ...;

    e.   a common policy in the sphere of agriculture and fisheries;

    f.   a common policy in the sphere of transport;

    g.   a system ensuring that competition in the common market is not distorted;

    h.   the approximation of the laws of the Member States to the extent required for the functioning of the common market;

    i.   a policy in the social sphere comprising a European Social Fund;

    j.   the strengthening of economic and social cohesion;

    k.   a policy in the sphere of the environment;

    l.   the strengthening of the competitiveness of Community industry;

    m. the promotion of research and technological development;

    n.   encouragement for the establishment and development of trans-European networks;

    o.   a contribution to the attainment of a high level of health protection;

    p.   a contribution to education and training of quality and to the flowering of the cultures of the Member States;

    q.   a policy in the sphere of development cooperation;

    r.   the association of the overseas countries and territories in order to increase trade and promote jointly economic and social development;

    s.   a contribution to the strengthening of consumer protection;

    t.   measures in the spheres of energy, civil protection and tourism.[20]

Important for equal rights, Article 6(a) prohibits discrimination:

6. a.   Within the scope of application of this Treaty, and without prejudice to any special provisions contained therein, any discrimination on grounds of nationality shall be prohibited.[21]

Further, in terms of the free movement of persons, services and capital, in particular workers, Article 48 provides:

48. 1.   Freedom of movement for workers shall be secured within the Community by the end of the transitional period at the latest.

    2.   Such freedom of movement shall entail the abolition of any discrimination based on nationality between workers of the Member

---

20   Treaty of Rome, at Article 3.

21   Ibid., at Article 6(a).

States as regards employment, remuneration and other conditions of
work and employment.

3. It shall entail the right, subject to limitations justified on grounds of
    public policy, public security or public health:
    a. to accept offers of employment actually made;
    b. to move freely within the territory of Member States for this
        purpose;
    c. to stay in a Member State for the purpose of employment in
        accordance with the provisions governing the employment of
        nationals of that State laid down by law, regulation or administrative
        action;
    d. to remain in the territory of a Member State after having been
        employed in that State, subject to conditions which shall be embodied
        in implementing regulations to be drawn up by the Commission.
4. The provisions of this Article shall not apply to employment in the
    public service.[22]

Important for women, in terms of equal pay, Article 119 states:

119. Each Member State shall during the first stage ensure and subsequently
     maintain the application of the principle that men and women should receive
     equal pay for equal work.

     For the purpose of this Article, 'pay' means the ordinary basic or
     minimum wage or salary and any other consideration, whether in cash or
     in kind, which the worker receives, directly or indirectly, in respect of his
     employment from his employer.

     Equal pay without discrimination based on sex means:
     a. that pay for the same work at piece rates shall be calculated on the basis
         of the same unit of measurement;
     b. that pay for work at time rates shall be the same for the same job.[23]

Maastricht Treaty

The Maastricht Treaty was signed on 7 February 1992 and entered into force on 1
November 1993, creating the European Union (EU). The EU became an internal
market of over 340 million people providing for the free movement of goods,
capital, services and citizens of Member States. The Maastricht Treaty affirms that
it marks a new stage in the process of European integration undertaken with the
establishment of the European Communities. It was designed to create a firm basis
for the construction of the future of Europe, by deepening the solidarity between
peoples while respecting the different histories, cultures and traditions. Further,

---

22   Ibid., at Article 48.
23   Ibid., at Article 119.

the Maastricht Treaty espoused the desire to enhance the democracy and efficient functioning of the institutions so as to enable them to better carry out, within a single institutional framework, the tasks entrusted to them. The foundations for a united Europe were laid on fundamental values including peace, unity, equality, freedom, solidarity and security, through intergovernmental cooperation and the creation of the three pillars of EC society. By the Maastricht Treaty, the European Union confirms its 'attachment to the principles of liberty, democracy and respect for human rights and fundamental freedoms and of the rule of law'.

According to Article A of the Maastricht Treaty, the Treaty 'marks a new stage in the process of creating an ever closer union among the peoples of Europe, in which decisions are taken as closely as possible to the citizen'.[24] Further, Article B states:

> B. The Union shall set itself the following objectives:
>
> to promote economic and social progress which is balanced and sustainable, in particular through the creation of an area without internal frontiers, through the strengthening of economic and social cohesion and through the establishment of economic and monetary union, ultimately including a single currency in accordance with the provisions of this Treaty;
>
> to assert its identity on the international scene, in particular through the implementation of a common foreign and security policy including the eventual framing of a common defence policy, which might in time lead to a common defence;
>
> to strengthen the protection of the rights and interests of the nationals of its Member States through the introduction of a citizenship of the Union;
>
> to develop close cooperation on justice and home affairs;
>
> to maintain in full the 'acquis communautaire' and build on it with ... the aim of ensuring the effectiveness of the mechanisms and the institutions of the Community.[25]

Treaty of Amsterdam

The Treaty of Amsterdam, the treaty establishing the European Community, amending previous treaties, was signed on 2 October 1997 and entered into force on 1 May 1999.[26] Important for all people, in order to combat maternity discrimination, Article 13, amending Article 6(a) of the Treaty of Rome for specificity:

> 13. Without prejudice to the other provisions of this Treaty and within the limits of the powers conferred by it upon the Community, the Council, acting

---

24 Maastricht Treaty, at Article A.
25 Ibid., at Article B.
26 Treaty of Amsterdam, at Article 141.

unanimously on a proposal from the Commission and after consulting the European Parliament, may take appropriate action to combat discrimination based on sex, racial or ethnic origin, religion or belief, disability, age or sexual orientation.[27]

Further, in terms of the free movement of persons, services and capital, in particular workers, Article 39, amending Article 48 of the Treaty of Rome, states:

39. 1. Freedom of movement for workers shall be secured within the Community.
    2. Such freedom of movement shall entail the abolition of any discrimination based on nationality between workers of the Member States as regards employment, remuneration and other conditions of work and employment.
    3. It shall entail the right, subject to limitations justified on grounds of public policy, public security or public health:
        a. to accept offers of employment actually made;
        b. to move freely within the territory of Member States for this purpose;
        c. to stay in a Member State for the purpose of employment in accordance with the provisions governing the employment of nationals of that State laid down by law, regulation or administrative action;
        d. to remain in the territory of a Member State after having been employed in that State, subject to conditions which shall be embodied in implementing regulations to be drawn up by the Commission.
    4. The provisions of this Article shall not apply to employment in the public service.[28]

Important for women, in terms of equal pay, Article 141, amending Article 119 of the Treaty of Rome, states:

141. 1. Each Member State shall ensure that the principle of equal pay for male and female workers for equal work or work of equal value is applied.
     2. For the purpose of this Article, 'pay' means the ordinary basic or minimum wage or salary and any other consideration, whether in cash or in kind, which the worker receives directly or indirectly, in respect of his employment, from his employer.

        Equal pay without discrimination based on sex means:
        a. that pay for the same work at piece rates shall be calculated on the basis of the same unit of measurement;

---

27 Ibid., at Article 13.
28 Ibid., at Article 39.

b. that pay for work at time rates shall be the same for the same job.

3. The Council, acting in accordance with the procedure referred to in Article 251, and after consulting the Economic and Social Committee, shall adopt measures to ensure the application of the principle of equal opportunities and equal treatment of men and women in matters of employment and occupation, including the principle of equal pay for equal work or work of equal value.

4. With a view to ensuring full equality in practice between men and women in working life, the principle of equal treatment shall not prevent any Member State from maintaining or adopting measures providing for specific advantages in order to make it easier for the under-represented sex to pursue a vocational activity or to prevent or compensate for disadvantages in professional careers.[29]

Treaty Establishing a Constitution for Europe and Charter of Fundamental Rights of the European Union

The Heads of State or Government of the then 25 Member States and the candidate countries signed the Treaty establishing a Constitution for Europe on 29 October 2004, but it was not ratified by all Member States of the enlarged Union. It was written in order to enable the European Union to ensure the well-being of citizens, and the defense of values and interests; to assume responsibilities as a leading international player; to fight unemployment and social exclusion more effectively; to promote sustainable economic growth; to respond to the challenges of globalization; to safeguard internal and external security; and to protect the environment. The Charter of Fundamental Rights of the European Union, part of the intended Constitution of Europe, has to be seen in the wider context of the European Union's long-lasting commitment to human rights and fundamental freedoms and of its policy in the areas of justice, freedom, security and social rights.

The Preamble of the Treaty 2004/C 310/01 establishing a Constitution for Europe states:

DRAWING INSPIRATION from the cultural, religious and humanist inheritance of Europe, from which have developed the universal values of the inviolable and inalienable rights of the human person, freedom, democracy, equality and the rule of law,

CONVINCED that, while remaining proud of their own national identities and history, the peoples of Europe are determined to transcend their former divisions and, united ever more closely, to forge a common destiny,

---

29   Ibid., at Article 141.

CONVINCED that, thus 'United in diversity', Europe offers them the best chance of pursuing, with due regard for the rights of each individual and in awareness of their responsibilities towards future generations and the Earth, the great venture which makes of it a special area of human hope,

DETERMINED to continue the work accomplished within the framework of the Treaties establishing the European Communities and the Treaty on European Union, by ensuring the continuity of the Community *acquis*,

WHO, having exchanged their full powers, found in good and due form.[30]

Article I-1 on the establishment of the Union states:

I-1. 1. Reflecting the will of the citizens and States of Europe to build a common future, this Constitution establishes the European Union, on which the Member States confer competences to attain objectives they have in common. The Union shall coordinate the policies by which the Member States aim to achieve these objectives, and shall exercise in the Community way the competences they confer on it.

2. The Union shall be open to all European States which respect its values and are committed to promoting them together.[31]

The Union's values are outlined in Article I-2:

I-2. The Union is founded on the values of respect for human dignity, liberty, democracy, equality, the rule of law and respect for human rights, including the rights of persons belonging to minorities. These values are common to the Member States in a society in which pluralism, non-discrimination, tolerance, justice, solidarity and equality between women and men prevail.[32]

Further, the Union's objectives are outlined in Article I-3:

I-3. 1. The Union's aim is to promote peace, its values and the well-being of its peoples.

2. The Union shall offer its citizens an area of freedom, security and justice without internal frontiers, and an internal market where competition is free and undistorted.

3. The Union shall work for the sustainable development of Europe based on balanced economic growth and price stability, a highly competitive social market economy, aiming at full employment and social progress,

---

30 Treaty establishing a Constitution for Europe, at the Preamble.
31 Ibid., at Article I-1.
32 Ibid., at Article I-2.

and a high level of protection and improvement of the quality of the environment. It shall promote scientific and technological advance.

It shall combat social exclusion and discrimination, and shall promote social justice and protection, equality between women and men, solidarity between generations and protection of the rights of the child.

It shall promote economic, social and territorial cohesion, and solidarity among Member States.

It shall respect its rich cultural and linguistic diversity, and shall ensure that Europe's cultural heritage is safeguarded and enhanced.

4. In its relations with the wider world, the Union shall uphold and promote its values and interests. It shall contribute to peace, security, the sustainable development of the Earth, solidarity and mutual respect among peoples, free and fair trade, eradication of poverty and the protection of human rights, in particular the rights of the child, as well as to the strict observance and the development of international law, including respect for the principles of the United Nations Charter.

5. The Union shall pursue its objectives by appropriate means commensurate with the competences which are conferred upon it in the Constitution.[33]

Important for equal rights, fundamental freedoms and non-discrimination are upheld in Article I-4:

I-4.1. The free movement of persons, services, goods and capital, and freedom of establishment shall be guaranteed within and by the Union, in accordance with the Constitution.

2. Within the scope of the Constitution, and without prejudice to any of its specific provisions, any discrimination on grounds of nationality shall be prohibited.[34]

The primacy of Union law is emphasized in Article I-6:

I-6. The Constitution and law adopted by the institutions of the Union in exercising competences conferred on it shall have primacy over the law of the Member States.[35]

Further, relations between the Union and Member States are contained in Article I-5:

I-5.1. The Union shall respect the equality of Member States before the Constitution as well as their national identities, inherent in their

---

33　Ibid., at Article I-3.
34　Ibid., at Article I-4.
35　Ibid., at Article I-6.

fundamental structures, political and constitutional, inclusive of regional and local self-government. It shall respect their essential State functions, including ensuring the territorial integrity of the State, maintaining law and order and safeguarding national security.

2. Pursuant to the principle of sincere cooperation, the Union and the Member States shall, in full mutual respect, assist each other in carrying out tasks which flow from the Constitution.

    The Member States shall take any appropriate measure, general or particular, to ensure fulfilment of the obligations arising out of the Constitution or resulting from the acts of the institutions of the Union.

    The Member States shall facilitate the achievement of the Union's tasks and refrain from any measure which could jeopardise the attainment of the Union's objectives.[36]

The Preamble of the Charter of Fundamental Rights of the European Union, part of the Constitution of Europe, states:

The peoples of Europe, in creating an ever closer union among them, are resolved to share a peaceful future based on common values.

Conscious of its spiritual and moral heritage, the Union is founded on the indivisible, universal values of human dignity, freedom, equality and solidarity; it is based on the principles of democracy and the rule of law. It places the individual at the heart of its activities, by establishing the citizenship of the Union and by creating an area of freedom, security and justice.

The Union contributes to the preservation and to the development of these common values while respecting the diversity of the cultures and traditions of the peoples of Europe as well as the national identities of the Member States and the organisation of their public authorities at national, regional and local levels; it seeks to promote balanced and sustainable development and ensures free movement of persons, goods, services and capital, and the freedom of establishment.

To this end, it is necessary to strengthen the protection of fundamental rights in the light of changes in society, social progress and scientific and technological developments by making those rights more visible in a Charter.

This Charter reaffirms, with due regard for the powers and tasks of the Community and the Union and the principle of subsidiarity, the rights as they result, in particular, from the constitutional traditions and international obligations common to the Member States, the Treaty on European Union, the Community

---

36   Ibid., at Article I-5.

Treaties, the European Convention for the Protection of Human Rights and Fundamental Freedoms, the Social Charters adopted by the Community and by the Council of Europe and the case law of the Court of Justice of the European Communities and of the European Court of Human Rights.

Enjoyment of these rights entails responsibilities and duties with regard to other persons, to the human community and to future generations.

The Union therefore recognises the rights, freedoms and principles set out hereafter.[37]

Importantly, equality before the law is contained in Article II-80:

II-80. Everyone is equal before the law.[38]

Further, Article II-81 deals with non-discrimination:

II-81. 1. Any discrimination based on any ground such as sex, race, colour, ethnic or social origin, genetic features, language, religion or belief, political or any other opinion, membership of a national minority, property, birth, disability, age or sexual orientation shall be prohibited.
2. Within the scope of application of the Treaty establishing the European Community and of the Treaty on European Union, and without prejudice to the special provisions of those Treaties, any discrimination on grounds of nationality shall be prohibited.[39]

Continuing on, importantly, Article III-118 states:

III-118. In defining and implementing the policies and activities referred to in this Part, the Union shall aim to combat discrimination based on sex, racial or ethnic origin, religion or belief, disability, age or sexual orientation.[40]

Finally, Article III-124 provides for measures for combating discrimination:

III-124. 1. Without prejudice to the other provisions of the Constitution and within the limits of the powers assigned by it to the Union, a European law or framework law of the Council may establish the measures needed to combat discrimination based on sex, racial or ethnic origin, religion

---

37 Treaty establishing a Constitution for Europe, the Charter of Fundamental Rights, at the Preamble.
38 Ibid., at Article II-80.
39 Ibid., at Article II-81.
40 Ibid., at Article III-118.

or belief, disability, age or sexual orientation. The Council shall act unanimously after obtaining the consent of the European Parliament.

2.   By way of derogation from paragraph 1, European laws or framework laws may establish basic principles for Union incentive measures and define such measures, to support action taken by Member States in order to contribute to the achievement of the objectives referred to in paragraph 1, excluding any harmonisation of their laws and regulations.[41]

Treaty of Lisbon

Finally, the Treaty of Lisbon amending the Treaty on European Union and the Treaty establishing the European Community was signed at Lisbon on 13 December 2007, after the rejection of the Constitution for Europe, in order to enhance the efficiency of the decision-making process and democratic participation in a Union of 27 Member States. The Preamble of the Treaty of Lisbon, which came into effect on 1 December 2009, states:

DRAWING INSPIRATION from the cultural, religious and humanist inheritance of Europe, from which have developed the universal values of the inviolable and inalienable rights of the human person, freedom, democracy, equality and the rule of law.[42]

Specifically, Article 5(b) notes:

5.   b.   In defining and implementing its policies and activities, the Union shall aim to combat discrimination based on sex, racial or ethnic origin, religion or belief, disability, age or sexual orientation.[43]

The Treaty of Lisbon hoped to provide for: a more democratic and transparent Europe, with a strengthened role for the European Parliament and national parliaments, more opportunities for citizens to have their voices heard and a clearer sense of who does what at European and national level; a more efficient Europe, with simplified working methods and voting rules, streamlined and modern institutions for a European Union of 27 members and an improved ability to act in areas of major priority for today's Union; a Europe of rights and values, freedom, solidarity and security, promoting the Union's values, introducing the Charter of Fundamental Rights into European primary law, providing for new solidarity mechanisms and ensuring better protection of European citizens; and Europe as an actor on the global stage by bringing together Europe's external policy tools, both when developing and deciding new policies, harnessing Europe's economic,

---

41   Ibid., at Article III-124.
42   Treaty of Lisbon, at the Preamble.
43   Ibid., at Article 5(b).

humanitarian, political and diplomatic strengths to promote European interests and values worldwide, while respecting the particular interests of the Member States in Foreign Affairs.

European Law and the European Court of Justice

The extension of civil rights marks another step toward European integration. The concept of citizenship is based on the principle that nationals of Member States have certain rights to move freely across national borders in the common market. Freedom of movement, under the Treaty of Rome, applied only to certain economic categories of workers, the self-employed and service providers. This, however, was expanded by the Treaty of Amsterdam and the European Court of Justice, which had a profound impact on employment. There are five European Union (EU) institutions, each playing a specific role, namely: the European Parliament, which is elected by the citizens of the Member States; the Council of the European Union, which represents the governments of the Member States; the European Commission, which is the executive body; the European Court of Justice, which ensures compliance with the law; and the Court of Auditors, which controls sound and lawful management of the European Union budget. There are five other important bodies, namely: the European Economic and Social Committee, which expresses the opinions of organized civil society on economic and social issues; the Committee of the Regions, which expresses the opinions of regional and local authorities; the European Central Bank, which is responsible for monetary policy and managing the Euro; the European Ombudsman, who deals with citizens' complaints about maladministration by any European Union institution or body; and the European Investment Bank, which helps achieve European Union objectives by financing investment projects. A number of agencies and other bodies complete the system.[44]

Specifically, the Commission is responsible for making legislative proposals, executing policies and monitoring the compliance of Member States with their obligations. It is the driving force behind European integration by its right of initiative. It is also the guardian of the Treaties by its right to intervene with Member States and to demand compliance with their obligations. If Member States breach their Treaty obligations, they will face Commission action and possible legal proceedings in the European Court of Justice. As assistance to the European Court of Justice, the Commission is the European Union watchdog for the observance of the Treaties, as it originates and administers European Union law. The Council of Ministers is composed of representatives of Member State governments, and decides on Commission proposals. It is the Union's legislator, with all decisions involving new policies requiring unanimity. The Assembly is charged with proposing, to the Council, arrangements for universal direct

---

44   Nicoll, William and Salmon, Trevor, *Understanding the New European Community*, Prentice Hall, Exeter, 1994, p.97.

elections. In addition, the Council, in turn, commends them to the Member States for adoption under constitutional procedures. The Assembly is consultative and can, if it has a sufficient majority, express its non-confidence in the commission by dismissing it.

The European Court of Justice (ECJ) is the European Union's supreme constitutional authority. It renders judgments on the obligations of the institutions, Member States and citizens. The very existence of the European Union is conditional on the recognition of the binding nature of its rules, by the Member States, by the institutions, and by individuals. European Union law has successfully embedded itself thoroughly in the legal life of the Member States through the supervision of the European Court of Justice. The founding European Treaties are the primary source of European Union law, and therein is found the central jurisdiction of the European Court of Justice. European Union law involves primary law, namely Treaties, and secondary law, namely legislative acts, both of which are binding on national governments and take precedence over national law. The nature of the European Union, its existence and its functions, demand a consistent application of European Union law between Member States.

The ECJ was to provide the legal sanctions for the carrying out of the Treaties. Before the European Community and the European Union, courts operating beyond national boundaries were constrained by international agreement, such as the International Court of Justice. In essence, European Union citizens are affected by two legal systems, national and European Union law. The courts of law must apply both systems of law where relevant, and if there is a conflict, the European Union law takes precedence. The supremacy of European Union law is implicit in the nature of the European Union, since its existence and functioning require its application. European Union law is directly applicable to Member States, and there is no requirement that it be passed into national law for its validity, since the rights and obligations accrue directly to European Union citizens.

The primacy of European Union law and its direct applicability are distinctive features of the European Union, turning freedoms into rights. It is a system of laws, which is directly applicable to people and institutions in Member States, and is invoked in national courts. European Union law touches on many aspects of national life, including immigration, control of foreign workers, and matters relating to equality. Thus, national law has been challenged or influenced by European Union law, which is enforced and overseen by the European Court of Justice. This surrender of sovereignty cannot be reversed by measures taken by national authorities in conflict with European Union law, relinquishing far-reaching powers to an independent legal order, which binds Member States. Points of law and the interpretation of Treaties are decided by the European Court of Justice, the European Union's judicial institution having jurisdiction over disputes concerning the Member States. Often, the national court is faced with issues such as the interpretation of a Treaty, the validity of acts or the lack of a judicial remedy under national law. If a nation State's court decides that a question of European Union law needs to be answered before it can render a judgment, it can go before the European Court of Justice for a ruling. The European Union Treaties are part of the domestic law of the State, and as such, they impinge on the finality of national court decisions.

Where European Union law has direct effect, it will take precedence over domestic law in such cases as equality in employment. Under national law, the national court of the Member State is within its limits of discretion, when interpreting domestic law. However, domestic law must be in accord with the requirements of European Union law, and if this is not possible, then domestic law is inapplicable. This, therefore, is a strong incentive for national courts to rule against maternity discrimination. The European Union can legislate directly through regulations, which are binding in law and are automatically incorporated into the national legal systems of Member States, without the need for specific individual ratification. It can also work through the legal systems of the Member States, by the use of the Commission, which implements directives with broad objectives. Although directives require some legal action, such as legislation, by the Member States before they become national law, they are laws transposed into Member States' legislation to enforce Treaty principles. Importantly, decisions by the European Court of Justice are binding as force of law, whereas recommendations and opinions by the Council of Ministers or the Commission are not.

European Union legislation establishes that a citizen of the European Union should not be discriminated against in the workplace. In employment, discrimination can occur in two ways: direct discrimination when people are treated differently solely on the basis of a discriminatory ground; and indirect discrimination when people are treated differently because of an apparently neutral provision, criterion or practice determining recruitment, pay, working conditions, dismissal, and social security in practice disadvantaging a substantially higher proportion of the members of one group. Such provisions, criteria or practices are prohibited under European Union law, unless it is proven that they are justified by objective reasons in no way related to maternity discrimination. In examining positive action, European Union law allows European Union countries and companies to undertake several initiatives to counter maternity discrimination. While there is no official definition of positive action, it does include all measures which are designed to counter the effects of past disadvantages and existing discrimination, and to promote equality of opportunity in the field of employment. Historically, there have been discriminatory policies directly on their face or indirectly, applied to different groups. Positive action is needed not only to help guarantee equality, but also to combat the perpetuation of traditional discriminatory attitudes so as to ensure access to equal opportunities for all.

The European Court of Justice is at the heart of the legal system, and ensures that European Union law is observed in the interpretation and application of the Treaties. Its judgments are binding on Member States. The court reviews the lawfulness of acts of Council, the Commission, the Member States' governments and citizens. National laws in conflict with European Union law may be declared invalid by the European Court of Justice. Appeals against acts of an institution or a Member State can be lodged by any other institution, government, firm or individual citizen directly affected.

Two types of case may be brought before the European Court of Justice, namely direct actions, brought directly before the Court by the Commission, other European Union institutions or a Member State, or preliminary rulings, requested by courts or tribunals in the Member States on a question of European Union law. The European Court of Justice may hear a variety of cases involving: annulment of binding legal acts; failure to act; infringement of the European Union Treaties under Article 33, in order to have Commission decisions or recommendations declared void for lack of competence, infringement of an essential procedural requirement, the Treaty or any rule of law relating to its application, or misuse of powers; preliminary rulings, in which national courts petition the Court of Justice for a ruling on a point of European Union law, binding in the case; damages; and application of staff regulations. The Treaties state that the European Union's legal system, which must not be impeded by any State, applies throughout the European Union.

The legal order is called the 'originality' of the European Union, which is the jurisdiction of the constitutional court, the European Court of Justice. The Court's decisions are made by majority vote, presented in open court. The judgments are directly applicable to Member States and are enforceable through the national courts. The Court of Justice located in Luxembourg may sit in plenary session, when a Member State or a European Union institution is a party to the proceeding and so requests or when a case is considered complex and important, or may sit in chamber. Since all the official languages of the European Union are used at some point, the Court provides for a large translation and interpretation service. The Court is also assisted by an Advocate General, as *amicus curiae* acting as an independent judicial observer representing the public interest, who makes a reasoned presentation of the case before the Court, gives a summary of the submissions of the parties, puts forth observations of oral hearings, statute law and previous cases, and offers an opinion, which although published is not binding on the Court. In order to enable the Court of Justice to concentrate its activities on the fundamental task of ensuring uniform interpretation of European Union law, a Court of First Instance was established in 1989, which has jurisdiction over actions brought by individuals and companies against decisions of the European Union institutions and agencies, and these judgments are in turn subject to appeal before the European Court of Justice on a point of law.

As the arbiter of European Union law, the European Court of Justice, with its power, has strengthened the European Union as a political system, and defiance of its rulings has been exceptional. By creating a body of independent European Union law, the European Union has promoted its survival, by requiring harmonization of the laws of the Member States. The national courts are, therefore, responsible for aligning national law with European Union law. The Treaties are a comprehensive code of law, which set out the rights and duties of governments and individuals, and from which rights and remedies can be deduced. Interestingly, for the European Court of Justice, the European Union's common aims count more than a literal construction of legal texts, and in turn, the legal character of the European Union is concerned with influencing, shaping and controlling the legislative output of the European Union. Fundamental rights are part of the bedrock of the European Union's legal order. The European Court of Justice held that the protection of such rights, while inspired by the constitutional traditions common to Member States, must be ensured within the framework of the structure and objectives of the European Union (*Internationale Handelsgesellschaft* [1970] ECR 1125, [1972] CMLR 255).[45] Importantly, in a seminal case, the European Court of Justice stated:

> The integration into the laws of each Member State of provisions which derive from the Community, and more generally the terms and the spirit of the Treaty, make it impossible for the States, as a corollary, to accord precedence to a unilateral and subsequent measure over a legal system accepted by them on a basis of reciprocity ... The executive force of Community law cannot vary from one State to another ... without jeopardising the attainment of the object of the Treaty ... It follows from all these observations that the law stemming from the treaty, an independent source of law, could not, because of its special and original nature, be overridden by domestic legal provisions, however framed, without being deprived of its character as Community law and without the legal basis of the Community itself being called into question (*Costa v. ENEL* [1964] CMLR 425).[46]

In terms of the burden of proof, in the European Court of Justice, the plaintiff has the burden of showing, in indirect cases, that a neutral policy has a disproportionate impact (*Teuling v. Bredrijfsvereniging*, [1987] ECR 2497).[47] The burden is then shifted to the defendant who must justify this by objective reasons other than discrimination. The plaintiff must then show that the explanation is not effective for the purpose, or that there is an alternative provision to accomplish it in a manner that has a less discriminatory impact. Otherwise, if there is a difference in treatment, it must be justified by objective factors other than discrimination. If a provision is neutral on its terms, but factually disadvantages a particular group, an employer bears the burden of justification. The European Court of Justice requires a showing of objective justification as a defense to discrimination.

European Convention for the Protection of Human Rights and Fundamental Freedoms (ECHR)

Crucially for human rights, the European Convention for the Protection of Human Rights and Fundamental Freedoms came into being on 4 November 1950, which affords protection against discrimination. In the Preamble of the European

---

45   *Internationale Handelsgesellschaft* [1970] ECR 1125, [1972] CMLR 255.
46   *Costa v. ENEL* [1964] CMLR 425.
47   *Teuling v. Bredrijfsvereniging* [1987] ECR 2497.

Convention for the Protection of Human Rights and Fundamental Freedoms, the Governments signatory hereto, being Members of the Council of Europe, undertake the agreement:

> Considering the Universal Declaration of Human Rights proclaimed by the General Assembly of the United Nations on 10th December 1948;
>
> Considering that this Declaration aims at securing the universal and effective recognition and observance of the Rights therein declared;
>
> Considering that the aim of the Council of Europe is the achievement of greater unity between its Members and that one of the methods by which the aim is to be pursued is the maintenance and further realisation of Human Rights and Fundamental Freedoms;
>
> Reaffirming their profound belief in those Fundamental Freedoms which are the foundation of justice and peace in the world and are best maintained on the one hand by an effective political democracy and on the other by a common understanding and observance of the Human Rights upon which they depend;
>
> Being resolved, as the Governments of European countries which are like-minded and have a common heritage of political traditions, ideals, freedom and the rule of law to take the first steps for the collective enforcement of certain of the Rights stated in the Universal Declaration.[48]

Article 1 guarantees:

> 1. The High Contracting Parties shall secure to everyone within their jurisdiction the rights and freedoms defined.[49]

The prohibition of discrimination is guaranteed under Article 14:

> 14. The enjoyment of the rights and freedoms set forth in this Convention shall be secured without discrimination on any ground such as sex, race, colour, language, religion, political or other opinion, national or social origin, association with a national minority, property, birth or other status.[50]

The right to an effective remedy is secured by Article 13:

---

48 European Convention for the Protection of Human Rights and Fundamental Freedoms (ECHR), at the Preamble.

49 Ibid., at Article 1.

50 European Convention for the Protection of Human Rights and Fundamental Freedoms (ECHR), at Article 14.

13. Everyone whose rights and freedoms as set forth in this Convention are violated shall have an effective remedy before a national authority notwithstanding that the violation has been committed by persons acting in an official capacity.[51]

Further, Article 17 provides for the prohibition of abuse of rights:

17. Nothing in this Convention may be interpreted as implying for any State, group or person any right to engage in any activity or perform any act aimed at the destruction of any of the rights and freedoms set forth herein or at their limitation to a greater extent than is provided for in the Convention.[52]

Importantly, the European Court of Human Rights is established under Article 19:

19. To ensure the observance of the engagements undertaken by the High Contracting Parties in the Convention and the Protocols thereto, there shall be set up a European Court of Human Rights, hereinafter referred to as 'the Court'. It shall function on a permanent basis.[53]

Article 32 outlines the jurisdiction of the Court:

32. 1. The jurisdiction of the Court shall extend to all matters concerning the interpretation and application of the Convention and the protocols thereto which are referred to it as provided in Articles 33, 34 and 47.
2. In the event of dispute as to whether the Court has jurisdiction, the Court shall decide.[54]

Article 27 outlines the structure of the Committees, the Chambers and the Grand Chamber:

27. 1. To consider cases brought before it, the Court shall sit in committees of three judges, in Chambers of seven judges and in a Grand Chamber of seventeen judges. The Court's Chambers shall set up committees for a fixed period of time.
2. There shall sit as an ex officio member of the Chamber and the Grand Chamber the judge elected in respect of the State Party concerned or, if there is none or if he is unable to sit, a person of its choice who shall sit in the capacity of judge.

---

51 Ibid., at Article 13.
52 Ibid., at Article 17.
53 Ibid., at Article 19.
54 Ibid., at Article 32.

3. The Grand Chamber shall also include the President of the Court, the Vice-Presidents, the Presidents of the Chambers and other judges chosen in accordance with the rules of the Court. When a case is referred to the Grand Chamber under Article 43, no judge from the Chamber which rendered the judgment shall sit in the Grand Chamber, with the exception of the President of the Chamber and the judge who sat in respect of the State Party concerned.[55]

Inter-State cases are provided for under Article 33:

33. Any High Contracting Party may refer to the Court any alleged breach of the provisions of the Convention and the protocols thereto by another High Contracting Party.[56]

Individual applications are provided for under Article 34:

34. The Court may receive applications from any person, non-governmental organisation or group of individuals claiming to be the victim of a violation by one of the High Contracting Parties of the rights set forth in the Convention or the protocols thereto. The High Contracting Parties undertake not to hinder in any way the effective exercise of this right.[57]

Further, third party intervention is provided for under Article 36:

36. 1. In all cases before a Chamber or the Grand Chamber, a High Contracting Party one of whose nationals is an applicant shall have the right to submit written comments and to take part in hearings.
    2. The President of the Court may, in the interest of the proper administration of justice, invite any High Contracting Party which is not a party to the proceedings or any person concerned who is not the applicant to submit written comments or take part in hearings.[58]

Article 35 contains the admissibility of evidence criteria:

35. 1. The Court may only deal with the matter after all domestic remedies have been exhausted, according to the generally recognised rules of international law, and within a period of six months from the date on which the final decision was taken.

---

55 Ibid., at Article 27.
56 Ibid., at Article 3.
57 Ibid., at Article 34.
58 Ibid., at Article 36.

2. The Court shall not deal with any application submitted under Article 34 that:
    a. is anonymous; or
    b. is substantially the same as a matter that has already been examined by the Court or has already been submitted to another procedure of international investigation or settlement and contains no relevant new information.
3. The Court shall declare inadmissible any individual application submitted under Article 34 which it considers incompatible with the provisions of the Convention or the protocols thereto, manifestly ill-founded, or an abuse of the right of application.
4. The Court shall reject any application which it considers inadmissible under this Article. It may do so at any stage of the proceedings.[59]

Further, Article 37 contains the striking out of applications:

37. 1. The Court may at any stage of the proceedings decide to strike an application out of its list of cases where the circumstances lead to the conclusion that:
    a. the applicant does not intend to pursue his application; or
    b. the matter has been resolved; or
    c. for any other reason established by the Court, it is no longer justified to continue the examination of the application.
    However, the Court shall continue the examination of the application if respect for human rights as defined in the Convention and the protocols thereto so requires.
2. The Court may decide to restore an application to its list of cases if it considers that the circumstances justify such a course.[60]

Article 38 outlines the examination of the case and friendly settlement proceedings:

38. 1. If the Court declares the application admissible, it shall:
    a. pursue the examination of the case, together with the representatives of the parties, and if need be, undertake an investigation, for the effective conduct of which the States concerned shall furnish all necessary facilities;
    b. place itself at the disposal of the parties concerned with a view to securing a friendly settlement of the matter on the basis of respect for human rights as defined in the Convention and the protocols thereto.

---

59 Ibid., at Article 35.
60 Ibid., at Article 37.

2. Proceedings conducted under paragraph 1.b shall be confidential.[61]

Further, Article 39 outlines the finding of a friendly settlement:

39. If a friendly settlement is effected, the Court shall strike the case out of its list by means of a decision which shall be confined to a brief statement of the facts and of the solution reached.[62]

Public hearings and access to documents are provided for under Article 40:

40. 1. Hearings shall be in public unless the Court in exceptional circumstances decides otherwise.
    2. Documents deposited with the Registrar shall be accessible to the public unless the President of the Court decides otherwise.[63]

Further, Article 41 provides for just satisfaction:

41. If the Court finds that there has been a violation of the Convention or the protocols thereto, and if the internal law of the High Contracting Party concerned allows only partial reparation to be made, the Court shall, if necessary, afford just satisfaction to the injured party.[64]

Importantly, final judgments are contained in Article 44:

44. 1. The judgment of the Grand Chamber shall be final.
    2. The judgment of a Chamber shall become final:
        a. when the parties declare that they will not request that the case be referred to the Grand Chamber; or
        b. three months after the date of the judgment, if reference of the case to the Grand Chamber has not been requested; or
        c. when the panel of the Grand Chamber rejects the request to refer under Article 43.
    3. The final judgment shall be published.[65]

Further, reasons for judgments and decisions are contained in Article 45:

45. 1. Reasons shall be given for judgments as well as for decisions declaring applications admissible or inadmissible.

---

61 Ibid., at Article 38.
62 Ibid., at Article 39.
63 Ibid., at Article 40.
64 Ibid., at Article 41.
65 Ibid., at Article 44.

> 2. If a judgment does not represent, in whole or in part, the unanimous opinion of the judges, any judge shall be entitled to deliver a separate opinion.[66]

In addition, binding force and execution of judgments are contained in Article 46:

> 46. 1. The High Contracting Parties undertake to abide by the final judgment of the Court in any case to which they are parties.
>   2. The final judgment of the Court shall be transmitted to the Committee of Ministers, which shall supervise its execution.[67]

Finally, Article 47 provides for advisory opinions:

> 47. 1. The Court may, at the request of the Committee of Ministers, give advisory opinions on legal questions concerning the interpretation of the Convention and the protocols thereto.
>   2. Such opinions shall not deal with any question relating to the content or scope of the rights or freedoms defined in Section I of the Convention and the protocols thereto, or with any other question which the Court or the Committee of Ministers might have to consider in consequence of any such proceedings as could be instituted in accordance with the Convention.
>   3. Decisions of the Committee of Ministers to request an advisory opinion of the Court shall require a majority vote of the representatives entitled to sit on the Committee.[68]

In addition, the Preamble of Protocol No.1, entitled Enforcement of Certain Rights and Freedoms not included in Section I of the Convention, states that:

> The Governments signatory hereto, being Members of the Council of Europe, Being resolved to take steps to ensure the collective enforcement of certain rights and freedoms other than those already included in Section I of the Convention for the Protection of Human Rights and Fundamental Freedoms signed at Rome on 4th November, 1950 (hereinafter referred to as 'the Convention'), Have agreed as follows.[69]

Further, important for equal rights, in the Preamble of the Protocol No. 12 to the European Convention for the Protection of Human Rights and Fundamental

---

66 Ibid., at Article 45.

67 Ibid., at Article 46.

68 Ibid., at Article 47.

69 European Convention for the Protection of Human Rights and Fundamental Freedoms as amended by Protocol No. 1, at the Preamble.

Freedoms, the Member States of the Council of Europe signatory hereto, undertake the agreement:

> Having regard to the fundamental principle according to which all persons are equal before the law and are entitled to the equal protection of the law;
>
> Being resolved to take further steps to promote the equality of all persons through the collective enforcement of a general prohibition of discrimination by means of the Convention for the Protection of Human Rights and Fundamental Freedoms signed at Rome on 4 November 1950 (hereinafter referred to as 'the Convention');
>
> Reaffirming that the principle of non-discrimination does not prevent States Parties from taking measures in order to promote full and effective equality, provided that there is an objective and reasonable justification for those measures.[70]

Article 1 outlines the general prohibition against discrimination:

> 1. 1. The enjoyment of any right set forth by law shall be secured without discrimination on any ground such as sex, race, colour, language, religion, political or other opinion, national or social origin, association with a national minority, property, birth or other status.
>   2. No one shall be discriminated against by any public authority on any ground such as those mentioned in paragraph 1.[71]

It is noteworthy that the words 'other status' in Article 14 of the ECHR should include maternity discrimination, and such a specific inclusion was considered unnecessary from a legal point of view, since the list of non-discrimination grounds is not exhaustive, and since inclusion of any particular additional ground might give rise to unwarranted *a contrario* interpretations as regards discrimination based on grounds not so included. According to the Explanatory Memorandum prepared by the Council of Europe, the expression 'any right set forth by law' in Article 1 of Protocol 12 is meant to cover: (i) the enjoyment of any right specifically granted to an individual by national law; (ii) the enjoyment of a right which may be inferred from a clear obligation of a public authority under national law, such as where a public authority is obliged under national law to behave in a particular manner; (iii) the exercise of a discretionary power by a public authority; and (iv) any other act or omission by a public authority. The prime objective of Article 1 is to embody a negative obligation on public authorities not to discriminate; it does

---

70 European Convention for the Protection of Human Rights and Fundamental Freedoms as amended by Protocol No. 12, at the Preamble.

71 Ibid., at Article 1.

not impose a general positive obligation to take measures to prevent or prohibit all instances of discrimination between private persons. On the other hand, the duty to 'secure' might entail a positive obligation where there is a clear gap in protection from discrimination under domestic law, and would oblige a ratifying State to secure protection against discrimination on all the proscribed grounds, including maternity.

European Social Charter

The European Social Charter promotes the right of workers to equal opportunities and equal treatment in matters of employment and occupation without discrimination. It espouses the notion of 'equal pay for work of equal value', and also provides for the equal treatment with regard to access to employment, vocational training, promotion and working conditions, aimed at eliminating all discrimination, both direct and indirect, in the world of work, providing for opportunities for positive measures. In the Preamble to the European Social Charter of 18 October 1961, the governments signatory hereto, being members of the Council of Europe, undertake the agreement:

> Considering that the aim of the Council of Europe is the achievement of greater unity between its members for the purpose of safeguarding and realising the ideals and principles which are their common heritage and of facilitating their economic and social progress, in particular by the maintenance and further realisation of human rights and fundamental freedoms;

> Considering that in the Convention for the Protection of Human Rights and Fundamental Freedoms signed at Rome on 4th November 1950, and the Protocol thereto signed at Paris on 20th March 1952, the member States of the Council of Europe agreed to secure to their populations the civil and political rights and freedoms therein specified;

> Considering that the enjoyment of social rights should be secured without discrimination on grounds of race, colour, sex, religion, political opinion, national extraction or social origin;

> Being resolved to make every effort in common to improve the standard of living and to promote the social well-being of both their urban and rural populations by means of appropriate institutions and action.[72]

In the Preamble to the European Social Charter (revised) of 3 May 1996, the governments signatory thereto, being members of the Council of Europe, undertake the agreement:

---

72   European Social Charter, at the Preamble.

... Considering that in the European Social Charter opened for signature in Turin on 18 October 1961 and the Protocols thereto, the member States of the Council of Europe agreed to secure to their populations the social rights specified therein in order to improve their standard of living and their social well-being;

Recalling that the Ministerial Conference on Human Rights held in Rome on 5 November 1990 stressed the need, on the one hand, to preserve the indivisible nature of all human rights, be they civil, political, economic, social or cultural and, on the other hand, to give the European Social Charter fresh impetus.[73]

Important for all workers, under Part I, several rights and principles are espoused:

The Parties accept as the aim of their policy, to be pursued by all appropriate means both national and international in character, the attainment of conditions in which the following rights and principles may be effectively realised:

1. Everyone shall have the opportunity to earn his living in an occupation freely entered upon.
2. All workers have the right to just conditions of work.
3. All workers have the right to safe and healthy working conditions.
4. All workers have the right to a fair remuneration sufficient for a decent standard of living for themselves and their families.
5. All workers and employers have the right to freedom of association in national or international organisations for the protection of their economic and social interests.
6. All workers and employers have the right to bargain collectively.
7. Children and young persons have the right to a special protection against the physical and moral hazards to which they are exposed.
8. Employed women, in case of maternity, have the right to a special protection.
9. Everyone has the right to appropriate facilities for vocational guidance with a view to helping him choose an occupation suited to his personal aptitude and interests.
10. Everyone has the right to appropriate facilities for vocational training.
11. Everyone has the right to benefit from any measures enabling him to enjoy the highest possible standard of health attainable.
12. All workers and their dependents have the right to social security.
13. Anyone without adequate resources has the right to social and medical assistance.
14. Everyone has the right to benefit from social welfare services.

---

73   European Social Charter (revised), at the Preamble.

15. Disabled persons have the right to independence, social integration and participation in the life of the community.
16. The family as a fundamental unit of society has the right to appropriate social, legal and economic protection to ensure its full development.
17. Children and young persons have the right to appropriate social, legal and economic protection.
18. The nationals of any one of the Parties have the right to engage in any gainful occupation in the territory of any one of the others on a footing of equality with the nationals of the latter, subject to restrictions based on cogent economic or social reasons.
19. Migrant workers who are nationals of a Party and their families have the right to protection and assistance in the territory of any other Party.
20. All workers have the right to equal opportunities and equal treatment in matters of employment and occupation without discrimination on the grounds of sex.
21. Workers have the right to be informed and to be consulted within the undertaking.
22. Workers have the right to take part in the determination and improvement of the working conditions and working environment in the undertaking.
23. Every elderly person has the right to social protection.
24. All workers have the right to protection in cases of termination of employment.
25. All workers have the right to protection of their claims in the event of the insolvency of their employer.
26. All workers have the right to dignity at work.
27. All persons with family responsibilities and who are engaged or wish to engage in employment have a right to do so without being subject to discrimination and as far as possible without conflict between their employment and family responsibilities.
28. Workers' representatives in undertakings have the right to protection against acts prejudicial to them and should be afforded appropriate facilities to carry out their functions.
29. All workers have the right to be informed and consulted in collective redundancy procedures.
30. Everyone has the right to protection against poverty and social exclusion.
31. Everyone has the right to housing.[74]

Under Part II, the right to work is provided for in Article 1:

1. With a view to ensuring the effective exercise of the right to work, the Parties undertake:

---

74 Ibid., at Part I.

1. to accept as one of their primary aims and responsibilities the achievement and maintenance of as high and stable a level of employment as possible, with a view to the attainment of full employment;
2. to protect effectively the right of the worker to earn his living in an occupation freely entered upon;
3. to establish or maintain free employment services for all workers;
4. to provide or promote appropriate vocational guidance, training and rehabilitation.[75]

Further, Article 4 guarantees the right to a fair remuneration and equal pay:

4. With a view to ensuring the effective exercise of the right to a fair remuneration, the Parties undertake:
   1. to recognise the right of workers to a remuneration such as will give them and their families a decent standard of living;
   2. to recognise the right of workers to an increased rate of remuneration for overtime work, subject to exceptions in particular cases;
   3. to recognise the right of men and women workers to equal pay for work of equal value;
   4. to recognise the right of all workers to a reasonable period of notice for termination of employment;
   5. to permit deductions from wages only under conditions and to the extent prescribed by national laws or regulations or fixed by collective agreements or arbitration awards. The exercise of these rights shall be achieved by freely concluded collective agreements, by statutory wage-fixing machinery, or by other means appropriate to national conditions.[76]

In addition, Article 24 provides for termination of employment under appropriate means:

24. It is understood that for the purposes of this article the terms 'termination of employment' and 'terminated' mean termination of employment at the initiative of the employer.
   1. It is understood that this article covers all workers but that a Party may exclude from some or all of its protection the following categories of employed persons:
      a. workers engaged under a contract of employment for a specified period of time or a specified task;
      b. workers undergoing a period of probation or a qualifying period of employment, provided that this is determined in advance and is of a reasonable duration;

---

75   Ibid, at Part II, Article 1.
76   Ibid., at Article 4.

    c. workers engaged on a casual basis for a short period.

2. For the purpose of this article the following, in particular, shall not constitute valid reasons for termination of employment:

    a. trade union membership or participation in union activities outside working hours, or, with the consent of the employer, within working hours;

    b. seeking office as, acting or having acted in the capacity of a workers' representative;

    c. the filing of a complaint or the participation in proceedings against an employer involving alleged violation of laws or regulations or recourse to competent administrative authorities;

    d. race, colour, sex, marital status, family responsibilities, pregnancy, religion, political opinion, national extraction or social origin;

    e. maternity or parental leave;

    f. temporary absence from work due to illness or injury.

3. It is understood that compensation or other appropriate relief in case of termination of employment without valid reasons shall be determined by national laws or regulations, collective agreements or other means appropriate to national conditions.[77]

Pursuant to Article 22, the Parties undertake to adopt or encourage measures enabling all workers, in accordance with national legislation and practice, to contribute to the determination and the improvement of the working conditions, work organization and working environment; to the protection of health and safety within the undertaking; to the organization of social and sociocultural services and facilities within the undertaking; and to the supervision of the observance of regulations on these matters.[78]

Finally, importantly, under Part V, Article E is a provision on non-discrimination:

> The enjoyment of the rights set forth in this Charter shall be secured without discrimination on any ground such as race, colour, sex, language, religion, political or other opinion, national extraction or social origin, health, association with a national minority, birth or other status.[79]

The right of all individuals to equality before the law and to protection from discrimination is a fundamental right which is essential in order to allow any democratic society to function properly, since it helps to achieve the objectives of promoting economic and social progress, and a high level of employment by increasing economic and social cohesion. When women became more militant in

---

77   Ibid., at Article 24.

78   Ibid., at Article 22.

79   Ibid., at Part V, Article E.

the 1970s, the Community began to adopt a more positive attitude toward women's rights. Community legislation, through Council Directives, reinforced the general legal provisions for equal pay and equal treatment. A series of directives have been adopted aimed at ensuring equal opportunities and treatment for men and women. The Council Directives require the Member States to realign their national laws in providing recourse to the courts, and importantly prohibit any possible retribution against those who pursue a judicial action: Member States shall introduce into their national legal systems such measures as are necessary to enable all persons who consider themselves wronged by failure to apply them the principle to pursue their claims by judicial process after possible recourse to other competent authorities. Member States shall take the necessary measures to protect employees against dismissal by the employer as a reaction to a complaint within the undertaking or to any legal proceedings aimed at enforcing compliance with the principle.

Council Recommendation 84/635/EEC on the Promotion of Positive Action for Women

Article 1 of the Council Recommendation states:

1. To adopt a positive action policy designed to eliminate existing inequalities affecting women in working life and to promote a better balance between the sexes in employment,
   a. to eliminate or counteract the prejudicial effects on women in employment or seeking employment which arise from existing attitudes, behaviours and structures based on the idea of a traditional division of roles in society between men and women;
   b. to encourage the participation of women in various occupations in those sectors of working life where they are at present under-represented, particularly in the sectors of the future, and at higher levels of responsibility in order to achieve better use of all human resources.[80]

Further, Article 4 goes on to enumerate positive action measures:

4. To take steps to ensure that positive action includes as far as possible actions having a bearing on the following aspects:
   - informing and increasing the awareness of both the general public and the working world of the need to promote equality of opportunity for working women,
   - respect for the dignity of women at the workplace,
   - qualitative and quantitative studies and analyses of the position of women on the labour market,

---

[80] Council Recommendation 84/635/EEC of 13 December 1984 on the promotion of positive action for women, at Article 1.

- diversification of vocational choice, and more relevant vocational skills, particularly through appropriate vocational training, including the implementation of supporting measures and suitable teaching methods,
- measures necessary to ensure that placement, guidance and counselling services have sufficient skilled personnel to provide a service based on the necessary expertise in the special problems of unemployed women,
- encouraging women candidates and the recruitment and promotion of women in sectors and professions and at levels where they are underrepresented, particularly as regards positions of responsibility,
- adapting working conditions; adjusting the organisation of work and working time,
- encouraging supporting measures such as those designed to foster greater sharing of occupational and social responsibilities,
- active participation by women in decision making bodies, including those representing workers, employers and the self-employed.[81]

Council Decision 2000/750/EC Establishing a Community Action Program to Combat Discrimination (2001 to 2006)

Important for equal rights in general and equal rights for women in particular, the Preamble of Council Decision 2000/750/EC Establishing a community action program to combat discrimination states:

1. The European Union is founded on the principles of liberty, democracy, respect for human rights and fundamental freedoms, and the rule of law, principles which are common to all Member States. In accordance with Article 6(2) of the Treaty on European Union, the Union should respect fundamental rights as guaranteed by the European Convention for the Protection of Human Rights and Fundamental Freedoms and as derived from the shared constitutional traditions common to the Member States, as general principles of Community law.
2. The European Parliament has strongly and repeatedly urged the European Union to develop and strengthen its policy in the field of equal treatment and equal opportunities across all grounds of discrimination.
5. The different forms of discrimination cannot be ranked: all are equally intolerable. The programme is intended both to exchange existing good practice in the Member States and to develop new practice and policy for combating discrimination, including multiple discrimination. This Decision may help to put in place a comprehensive strategy for combating all forms of discrimination on different grounds, a strategy which should henceforward be developed in parallel.

---

81 Ibid., at Article 4.

9. Many non-governmental organisations at European level have experience and expertise in fighting discrimination, as well as acting at European level as the advocates of people who are exposed to discrimination. They can therefore make an important contribution towards a better understanding of the diverse forms and effects of discrimination and to ensuring that the design, implementation and follow-up of the programme take account of the experience of people exposed to discrimination.

11. It is necessary, in order to reinforce the added value of Community action, that the Commission, in cooperation with the Member States, should ensure, at all levels, the coherence and complementarity of actions implemented in the framework of this Decision and other relevant Community policies, instruments and actions, in particular those in the fields of education and training and equal opportunities between men and women under the European Social Fund and those to promote social inclusion. Consistency and complementarity with the relevant activities of the European Monitoring Centre on Racism and Xenophobia should also be ensured.[82]

Objectives of the program are outlined in Article 2:

2. Within the limits of the Community's powers, the programme shall support and supplement the efforts at Community level and in the Member States to promote measures to prevent and combat discrimination whether based on one or on multiple factors, taking account, where appropriate, of future legislative developments. It shall have the following objectives:

   a. to improve the understanding of issues related to discrimination through improved knowledge of this phenomenon and through evaluation of the effectiveness of policies and practice;

   b. to develop the capacity to prevent and address discrimination effectively, in particular by strengthening organisations' means of action and through support for the exchange of information and good practice and networking at European level, while taking into account the specific characteristics of the different forms of discrimination;

   c. to promote and disseminate the values and practices underlying the fight against discrimination, including through the use of awareness-raising campaigns.[83]

Finally, Article 3 stipulates the Community actions to be undertaken:

3. 1. With a view to achieving the objectives set out in Article 2, the following actions may be implemented within a transnational framework:

---

82 Council Decision 2000/750/EC of 27 November 2000 establishing a Community Action Program to Combat Discrimination (2001 to 2006), at the Preamble.

83 Ibid., at Article 2.

a. analysis of factors related to discrimination, including through studies and the development of qualitative and quantitative indicators and benchmarks, in accordance with national law and practices, and the evaluation of anti-discrimination legislation and practice, with a view to assessing its effectiveness and impact, with effective dissemination of the results;

b. transnational cooperation and the promotion of networking at European level between partners active in the prevention of, and the fight against, discrimination, including non-governmental organisations;

c. awareness-raising, in particular to emphasise the European dimension of the fight against discrimination and to publicise the results of the programme, in particular through communications, publications, campaigns and events.[84]

Council Directive 97/80/EC on the Burden of Proof in Cases of Discrimination Based on Sex

The directive known as the Burden of Proof Directive requires any necessary changes in Member States' judicial systems to ensure more effective implementation of the principle of equal treatment.[85] According to Article 1, the aim of this Directive shall be to ensure that the measures taken by the Member States to implement the principle of equal treatment are made more effective, in order to enable all persons who consider themselves wronged because the principle of equal treatment has not been applied to them to have their rights asserted by judicial process after possible recourse to other competent bodies.[86]

Article 2 defines equal treatment and indirect discrimination:

2. 1. For the purposes of this Directive, the principle of equal treatment shall mean that there shall be no discrimination whatsoever based on sex, either directly or indirectly.

2. For purposes of the principle of equal treatment referred to in paragraph 1, indirect discrimination shall exist where an apparently neutral provision, criterion or practice disadvantages a substantially higher proportion of the members of one sex unless that provision, criterion or practice is appropriate and necessary and can be justified by objective factors unrelated to sex.[87]

---

84 Ibid., at Article 3.
85 Council Directive 97/80/EC of 15 December 1997 on the burden of proof in cases of discrimination based on sex.
86 Ibid., at Article 1.
87 Ibid., at Article 2.

In terms of the burden of proof, Article 4 holds:

> 4. 1. Member States shall take such measures as are necessary, in accordance with their national judicial systems, to ensure that, when persons who consider themselves wronged because the principle of equal treatment has not been applied to them establish, before a court or other competent authority, facts from which it may be presumed that there has been direct or indirect discrimination, it shall be for the respondent to prove that there has been no breach of the principle of equal treatment.
>   2. This Directive shall not prevent Member States from introducing rules of evidence which are more favourable to plaintiffs.[88]

Council Directive 2000/78/EC Establishing a General Framework for Equal Treatment in Employment and Occupation

Important for equal rights in employment, the Preamble of Council Directive 2000/78/EC Establishing a General Framework for Equal Treatment in Employment and Occupation states:

> The Council of the European Union,
> Having regard to the Treaty establishing the European Community, and in particular Article 13 thereof,
> Having regard to the proposal from the Commission,
> Having regard to the Opinion of the European Parliament,
> Having regard to the Opinion of the Economic and Social Committee,
> Having regard to the Opinion of the Committee of the Regions,
>
> Whereas:
> 1. In accordance with Article 6 of the Treaty on European Union, the European Union is founded on the principles of liberty, democracy, respect for human rights and fundamental freedoms, and the rule of law, principles which are common to all Member States and it respects fundamental rights, as guaranteed by the European Convention for the Protection of Human Rights and Fundamental Freedoms and as they result from the constitutional traditions common to the Member States, as general principles of Community law.
> 4. The right of all persons to equality before the law and protection against discrimination constitutes a universal right recognised by the Universal Declaration of Human Rights, the United Nations Convention on the Elimination of All Forms of Discrimination against Women, United Nations Covenants on Civil and Political Rights and on Economic, Social and Cultural Rights and by the European Convention for the Protection of

---

88 Ibid., at Article 4.

Human Rights and Fundamental Freedoms, to which all Member States are signatories. Convention No 111 of the International Labour Organization (ILO) prohibits discrimination in the field of employment and occupation.

6. The Community Charter of the Fundamental Social Rights of Workers recognises the importance of combating every form of discrimination, including the need to take appropriate action for the social and economic integration of elderly and disabled people.

7. The EC Treaty includes among its objectives the promotion of coordination between employment policies of the Member States. To this end, a new employment chapter was incorporated in the EC Treaty as a means of developing a coordinated European strategy for employment to promote a skilled, trained and adaptable workforce.

8. The Employment Guidelines for 2000 agreed by the European Council at Helsinki on 10 and 11 December 1999 stress the need to foster a labour market favourable to social integration by formulating a coherent set of policies aimed at combating discrimination against groups such as persons with disability. They also emphasise the need to pay particular attention to supporting older workers, in order to increase their participation in the labour force.

9. Employment and occupation are key elements in guaranteeing equal opportunities for all and contribute strongly to the full participation of citizens in economic, cultural and social life and to realising their potential.

15. The appreciation of the facts from which it may be inferred that there has been direct or indirect discrimination is a matter for national judicial or other competent bodies, in accordance with rules of national law or practice. Such rules may provide, in particular, for indirect discrimination to be established by any means including on the basis of statistical evidence.

17. This Directive does not require the recruitment, promotion, maintenance in employment or training of an individual who is not competent, capable and available to perform the essential functions of the post concerned or to undergo the relevant training, without prejudice to the obligation to provide reasonable accommodation for people with disabilities.

28. This Directive lays down minimum requirements, thus giving the Member States the option of introducing or maintaining more favourable provisions. The implementation of this Directive should not serve to justify any regression in relation to the situation which already prevails in each Member State.

30. The effective implementation of the principle of equality requires adequate judicial protection against victimisation.

32. Member States need not apply the rules on the burden of proof to proceedings in which it is for the court or other competent body to investigate the facts of the case. The procedures thus referred to are those in which the plaintiff is not required to prove the facts, which it is for the court or competent body to investigate.

33. Member States should promote dialogue between the social partners and, within the framework of national practice, with non-governmental organisations to address different forms of discrimination at the workplace and to combat them.
35. Member States should provide for effective, proportionate and dissuasive sanctions in case of breaches of the obligations under this Directive,

Has adopted this Directive.[89]

The scope of the Directive is outlined in Article 3:

3. 1. Within the limits of the areas of competence conferred on the Community, this Directive shall apply to all persons, as regards both the public and private sectors, including public bodies, in relation to:
    a. conditions for access to employment, to self-employment or to occupation, including selection criteria and recruitment conditions, whatever the branch of activity and at all levels of the professional hierarchy, including promotion;
    b. access to all types and to all levels of vocational guidance, vocational training, advanced vocational training and retraining, including practical work experience;
    c. employment and working conditions, including dismissals and pay;
    d. membership of, and involvement in, an organisation of workers or employers, or any organisation whose members carry on a particular profession, including the benefits provided for by such organisations.[90]

Importantly, the concept of discrimination is defined under Article 2:

2. 1. For the purposes of this Directive, the 'principle of equal treatment' shall mean that there shall be no direct or indirect discrimination whatsoever on any of the grounds referred to in Article 1.
   2. For the purposes of paragraph 1:
    a. direct discrimination shall be taken to occur where one person is treated less favourably than another is, has been or would be treated in a comparable situation, on any of the grounds referred to in Article 1;
   3. Harassment shall be deemed to be a form of discrimination within the meaning of paragraph 1, when unwanted conduct related to any of the grounds referred to in Article 1 takes place with the purpose or effect of

---

89   Council Directive 2000/78/EC Establishing a General Framework for Equal Treatment in Employment and Occupation, at the Preamble.
90   Ibid., at Article 3.

violating the dignity of a person and of creating an intimidating, hostile, degrading, humiliating or offensive environment. In this context, the concept of harassment may be defined in accordance with the national laws and practice of the Member States.

4. An instruction to discriminate against persons on any of the grounds referred to in Article 1 shall be deemed to be discrimination within the meaning of paragraph 1.[91]

Further, Article 11 guards against victimization:

11. Member States shall introduce into their national legal systems such measures as are necessary to protect employees against dismissal or other adverse treatment by the employer as a reaction to a complaint within the undertaking or to any legal proceedings aimed at enforcing compliance with the principle of equal treatment.[92]

However, Article 4 contains genuine occupational requirements:

4. 1. Notwithstanding Article 2(1) and (2), Member States may provide that a difference of treatment which is based on a characteristic related to any of the grounds referred to in Article 1 shall not constitute discrimination where, by reason of the nature of the particular occupational activities concerned or of the context in which they are carried out, such a characteristic constitutes a genuine and determining occupational requirement, provided that the objective is legitimate and the requirement is proportionate.[93]

Further, Article 8 provides for minimum requirements:

8. 1. Member States may introduce or maintain provisions which are more favourable to the protection of the principle of equal treatment than those laid down in this Directive.

2. The implementation of this Directive shall under no circumstances constitute grounds for a reduction in the level of protection against discrimination already afforded by Member States in the fields covered by this Directive.[94]

Positive action is provided for under Article 7:

---

91 Ibid., at Article 2.
92 Ibid., at Article 11.
93 Ibid., at Article 4.
94 Ibid., at Article 8.

7. 1. With a view to ensuring full equality in practice, the principle of equal treatment shall not prevent any Member State from maintaining or adopting specific measures to prevent or compensate for disadvantages linked to any of the grounds referred to in Article 1.[95]

Importantly, in terms of remedies and enforcement, Article 9 provides for defense of rights:

9. 1. Member States shall ensure that judicial and/or administrative procedures, including where they deem it appropriate conciliation procedures, for the enforcement of obligations under this Directive are available to all persons who consider themselves wronged by failure to apply the principle of equal treatment to them, even after the relationship in which the discrimination is alleged to have occurred has ended.

   2. Member States shall ensure that associations, organisations or other legal entities which have, in accordance with the criteria laid down by their national law, a legitimate interest in ensuring that the provisions of this Directive are complied with, may engage, either on behalf or in support of the complainant, with his or her approval, in any judicial and/or administrative procedure provided for the enforcement of obligations under this Directive.[96]

The burden of proof is detailed in Article 10:

10. 1. Member States shall take such measures as are necessary, in accordance with their national judicial systems, to ensure that, when persons who consider themselves wronged because the principle of equal treatment has not been applied to them establish, before a court or other competent authority, facts from which it may be presumed that there has been direct or indirect discrimination, it shall be for the respondent to prove that there has been no breach of the principle of equal treatment.[97]

Article 16 provides for compliance:

16. Member States shall take the necessary measures to ensure that:
   a. any laws, regulations and administrative provisions contrary to the principle of equal treatment are abolished;
   b. any provisions contrary to the principle of equal treatment which are included in contracts or collective agreements, internal rules of undertakings or rules governing the independent occupations and

---

95 Ibid., at Article 7.
96 Ibid., at Article 9.
97 Ibid., at Article 10.

professions and workers' and employers' organisations are, or may be, declared null and void or are amended.[98]

Finally, Article 17 deals with sanctions:

> 17. Member States shall lay down the rules on sanctions applicable to infringements of the national provisions adopted pursuant to this Directive and shall take all measures necessary to ensure that they are applied. The sanctions, which may comprise the payment of compensation to the victim, must be effective, proportionate and dissuasive. Member States shall notify those provisions to the Commission by 2 December 2003 at the latest and shall notify it without delay of any subsequent amendment affecting them.[99]

Council Directive 96/34/EC Establishing a General Framework Agreement on Parental Leave

The Parental Leave Directive provides for all parents of children up to a given age to be defined by Member States, to be given parental leave. Important for equal rights, in the Preamble of directive, it is stated:

> The Council of the European Union,
> Having regard to the Agreement on social policy, annexed to the Protocol (No 14) on social policy, annexed to the Treaty establishing the European Community, and in particular Article 4 (2) thereof,
>
> Having regard to the proposal from the Commission,
>
> 1. Whereas on the basis of the Protocol on social policy, the Member States, with the exception of the United Kingdom of Great Britain and Northern Ireland, (hereinafter referred to as the Member States), wishing to pursue the course mapped out by the 1989 Social Charter have concluded an Agreement on social policy amongst themselves;
> 2. Whereas management and labour may, in accordance with Article 4 (2) of the Agreement on social policy, request jointly that agreements at Community level be implemented by a Council decision on a proposal from the Commission;
> 3. Whereas paragraph 16 of the Community Charter of the Fundamental Social Rights of Workers on equal treatment for men and women provides, inter alia, that measures should also be developed enabling men and women to reconcile their occupational and family obligations;

---

98 Ibid., at Article 16.
99 Ibid., at Article 17.

4. Whereas the Council, despite the existence of a broad consensus, has not been able to act on the proposal for a Directive on parental leave for family reasons (1), as amended (2) on 15 November 1984;

5. Whereas the Commission, in accordance with Article 3 (2) of the Agreement on social policy, consulted management and labour on the possible direction of Community action with regard to reconciling working and family life;

6. Whereas the Commission, considering after such consultation that Community action was desirable, once again consulted management and labour on the substance of the envisaged proposal in accordance with Article 3 (3) of the said Agreement;

7. Whereas the general cross-industry organisations (Unice, CEEP and the ETUC) informed the Commission in their joint letter of 5 July 1995 of their desire to initiate the procedure provided for by Article 4 of the said Agreement;

8. Whereas the said cross-industry organisations concluded, on 14 December 1995, a framework agreement on parental leave; whereas they have forwarded to the Commission their joint request to implement this framework agreement by a Council Decision on a proposal from the Commission in accordance with Article 4 (2) of the said Agreement;

9. Whereas the Council, in its Resolution of 6 December 1994 on certain aspects for a European Union social policy; a contribution to economic and social convergence in the Union (3), asked the two sides of industry to make use of the possibilities for concluding agreements, since they are as a rule closer to social reality and to social problems; whereas in Madrid, the members of the European Council from those States which have signed the Agreement on social policy welcomed the conclusion of this framework agreement;

10. Whereas the signatory parties wanted to conclude a framework agreement setting out minimum requirements on parental leave and time off from work on grounds of force majeure and referring back to the Member States and/or management and labour for the definition of the conditions under which parental leave would be implemented, in order to take account of the situation, including the situation with regard to family policy, existing in each Member State, particularly as regards the conditions for granting parental leave and exercise of the right to parental leave;

11. Whereas the proper instrument for implementing this framework agreement is a Directive within the meaning of Article 189 of the Treaty; whereas it is therefore binding on the Member States as to the result to be achieved, but leaves them the choice of form and methods;

12. Whereas, in keeping with the principle of subsidiarity and the principle of proportionality as set out in Article 3b of the Treaty, the objectives of this Directive cannot be sufficiently achieved by the Member States and can therefore be better achieved by the Community; whereas this Directive is confined to the minimum required to achieve these objectives and does not go beyond what is necessary to achieve that purpose;

13. Whereas the Commission has drafted its proposal for a Directive, taking into account the representative status of the signatory parties, their mandate and the legality of the clauses of the framework agreement and compliance with the relevant provisions concerning small and medium-sized undertakings;

14. Whereas the Commission, in accordance with its Communication of 14 December 1993 concerning the implementation of the Protocol on social policy, informed the European Parliament by sending it the text of the framework agreement, accompanied by its proposal for a Directive and the explanatory memorandum;

15. Whereas the Commission also informed the Economic and Social Committee by sending it the text of the framework agreement, accompanied by its proposal for a Directive and the explanatory memorandum;

16. Whereas clause 4 point 2 of the framework agreement states that the implementation of the provisions of this agreement does not constitute valid grounds for reducing the general level of protection afforded to workers in the field of this agreement. This does not prejudice the right of Member States and/or management and labour to develop different legislative, regulatory or contractual provisions, in the light of changing circumstances (including the introduction of non-transferability), as long as the minimum requirements provided for in the present agreement are complied with;

17. Whereas the Community Charter of the Fundamental Social Rights of Workers recognises the importance of the fight against all forms of discrimination, especially based on sex, colour, race, opinions and creeds;

18. Whereas Article F (2) of the Treaty on European Union provides that 'the Union shall respect fundamental rights, as guaranteed by the European Convention for the Protection of Human Rights and Fundamental Freedoms signed in Rome on 4 November 1950 and as they result from the constitutional traditions common to the Member States, as general principles of Community law;

19. Whereas the Member States can entrust management and labour, at their joint request, with the implementation of this Directive, as long as they take all the necessary steps to ensure that they can at all times guarantee the results imposed by this Directive;

20. Whereas the implementation of the framework agreement contributes to achieving the objectives under Article 1 of the Agreement on social policy,

Has adopted this Directive.[100]

Article 1 deals with the implementation of the framework agreement and states:

---

100 Council Directive 96/34/EC Establishing a General Framework Agreement on Parental Leave, at the Preamble.

1. The purpose of this Directive is to put into effect the annexed framework agreement on parental leave concluded on 14 December 1995 between the general cross-industry organisations (Unice, CEEP and the ETUC).[101]

In terms of final provisions, Article 2 states:

2. 1. The Member States shall bring into force the laws, regulations and administrative provisions necessary to comply with this Directive by 3 June 1998 at the latest or shall ensure by that date at the latest that management and labour have introduced the necessary measures by agreement, the Member States being required to take any necessary measure enabling them at any time to be in a position to guarantee the results imposed by this Directive. They shall forthwith inform the Commission thereof.
    2. The Member States may have a maximum additional period of one year, if this is necessary to take account of special difficulties or implementation by a collective agreement.
        They must forthwith inform the Commission of such circumstances.
    3. When Member States adopt the measures referred to in paragraph 1, they shall contain a reference to this Directive or be accompanied by such reference on the occasion of their official publication. The methods of making such reference shall be laid down by Member States.[102]

In the Annex, the Preamble of the Framework Agreement on Parental Leave states:

The enclosed framework agreement represents an undertaking by Unice, CEEP and the ETUC to set out minimum requirements on parental leave and time off from work on grounds of force majeure, as an important means of reconciling work and family life and promoting equal opportunities and treatment between men and women.

ETUC, Unice and CEEP request the Commission to submit this framework agreement to the Council for a Council Decision making these minimum requirements binding in the Member States of the European Community, with the exception of the United Kingdom of Great Britain and Northern Ireland.[103]

The General Considerations are outlined under Section 1:

---

101   Ibid., at Article 1.
102   Ibid., at Article 2.
103   Ibid., Annex, at the Preamble.

1. 1. Having regard to the Agreement on social policy annexed to the Protocol on social policy, annexed to the Treaty establishing the European Community, and in particular Articles 3 (4) and 4 (2) thereof;

    2. Whereas Article 4 (2) of the Agreement on social policy provides that agreements concluded at Community level shall be implemented, at the joint request of the signatory parties, by a Council decision on a proposal from the Commission;

    3. Whereas the Commission has announced its intention to propose a Community measure on the reconciliation of work and family life;

    4. Whereas the Community Charter of Fundamental Social Rights stipulates at point 16 dealing with equal treatment that measures should be developed to enable men and women to reconcile their occupational and family obligations;

    5. Whereas the Council Resolution of 6 December 1994 recognises that an effective policy of equal opportunities presupposes an integrated overall strategy allowing for better organisation of working hours and greater flexibility, and for an easier return to working life, and notes the important role of the two sides of industry in this area and in offering both men and women an opportunity to reconcile their work responsibilities with family obligations;

    6. Whereas measures to reconcile work and family life should encourage the introduction of new flexible ways of organising work and time which are better suited to the changing needs of society and which should take the needs of both undertakings and workers into account;

    7. Whereas family policy should be looked at in the context of demographic changes, the effects of the ageing population, closing the generation gap and promoting women's participation in the labour force;

    8. Whereas men should be encouraged to assume an equal share of family responsibilities, for example they should be encouraged to take parental leave by means such as awareness programmes;

    9. Whereas the present agreement is a framework agreement setting out minimum requirements and provisions for parental leave, distinct from maternity leave, and for time off from work on grounds of force majeure, and refers back to Member States and social partners for the establishment of the conditions of access and detailed rules of application in order to take account of the situation in each Member State;

    10. Whereas Member States should provide for the maintenance of entitlements to benefits in kind under sickness insurance during the minimum period of parental leave;

    11. Whereas Member States should also, where appropriate under national conditions and taking into account the budgetary situation, consider the maintenance of entitlements to relevant social security benefits as they stand during the minimum period of parental leave;

12. Whereas this agreement takes into consideration the need to improve social policy requirements, to enhance the competitiveness of the Community economy and to avoid imposing administrative, financial and legal constraints in a way which would impede the creation and development of small and medium-sized undertakings;

13. Whereas management and labour are best placed to find solutions that correspond to the needs of both employers and workers and must therefore have conferred on them a special role in the implementation and application of the present agreement,

The signatory Parties have agreed the following.[104]

Clause 1 states the purpose and scope of the agreement:

1. 1. This agreement lays down minimum requirements designed to facilitate the reconciliation of parental and professional responsibilities for working parents.

   2. This agreement applies to all workers, men and women, who have an employment contract or employment relationship as defined by the law, collective agreements or practices in force in each Member State.[105]

Importantly, Clause 2 protects parental leave:

2. 1. This agreement grants, subject to clause 2.2, men and women workers an individual right to parental leave on the grounds of the birth or adoption of a child to enable them to take care of that child, for at least three months, until a given age up to 8 years to be defined by Member States and/or management and labour.

   2. To promote equal opportunities and equal treatment between men and women, the parties to this agreement consider that the right to parental leave provided for under clause 2.1 should, in principle, be granted on a non-transferable basis.

   3. The conditions of access and detailed rules for applying parental leave shall be defined by law and/or collective agreement in the Member States, as long as the minimum requirements of this agreement are respected. Member States and/or management and labour may, in particular:

      a. decide whether parental leave is granted on a full-time or part-time basis, in a piecemeal way or in the form of a time-credit system;

      b. make entitlement to parental leave subject to a period of work qualification and/or a length of service qualification which shall not exceed one year;

---

104 Ibid., at Section 1.
105 Ibid., at Clause 1.

  c. adjust conditions of access and detailed rules for applying parental leave to the special circumstances of adoption;

  d. establish notice periods to be given by the worker to the employer when exercising the right to parental leave, specifying the beginning and the end of the period of leave;

  e. define the circumstances in which an employer, following consultation in accordance with national law, collective agreements and practices, is allowed to postpone the granting of parental leave for justifiable reasons related to the operation of the undertaking (e.g. where work is of a seasonal nature, where a replacement cannot be found within the notice period, where a significant proportion of the workforce applies for parental leave at the same time, where a specific function is of strategic importance). Any problem arising from the application of this provision should be dealt with in accordance with national law, collective agreements and practices;

  f. in addition to (e), authorise special arrangements to meet the operational and organisational requirements of small undertakings.

4. In order to ensure that workers can exercise their right to parental leave, Member States and/or management and labour shall take the necessary measures to protect workers against dismissal on the grounds of an application for, or the taking of, parental leave in accordance with national law, collective agreements or practices.

5. At the end of parental leave, workers shall have the right to return to the same job or, if that is not possible, to an equivalent or similar job consistent with their employment contract or employment relationship.

6. Rights acquired or in the process of being acquired by the worker on the date on which parental leave starts shall be maintained as they stand until the end of parental leave. At the end of parental leave, these rights, including any changes arising from national law, collective agreements or practice, shall apply.

7. Member States and/or management and labour shall define the status of the employment contract or employment relationship for the period of parental leave.

8. All matters relating to social security in relation to this agreement are for consideration and determination by Member States according to national law, taking into account the importance of the continuity of the entitlements to social security cover under the different schemes, in particular health care.[106]

Clause 3 covers time off from work on grounds of *force majeure*:

---

106 Ibid., at Clause 2.

3. 1. Member States and/or management and labour shall take the necessary measures to entitle workers to time off from work, in accordance with national legislation, collective agreements and/or practice, on grounds of force majeure for urgent family reasons in cases of sickness or accident making the immediate presence of the worker indispensable.

   2. Member States and/or management and labour may specify the conditions of access and detailed rules for applying clause 3.1 and limit this entitlement to a certain amount of time per year and/or per case.[107]

Final provisions are outlined in Clause 4:

4. 1. Member States may apply or introduce more favourable provisions that those set out in this agreement.

   2. Implementation of the provisions of this agreement shall not constitute valid grounds for reducing the general level of protection afforded to workers in the field covered by this agreement. This shall not prejudice the right of Member States and/or management and labour to develop different legislative, regulatory or contractual provisions, in the light of changing circumstances (including the introduction of non-transferability), as long as the minimum requirements provided for in the present agreement are complied with.

   3. The present agreement shall not prejudice the right of management and labour to conclude, at the appropriate level including European level, agreements adapting and/or complementing the provisions of this agreement in order to take into account particular circumstances.

   4. Member States shall adopt the laws, regulations and administrative provisions necessary to comply with the Council decision within a period of two years from its adoption or shall ensure that management and labour (1) introduce the necessary measures by way of agreement by the end of this period. Member States may, if necessary to take account of particular difficulties or implementation by collective agreement, have up to a maximum of one additional year to comply with this decision.

   5. The prevention and settlement of disputes and grievances arising from the application of this agreement shall be dealt with in accordance with national law, collective agreements and practices.

   6. Without prejudice to the respective role of the Commission, national courts and the Court of Justice, any matter relating to the interpretation of this agreement at European level should, in the first instance, be referred by the Commission to the signatory parties who will give an opinion.[108]

---

107   Ibid., at Clause 3.
108   Ibid., at Clause 4.

Council Directive 86/613/EEC on the Application of the Principle of Equal Treatment between Men and Women Engaged in an Activity, including Agriculture, in a Self-employed Capacity, and on the Protection of Self-employed Women during Pregnancy and Motherhood

The Directive covers self-employed workers, that is all persons pursuing a gainful activity for their own account, under the conditions laid down by national law, and defines the principle of equal treatment as implying the absence of all discrimination on grounds of sex, either directly or indirectly, by reference in particular to marital or family status. In the Preamble of the directive, it is stated:

> The Council of the European Communities,
>
> Having regard to the Treaty establishing the European Economic Community, and in particular Articles 100 and 235 thereof,
>
> Having regard to the proposal from the Commission (1),
>
> Having regard to the opinion of the European Parliament (2),
>
> Having regard to the opinion of the Economic and Social Committee (3),
>
> Whereas, in its resolution of 12 July 1982 on the promotion of equal opportunities for women (4), the Council approved the general objectives of the Commission communication concerning a new Community action programme on the promotion of equal opportunities for women (1982 to 1985) and expressed the will to implement appropriate measures to achieve them;
>
> Whereas action 5 of the programme referred to above concerns the application of the principle of equal treatment to self-employed women and to women in agriculture;
>
> Whereas the implementation of the principle of equal pay for men and women workers, as laid down in Article 119 of the Treaty, forms an integral part of the establishment and functioning of the common market;
>
> Whereas on 10 February 1975 the Council adopted Directive 75/117/EEC on the approximation of the laws of the Member States relating to the application of the principle of equal pay for men and women (5);
>
> Whereas, as regards other aspects of equality of treatment between men and women, on 9 February 1976 the Council adopted Directive 76/207/EEC on the implementation of the principle of equal treatment for men and women as regards access to employment, vocational training and promotion, and working conditions (6) and on 19 December 1978 Directive 79/7/EEC on the progressive implementation of the principle of equal treatment for men and women in matters of social security (7);
>
> Whereas, as regards persons engaged in a self-employed capacity, in an activity in which their spouses are also engaged, the implementation of the principle of equal treatment should be pursued through the adoption of detailed provisions designed to cover the specific situation of these persons;

Whereas differences persist between the Member States in this field, whereas, therefore it is necessary to approximate national provisions with regard to the application of the principle of equal treatment;

Whereas in certain respects the Treaty does not confer the powers necessary for the specific actions required;

Whereas the implementation of the principle of equal treatment is without prejudice to measures concerning the protection of women during pregnancy and motherhood,

Has adopted this Directive.[109]

Article 1 covers the aims and scope of the directive:

> 1. The purpose of this Directive is to ensure, in accordance with the following provisions, application in the Member States of the principle of equal treatment as between men and women engaged in an activity in a self-employed capacity, or contributing to the pursuit of such an activity, as regards those aspects not covered by Directives 76/207/EEC and 79/7/EEC.[110]

Article 2 deals with the application of the directive:

> 2. a. self-employed workers, i.e. all persons pursuing a gainful activity for their own account, under the conditions laid down by national law, including farmers and members of the liberal professions;
>   b. their spouses, not being employees or partners, where they habitually, under the conditions laid down by national law, participate in the activities of the self-employed worker and perform the same tasks or ancillary tasks.[111]

Equal treatment is covered under Article 3:

> 3. For the purposes of this Directive the principle of equal treatment implies the absence of all discrimination on grounds of sex, either directly or indirectly, by reference in particular to marital or family status.[112]

Article 4 calls for the elimination of discriminatory provisions:

---

109 Council Directive 86/613/EEC of 11 December 1986 on the application of the principle of equal treatment between men and women engaged in an activity, including agriculture, in a self-employed capacity, and on the protection of self-employed women during pregnancy and motherhood, at the Preamble.

110 Ibid., at Article 1.

111 Ibid., at Article 2.

112 Ibid., at Article 3.

4. As regards self-employed persons, Member States shall take the measures necessary to ensure the elimination of all provisions which are contrary to the principle of equal treatment as defined in Directive 76/207/EEC, especially in respect of the establishment, equipment or extension of a business or the launching or extension of any other form of self-employed activity including financial facilities.[113]

Article 8 deals with access to services during pregnancy or motherhood:

8. Member States shall undertake to examine whether, and under what conditions, female self-employed workers and the wives of self-employed workers may, during interruptions in their occupational activity owing to pregnancy or motherhood,
    –   have access to services supplying temporary replacements or existing national social services, or
    –   be entitled to cash benefits under a social security scheme or under any other public social protection system.[114]

Finally, Article 9 calls for national legal implementation:

9. Member States shall introduce into their national legal systems such measures as are necessary to enable all persons who consider themselves wronged by failure to apply the principle of equal treatment in self-employed activities to pursue their claims by judicial process, possibly after recourse to other competent authorities.[115]

Council Directive 92/85/EEC on the Introduction of Measures to Encourage Improvements in the Safety and Health at Work of Pregnant Workers and Workers who have Recently given Birth or are Breastfeeding

The Pregnant Workers Directive requires minimum measures to improve the safety and health at work of pregnant women, and women who have recently given birth or are breastfeeding, including a right to maternity leave. It extends the rights of all pregnant women to at least 14 weeks maternity leave, regardless of length of service, with all contractual rights and benefits maintained during the maternity leave period, and employment protection throughout pregnancy and maternity leave.[116]

Definitions are covered under Article 2:

---

113   Ibid., at Article 4.
114   Ibid., at Article 8.
115   Ibid., at Article 9.
116   Council Directive 92/85/EEC of 19 October 1992 on the introduction of measures to encourage improvements in the safety and health at work of pregnant workers

2. For the purposes of this Directive:

    a. pregnant worker shall mean a pregnant worker who informs her employer of her condition, in accordance with national legislation and/or national practice;

    b. worker who has recently given birth shall mean a worker who has recently given birth within the meaning of national legislation and/or national practice and who informs her employer of her condition, in accordance with that legislation and/or practice;

    c. worker who is breastfeeding shall mean a worker who is breastfeeding within the meaning of national legislation and/or national practice and who informs her employer of her condition, in accordance with that legislation and/or practice.[117]

Article 4 covers assessment and information:

4. 1. For all activities liable to involve a specific risk of exposure to the agents, processes or working conditions of which a non-exhaustive list is given in Annex I, the employer shall assess the nature, degree and duration of exposure, in the undertaking and/or establishment concerned, of workers within the meaning of Article 2, either directly or by way of the protective and preventive services referred to in Article 7 of Directive 89/391/EEC, in order to:

    –   assess any risks to the safety or health and any possible effect on the pregnancies or breastfeeding of workers within the meaning of Article 2,

    –   decide what measures should be taken.

    2. Without prejudice to Article 10 of Directive 89/391/EEC, workers within the meaning of Article 2 and workers likely to be in one of the situations referred to in Article 2 in the undertaking and/or establishment concerned and/or their representatives shall be informed of the results of the assessment referred to in paragraph 1 and of all measures to be taken concerning health and safety at work.[118]

Article 5 requires action further to the results of the assessment:

5. 1. Without prejudice to Article 6 of Directive 89/391/EEC, if the results of the assessment referred to in Article 4 (1) reveal a risk to the safety or health or an effect on the pregnancy or breastfeeding of a worker within the meaning of Article 2, the employer shall take the necessary measures

---

and workers who have recently given birth or are breastfeeding (tenth individual Directive within the meaning of Article 16 (1) of Directive 89/391/EEC).

117   Ibid., at Article 2.

118   Ibid., at Article 4.

to ensure that, by temporarily adjusting the working conditions and/or the working hours of the worker concerned, the exposure of that worker to such risks is avoided.

2. If the adjustment of her working conditions and/or working hours is not technically and/or objectively feasible, or cannot reasonably be required on duly substantiated grounds, the employer shall take the necessary measures to move the worker concerned to another job.

3. If moving her to another job is not technically and/or objectively feasible or cannot reasonably be required on duly substantiated grounds, the worker concerned shall be granted leave in accordance with national legislation and/or national practice for the whole of the period necessary to protect her safety or health.

4. The provisions of this Article shall apply mutatis mutandis to the case where a worker pursuing an activity which is forbidden pursuant to Article 6 becomes pregnant or starts breastfeeding and informs her employer thereof.[119]

Article 6 covers cases in which exposure is prohibited:

6. In addition to the general provisions concerning the protection of workers, in particular those relating to the limit values for occupational exposure:

1. Pregnant workers within the meaning of Article 2 (a) may under no circumstances be obliged to perform duties for which the assessment has revealed a risk of exposure, which would jeopardise safety or health, to the agents and working conditions listed in Annex II, Section A;

2. Workers who are breastfeeding, within the meaning of Article 2 (c), may under no circumstances be obliged to perform duties for which the assessment has revealed a risk of exposure, which would jeopardise safety or health, to the agents and working conditions listed in Annex II, Section B.[120]

Night work is prohibited under Article 7:

7. 1. Member States shall take the necessary measures to ensure that workers referred to in Article 2 are not obliged to perform night work during their pregnancy and for a period following childbirth which shall be determined by the national authority competent for safety and health, subject to submission, in accordance with the procedures laid down by the Member States, of a medical certificate stating that this is necessary for the safety or health of the worker concerned.

---

119 Ibid., at Article 5.
120 Ibid., at Article 6.

2. The measures referred to in paragraph 1 must entail the possibility, in accordance with national legislation and/or national practice, of:

    a. transfer to daytime work; or

    b. leave from work or extension of maternity leave where such a transfer is not technically and/or objectively feasible or cannot reasonably by required on duly substantiated grounds.[121]

Maternity leave is protected under Article 8:

8. 1. Member States shall take the necessary measures to ensure that workers within the meaning of Article 2 are entitled to a continuous period of maternity leave of a least 14 weeks allocated before and/or after confinement in accordance with national legislation and/or practice.

    2. The maternity leave stipulated in paragraph 1 must include compulsory maternity leave of at least two weeks allocated before and/or after confinement in accordance with national legislation and/or practice.[122]

Further, time off for ante-natal examinations is guaranteed under Article 9:

9. Member States shall take the necessary measures to ensure that pregnant workers within the meaning of Article 2 (a) are entitled to, in accordance with national legislation and/or practice, time off, without loss of pay, in order to attend ante-natal examinations, if such examinations have to take place during working hours.[123]

Finally, in terms of prohibition of dismissal, Article 10 states:

10. In order to guarantee workers, within the meaning of Article 2, the exercise of their health and safety protection rights as recognised under this Article, it shall be provided that:

    1. Member States shall take the necessary measures to prohibit the dismissal of workers, within the meaning of Article 2, during the period from the beginning of their pregnancy to the end of the maternity leave referred to in Article 8 (1), save in exceptional cases not connected with their condition which are permitted under national legislation and/or practice and, where applicable, provided that the competent authority has given its consent;

    2. if a worker, within the meaning of Article 2, is dismissed during the period referred to in point 1, the employer must cite duly substantiated grounds for her dismissal in writing;

---

121   Ibid., at Article 7.
122   Ibid., at Article 8.
123   Ibid., at Article 9.

> 3. Member States shall take the necessary measures to protect workers, within the meaning of Article 2, from consequences of dismissal which is unlawful by virtue of point 1.[124]

The European Union is at a crossroads challenged to adapt the vision of the 'founding fathers' that was first designed for six Member States to a future union of over 20 States. In essence, Europe is now the biggest frontier-free market in the world. The single market removed three types of barriers to free movement, namely: physical, technical and fiscal. The four freedoms of the Union, for goods, services, people and capital, have become a reality. Further, the new single currency, the euro, was introduced as legal tender on 1 January 1999 and replaced the currencies of those Member States in agreement on 1 January 2002. Currently, the Member States of the European Union are: Austria, Belgium, Denmark, Finland, France, Germany, Greece, Ireland, Italy, Luxembourg, the Netherlands, Portugal, Spain, Sweden and the United Kingdom; and since 1 May 2004, Cyprus (Greek part), the Czech Republic, Estonia, Hungary, Latvia, Lithuania, Malta, Poland, Slovakia and Slovenia, which expanded it from 15 to 25 Member States; and since 1 January 2007, Bulgaria and Romania, bringing the number to 27 Member States. Candidate countries are Croatia, the Former Yugoslav Republic of Macedonia, and Turkey. The remaining European countries which are not Member States of the European Union are Albania, Andorra, Belarus, Bosnia-Herzegovina, Iceland, Liechtenstein, Moldova, Monaco, Montenegro, Norway, Russia, San Marino, Serbia, Switzerland, Ukraine and Vatican City.

The criteria used for a nation to secure membership in the ever-growing European Union are: (1) democratic institutions and the rule of law, with respect for human rights and minorities within the borders; (2) a functioning market economy capable of competing within the union's single market; and (3) the acceptance of obligations of membership, signing onto the union's body of rules. The latter is perhaps the most important criterion for equal rights and their enforcement. European enlargement has increased the population of the European Union to roughly 500 million inhabitants, the third most populated political entity in the world after China and India.[125] The European Union's share of the world population is falling, though. If current trends for fertility, mortality and migration continue, the European Union population will peak in the year 2025 and revert to its current level in the year 2050. The socioeconomic conditions in the EU-15 countries have been marked by steady improvements in employment and real income since 1995. Furthermore, significant progress has been recorded in reducing disparities both among countries and among regions within the countries. Moreover, the new Member States are well placed for pursuing faster economic growth after enlargement, thereby making progress in achieving real convergence.

---

124   Ibid., at Article 10.

125   Commission Report on the Social Situation in the European Union, Report on social protection in Europe.

In the area of social cohesion, the differences between the EU-15 countries and the new Member States are particularly pronounced. With enlargement, income disparities increased considerably. Whereas income differentials between the EU-15 countries and regions diminished significantly, they rose among the new Member States, and so the European Union must therefore address the new east–west divide resulting from enlargement. Employment levels in the EU-15 countries, a major determining factor of economic and social inclusion, still show a north–south divide, which has significant implications for the social situation. With enlargement, the lower employment rates in several regions of the south will be mirrored in the east due to the effects of restructuring and job losses in agriculture and industry. This substantial reduction of jobs in these sectors has not yet been compensated for by the growth of services.

As for investing in education, the new Member States are outperforming the majority of the EU-15 countries in upper secondary education. However, the EU-15 countries produce better results when it comes to tertiary education. Disparities as regards life-long learning and familiarity with information and communication technologies (ICT), more current in the EU-15 countries, also exist. Satisfaction with life also differs considerably between the EU-15 countries and the 10 new Member States, the latter being significantly less satisfied with their personal safety and social life. The instruments of social protection aim to reduce poverty, promote social and civil dialogue, create jobs and tackle regional and social disparities in a strategic fashion. With the support of European Union policies, these advantages will become the basis of a powerful driving force of economic growth and social progress within the enlarged Union.[126]

Overall, legislation and education have proven to help overcome some discrimination. The European Union has provided important contributions to the ending of maternity discrimination in the coming together of people of different nations, and equality in employment is a real commitment for the Member States. The right of all individuals to equality before the law and to protection from discrimination is a fundamental principle of all democratic societies.[127] Establishing an effective set of laws against discrimination is an essential part of stamping out unfair treatment, but laws themselves are not enough. If discrimination is to be eliminated, attitudes and behavior must also change. A European Union-wide action program against discrimination was developed, with its purpose to support activities which combat discrimination and to raise awareness as to measures being taken across the Union to tackle it.

According to the 57th Eurobarometer survey on discrimination, few respondents reported personally experiencing discrimination on any of the six grounds explored,

---

126   Ibid.

127   Eurobarometer 57, *Discrimination in Europe, For Diversity Against Discrimination*, Alan Marsh and Melahat Sahin-Dikmen, The European Opinion Research Group (EEIG) for the European Commission Directorate General Employment and Social Affairs.

but the most often cited ground for discrimination was age (5%), followed by race or ethnicity (3%), religion or beliefs (2%), physical disability, learning difficulties or mental illness (2%), and sexual orientation (less than 1%).[128] Young people, the better educated and those on the left of the political spectrum were more likely to report having experienced discrimination. Further, those who personally experienced discrimination, young people and respondents with leftist political views were significantly more likely to report witnessing discrimination. The most often cited ground for witnessed discrimination was race or ethnicity (22%), followed by learning difficulties or mental illness (12%), physical disability (11%), religion or beliefs (9%), age (6%) and sexual orientation (6%). The young, better-educated and non-manually-employed women are more likely to oppose discrimination, older male manual workers with little education less so, but there is no clear evidence that the tendency to believe discrimination right or wrong, or to attribute such views to others, is socially determined to any great degree.[129] However, despite widespread legal protection, discrimination continues to exist and further efforts are needed to ensure that the right not to be discriminated against is implemented effectively in an enlarged European Union. Therefore, 2007 was designated as the European Year of Equal Opportunities for All, with the aim to inform people of their rights, to celebrate diversity and to promote equal opportunities for everyone in the European Union. A large proportion of Europeans are still of the opinion that discrimination is widespread in their country.[130] There is very broad support among European Union citizens for adopting measures that provide equal opportunities for everyone in the field of employment.

In the European Employment Strategy, the European Union has set out to combat unemployment and significantly increase the employment rate of Europe on a lasting basis. 'Flexicurity' strategies imply political choices between various aspects of flexibility and security, especially important for women workers. The flexicurity model remains in line with the central elements of the European Union strategy for sustainable economic growth with more jobs, better jobs and greater social cohesion. Policy measures must focus on making the labor market more open to all workers, rather than putting the blame for their exclusion from employment on them. Seen as an integral part of the macroeconomic policy mix, flexicurity should be an additional tool strengthening the European social model, which promotes strong social protection, gender equalities, high living standards and quality of life, social cohesion, and measures to combat exclusion, both from the labor market and within society. Assuring a flexible approach towards employees not only attracts the best workers, but it also contributes to achieving employment targets and reducing barriers to the labor market by making employment accessible to more people. The effects of policies related to flexicurity on vulnerable groups

---

128   Marsh, Alan, Sahin-Dikmen, Mehalat, *Discrimination in Europe*, Policy Studies Institute, London.

129   Ibid.

130   Special Eurobarometer 263 Discrimination in the European Union, 2007.

must be adequately considered as should the interconnected dimensions of social cohesion, non-discrimination and equality. Flexible and short-term contracts should not lead to increased discrimination in employment by providing a rationale to terminate employment and becoming a substitute for discrimination. A two-fold responsibility exists: on the employer side, this responsibility lies in the provision of suitable working conditions accommodating diverse practices, of adequate early warning systems, and of the availability of training and support to workers to find future employment; on the employee side, there is an individual responsibility to remain continuously employable.[131] Thus, it will be necessary to develop incentives to change people's behavior with regard to maternity issues and to combat discrimination.

Conclusion

It is important that equality be achieved in securing access to jobs, which are commensurate with skill levels. Some groups, namely women, are still lagging behind due to horizontal segregation, and vertical segregation, with difficulty acceding to higher positions in the occupational hierarchy. The system has failed to reward skills and even provides guises for discrimination. The demographic changes on the horizon will bring about a further need for qualified workers. However, some remain underutilized, considered as reserve labor. This attitude is a barrier to progressive legislation. Although European laws have gone a long way to improving the plight of many in the European Union, in reality, some have yet to enjoy the equality they are entitled to in theory. The European Union is a political structure, which emerged out of a general act of will of heterogeneous States. It is ultimately dependent on statements of general principle. Therefore, European Union law is the motor to enable the European Union to move toward its ultimate aim, the 'ever closer union'. European Union is based on partnership, cooperation and mutual dependence. The concern is to enhance the social, economic and cultural welfare of all citizens in an atmosphere of peace. This, thereby, advances the cause for maternity rights in stamping out discrimination of any kind, including maternity discrimination, through the effective use of laws and the courts, in the pursuit of *Pregnant Pause*.

---

131   Ibid.

Chapter 10
Conclusion

In the quest for appreciation for maternity issues in *Pregnant Pause*, a deep embedded patriarchal authority is still keeping society on the designated track, as *de jure* discrimination has given way to *de facto* discrimination, and in essence, inequality, once obvious and accepted, is now hidden and protected in a most dangerous way. Since within society there is an *a priori* assumption of freedom and impartiality, the burden is high on the attackers of this universal opinion. Human inequality both encompasses maternity discrimination and conceals it, and although other types of discrimination exist apart from maternity inequality, discrimination which is so blatant and open as to focus on one's maternity characteristics is most persistent and threatening to society. Therefore, seeking out inequality and bringing it to the forefront of microscopic debate can only serve to advance all quests for equality.

Both legislation and the court system have made inroads into maternity discrimination. It is important to have adequate legislation to influence conduct and outcomes, as well as an appropriate legal system to achieve favorable and enforceable results. By cooperating and learning from other similarly disadvantaged groups in the fight for equality of opportunity, more advances can be made in the fight for maternity equality. We will never totally correct the injustices of the past or of the present. However, in the pursuit of appreciation for maternity issues, as well as a better understanding of the importance of adequate legislation, future endeavors in the field will help to improve the situation for all people.

Countries around the world have made important progress in the development of equal rights. Equality rights legislation and court challenges are required in order to improve the situation of all in the workplace. The desire is for equal human rights for all. Maternity discrimination is an equal opportunity discrimination as it cuts across race, language, age, religion, disability, sexual orientation, and even gender as fathers are affected too. Therefore, the law needs to be enforced by way of the courts to achieve greater equality in an effort to modify historical attitudes, so that nations conform to certain standards. There should be real freedom to choose one's amount of participation in the workforce in the pursuit of flexibility as to a just remuneration and access to employment.

Further, taking into account the fact that continuing inequalities and noticeable progress coexist, rethinking employment policies is necessary in order to integrate the maternity perspective, not only to address any negative implications of current patterns of work and employment, but also to draw attention to a wider range of opportunities. Governments and other actors need to promote an active and visible policy of mainstreaming the *Pregnant Pause* perspective into all policies and programs.

The central importance of equality legislation in order to bring about change is evident and indeed critical. Our very rights as human beings emanate from the word of the law and the interpretation given by the highest courts in the land. Therefore, it is imperative that the struggle for maternity equality encompasses the legal system. The concept of total equality has never truly existed, nor was it ever meant to be anything more than empty promises of change. Absolute equality is not sought in this book, nor is it realistic. However, in a feeling of mutual respect for individual differences, a better equality among humans is possible and desirable through society's laws and legal institutions.

The keys to the future are the implementation and development of the law, the deepening in understanding of specific legal issues relating to employment discrimination, and the raising of the level of awareness of legal rights and obligations. In addition, a continuing exchange of experience and expertise needs to occur on the international front for mutual benefit among all groups in order to best serve the fight for maternity equality. We must all strive to promote and improve the situation of all humans through networks of awareness, in the raising of initiatives, the dissemination of information and the provision of support for equality. In addition, there needs to be a full employment policy for the integration of all humans into the labor market, the reduction of barriers to access and participation in employment, the improvement in the quality of employment through education, training and management of resources, and the improvement in the status of all in society for a change of attitudes and a lasting progress.[1]

Further, we must learn from other groups' experiences in the fight for equality. As such, like the civil rights' movement, the women's liberation movement and the disability movement, in examining legislation, we should take into account the maternity and the women's movement, and specifically its advancements in equal rights in general and appreciation for maternity issues. Therefore, in the struggle to secure equal rights for all, the consultation process must include input from other groups for strategic purposes in order to strengthen the cause. The process must be one of inclusion, not exclusion.

It is realistic to say that inequality in general exists, but especially inequality of opportunity within the labor force. This is to be expected, since not all humans have occupied a major role in the employment sphere. In addition to this, laws have been enacted and courts have enforced them in a traditionally younger white male non-disability dominant way. However, all humans too need to be a rallying symbol of political and economic force, so that equality can become a reality. The impact of equality legislation will depend on the legislative provisions as well as the effectiveness of the legislation's enforcement.

---

1   Commission of the European Communities, *Promotion of Positive Action*, Brussels, p.4.

The full and equal enjoyment of all human rights and fundamental freedoms should be a priority for all and is essential for the advancement of all. Equal rights are explicitly mentioned in the Preamble to the Charter of the United Nations, and all the major international human rights instruments include or should include maternity as one of the grounds upon which States may not discriminate. Unless the human rights of all are fully recognized and effectively protected, applied, implemented and enforced in national and international law as well as in national practice in family, civil, penal, labor and commercial codes and administrative rules and regulations, they will exist in name only.[2]

It is evident that we are moving in the right direction, since some change has taken place. However, further change is necessary and plausible. Only by working on the very thing that controls and defines all of our lives, the law, can further progress be made.

Once again, the memorable words of the Rev. Martin Luther King Jr. in his struggle for civil rights are most relevant today in the struggle for equality for those who are discriminated against, including maternity discrimination in the pursuit of *Pregnant Pause*:

> I have a dream that one day every valley shall be exalted, every hill and mountain shall be made low, the rough places shall be made plain, and the crooked places shall be made straight and the glory of the Lord will be revealed and all flesh shall see it together. This is our hope ... And when we allow freedom to ring, when we let it ring from every village and hamlet, from every state and city, we will be able to speed up that day when all of God's children ... will be able to join hands and to sing in the words of the old Negro spiritual, 'Free at last, free at last; thank God Almighty, we are free at last'.[3]

---

2 United Nations, *Beijing Declaration and Platform for Action*.

3 King Jr., Martin Luther, *March on Washington*, 1963.

Bibliography

African Charter on Human and Peoples' Rights, 1981.

American Convention on Human Rights, 1978.

American Declaration of the Rights and Duties of Man, 1948.

American Federation of State, County and Municipal Employees v. Washington, 770 F.2d. 1401 (1985).

American Nurses Association v. State of Illinois, 783 F.2d. 716 (1985).

Anti-Discrimination Act, Australia, 1991.

Australia Census.

Australia's Beijing Plus Five Action Plan 2001–2005.

Axworthy, Lloyd (1988), 'Free Trade, the Costs for Canada', in A.R. Riggs and Tom Velk, *Canadian-American Free Trade: (The Sequel) Historical, Political and Economic Dimensions*, The Institute for Research on Public Policy, Montreal.

Baird, Marian, University of Sydney, *Valuing Parenthood, Options for Paid Maternity Leave*, Australia Review of Public Affairs, 14 June 2002.

Ballard v. United States, 329 U.S. 187 (1946).

Basi v. Canadian National Railway (1984), 9 CHRR 4. D/5029 (CHR Tribunal).

Basic Conditions of Employment Act, South Africa, 1997.

Bill of Rights Act, New Zealand, 1990.

Blake v. Ministry of Correctional Services and Mimico Correctional Institute (1984), 5 CHRR D/2417 (Ontario).

Board of Trustees of Keene State College v. Sweeney, 439 US 24 (1978).

Bradwell v. State, 16 Wall. 130 (1873).

Brecher, Irving (1987), 'The Free Trade Initiative, On Course or Off', in A.R. Riggs and Tom Velk, *Canadian-American Free Trade: Historical, Political and Economic Dimensions*, The Institute for Research in Public Policy, Montreal.

Brennan v. City Stores, 479 F.2d. 235 (1973).

British North America Act, Canada, 1867.

Campbell, Bruce (1993), *Free Trade, Destroyer of Jobs*, Canadian Centre for Policy Alternatives, Ottawa.

Canada Census.

Canada Employment Equity Act, Canada, 1995.

Canada–United States Free Trade Agreement, 1989.

Canadian Advisory Council on the Status of Women (1992), *Feminist Guide to the Canadian Constitution*, Ottawa.

Canadian Bill of Rights, Canada, 1960.

Canadian Constitution, Canada, 1982.

Canadian Constitution, Canadian Charter of Rights and Freedoms, Canada, 1982.

Canadian Human Rights Act, Canada, 1978.

Cassin, René (1969), *From the Ten Commandments to the Rights of Man*, France.

Central Alberta Dairy Pool v. Alberta (Human Rights Commission) [1990] 2 S.C.R. 489.

Charter of the Organization of African Unity, 1963.

Civil Rights Act, United States, 1964.

Cohen, Gary L., *Women Entrepreneurs*, Perspectives.

Coleman, Frank (1977), *Hobbes and America*, University of Toronto, Toronto.

Commission of the European Communities, *Employment in Europe*, Brussels.

Commission of the European Communities, *Equal Opportunity for Women and Men*, Brussels.

Commission of the European Communities, *Europe*, Brussels.

Commission of the European Communities, *Promotion of Positive Action*, Brussels.

Commission of the European Communities, *The Position of Women on the Labour Market*.

Commission Report on the Social Situation in the European Union, Report on Social Protection in Europe.

Commonwealth of Australia, *Women*.

Commonwealth Office, *Advancing the Commonwealth Agenda for Gender Equality into the New Millennium (2000–2005)*.

Commonwealth Office of the Status of Women, Australia.

Commonwealth Secretariat, *Commonwealth Plan*.

Constitución Política de los Estados Unidos Mexicanos, Mexico.

Constitution of Ireland, Ireland, 1937.

Constitution of South Africa, 1996.

Corning Glass Works v. Brennan, 417 US 188 (1974).

Costa v. ENEL [1964] CMLR 425.

Council Decision 2000/750/EC of 27 November 2000 establishing a Community Action Program to Combat Discrimination (2001 to 2006).

Council Directive 86/613/EEC of 11 December 1986 on the application of the principle of equal treatment between men and women engaged in an activity, including agriculture, in a self-employed capacity, and on the protection of self-employed women during pregnancy and motherhood.

Council Directive 92/85/EEC of 19 October 1992 on the introduction of measures to encourage improvements in the safety and health at work of pregnant workers and workers who have recently given birth or are breastfeeding (tenth individual Directive within the meaning of Article 16 (1) of Directive 89/391/EEC).

Council Directive 96/34/EC Establishing a General Framework Agreement on Parental Leave.

Council Directive 97/80/EC of 15 December 1997 on the burden of proof in cases of discrimination based on sex.

Council Directive 2000/78/EC Establishing a General Framework for Equal Treatment in Employment and Occupation.

Council Recommendation 84/635/EEC of 13 December 1984 on the promotion of positive action for women.

Cox, Archibald (1967), *Civil Rights, the Constitution and the Court*, Harvard University Press, Cambridge.

Cox, Archibald (1976), *The Role of the Supreme Court in American Government*, Oxford University Press, New York.

Craig v. Boren, 429 U.S. 190 (1976).

Crompton, Susan, and Geran, Leslie, *Women as Main Wage-Earners*, Perspectives.

d'Aquino, Thomas (1987), 'Truck and Trade with the Yankees, The Case for a Canada-U.S. Comprehensive Trade Agreement', in A.R. Riggs and Tom Velk, *Canadian-American Free Trade: Historical, Political and Economic Dimensions*, The Institute for Research on Public Policy, Montreal.

Daltrop, Anne (1982), *Political Realities, Politics and the European Community*, Longman, London.

Dandridge v. William, 397 U.S. 471, 485 (1970).

Davis v. Passman, 442 US 228 (1979).

Declaration of Independence, United States, 1776.

Department of Justice, Equality & Law Reform, *Developing Sectoral Strategies to Address Gender Pay Gaps*.

Department of Labour New Zealand and Research New Zealand, *Parental Leave in New Zealand 2005/2006 Evaluation*.

Department of Trade and Industry, Great Britain, *Key Facts about Women in the Labour Market*.

Directive 2002/73/EC of the European Parliament and of the Council of 23 September 2002 amending Council Directive 76/207/EEC on the implementation of the principle of equal treatment for men and women as regards access to employment, vocational training and promotion, and working conditions.

Discrimination Act, Australia, 1991.

Easterbrook, W.T. and Aitken, Hugh (1976), *Canadian Economic History*, Macmillan, Toronto.

Economic Commission for Africa, *Economic Report on Africa*.

Ely, J. (1980), *Democracy and Distrust*, Harvard University Press, Cambridge.

Employment Contracts Act, New Zealand, 1991.

Employment Equality Act, Ireland, 1998.

Employment Equity Act, South Africa, 1998.

Employment Relations Act, New Zealand, 2000.

Employment Rights Act, UK, 1996.

Equal Opportunities Commission, *Code of Practice on Equal Pay*, UK.

Equal Opportunities Commission, *Facts About Women and Men in Great Britain*.

Equal Opportunities Commission, *Facts About Women and Men in Scotland*.

Equal Opportunities Commission, *Facts About Women and Men in Wales*.

Equal Opportunities Commission, *Women and Men in Britain, Pay and Income.*

Equal Pay Act, UK, 1970.

Equal Pay Act, United States, 1963.

Equal Status Act, Ireland, 2000.

Equality Act, UK, 2006.

Eurobarometer 57, *Discrimination in Europe, For Diversity Against Discrimination,* Alan Marsh and Melahat Sahin-Dikmen, The European Opinion Research Group (EEIG) for the European Commission Directorate General Employment and Social Affairs.

European Convention for the Protection of Human Rights and Fundamental Freedoms, 1950.

European Convention for the Protection of Human Rights and Fundamental Freedoms as amended by Protocol No. 1, 1950.

European Convention for the Protection of Human Rights and Fundamental Freedoms as amended by Protocol No. 12, 2000.

European Social Charter, 1961.

European Social Charter (revised), 1996.

Eurostat, *Yearbook, Statistical Guide to Europe*, Brussels.

Family and Medical Leave Act, United States, 1993.

Federalist Papers, United States, 1787–1788.

Fried, Morton (1967), *The Evolution of Political Society*, Random House, New York.

Frontiero v. Richardson, 411 U.S. 677 (1973).

Fry, Earl (1987), 'Trends in Canada-U.S. Free Trade Discussions', in A.R. Riggs and Tom Velk, *Canadian-American Free Trade: Historical, Political and Economic Dimensions*, The Institute for Research in Public Policy, Montreal.

F.S. Royster Guano Co. v. Com of Virginia, 253 U.S. 412, 415 (1920).

General Agreement on Tariffs and Trade, 1947.

Goesaert v. Cleary, 335 U.S. 464, 466 (1948).

Gornick, Janet C. and Schmitt, John (2008), *Parental Leave Policies in 21 Countries, Assessing Generosity and Gender Equality*, September.

Gould, Elise, *Economic Snapshot for May 6, 2009, No paid leave for new U.S. moms.*

Government of Australia, *Australia's Beijing Plus Five Action Plan 2001–2005.*

Government of Australia, *Implementation of the Beijing Platform for Action.*

Government of Canada, *The North American Free Trade Agreement At A Glance*, Ottawa.

Government of Canada (2002), *NAFTA at Eight*, Ottawa.

Government of the United Kingdom, *Equality in Practice*, 2002.

Griffin Cohen, Marjorie (1987), *Free Trade and the Future of Women's Work, Manufacturing and Service Industries*, Garamond Press, Toronto.

Griggs v. Duke Power Co., 401 US 424 (1971).

Habermas, Jurgen (1998), *Between Facts and Norms*, MIT Press, Massachusetts.

Hamelin, Jean (1976), *Histoire du Québec*, Edisem, St. Hyacinthe.

Harris, Diana K. (2005), 'Age Norms', in Erdman B. Palmore, Laurence Branch, Diana K. Harris, *Encyclopedia of Ageism*, The Haworth Press, Inc., New York.

Harris, Richard (1988), 'Some Observations on the Canada-U.S. Free Trade Deal', in A.R. Riggs and Tom Velk, *Canadian-American Free Trade: (The Sequel) Historical, Political and Economic Dimensions*, The Institute for Research on Public Policy, Montreal.

Hatfield, Robert, *Duty to Accommodate*, Just Labour, vol. 5 (Winter 2005).

Hornstein, Zmira, *Outlawing age discrimination: Foreign lessons, UK choices*, The Policy Press.

Hoyt v. Florida, 368 U.S. 57, 62 (1961).

Human Resources Development Canada, Labour Program.

Human Resources and Social Development Canada.

Human Rights Act, Australia, 2004.

Human Rights Act, New Zealand, 1993.

Human Rights Act, UK, 1998.

Human Rights and Equal Opportunity Commission Act, Australia, 1986.

Hurtig, Mel (1991), *The Betrayal of Canada*, Stoddart Publishing, Toronto.

Institute for Women's Policy Research, *Maternity Leave in the United States, Paid Parental Leave Is Still Not Standard, Even Among the Best U.S. Employers*.

Inter-American Democratic Charter, 2001.

Interim Constitution of South Africa, Schedule 4.

Internationale Handelsgesellschaft, [1970] ECR 1125, [1972] CMLR 255.

Ireland Census.

Johnson, Tallese D., *Maternity Leave and Employment Patterns, 2007*, U.S. Census Bureau, Washington, D.C.

Kahn v. Shevin, 416 U.S. 351, 355 (1974).

King Jr., Martin Luther (1963), *March on Washington*.

Kirchberg v. Feenstra, 450 U.S. 455 (1981).

Labor Canada (1986), *Equal Pay for Work of Equal Value*, Ottawa.

Laun, Louis (1987), 'U.S.-Canada Free Trade Negotiations: Historical Opportunities', in A.R. Riggs and Tom Velk, *Canadian-American Free Trade: Historical, Political and Economic Dimensions*, The Institute for Research in Public Policy, Montreal.

Layton, Robert (1987), 'Why Canada Needs Free Trade', in A.R. Riggs and Tom Velk, *Canadian-American Free Trade: Historical, Political and Economic Dimensions*, The Institute for Research in Public Policy, Montreal.

Ley Federal de Trabajo, Mexico.

Ley del Seguro Social, Mexico.

Lindsley v. Natural Carbonic Gas Co., 220 U.S. 61, 78 (1911).

Lipsey, Richard (1987), 'Canada's Trade Options', in A.R. Riggs and Tom Velk, *Canadian-American Free Trade: Historical, Political and Economic Dimensions*, The Institute for Research in Public Policy, Montreal.

Maastricht Treaty, 1992.

Magna Carta, Great Britain, 1215.

Mandel, Michael (1989), *The Charter of Rights and the Legalization of Politics in Canada*, Wall & Thompson, Toronto.

Marbury v. Madison, 1 Cranch 137 (1803).

Marsh, Alan and Sahin-Dikmen, Mehalat, *Discrimination in Europe*, Policy Studies Institute, London.

Maternity Protection Act, Ireland, 1994.

Maternity Protection (Amendment) Act, Ireland, 2004.

McCullough v. Maryland, 4 Wheaton 415 (1819).

McDonnell Douglas Corp. v. Green, 411 US 792 (1973).

McGill University Institute for Health and Social Policy, 2009.

McGowan v. Maryland, 366 U.S. 420 (1961).

McPhail, Brenda (1985), *NAFTA Now*, University Press of America, Lanham.

Meiorin: British Columbia (Public Service Employee Relations Commission) (BCPSERC) v. The British Columbia Government and Service Employees Union (BCGSEU) [1999], 35 C.H.R.R. D/257 (S.C.C.).

Merrett, Christopher (1996), *Free Trade, Neither Free Nor About Trade*, Black Rose Books, New York.

Metropolis Theatre Co. v. City of Chicago, 228 U.S. 61, 69 (1913).

Mexican Investment Board (1994), *Mexico Your Partner for Growth, Regulatory Reform and Competition Policy, Setting the Incentives for an Efficient Economy*, Mexico.

Minister of Industry, *Canada Yearbook*.

Ministry of Women's Affairs, New Zealand.

Murphy v. Miller Brewer Co., 307 F.Supp. 829 (1969).

Nader, Ralph (1993), *The Case Against Free Trade*, Earth Island Press, San Francisco.

National Foundation for Australian Women.

Neufeld, E.P. (1987), 'Financial and Economic Dimensions of Free Trade', in A.R. Riggs and Tom Velk, *Canadian-American Free Trade: Historical, Political and Economic Dimensions*, The Institute for Research on Public Policy, Montreal.

New Zealand Census.

Nicoll, William and Salmon, Trevor (1994), *Understanding the New European Community*, Prentice Hall, Exeter.

North, Arthur (1964), *The Supreme Court, Judicial Process and Judicial Politics*, Appleton Century Crofts, New York.

North American Agreement on Labor Cooperation, 1993.

North American Free Trade Agreement, 1994.

Ontario Human Rights Commission v. Simpsons-Sears Ltd., [1985] SCR 536.

Orr v. Orr, 440 U.S. 268 (1979).

Pope John XXIII (1963), *Pacem in Terris*, Rome.

Pope John Paul II (1981), *Laborem Exercens*, Rome.

Pregnancy Discrimination Act, United States, 1978.

President John F. Kennedy.

Promotion of Equality and Prevention of Unfair Discrimination Act, South Africa, 2000.

Protocol on the Rights of Women in Africa, 2003.

Protocol to the African Charter on Human and Peoples' Rights on the Establishment of an African Court on Human and Peoples' Rights, 2003.

Quebec Charter of Rights and Freedoms.

Raynauld, Andre (1987), 'Looking Outward Again', in A.R. Riggs and Tom Velk, *Canadian-American Free Trade: Historical, Political and Economic Dimensions*, The Institute for Research on Public Policy, Montreal.

Reed v. Reed, 404 U.S. 71 (1971).

Regina v. Oakes, [1986] 1 S.C.R. 103.

Sack, Shelley, Deloitte & Touche, 2002.

San Antonio Independent School Division v. Rodriguez, 411 U.S. 1, 16 (1973).

Schlesinger v. Ballard, 419 U.S. 498 (1975).

Sex Discrimination Act, Australia, 1984.

Sex Discrimination Act, UK, 1975.

Shakes v. Rex Pak Ltd. (1982), 3 CHRR D/1001.

Soldatos, P. (1988), 'Canada's Foreign Policy in Search of a Fourth Option: Continuity and Change in Orientation Towards the U.S.', in A.R. Riggs and Tom Velk, *Canadian-American Free Trade: (The Sequel) Historical, Political and Economic Dimensions*, The Institute for Research on Public Policy, Montreal.

South African Census.

Spaulding v. University of Washington, 740 F.2d. 686 (1984).

Special Eurobarometer 263 Discrimination in the European Union, 2007.

Stanton v. Stanton, 421 U.S. 7 (1975).

Statistics Canada, *Women in the Labour Force*.

Statute of the Inter-American Court on Human Rights, 1980.

Stone, Frank (1987), 'Removing Barriers to Canada', in A.R. Riggs and Tom Velk, *Canadian-American Free Trade: Historical, Political and Economic Dimensions*, The Institute for Research on Public Policy, Montreal.

Taylor v. Louisiana, 419 U.S. 522 (1975).

Teuling v. Bredrijfsvereniging [1987] ECR 2497.

Treaty establishing a Constitution for Europe, 2004.

Treaty of Amsterdam, 1997.

Treaty of Lisbon, 2007.

Treaty of Paris, 1951.

Treaty of Rome, 1957.

Treaty of Waitangi, New Zealand, 1840.

Unemployment Insurance Act, South Africa, 2001.

United Kingdom Census.

United Nations (1945), Charter of the United Nations.

United Nations (1945), Statute of the International Court of Justice.

United Nations (1948), Universal Declaration of Human Rights.

United Nations (1951), Equal Remuneration Convention (ILO C100).

United Nations (1958), Discrimination (Employment and Occupation) Convention (ILO C111).

United Nations (1964), Employment Policy Convention (ILO C122).

United Nations (1965), International Convention on the Elimination of All Forms of Racial Discrimination.

United Nations (1966), International Covenant on Civil and Political Rights.

United Nations (1966), International Covenant on Economic, Social and Cultural Rights.

United Nations (1966), Optional Protocol to the International Covenant on Civil and Political Rights.

United Nations (1979), Convention on the Elimination of all Forms of Discrimination Against Women.

United Nations (1995), *Beijing Declaration and Platform for Action*.

United Nations (1999), Optional Protocol to the Convention on the Elimination of All Forms of Discrimination against Women.

United Nations, *Demographic Yearbook*.

United Nations Development Program, *Human Development Report*, Oxford University Press, Oxford.

United Nations, Maternity Leave by Country.

United Nations, Maternity Protection Act (ILO C3, C103, C183).

United Nations, *The World's Women: Trends and Statistics*.

United Nations Women Watch, *Beijing+5 Process and Beyond*.

United Nations Women Watch, *Commitments of Governments to Implement the Beijing Platform for Action*.

United States Census.

United States Census Bureau, *Statistical Abstract*.

United States Census Bureau, *Women in the United States*.

United States Constitution, United States, 1776.

Velk, Tom and Riggs, A.R. (1987), 'The Ongoing Debate Over Free Trade', in A.R. Riggs and Tom Velk, *Canadian-American Free Trade: Historical, Political and Economic Dimensions*, The Institute for Research on Public Policy, Montreal.

Watkins, Mel (1989), 'The Political Economy of Growth', in Wallace Clement and Glen Williams, *The New Canadian Political Economy*, McGill-Queen's University Press, Kingston.

Whitehouse, G., M. Baird and C. Diamond (2006), *Highlights from The Parental Leave in Australia Survey*, December.

Wigle, Randall (1987), 'The Received Wisdom of the Canada-U.S. Free Trade Qualifications', in A.R. Riggs and Tom Velk, *Canadian-American Free Trade: Historical, Political and Economic Dimensions*, The Institute for Research in Public Policy, Montreal.

Wirth, L. (1945), 'The Problem of Minority Groups', in R. Linton (ed.), *The Science of Man in the World Crisis*, Columbia University Press, New York.

Women and Equality Unit, *Key Indicators of Women's Position in Britain*.

Workplace Relations Act, Australia, 1996.
Workplace Relations Amendment (Paid Maternity Leave) Bill 2002.

Index